Indus Valley

Melukhkha

F

Magan

INDIAN OCEAN

THE ARCHAEOLOGY
OF THE ARABIAN GULF

THE EXPERIENCE OF ARCHAEOLOGY

Series editor: Andrew Wheatcroft
University of Stirling

Rome and its Empire
Stephen Johnson

The Near East: Archaeology in the 'Cradle of Civilization'
Charles Keith Maisels

THE ARCHAEOLOGY
OF THE ARABIAN GULF

c. 5000–323 BC

Michael Rice

London and New York

First published in 1994
by Routledge
11 New Fetter Lane, London EC4P 4EE

Simultaneously published in the USA and Canada
by Routledge Inc.
29 West 35th Street, New York, NY 10001

Typeset in Garamond 10/12 by Florencetype Ltd, Kewstoke, Avon
Printed and bound in Great Britain by T J Press Ltd, Padstow, Cornwall

British Library Cataloguing in Publication Data
A catalogue for this book is available from the British Library

Library of Congress Cataloging in Publication Data
Rice, Michael
The archaeology of the Arabian Gulf / Michael Rice
p.   cm.
Includes bibliographical references and index.
1. Persian Gulf Region—Antiquities.   2. Persian Gulf Region—
Civilization.   I. Title.
DS211.R53   1994
953.6--dc20   93-7006

ISBN 0-415-032687

CONTENTS

LIST OF ILLUSTRATIONS

INTRODUCTION

This book is the product of many years' involvement in the affairs of the Arabian peninsula and Gulf states with whose past it is concerned, particularly with the state of Bahrain, which lies at the centre of the Gulf, as much historically as geographically. My involvement has swung, on the one hand, between a concern with the contemporary politics of the region and, in particular, with some of the issues which have arisen from the dependence of so much of the western world on its oil reserves and, on the other, with the uncovering of its extraordinary antiquity. It is perhaps difficult to imagine two such extreme perspectives, but straddling them has given me considerable happiness and only occasional discomfort. I have learned much about the people of the region, who have become my friends, and I believe I have gained some understanding of the role which eastern Arabia and the Gulf played in the development of many of the beliefs which are common to those of us who draw our cultural inheritance from the lands which lie to the west of the Zagros mountains.

The archaeology of the Arabian peninsula is very largely a new discipline. I have been singularly fortunate in having been involved with it over the period of its greatest activity, in the past thirty years or so. My interest in the archaeology of the ancient world long preceded my first visit to the Gulf, back in the early 1960s. When I came to Bahrain, I became aware of the remarkable work of the Danish Expeditions, promoted by the Forhistorisk Museum at Moesgard, an idyllic place near Aarhus in Jutland. The Danes had already been working in and around Bahrain for some years when I arrived. In common with the excavators I was alarmed at the risks to which a lack of understanding of the importance of Bahrain's antiquities exposed the sites and the increasing quantity of artefacts which was being excavated from them. I urged my friends in the Government of Bahrain (even then a particularly enlightened one) to cause a museum to be built, both to house the products of the excavations and to set them, and the archaeology of Bahrain itself, into some sort of coherent context, one that I, for example, might understand.

Eventually, and somewhat to my surprise, the Government asked my colleagues and me, who had some modest experience of design and communications, to prepare the museum. This we did working closely with Geoffrey Bibby, of the Danish Expedition; his book, *Looking for Dilmun*, tells of the work of the expeditions in Bahrain and in other of the Gulf states. The museum was housed initially in the Government's own headquarters building, later to be moved to what had been the RAF Officers' Mess at Muharraq, Bahrain's sister island. It was well received. We were able to work with a free hand and to introduce ideas then only beginning to be employed in contemporary museum design.

My colleagues and I have been deeply immersed in Arabia's past since that time and in communicating it to the present day, as a result of this well-omened Bahraini precedent. Over the intervening years we have designed and installed museums in Qatar, Oman and Saudi Arabia. We have also been concerned with the making of films on the region's past and in two other particularly satisfying activities. These have been the launching and editorial preparation of two important academic journals concerned with Arabia's archaeology,[1] and helping in the creation, staffing or development of Departments of Antiquities for several of the states. The direction of the Departments is now the responsibility of people from the states themselves; the journals too, increasingly, are being locally edited and produced and this is entirely as it should be.

In the course of planning the various museums for which we have been responsible, we are naturally much concerned with the research which must underlie any well-conceived museum exhibition. In some cases we carry out the research ourselves, or at least direct it; in others we work closely with the ever-increasing number of specialist scholars in the peninsula states, in Britain, Europe and the United States, who are now engaged on studies relating to the past of Arabia and the Gulf.

One of the compensations of working in museums in Arabia and the Gulf is that the people who use them are prepared to read far longer explanatory texts than would many western audiences. To people who are as involved with communications as my colleagues and I, this is highly satisfactory. It is also the reason for a great deal of the basic material of this book being readily accessible, not least to me.

I was also responsible for the planning, organization and publication of a major archaeological and historical conference which was held in Bahrain in December 1983. The published Proceedings of the conference[2] will provide the basis for a great deal of new research for many years to come: the findings of several of the distinguished scholars who took part will be a revelation to many. These papers and the several books which have been published in recent years have been of great help to me in preparing this text. I have also been assisted immeasurably by the work which we have collectively undertaken in preparing the six local museums with which the Department of Antiquities and Museum of Saudi Arabia entrusted us; this project is further described in Chapter 2. I am particularly grateful to my colleagues, Derek Dalby, my partner for many years, and Will Facey, who was responsible for the co-ordination of much of the research which has gone into making the museums the well-rounded institutions which I believe they are.

I am conscious that, despite my own considerable commitment to the region and its archaeology, it is very largely the findings of other men that I am presenting here. It used to be said that there were two sorts of archaeologists, 'diggers' and 'classifiers'. I suppose I might scrape into the latter category, but I would rather plead for a third to be accepted, that of the 'presenters', and I will contentedly take a modest place amongst them. In archaeology the presenters are those who communicate the lives of those who lived long ago to those who live today.

I acknowledge most gratefully a debt to those scholars whose work forms the substance of this book. Such facts as there are, are theirs; much of the interpretation is mine and I have attempted to make it clear where this is the case. The errors and omissions are wholly my own.

Michael Rice

PREFACE

The invasion of Kuwait by Iraq in August 1990 served to remind us how vital the Gulf and eastern Arabia have become to the prosperity of much of the world. This concern was signalled by the unprecedented ferocity of the Allies' response to Iraq's annexation of Kuwait; if some saw the Allied response as demonstrating a double standard when dealing with the politics of a part of the world which has suffered more than most from the intervention of foreign interests, it was generally respected as the necessary reaction to the absorption of a small, independent state by a larger, more aggressive neighbour. Most right-thinking people, in consequence, applauded the effect of the Allied effort if they did not always admire its methods of operation or the morality which seemed sometimes to be underlying it.

The attack on Kuwait also revealed how very little was known about the past of a part of the world which suddenly became the almost totally absorbing focus of international media attention. Given the fact that for more than half a century much of the industrial world has been powered by fossil hydrocarbon extracted from this very region, such a lack of awareness of its rich history was surprising and not a little deplorable, the more so when its unique contribution to the history of our species is apprehended.

One of the ironies of the war in the Gulf was the discovery by many that the Gulf states represent a much more coherent historical entity than does much of the land between the Twin Rivers, which is today called Iraq. The heritage which the world still enjoys from the successive civilizations of Mesopotamia is immense. However, whereas the Gulf culture, known to history as *Dilmun* and the principal subject of this book, survived as a distinct entity from its first appearance in eastern Arabia at the end of the fourth millennium BC down to Islamic times and to the present day through the modern states which are its successors, the land of Mesopotamia was ever fractious and was rarely brought under the control of one power centre. The city state, often bounded by a few hundred acres, was the characteristic Sumerian political unit: the Akkadian 'empire' lasted for a century or so, and the Babylonians and Assyrians came and went almost as swiftly, despite the powerful, often brutal impact which they made on the history of the Near East.

It is perhaps facile to search for historical parallels over long periods of human history but the northern headlands of the Gulf have been a disputed area for at least four thousand years, though not, again ironically, the region which today is represented by the State of Kuwait: that was, from around 2000 BC, part of Dilmun and hence ineluctably part of the Gulf. The Shatt al Arab however, to the east, marking the frontier between Iraq and Iran, was the cause of the final destruction of the benign civilization of Sumer when the king of Elam, in Iran, took captive Ibbi-Sin, the king of Ur, of the last native Sumerian dynasty around the year 2006 BC.

But the quarrels of Mesopotamians and Iranians are not the true measure of the importance of the Gulf in human history. Rather its contributions to the widening of man's perceptions of the world around him should be recognized in the vitality of myth, the enthusiasm of the quest, the challenge and invention of commerce, in art and literature and in the mystery of the origins of the way of life in which our species has elected to live.

A great deal has happened in the archaeology of the Gulf over the past decade or so since first I began to publish it. It is now possible to speak of the Gulf in antiquity as one coherent region and to extend the story of its people over the entire range of recorded history and beyond. It is this story which this book attempts to tell.

ACKNOWLEDGEMENTS

The author gratefully acknowledges the following: the Department of Antiquities and Museums, the State of Bahrain; the Department of Antiquities and Museums, the Kingdom of Saudi Arabia; the Department of Antiquities and Museums, the State of Kuwait; the Department of Antiquities and Museums, the United Arab Empires, the Department of Antiquities and Museums, Sultanate of Oman, the State of Qatar; Bahrain National Museum; the CNRS; the Forhistorisk Museum, Moesgard; the Louvre Museum; the Museum of Archaeology and Ethnography, Riyadh; the Royal Asiatic Society; the Trustees of the British Museum; the University of Chicago Press; Indiana University Press; Princeton University Press; E. Benn Ltd; E.J. Brill; Faber & Faber Ltd; Penguin Books Ltd; Thames & Hudson Ltd; the *Illustrated London News*; The Directors, The London-Bahrain Expedition; Dr D. B. Doe; Mrs Shirley Kay; Dr Paolo Costa and, in particular, my colleague Ian Cook of Graphic Design International for the maps.

1

THE ARABIAN GULF
IN ANTIQUITY

Four thousand years ago a man walked barefoot across the newly plastered floor of a curious building on a small island, close to the placid waters of an enclosed and distant sea.[1] What manner of man he was we have no way of knowing, except, a little absurdly, that his feet were remarkably large; we know, too, that he was not alone, for he was one of several to walk over the plaster laid down on the floor, and that one of his companions was a dog. Whether he was a labourer engaged on the construction of the building (though surely a singularly careless one), or a stranger who did not know of the work which was in progress so close to the whispering sea and, perhaps at night and in the darkness, stumbled across the still damp surface, are now beyond speculation.

In this remote episode it is the location, and not the walker by the shore, which is important; the building was a sacred place, part of a complex of monumental buildings raised to the glory of gods who, at the time when the careless (or perhaps deliberate) feet crossed the plaster floor, had already been worshipped there for upwards of 500 years in handsome stone-built temples and, in less substantial structures, perhaps for longer still. From the middle years of the third millennium BC a temple had stood upon this site, skirted by palm-trees and lapped by the nearby, shallow sea. Here men had sought both to honour and to propitiate the forces of nature and the unknown which they eternalized as gods. It is possible only to guess at the name of the principal divinity who was commemorated in this ancient place; but everything that now is known about it leads to the conviction that he was a great god, the lord and protector of a people for long totally forgotten, without whose lives the world would not be quite as it is today.

The temples on this distant island stand at a special point in time and space: from the earliest of them to the latest they span one of those periods in human history when the most intense social, technological and cultural changes were set in train. It will perhaps surprise some to be told that the island and its temples lie close to the origins of the modern world; the search for their own origins was a preoccupation of the people most closely identified with the mysteries enshrined in the temples.[2] That search itself forms part of the substance of this study.

The island itself is both the geographical centre as well as the focus of much legend and of elaborate religious cults. Its oecumene, if that is not too pretentious a word for so modest a land, stretched far to the north, deep into Iraq, and southwards out into the Indian Ocean beyond the horizons of the Arabian peninsula, of which it is a geographical dependency.

The island lies in the shallow waters of the Arabian (sometimes called the Persian) Gulf: today it is called Bahrain. In ancient times it was variously named: Dilmun, Tilmun, Tylos, Awad, Samak, Awal,[3] but whatever its name, it was the epicentre of a region which was to exercise a profound influence on the history of the western world. That region was bounded by the marshlands of southern Iraq to the north and, to the south, by the mountains of Oman; between these points on the western littoral of the Arabian peninsula lies the scatter of little shaikhdoms which make up the states of the Gulf. To the east is Iran.

Only in the very recent past has the rest of the world been reminded even of the existence of this small part of it and then not for reasons of its high antiquity nor for any contribution which it may have made to an under-standing of some of the most deep-seated preoccupations of mankind. For its people, entire millennia passed in neglect and forgetfulness. Fifty years ago or less the Arabian shores of the Gulf supported some of the least endowed of the world's populations, living in tiny settlements on the edge of the harsh and inhospitable desert.[4] With infinite toil and in the face of an often merciless climate, its people wrested a bare subsistence from the sea and the lean herds of goat and camel which the land could barely nourish. But in modern times the kaleidoscope of human fortune has shattered and reformed totally; today the people of the Gulf enjoy per capita incomes which are amongst the highest in the world and a level of prosperity and social welfare which makes them the object of the often malicious envy of those who have been less favoured by the caprice of fate.

It was, of course, oil which effected this phenomenal transformation, from abject poverty to wealth limited only by the extent of the black lakes on which much of south-western Asia floats. With the accession of such great riches came the interplay of politics and the complex games of more power-ful nations which quickly saw the control of the Gulf lands as a prize worth any amount of conflict and chicanery.

Half a century of external influence has marked the region's most recent history, an influence not always entirely maleficent. But, curiously, in all that time and with the hordes of western officials, engineers, buccaneers, businessmen and their attendant flocks of journalists, academics and all manner of miscellaneous commentators who followed in their train, few people ever gave thought to what had preceded the Gulf's sudden plunge into the twentieth century.

To their credit, however, some few did. Archaeological excavation of a sort had been carried out, with varying degrees of intensity, efficiency and perception, for over a century, notably in Bahrain.[5] The work of more recent years and the improved techniques of excavation and analysis now available to the archaeologist's hand are beginning, if still only dimly, to suggest the profoundly important role which this region played in the early centuries of the development of urban cultures and in their diffusion over formidable distances.

As with so many other disciplines, in the past twenty years archaeology has witnessed the recasting of many of its most fervently defended concepts of earlier times. Archaeology is concerned with the extraction and evaluation of those material evidences of the past which can either be recovered or reconstructed. More scientific methodology, a greater awareness among many of the nations, the successors of the ancient cultures, of the significance of their heritage, and the sophisticated processing and publication of the results of an ever-increasing number of excavations throughout the world, have contributed to the transformation of what modern man believes he knows about his predecessors and hence about his own origins. At the same time there has been, amongst all types and conditions of humanity, an immeasurably increased awareness of and concern for the origins of these societies which have been constructed, in the course of an uncertain progress from a brute nature to the prospect, diminishing though it must seem to be in our own time, of enlightenment. Ironically, two of the less elevating accessories of our contemporary culture, television and tourism, have done much to make the public at large aware of antiquity.

The Near East, despite increasing competition from other areas, is still the most profitable region for the study of man's past. But the inevitable shortcomings of the reliance by archaeology on the evidence which is actually available is nowhere more tellingly demonstrated than in the case of Arabia's position in scholarship. Until very recently few works of general archaeological or historical reference contained any mention of the Gulf in their indices, or indeed of Arabia in pre-Islamic times at all, except perhaps for the trade in aromatics. This was usually mentioned incidentally, with perhaps a passing reference to the southern Arabian kingdoms which grew out of its prosperity. But beyond these glances, virtually nothing.

Thus Henri Frankfort, one of the most perceptive of the archaeologists of this century, could write in the preface to *The Birth of Civilisation in the Ancient Near East*: 'I have confined myself to Egypt and Mesopotamia, the cultural centres of the Ancient Near East; for in the peripheral regions civilisation arose late and was always, to some extent, derivative.'[6]

In this case Frankfort was, to a degree, misguided. He was, however, hardly likely to think otherwise for, in his day, the evidence was scarcely available for a more enlightened or informed view to prevail, though some scholars did perceive, however dimly, that Arabia and its littorals represented a blank page in man's history which demanded to be filled. Since his study was written, of course, other regions such as Anatolia, the Levant, even the far west of Europe, have come to be revalued and their contribution to the development of that confusing concept, civilization, accepted as far greater than Frankfort could ever have realized.

It might be imagined that it would be difficult to overlook the Arabian peninsula, the 'Island of the Arabs', that great land mass which divides Africa from Asia and which in surface area is approximately the size of western Europe. Yet historians and archaeologists had largely succeeded in doing this, from late Roman times to the very recent past. Such neglect is careless, to say the least, the more so because by no stretch of even the most perverse imagination could Arabia ever really have been said to be *terra incognita*. For over 1,400 years now it has been the focus of one of the most pervasive and powerful of the world's faiths, whose adherents are enjoined to travel to the Arabian holy places at least once in their lifetimes. This fact alone has meant the accumulation of a gigantic traffic of humanity and of experience over the centuries; that traffic's existence at least has been well known to Europeans since Crusader times, if not before.[7]

Nor has Arabia experienced any lack of spirited, if variously motivated, foreigners who have sought to penetrate the peninsula's interior wastelands of sand and wind-scoured rock. From them has descended the enduring myth of the dauntless, fierce but noble-hearted tent dwellers, customarily but inaccurately called the 'Bedouin'. The desert was furrowed with the tracks of all manners and conditions of purposeful explorers, seeking who knows what enchantment or release in the harsh purity of Arabia's empty spaces.

But, for whatever reason, few of Arabia's explorers were even of a modest archaeological bent. Admittedly the pickings were sparse when compared with Egypt, the Levant or Mesopotamia; politics, too, largely ignored Arabia in the nineteenth century, the high point of Near Eastern exploration and western exploitation, leaving the peninsula generally, with the exception of its western littoral and the south which controlled the route to India, to slumber under the formidable power of the Ottoman Empire. Egypt had been opened to the West and to the pursuits of scholars, first by Napoleon's expedition ('Four thousand years look down on you, Soldiers') and then by Mohammad Ali's Europeanizing policies. Mesopotamia attracted an early interest and her sites were being dug, however inexpertly, early in the nineteenth century. But, as was most markedly the case in the Levant and the Syro-Palestinian desert, one of the primary motivations for archaeological activity in the Land of the Two Rivers was to prove the historicity of the Bible.

The Biblical orientation of much European archaeology survived well into the twentieth century; the Bible was still considered a primary, if somewhat selective, source of an understanding of the ways of the ancient world, before the Redemption. All over the lands of the ancient Near East there continued to plod, sometimes in extreme discomfort but always in confident certainty, an army of learned men. They were often clergymen who espoused passionately the claims of this or that small piece of desert or river bank as the site of such and such a recorded intervention of the Divine in the affairs of man. That the topography usually did not fit, at least according to the Bible's directions, did not deter them at all.

Sadly, the winds of time have, as often as not, blown away the theories that they laboured so hard to construct. But Arabia shared rarely in these Biblical excursions, mostly, perhaps, because, other than in certain instances, Arabian sites do not feature largely in the Biblical record, and even taking into account the often over-excited terms which seem to have determined the character of much Biblical archaeology, there were few scholars who would readily venture into such unpromising territory. Then, of course, there was the uncomfortable fact that Arabia was firmly held, as it were, by the competition, which, despite all the efforts of the missionary societies of the day, had shown a marked and peremptory disinclination to accept the precepts of Christian proselytizers and firmly resisted any attempt by infidels to involve themselves with the exclusive land of Arabia. From this land, in its inhabitants' view, had sprung the last and greatest of the Prophets and the ultimate Revelation of God's purpose to man. Ideological constraints, too, militated against the unearthing of the material evidences of 'the Age of Ignorance', which to the devout Muslim was represented by the whole course of human history prior to AD 622. Deep revulsion was also expressed at the actions of those who disturbed the tombs of the dead, even if they were not, in strict terms, the burials of believers.

Then, of course, there was the simple but compelling fact of Arabia's extreme physical discomfort. Whilst this did not actually discourage all interested scholars, it may be that the pleasures of excavation in the Nile Valley or by the shores of the sun-blessed Aegean were discernibly greater than those attending similar work in Arabia. There were also the discommoding facts of the sheer immensity of the desert and the lack of enthusiasm towards foreigners looking for gold (for the search for gold is a fact well known to every desert-dweller about every archaeologist) which was demonstrated, sometimes fatally for the would-be searchers, by its people.

Arabian archaeology is in fact essentially a twentieth-century phenomenon; indeed, with one or two exceptions, it is to all intents and purposes a post-World War II development. It is one of the less immediately predictable by-products of the exploitation of the Arabian peninsula's staggering reserves of fossil hydrocarbons, the oil for which the industrial world so desperately thirsts. It is pertinent to this study that the reserves of Arabia's oil are located beneath the eastern province of Saudi Arabia and the states of the peninsula's eastern littoral which form the substance of this book. Commerce, in any serious, organized sense, began here, more than 4,000 years ago; it is the pursuit of commercial gain which has brought the region back to the consciousness of the world.

The unremitting pursuit of the one resource which is all that most of the oil-bearing lands possess has been, generally speaking, equivocal. The West has almost exhausted itself in devising machines and whole economies which depend upon this sole resource of a people whose consequent prosperity is not only dependent upon those very machines and economies, but is also often bitterly resented. Now, the political power deriving from the owner-ship of so much of the world's energy resources has given the states of the Arabian peninsula a disconcerting influence on the lives of a substantial portion of the people who live on this planet. It is perhaps as well to try to understand something of their history. In doing so, we will find that we are discovering much about our own.

Thus far we have spoken of Arabia and the Arabian peninsula. Now we must become a little more specific, narrowing the focus down to one particular part of the peninsula with which this study will be concerned. This region is that which contains, in contemporary geopolitical terms, Kuwait, the Eastern Province of the Kingdom of Saudi Arabia, the State of Qatar, the archipelago of islands which comprise the State of Bahrain, the seven shaikhdoms of the United Arab Emirates and the Sultanate of Oman. Collectively this region is described as 'eastern Arabia'; it is also the western littoral of that inland sea, the gulf which divides Arabia from Iran and which, by reason of the controversy which attends whichever territorial adjective (Arabian or Persian) is employed to identify it, is most generally described simply as 'the Gulf'. This results in the infinite confusion of those living in the Americas, to whom the term generally has meant the Gulf of Mexico. Perhaps the conflict in the Arabian Gulf following the invasion of Kuwait will have served to identify it, for all nations.

This story is therefore concerned with the antiquity of eastern Arabia and of the Gulf. As such it is partial and limited, necessarily disregarding by far the largest part of the Arabian peninsula and concentrating only on one quadrant of it. There are three main reasons why this should be so.

The first is that, compared with the rest of Arabia, the eastern quadrant has generally been far better researched, to the extent at least that it is possible to lay out, with reasonable assurance, a historical sequence for it based on the evidence brought to light by the combination of chance and archaeology. For the past fifty years or thereabouts, access for non-Muslims to eastern Arabia has also been much easier than to any other part of the peninsula. Because they are the oil-producing regions of Arabia, the states have all maintained a substantial and increasing degree of contact with the outside world, sustaining significant populations of foreigners, including Europeans and Americans. Second, the opportunities for a ful-filled social and cultural life have in the past been limited in these parts, often notably so. In consequence the foreigners living in eastern Arabia have frequently turned to archaeology by way of diversion. The third factor provides the essence of this book: in eastern Arabia and the Gulf lies much of the earliest mythical and conceptual material which informs many of the most profoundly rooted beliefs of the modern world and of the iconography which illuminates them.

In the early years the foreign, if originally largely amateur, preoccupation with archaeology led in time to an awareness by professional archaeologists that the region did contain important and hitherto largely overlooked material. Gradually professional teams began to work there, in several of the states freely and with official support and involvement.

By geomorphological chance, a very substantial part of the world's reserves of fossil hydrocarbons, in oil-bearing strata laid down hundreds of millions of years ago, lies under these peninsula states. The earliest commercial exploitation of oil from the Arabian Gulf took place in 1932 when the first commercial quantities were exported from Bahrain:[8] in the light of what will be seen to be the almost mystical role which Bahrain has exercised in the region as a land of the beginning of things, this chance seems peculiarly appropriate. Since 1932 the region has become one of the most sought-after commercial and financial markets on the globe. It would nonetheless be an exaggeration to describe the Gulf states today as the very centre of the world's trade: it would not have been so great an exaggeration 4,000 years ago.

Throughout much of the third millennium BC and into the early centuries of the second, the Gulf was part (arguably the most important part) of the principal highway for the movement of international trade. The route ran from western Anatolia, down the twin rivers of Mesopotamia, the Tigris and the Euphrates, through the Gulf to Pakistan and up the Indus Valley riverine system to huge, forbiddingly monumental cities such as Harappa and Moenjo-Daro. This route may also have touched or have been connected with others to even more distant regions; westwards the traders may have penetrated to the Nile Valley.

Thus the Gulf played a major role in that extraordinary period, from c. 3300 BC to c. 2200 BC, when a great surge of energy seems to have possessed the populations of the Nile and the Tigris–Euphrates valleys and the lands contiguous with them, in consequence of which many of what have subsequently come to be regarded as the distinguishing marks of civilization and culture were first laid down. Indeed, no comparable period of dynamic change has been experienced by our species until the present century.

The organization of urban societies, the management and direction of large bodies of citizens, irrigation, the rapid advance of agriculture, the introduction of hierarchies, kingship, monumental architecture, writing (branching rapidly into administrative and literary usages), formalized rituals both religious and civil, the codification of laws, the specialization of crafts, the growth of defensive systems and military levies: indeed all the paraphernalia of developed societies which largely remained unchanged until our own day, either erupted into the world in this brief period of human history, or, during it, were refined out of recognition from their early forms. From this time everything was totally changed in the societies which experienced these phenomena and in those which have descended from them, including our own. From these Valley peoples, through a process of exceptional practical and intellectual energy, emerged the magnificent cultures of Pharaonic Egypt and of Sumer, the one arguably the most human, engaging and, paradoxically, the most majestic of ancient societies, the other the most inventive and dynamic.[9]

The discoveries of the post-war period have not diminished the splendour of the achievements of the two remarkable peoples who brought these cultures to birth; equally, they have revealed that, with regard to certain important aspects of what had seemed to be peculiarly their achievements, they were not, in fact, the first. Thus to the Sumerians is credited the origin of the curious human practice of building and living in cities; certainly the world had to wait for the emergence of the Sumerian city-states in the early third millennium for the particular form of city, in hierarchy, organization and structure, that modern man would recognize as something like his own. But thousands of years before even the earliest of Sumerian cities was raised up at Eridu, on a small island in the extreme south of the Mesopotamian marshlands, a 10-acre fortified settlement had been built at Jericho (c. 9000 BC)[10] far away to the west in Palestine. Great watch-towers guarded Jericho's walls against the incursion of the wild desert tribes who sought control of the wells which the people of Jericho had tapped and organized for their economy in the tenth millennium before the Christian era. Perhaps more remarkable still, 3,000 years before the first tentative temples began to be raised beside the god-infested Nile, painted shrines with the evidence of elaborate rites and worship were set up within the town (for it is difficult to use another word to describe it) that flourished on the Anatolian plains at Çatal Hüyük, on a site more than three times larger than Jericho.[11]

Even in this remote and obscure period of man's development, at least 7,000 years ago, sophisticated art, so much the most surprising of man's achievements, flourished. The carvings and paintings of these lonely Anatolian townsmen have a strange and chilling quality. Their principal divinity seems to have been a goddess, massive and fecund, who, with her boy-consort, is portrayed supported by leopards, her power manifest in bulls: somehow, terror never seems to be very far distant from her and the creatures that attend her.[12] A high bull-cult seems to have been one of the characteristic practices of Çatal Hüyük, one which was to have a profound influence on cultures as far distant as the islands in the Gulf, Egypt and Crete in the Aegean. After a few centuries of richly productive life, the Anatolian settlements disappeared: a long night descended until a second dawn heralded the first appearance of those civilizations which were to set the pattern for all the ages which followed them. With the invention of writing, at its earliest in the middle of the fourth millennium, history begins and with it the record of urban man.

There was a time in man's experience when everything was new under the sun. To many people, educated conventionally, the ancient world meant a subjective and often sentimentalized picture of life in a Greece and a Rome that never were. Such a view was fostered by nineteenth-century educationalists, often to satisfy their own emotional needs and frequently to warrant the moral and political ethics of the Europe of their day: Winckelmann, as it were, hand in hand with Dr Arnold. Otherwise, and with only a passing nod to the Egyptians (who were considered odd and rather disturbing), the problems of the remoter reaches of human history could be readily resolved by the simple reliance on Biblical revelation.

Myth, religious beliefs and fairy stories acknowledge no frontiers. Throughout human history most peoples have felt compelled irresistibly to seek a time when the world was young and free, when men and animals lived at one together, as in a world imagined by Savary. In this quest, so often identified with an imagined land of innocence and abundance, man proclaimed his protest against the debased, troubled and guilt-laden condition of his own humanity. Out of the need to explain his own existence came his hope that he was not entirely alone and that providence had some care of him. Thus man created, both as a means of consolation and because he was a highly creative animal much given to poetic expression, a series of splendid legends: in seeking for Eden, the primaeval garden of tranquillity and fulfilment, man revealed something of what, wistfully, he would have liked his world to be.

With the revelation of the geological age of the world, even the most besotted protagonists of the Biblican Eden began to lose confidence in their ability ever to discover precisely where man's sinful history had begun. But, little did they know it, help of a kind was on the way, galloping down the centuries. When it came, however, their plight was like that of the maiden who, saved from ravening beasts, finds that her most cherished bastion has fallen before the onslaught of her rescuer.

The discovery which demolished much Biblical scholarship of the day, and which accelerated its demotion from antiquarian pre-eminence to the relatively minor place it now occupies, was the unearthing of the earliest civilizations of the Mesopotamian plain lying between and around two great rivers, the Tigris and the Euphrates. This region had always ranked high among the contenders for the putative site of Eden, but its real history was hazy beyond the comparatively recent times dealt with by the historical books of the Jewish peoples. But in the second half of the nineteenth century Mesopotamian history was found to reach immeasurably beyond the time even of the Assyrians and Babylonians, the former of whom were regarded as so significant a people that their name was once given to the study of the entire region. At length, scholars who were not burdened with the necessity of proving the historicity of the Bible revealed in the Land of the Two Rivers a totally unsuspected culture, humane, highly sophisticated, sensitively literate, with hints of an architectural and artistic splendour which rivalled and perhaps even contributed to the majesty of Old Kingdom Egypt.[13]

In the legends and myths of the mysterious inhabitants of this land the archetypal Eden was at last discovered, not indeed merely as a geographical location to be neatly sited upon a map, but as the Place where the Sun Rises, a land to be yearned for, the original home of gods and men. In short, there was now revealed the likely origin of the myth which had been echoed, probably more than 2,000 years after it had first been written down, by the authors of the Book of Genesis, who must stand, in this as in so many other cases, as amongst the most successful and respected of plagiarists.

As more was discovered about the people whose poetic insight created the myth of the terrestrial paradise, more was also revealed about many of the most deep-seated beliefs and hopes of their successors. These beliefs, descending through the camp-fire stories of the nomadic tribes who lived belligerently on the periphery of the vastly superior cultures, passed in turn to the Hebrews, the Greeks and the Romans and so to the world of our time.

The early inhabitants of southern Mesopotamia called their land 'Sumer', or more precisely, they articulated it as 'Shumer'. They also called themselves, to our ears simply and engagingly, 'the black-headed folk'. Theirs is the earliest great civilization yet to be revealed in any detail: their legacy to us is almost incalculable and yet they remain relatively unknown when compared, for example, with their near and splendid contemporaries, the Egyptians. This may be because the marvellous inheritance of ancient Egypt has come down to us in stone and metal whilst the Sumerians left a gift of words, ideas and legends which has only been revealed as theirs 4,000 years after they ceased to exist as a nation. Their most stupendous innovation, which is Sumer's special glory, was the creation of writing: at least no earlier system of writing than theirs is known. Had the Sumerians done nothing else, mankind would eternally have been in their debt for what is perhaps the most benign of all great inventions. But they did much, much more.[14]

The discovery that the myth of Eden had its origins in the records of the Sumerians began another quest, this time for the site of *their* earthly paradise, the name of which is transliterated today as *Dilmun*. Sumerologists were on rather firmer ground than their Biblical predecessors, for it rapidly became obvious that to the Sumerians, and to their Akkadian, Babylonian, Kassite and Assyrian successors, Dilmun was both a mythical land and a geographical location.

The Hebrews did not make their Garden of Paradise a market-place, yet the Sumerian legends of man's primaeval existence in the blissful Land of the Living (one of the most frequent of Dilmun's epithets) were matched by matter-of-fact records of the shipments of dates and onions, stone, metal, timber and pearls from Dilmun. For those who find such quests down the byways of scholarship agreeable, Dilmun was a land well worth the search, more human in scale than Eden, happier by far in its legacy to men. The discountenanced band of scholars who had so earnestly sought for the Biblical Eden were given some small vindication by their Sumerological successors: at least a Paradise land existed after all, even if its gateway was more likely to be guarded by a customs official than by an angel with a flaming sword.

In fact, any distinction between the mythical and the mercantile Dilmun is artificial and unwarranted by any of the Sumerian sources. Goddesses and sea captains are as indiscriminately mingled in the literary remains as they were in Liddell and Scott's first Greek exercises of long ago. Dilmun's products include, variously, copper, dates, onions shipped to the metropolis of Ur, and an entire cycle of vegetation brought to birth in the place of the assembly of the gods. It is the home of Ziusudra, the Sumerian prototype of Noah, and of petty kings bowing respectfully before the pretensions of their Mesopotamian self-proclaimed overlords.

ON THE LOCATION OF DILMUN

For the past century or so there has been occasional but serious academic argument on the issue of where Dilmun might be sited.[15] Allowing even for the asperity with which such disputes seem always to be conducted, the argument over Dilmun cannot be said to have raged, for Dilmunology is a modest science.

From the later years of the nineteenth century onwards, academic opinion has decided that the metropolis of Dilmun, the terrestrial paradise and the flourishing entrepôt, was for much of its history located in Bahrain, whose name in Arabic means 'the place of the two seas'. But from time to time the term embraced much more extensive territories than the archipelago of islands with which the name is associated today.

One of the most frequently employed epithets of the Gulf itself was the Sea of the Rising Sun. This demonstrates the danger of taking the ancients seriously in the matter of geographical descriptions. No one could believe the Sumerians to be so obtuse or so unobservant as to imagine that the sun rose to the due south of their land, which could be the only conclusion if 'sea of the rising sun' is taken literally.

The question will be asked later in this study whether the Sumerians came to Mesopotamia from the south: if, as is at least possible, they came along a route skirting the westerly shores of the Gulf, it is conceivable that the Gulf was given this description by its earliest navigators, moored perhaps on the Arabian foreshore and looking out towards the easterly sky. From the Arabian mainland, the sun may well appear to rise across the sea, out of Bahrain itself, whose central prominence, the Jebal Dukhan, would be struck by its first rays: it is a perhaps questionable proposition but one that is not wholly insupportable. The axis of the Gulf runs south to east: as a ship sails southwards down its waters the axis shifts more to west to east. Thus, in the latitude of Bahrain, sailing southwards towards the Straits of Hormuz, the sun would rise apparently out of the sea's eastern horizon. But similarly, from the latitude of Ur, one of the most significant Sumerian cities, at certain times of the year the sun would appear to rise to the south and east, in other words over the Arabian Gulf.[16]

According to the traditions of Sumer the date-palm was brought to their land from the Gulf. The Sumerians, understandably in the light of the barrenness of their own land, respected and sought after trees. They also destroyed many forests and plantations in the course of providing fuel for one of their staple industries, copper-smelting. But the palm-tree was supreme in their regard and was honoured in ritual and in legend.[17]

In a hymn dedicated to Ninsinna, the goddess proclaims the antiquity of her city, Isin, as greater even than that of Dilmun and says: 'My house, before Dilmun existed, was fashioned from palm tree.'[18] The goddess here acknowledges the extremely important part which the date-palm played in Sumerian belief and legend. Growing straight and tall, it was unequivocally the 'tree of life' to the Sumerians and as such is often portrayed in their art. By tradition the palm was brought from Dilmun, on whose own seals (the form of which probably originated in Bahrain) it is a frequent motif: it was extensively cultivated in well-planted groves all over Sumer. The people had early discovered the high calorific value of the date, and they practised artificial pollination in promoting its growth in their otherwise treeless land.

The date-palm (*Phoenix dactylifera*) is known to have been domesticated by 3000 BC in southern Iraq, another of the technological triumphs of the ever-inventive Sumerians. Though it is possible that the date palm does not now exist in a truly wild state, parts of coastal eastern Arabia support populations of uncultivated palms that are not traceable to formerly cultivated areas or to other activities of man. Some of these may be modified remnants of the original wild stock, and it is possible that the cultivated forms were developed here in the Arabian Gulf coastal region, as the Sumerians themselves believed.

The palm-trees of Dilmun were indeed so renowned that they entered the common parlance of the Sumerians, as the very criterion of excellence. Thus a king is said to be cherished 'like a date-palm of Dilmun'.[19] When glorifying the sacred city of Nippur, the domain of the master of the gods Enlil himself (and a sort of Sumerian Vatican in the precedence which it seemed to take over the other god-ruled metropolitan centres), a hymnodist observes 'My Nippur, before Dilmun existed the palm tree grew there.'[20] This is of course itself a celebration of Dilmun's own vaunted antiquity.

There is an evocative praise of trees from one of the Tammuz liturgies, which mentions Dilmun: Tammuz was Dummuzi, the Sumerian god of vegetation.

> In my right hand is a cedar, on my left is a cypress,
> My pregnant mother is a consecrated cedar
> A cedar of Hasur
> A dark tree of Tilmun.[21]

It is suggested that Hasur represents the source of the two great rivers of Sumer, the Tigris and the Euphrates, and Tilmun (as the Semitic form of Dilmun) is the place of their outpouring. This again is a reference to the idea that the underground springs of Bahrain (which will be further described below) and of the Hasa Province of Saudi Arabia were connected with the rivers and not, as we know to be the truth, part of the Arabian water-table.

The repeated references in Sumerian and Babylonian texts to Dilmun as an entrepôt, as an island dominion of the Mesopotamian kings in later times and, accepting that the eastern coast of what is now called Saudi Arabia was included from time to time in the geographical description, as the known source of the best dates in the ancient world, all confirm the view that Dilmun was situated in the Gulf, and Bahrain is the only wholly convincing site for its centre. If the Sumerians were, as has been suggested, an immigrant people in southern Mesopotamia, and if they came originally from the south, the only island landfall in the northern Gulf they could have made in what would have seemed to them to have been a dangerous and treacherous sea would have been Bahrain.

The little island would thus have evoked grateful memories from the people that it sheltered. The strange lowering rock outcrop in its centre, the Jebel Dukhan, the Mountain of Smoke, and the altogether surprising fresh-water springs which bubble up in the seas around the island, could well have added a touch of mystery and wonder to its shores. Clearly it was a land redolent of the gods.

Islands have always fascinated men and there is much evidence that all over the ancient world they enjoyed a special reputation and sanctity as lands of the gods. Several Mediterranean islands shared this attribution of holiness, many of them being provinces of the supposed Great Mother goddess of remote antiquity. The Gulf is not well supplied with islands and it is more likely, therefore, that any new people settling on its shores would single out the only significant one as a sanctuary. The wealth of evidence which has emerged in recent years as a result of the archaeological work carried out in Bahrain has revealed the full and remarkable extent of Bahrain's early history and its exceptional antiquity.[22]

Since the 1950s it has been demonstrated that, from the closing centuries of the third millennium BC, Bahrain was an important religious centre, important enough to be the site of great temple complexes, markedly but not exclusively Sumerian in influence. Typically Mesopotamian cult and every-day objects have been found there and more undoubtedly wait to be uncovered. At least one important city flourished there; three of the principal sites known so far, the Qala'at al-Bahrain, Barbar and Saar, are important by any archaeological standards.

In another respect Bahrain has a wholly unique claim to its inclusion in the annals of ancient history in the Near East: it is often described as the largest necropolis of the ancient world. In the north of the island the land surface is so pitted with burial mounds that it looks like the popular image of a long-dead planet. *One hundred and seventy thousand* tombs (perhaps more) are there, in which an ancient people, mysterious and, until very recently, quite unknown, were buried.

Dilmun is the location for the Sumerians' explanation of the origins of agriculture and irrigation: it is even thought of as the place from which originated the god who brought the secrets of science, writing and all the arts to Sumer.[23] It is also the place of assembly of the Sumerian high gods, who were much given to collective decision-making.

Whilst Dilmun's place in the historical records of Sumer and of its successor cultures the Akkadian and the Babylonian is important, the fact that it is found at the centre of the oldest surviving corpus of legends recorded in written form is surely particularly appealing today. Dilmun has an important place in the original Sumerian story of the Flood on which the Old Testament version is unquestionably based. The Flood legend is an episode in the world's first (and one of its greatest) epic histories, which introduces the most enduring and powerful figure of ancient legend, the heroic Gilgamesh.[24] His love for man takes him on the quest for the secret of the renewal of youth which he believes is to be found only in the blessed land of Dilmun, at the confluence of the waters where Ziusudra lives, on whom, alone of all mortals, the gods had conferred the gift of eternal life (see Chapter 10).

On another level entirely, the control of Dilmun's trade was a matter of concern and pride to the sovereigns of Mesopotamia. From its busy harbours, shipments were made of stone, metals, foodstuffs and other merchandise vital to Sumer's economy. The trade routes were kept open to southern Arabia and even possibly to Egypt; later and above all, Dilmun's ships plied eastwards to the extensive and perplexing civilization of the Indus Valley.

THE ARABIAN GULF

The Gulf, a narrow almost rectangular body of water 1,000 kilometres (600 miles) in length which, until its outpouring through the Straits of Hormuz into the Arabian Sea, is virtually an inland sea, does more than simply divide the Arabian peninsula from Iran (Map 1). At its head, its northern extremity,

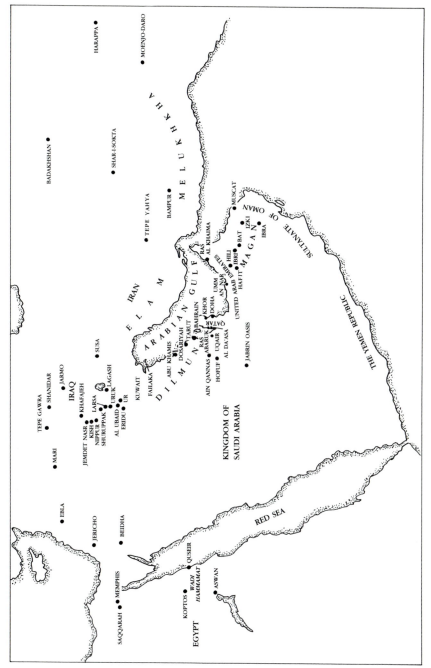

Map 1 The Arabian Gulf, Mesopotamia, Elam, the Indus Valley, showing the principal archaeological sites mentioned in the text.

15

in the marshlands where sky, lakes and sea all seem to merge into one, it is fed by the two great rivers of Mesopotamia, the Tigris and the Euphrates, on whose banks and extended canal irrigation systems so much of the early history of urban man was enacted. Geographically it is central to south-western Asia, linking the western edge of that great continent with the lands of the Iranian plateau and the Indian subcontinent. In ancient times the Gulf was called by a variety of names. As well as the Sea of the Rising Sun, it may also have been called the Waters of Death: if it is the Gulf on which Gilgamesh sailed in search of Ziusudra (see Chapter 10), this term would appear to have had some currency, though perhaps only of a literary sort. In Akkadian, towards the end of the third millennium, it was called *Tantum Shaplitum*. It was also called the Place of Crossing (a mysterious, ominous name) or perhaps the Place of Rule; the Bitter Sea may perhaps be a comment on the extreme salinity of the comparatively shallow waters of much of the Gulf, particularly in the summer months, whilst the Lower Sea was a term frequently employed from the late third millennium on, serving to differentiate it from the Upper Sea, the Mediterranean. These are both terms which reveal their Mesopotamian origins as well as heralding the eventual, gradual swing away from the Gulf to the Mediterranean as the world's principal artery of trade.

To Herodotus[25] and Alexander[26] the Gulf was the Erythraean Sea: 'Erythraean' means 'red' and confusingly, at this period and later, the stretch of water between Egypt and Arabia, now known as the Red Sea, was then called the Arabian Gulf; thus Ptolemy knew it.[27] To the Gulf waters were added the Red Sea *and* the Arabian Sea, all embraced within the term 'Erythraean' at various times.

By whatever name it might be known, the Gulf was, by early in the third millennium, the focus of considerable activity and development. Along the Arabian shore and particularly on the islands which nestle close to the coast, settlements were established which grew into sizeable and prosperous cities. The principal sites of such settlements, so far to be identified, have been found on Failaka island, a dependency of Kuwait; on Tarut, a small island close to the Saudi Arabian mainland; inland, around Abqaiq; on Bahrain island, at various times the political centre of the region; small settlements in Abu Dhabi and other of the states of the United Arab Emirates; and what appear to be several little townships in the Sultanate of Oman, where quantities of copper, the staple trade of the early Mesopotamian cities, were mined.

THE CITIES OF SUMER

The phenomenal growth of urban civilization in southern Mesopotamia, the most striking event of the late fourth millennium, was paradoxical in that the land in which the little cities of Sumer grew and flourished was almost wholly barren of the raw materials – wood, stone or metal-bearing ores – on which the cities depended for their rapidly developing manufacturing industries. These were already specialized and well organized, leading to the production of surplus, far beyond the needs of the citizens, or their ability to absorb them. The invention of the sailing-boat expanded the horizons of the river-based cities substantially, making it possible for them to mount expeditions over considerable distances both in search of the raw materials Mesopotamia lacked and to seek out markets for the disposal of the manufactured surplus which the cities' prosperous economies were turning out.

After the more tentative experience gained by the simpler, smaller river craft which no doubt occasionally ventured out on to the relatively open water of the lagoons with which southern Mesopotamia was liberally supplied, bolder experiments in marine design might be expected. The sail was developed and, as a consequence of boats being capable of moving before the wind, journeys of vastly increased range might be contemplated whilst substantially larger tonnages than could be driven by oarsmen could be built and sent out on wide-ranging voyages. The sailing-boats on which much of this far-ranging travel depended were nonetheless small: the displacement of one typical boat in the early second millennium (and it probably is representative of the earlier periods as well) is estimated as 19 tons.[28] Their range was limited by the amount of fresh water they could carry: their masters were cautious seamen, preferring, sensibly, to lug down the coast, stopping as frequently as they might, to take on water and fresh supplies for the next leg of the journey. Only the Arabian coast could give them the shelter and facilities they required: the Persian littoral was less favoured with natural harbours and inlets whilst its barren, rocky shore discouraged landfalls.

The differences between its two shores are what chiefly gave the whole Gulf its historic character. On its western littoral the islands gave shelter to ships, and provided fodder and water; they also acted as relatively secure bases for trade, both for trans-shipment and as entrepôts with the hinterland. On the western side the water is shallow and thus well suited for the loading and offloading of cargoes. On the eastern side, by contrast, the water is deep for the bed of the Gulf shelves steeply; the coast is often sheer and generally less hospitable than on the Arabian side. The islands on the eastern side of the Gulf, other than some of those near its mouth at the Gulf of Hormuz, seem not to have assumed the same importance as those on the Arabian side; many of them are barren.

The unique character of the Gulf, historically as much as archaeologically, is that it is a culture of islands, the only one of importance in the western hemisphere in antiquity. It is this fact which gives the Gulf in ancient times its special character and imbues it with qualities which make it quite different from any other of the high cultures of antiquity.

The little communities strung out along the eastern Arabian coast, once established, came to serve a variety of functions. First, they were convenient refuelling points, at least before the long haul from Oman to the mouth of the Indus Valley system far to the east; second, they provided access to the raw materials that Mesopotamia needed; third, they provided depots and outlets for manufactured goods that could be traded with the people of the hinterland.

In addition to their role as entrepôts, of places of trans-shipment either of raw materials or manufactured products, at least some of the coastal cities were themselves production centres. Thus, at one period, Bahrain sustained a copper-smelting industry, converting (in all probability) the ore which was mined in Oman and smelting it into ingots; it was also smelted in Oman itself. Agriculture, notably the cultivation of dates and onions, was an important element in the economy of eastern Arabia at least from the fourth millennium on, as was fishing, perhaps the most characteristic and the most typical way of life established in the region from the time of the very earliest settlements.[29]

Thus the presence, in the late fifth to early fourth millennium, of tiny stone tools from eastern Arabian sites, miniature awls and borers, suggests the existence of industralized pearl-fishing, the region's most important industry until well into recent times.[30] Oyster middens of great antiquity on Bahraini[31] and other sites suggest that the oyster-beds were fished for pearls and not simply for an elegant addition to the diet of the region's inhabitants. That fishing occupied a place in the Sumerians' ideological and philosophical make-up is demonstrated by the exceptional antiquity of fish-cults in the region and by the identification of at least one of the High Gods of Sumer, Enki, who has considerable connections with Bahrain and the Gulf, with fish and fishing.[32]

But like all other achievements of men, the paramountcy of the Gulf as a commercial waterway was destined to last for only a certain time. By the early centuries of the second millennium the axis of world politics and trade was already swinging away to the north and west, to the Levant, hence to the eastern Mediterranean and to the newly emerging lands of the Aegean. It is even possible that there was some form of population movement from the Gulf headlands into the Levantine coast, perhaps brought about by one of the marked, often short-term changes of climate to which the region seems always to have been subject, or by the inability of the coastal settlements to sustain the level of population developed during the late third millennium. Such a radical change may perhaps have come about as a consequence, in turn, of the invasions in the east and north which seem to have created havoc, in a time of general disunity and political confusion throughout near eastern lands, notably among the city-states of southern Mesopotamia, in the early centuries of the second millennium BC.

THE LATER HISTORY OF THE GULF

The Gulf and eastern Arabia sank into relative obscurity after the eighteenth/seventeenth centuries BC, with only an occasional incident or entry in a contemporary record to illuminate the apparent general gloom of the times. Mesopotamian rulers still claimed sovereignty over the Gulf as much by convention and the recollection of the splendours of past conquerors as by any real need to control what had become a literal backwater. For over a thousand years this situation persisted; then, from around the eighth century BC, there is evidence of a return of considerable prosperity to eastern Arabia and the Gulf islands.

This renaissance of the region, marked by the development of cities whose luxury and riches were proverbial, arose directly from the fortunes associated with the spice-trade, the extraordinary commerce in aromatics such as frankincense and myrrh which grow in abundance in southern Arabia and whose traffic gave rise to societies whose only purpose was to service the caravans, or to take tolls from them.[33] It was this trade, supported in particular by the large-scale domestication of the camel, making long-ranging land routes possible, comparable in extent even with the earlier sea routes, which drew Arabia again to the attention of the major world powers of the day.

The spice-trade was, in its own day, as important a factor in the economy of first-millennium Arabia as fossil hydrocarbons and the oil industry which has grown up to exploit them are to Arabia in the present day. Gerrha in eastern Arabia was founded around 690 BC: her inhabitants were said by Agatharchides to be the richest people in the world.

The last emperor of Babylon, Nabonidos (589–556 BC), established his capital at Tayma in northern Arabia and burials of neo-Babylonian date have been excavated on Bahrain. No doubt the Babylonians were there for purposes of trade, as inscriptions of the period make clear.[34]

THE GREEKS AND THE ORIGINS OF THE LEVANTINE CITIES

This return of Arabia to the consciousness of the larger world later coincided with the first waves of serious scientific curiosity, associated with the intellectual dynamism of the emerging Greek world. From the time of Herodotos onwards, accounts of the Gulf and eastern Arabia appear in the histories, geographies and other scientific treatises which the Greeks and their Roman successors delighted in producing.

At the beginning of his first book Herodotos considers the nature of the Greeks and 'the Asiatics' (the Persians, in other words) and the origins of their conflict. The Persians, he observes, put the responsibility for the quarrel on the Phoenicians who, the Persian learned men say, 'came to our seas from the sea which is called Red and having settled in the country which they still occupy at once begin to make long voyages'.[35] In Book VII, when he analyses the composition of Xerxes' forces he relates how 'the Phoenicians with the Syrians of Palestine, contributed 300 tribesmen . . . these people have a tradition that in ancient times they lived on the Persian Gulf but migrated to the Syrian coast, where they are found today.'[36]

The people of Tyre, that ancient and once splendid city, insisted on their Gulf origins. At one time the principal Bahrain island was called Tylos: it would be entirely consistent with philological precedent for the *l* to become an *r*. However, Tylos appears late in the record, certainly long after the establishment of Tyre. Even the Old Testament, not always to be relied on for its historical accuracy, preserves a memory of Tyre in association with 'Eden, the Garden of God'. Thus in Ezekiel the prophet says: 'O Tyre, you have said "I am perfect in beauty." Your borders are in the heart of the sea. . . . You were in Eden, the garden of God: every precious stone was your covering.'[37]

It may be observed that, in this translation at least, Tyre's borders are said to be 'in the heart of the sea' – a description not wholly appropriate for a coastal city, which could certainly not be said to be 'in the heart of the sea', but perfectly proper for an island.

Herodotos was not the only ancient author to examine and chronicle the Phoenicians' belief that they came originally from the coasts of the Gulf and, in particular, from the islands. Alexander's contemporary Androsthenes was one whose now lost work was extensively cited by other classical authors, of whom Strabo was the most influential. He records the tradition that the inhabitants of the Gulf islands in his time (the first century AD) believed that the Phoenician cities of Tyre and Arados were seeded by colonists from the Gulf islands which, in his time, bore the nearly identical names of Tylos and Arad (Bahrain and Muharraq as they are known today).

The evidence for a Gulf colonization of the Phoenician coast and the possible authenticity of the traditions here referred to have been reviewed in recent years.[38] This accepts the Phoenician tradition, as relayed by Herodotos, as a genuine expression of that people's belief about their origins; it also suggests that in late antiquity this belief about the origins of the Phoenicians was widespread.

There is a consideration which has been largely overlooked by other commentators. Strabo recalls a reference in the *Odyssey* in which Homer speaks of 'the Sidonians', in association with peoples who came from the shores of what is today called the Red Sea. Strabo suggests that these Sidonians are, in fact, not the inhabitants of the city of Sidon, but rather those who dwell in the Arabian Gulf, from whom the original Sidonians were descended. He draws the parallel between the Sidonians and the inhabitants of Tyre and Arad, as colonists in the same sense, from the Gulf islands.

In late antiquity, in the Graeco-Roman world at least, there was a widely held tradition concerning the origins of the Phoenician coastal cities, that they had been colonized from the Gulf islands. Herodotos even puts a date on when he thinks the original migration took place: 2,300 years before his day. Herodotos was writing in approximately 450 BC, so the migration would have taken place, roughly, in 2750 BC. This is firmly in the middle of the period when there is in fact little evidence of occupation at all in Bahrain, though there seems to have been a good deal going on in the eastern province of Saudi Arabia. However, it is specifically with the islands of the Gulf that the tradition deals and there is no reason to assume that it means anything other than what it says.

One aspect of historical writing often does reveal Herodotos as something less than his best: this is whenever he is dealing with chronology, a subject on which the ancients tended to be as shaky as in their understanding of direction or distance. If Herodotos' date is reduced by a thousand years (admittedly a fairly brutal reduction), the proposed date for the transfer of population from the Gulf to Phoenicia is then sited at the end of the first quarter of the second millennium, just when the high Dilmunite culture of the preceding 500 years or so seems to decline sharply. This is the point at which the Indus Valley cities no longer represent the lucrative and ready markets of the east and the Kassite mountain-dwellers came down on the cities of Babylonia and the Gulf. A migration at this date would be entirely plausible and, indeed, there is some evidence for it.

Later in this review of the Gulf in antiquity some consideration will be given to the place in its history of the island of Failaka, in the Bay of Kuwait. Failaka seems to have been associated particularly with religious festivals and cults which featured bulls. If Failaka was involved in this putative migration, which may well have been a relatively gradual process extending over several generations rather than any sort of mass exodus (although there *is* evidence of what seems to have been a hasty evacuation of the island in Old Babylonian times),[39] some of the cults associated with more western parts of the ancient world, including the bull-cults of Crete for example, a few centuries later, may have had their origins in the Gulf islands. It has already been suggested that one of the Gulf's frequent short-term climate changes may have been the occasion for the population finding it necessary to reduce the numbers of their parent settlement and setting out to find a new place in which to establish themselves. Since Dilmunite merchants had been travelling deep into northern Syria and southern Anatolia for centuries they would have been quite familiar with the Phoenician coast and with the rich lands which lay behind it.[40] Their predilection for coastal islands, too, would have been well met by the siting of what were to become Tyre and Arados.

The Gulf and its islands continued to figure spasmodically in the reports of the writers of late antiquity. After that period this corner of south-west Asia seems to have entered one of its periods of relative decline, certainly of obscurity. The reasons for the apparent decline may, once again, have been climatic or the consequences of war. The Muslim historians did not concern themselves with the times before Islam very much, though the Quran itself, as will be seen below, introduces an enigmatic and mysterious element into the region's history or, more exactly, into its mythology. Otherwise, long centuries passed during which any importance which once the region may have had was all but forgotten by the world.

After the splendid centuries of the Arab empires, when the thirst for trade drove Arab argosies across the world from the Gulf to China, the depredations of the Mongols, the rise of the Ottoman Empire, internal dissension and foreign invasion induced a strange lassitude in the lands of the Middle and Near East. Though occasional travellers penetrated Arabia and returned to tell curious tales of a remote people whose ways were markedly different from those of the western world, which was growing more and more confident of its role in the management of nations, the peninsula was allowed to slumber undisturbed. As the centuries rolled by, the heavy burden of the Ottoman bureaucracy bore down upon eastern Arabia, penetrating in its final years even to Qatar, just across the Gulf from Bahrain.

THE GULF IN THE MODERN AGE

The Gulf itself began to stir once again in the European consciousness during the eighteenth century. That most hardy and dedicated of travellers, the young Dane, Carsten Niebhur, travelled its length and included reports of it in his quite remarkable book, published in 1774 (in the French edition)[41] which attracted some mild attention among scholars and savants. The growing power of Britain in India was the factor which in time prompted the principal change in European attitudes, and it led in time to an awakening of scholarly interest in the region's past. In the later years of the eighteenth century, Britain, concerned with the need to protect her sea lanes to India, which were vital to the prosperity of her developing industrial cities, successfully eliminated French competition in Arabia and the lower reaches of the Gulf. The French presence had, for the while, seemed to pose a significant threat to what Britain had increasingly come to see as her necessary paramountcy in the area. The French had established a foothold in Muscat; in 1798 the British effected their expulsion and themselves entered into a treaty with the ruler of Oman.[42] Then another problem reared its head which was deemed to require British action: the nefarious activities of the celebrated pirates of the east Arabian coast.

'Pirates' is, of course, a term which the European interest in the area has applied to the freebooters who sailed the southern Gulf seas and who were a considerable nuisance to the free passage of the merchant ships sailing to and from the Indian Empire ports. Arab writers of the present day prefer to see them as independent-minded fighters for freedom, kicking against the presence of the colonial power which, with remarkable prescience, they are considered to have recognized as such a good deal earlier than most other peoples.[43]

The truth is more probably that, pirates or freedom fighters or whatever, they were really seaborne Badu who, like their land-based brothers, saw any strangers not directly under their protection as fair game. The rich cargoes that sailed to and from India, British and otherwise, also had the attraction of being carried by the ships of the infidel, making their seizure an act of piety as much as of profit.

A series of judicious treaties with the shaikhs of the Gulf coast eventually cut off the freebooters' land support. Gradually their activities ceased, their going marked by the occasional startlingly dramatic incident such as the case of the Qatari-based buccaneer, Rahma bin Jaber. Trapped at last in Khor after a lifetime of merciless harrying of the coastal ports and the shipping that served them, Rahma, with his 10-year-old son clasped to his breast, ignited a load of gunpowder in his hold and blew himself, his son and his ship to immortality in the year 1826, off the coast near Dammam in Saudi Arabia.

With the British maintaining a watchful eye on the seas around the Gulf and with British diplomatic activity directed largely towards the shaikhs who were the ancestors of the rulers of the modern states, matters remained relatively peaceful throughout the nineteenth century, punctuated only by the occasional flurry when a dynastic or clan dispute between the shaikhs and their followers might assume proportions which could not be ignored. Such occasions requiring British intervention were rare; Britain had, by virtue of the treaties which she had engineered with the shaikhs, made herself responsible for their relations with such foreign powers as might presume an interest in the area. Thus effectively she prevented any power other than herself from taking a real interest in what was going on in a corner of the world which was, in any case, in the eyes of most foreign observers, remote and insignificant.

In such circumstances it is not be be wondered at that most of the early archaeological survey and excavation in the Gulf was carried out by British scholars and amateurs. Although most of them, as will be seen, were diligent in reporting their work, the Gulf was not judged to be a rewarding area for research until well into the twentieth century.

2

THE PROGRESS OF GULF
ARCHAEOLOGY

Those who derive pleasure from the observation of ancient peoples and the places in which they lived find a special excitement in the descriptions of the first uncovering of the evidences of long buried and forgotten civilizations by those who originally identified them and who recorded the traces of their lives and deaths. The impact, the immediacy and, above all, the enthusiasm of the excavators' reports of those often small triumphs which later became the common currency of archaeology more than compensate for their occasional inaccuracy or, sometimes, downright fantasy. Nothing can detract from the excitement which a reading of Carter on Tutankhamun, Woolley on the Royal Graves at Ur, or Evans creating an entire world out of the mounds of Knossos (and, to a substantial degree, his imagination) instantly inspires. Happily, the story of the development of archaeological expedition and research in the Arabian Gulf begins with such a record.

In the winter of 1878, the first step in the archaeology of the Arabian Gulf was taken when a young British Officer, Captain E.L. Durand, came ashore at Muharraq, the smaller of the two principal islands of Bahrain in the Arabian Gulf, and then the seat of its commerce and government. His purpose was to undertake a survey of the island's antiquities, the first scientific review of Bahrain's past yet attempted, at least since Roman times or when Alexander sent his admirals to survey the Arabian coast and its islands. Captain E.L. Durand was First Assistant Resident, attached to the staff of Her Britannic Majesty's Political Resident, then based at Bushire, on the southern coast of Persia.

The appointment of 'Political Resident' was one of those somewhat imprecise titles with which British imperial servants were often labelled. It was a rank which was distinctly proconsular; its bearers, latterly, were entitled to the same formal courtesies as Ambassadors and indeed they outranked most. In the Gulf they were not merely the most senior political officials serving there, their writ running from Kuwait to Oman, but they also bore the burden of military command and were responsible for the British forces in the area. The post of Political Resident in the Gulf continued to be filled until the British withdrawal from their long-standing treaties of protection with the shaikhs of the Gulf in 1971. By that time the Gulf was the last posting in the British foreign service where the rank of Political Resident was still to be found; by then, and by a neat contortion of history, the seat of the Political Residence had shifted from Bushire to Bahrain itself.

In 1878 the Political Resident (then a less august rank than it was to become) was responsible not to the Foreign Office in London, but to the Government of India's Foreign Department in Calcutta. It was from this Department that Durand bore his mandate and it was to its Secretary, A.C. Lyall (later Sir Alfred and a Privy Councillor), that the Resident himself, Lieutenant-Colonel E.C. Ross (later Sir Edward) forwarded the report which Durand prepared at the conclusion of his mission.

Durand's report is the first document in the archaeology both of the Gulf and of the Bahrain islands; it is also one of the most important. It exists in two versions and an examination of them reveals certain telling differences between them.

The version which is most frequently quoted and which is generally used by archaeologists or commentators is the text as published in the *Journal of the Royal Asiatic Society* (new series), 12 (Part II), 1880, pp. 189–227, in which it is described as 'Extracts from Report on the Islands and Antiquities of Bahrain. by Captain Durand'.[1] Some twelve small pages of letterpress follow, punctuated by a reproduction of Bahrain's most celebrated artefact, the 'Durand stone', an Old Babylonian inscription recording the pious claim of one Rimum, who describes himself as the 'servant' of Dilmun's tutelary divinity. It is this discovery which is taken by most authorities to identify Bahrain decisively as the Dilmun of Sumerian and later myth and history. The identification was made by Sir Henry Rawlinson, perhaps the most distinguished specialist of his day in Mesopotamian studies, who appended a series of 'Notes' to the extracts from Durand's report and who was at that time the President and Director of the Royal Asiatic Society.[2]

This form of Durand's observations is an edited version of his full report which his superior official sent on to *his* superior in India.[3] There are several discrepancies between the two versions which are relevant and, in some cases, slightly surprising, for the official report is far more freely written; indeed, it is positively winsome in places. From the historical and archaeological standpoints, it is also much more extensive; perhaps Durand felt he was writing there for colleagues and friends who would understand more readily than the readers of the *Journal* both his scholarship and his more parenthetical comments on the pursuit of his studies in so remote and outlandish a location.

Further, the report contains an important element which the *Journal* article lacks: a number of fine illustrations, some full-page, others details inset into the text, all evidently prepared by Durand himself. By the evidence of the 100 or so drawings deposited in the India Office Library Durand was a competent water-colourist. Sadly, none of his Bahraini drawings seems to have survived.

The first illustration in the report is a map which shows the position of Bahrain (spelt in the map and throughout the text 'Bahrein') in the Gulf relative to the Qatar peninsula and the coast of what is now part of the Eastern Province of Saudi Arabia. The map has several features which make it unusual. It is evidently based on an earlier publication.

The principal island, Bahrain proper, is shown reasonably accurately. To the north-east lies the island of Muharraq, now linked to its larger partner by a causeway, then separated by a sea channel. To the west of Bahrain is shown the island of 'Umm en Hussan', presumably Umm Nassan. Various sites are marked on the Arabian coast further to the west. These include Geriyeh, Ojeir and Dohali Suhoa: no settlements of these names are known today though the last two probably conceal Ugair and Dohat-as-Salwa, whilst the first seems to recall the ancient and so far undiscovered emporium of Gerrha; the name may simply have been misinterpreted by Durand. The deep bay which lies behind Bahrain, between the Qatar peninsula and the mainland coast now called the Bay of Salwa, is shown on Durand's map with a dotted line; he was apparently uncertain of its outline when he prepared the map and speculated that the sea ran south and east, almost cutting off the Qatar peninsula. He identifies Al-Bida'a, the village which was the forerunner of Doha, Qatar's present-day capital.

More surprisingly he marked 'Khor el Udaid', an inlet of singular beauty, at the point where Qatar's territory today marches with that of the United Arab Emirates. It is difficult to reach, and it must be presumed that Durand has sailed round the Qatar coast to this point, though he makes it clear that he did not penetrate the Bay of Salwa.

A notable feature of the map is that the entire Qatar peninsula is marked 'El Bahrein'. When Durand landed Qatar was largely under the control of a remarkable shaikh of the Al-Thani family, Jassim bin Thani, whose 'pic-nic' in the desert in 1855 had been charmingly described by Palgrave in his *Travels in Central and Eastern Arabia*.[4] Shaikh Jassim lived on into the twentieth century and a notable description exists of him as a very old man riding out into the desert attended by a host of his sons, grandsons and retainers. However, in Durand's day, the Al-Khalifa princes in Bahrain considered that the city of Zubara in the north of Qatar, which they had founded in the eighteenth century during the migration of the Utub tribes, first to the east and then southwards, was their stronghold on the mainland and that they were the lawful rulers of the Qatar peninsula. This view they have indeed maintained to this day, especially as regards the disputed islands of Hawar. It would seem that at this point at least the Government of India, as the protecting power, agreed with them. In attaching the name 'Bahrein' to the Qatar peninsula, however, Durand was perpetuating a form of topographical nomenclature which was very ancient. Even in the earliest times, and certainly right down to the Islamic period, eastern Arabia had often been called by the same name as that of the principal island in the Bahrain group, which thus may be seen always to have been the dominant influence in the region.

Durand's report in its original version submitted to the Viceroy's office is a more elegant document than the *Journal* extracts. Each photograph is numbered in the manner of such productions; the pages are long, the typeface large and clear. Durand's remarks begin unpropitiously, at least as far as Bahrain's prospects for commerce are concerned.

> Trade – There is not much to be said about the trade of these islands.
>
> Pearls and dates are the chief, almost the only exports but the statistics are annually given in the reports. The import trade, consisting chiefly of rice, coffee and cloth, is mostly carried on by buniahs from Hindustan, those resident here being men in a very small way of business, the larger capitalists coming over for the pearl season only.
>
> The trade operations of these islands might be greatly extended under a settled Government; if for instance the British Government held them they would draw the trade of the whole Persian Gulf and be a trade centre, from which Persia and Arabia would be supplied and drained. I say boldly that there would be no merchants left in any of the ports subject to Native rule in the whole of the Gulf from Basrah to Maskat, except the agents necessary for clearing the customs and passing on consignments inland.
>
> A glance at the map will show that, with no labour to speak of, a most excellent harbour could be brought up to the very doors of the ware-houses, which might be built on land reclaimed from the sea.

This last comment is prophetic, if Durand means what his words seem to mean. In the light of Bahrain's more recent history, when a substantial increase in the habitable land presently available has been brought about by the Government's policy of land reclamation around the shores of Muharraq and the northern part of the principal Bahrain island, it is remarkable that Durand seems to have been proposing precisely the same thing in 1879.

> The land reclaimable stretches almost from the Portuguese fort to the island of Muharrak, and all that would be necessary to effect this would be a wall of stones carried out at low tide if necessary, and built up by degrees. During the present full moon and low tides I have seen the land dry to where the coral reefs sink abruptly into deep water.

Durand quotes Pliny's observation that the Arabs believed that the Euphrates debouched into the Gulf from an underground stream, surfacing in these parts. No doubt this was an attempt to explain the freshwater springs which rise up in the seabed and which may well account both for Bahrain's name in Arabic ('the two seas') and her reputation of special sanctity in ancient times. The report's quotation from Pliny reads 'Flumen per quod Euphratem emergere putant' whilst the *Journal*, more correctly, reads 'Euphraten flumen per quoddam Arabiae emergere putant.'

The occasional errors in the text printed in Calcutta, of which this seems to be one, suggest that Durand was able to proofread the *Journal* but not the report. Since the *Journal* extracts appear to be based on the report's actual text, Durand would have been able to correct any errors which had crept into the earlier version. An engaging example appears a little later in the report where the celebrated eighteenth-century French cartographer, D'Anville, is discovered quaintly disguised as 'Dr. Anville'. Many of the spellings, even of classical references, are eccentric and suggest that the report was printed without its author's supervision. The occasional inelegancies of language and *non sequiturs* in the text support this impression.

In the report Durand compares the underground waters in Bahrain with the Persian qanats but he evidently does not feel, in the *Journal*, that the reference supports his argument. He perhaps did not know of the existence of qanats in Bahrain; they were, until quite recent times, a notable factor in the island's agricultural economy.

A charming marginal drawing appears in the report to illustrate a comment he makes about the conduits of drinking water:

> The water is conducted from these various wells by ordinary unbanked channels, the larger of which have now come to look like natural streams. Where it is necessary to raise it this is done from wells by the ordinary skin bucket let down over a pulley and walked up to the cistern level by cattle pulling down an incline; from channels generally by leverage of a date trunk lightly swung by ropes to a frame, and balanced at one end by a basket of earth into which it is inserted, so that little exertion is required to lift up the water.

He captions his drawing, diffidently, 'something like this'. Durand permits himself a more vivid prose in the report than in the *Journal*. Thus the graves concealed within the mounds which are the principal focus of his archaeological interest ('dead-houses' he calls them) and the description of the dusty ground characterizing the region near the coast ('the relic', in the *Journal*'s words, 'probably of former habitations'), appears in the report as 'the cerecloth of dead races and habitations'.

The report contains some eighteen paragraphs devoted to a description of the plant and wildlife of the island. It seems from these descriptions that Durand liked animals and enjoyed their ways.

> The hares are about the size of a three-quarter grown English rabbit, very small and blood-locking [*sic*] with prominent eyes. This casty look is noticeable in every Arabian animal, man included. The Arab horse is well known, but the Arab greyhound of which a really good

specimen is seldom obtainable, is a most beautiful animal, so light and slender as to seem useless for work, but when going, appearing rather to fly than gallop. These hares are easily tamed; I had two, rescued from a hawk and a greyhound respectively, which after four days became so tame that they played about the room, hopping up occasionally to see what I was doing, and only retiring behind a box on the arrival of a stranger.

His description of the plight of the date plantations, even then a matter of concern, is clearly warmly felt:

Trees and Plants – Foremost amongst the trees is of course the date and some of the date-gardens are extremely fine. Many however are going and gone to ruin, the result of bad Government, and indeed in some places that were once flourishing gardens not a bearing tree remains.

Like many visitors to Arabia he dilates upon the hazards of camel-riding:

The camels are mostly from Arabia, though they are now bred here in the marshes. A few good ones for riding purposes are owned by the Sheikhs. These feed even when going at a sharp trot giving the un-accustomed rider an odd feeling of helplessness, as the long neck disappears in front and head becomes mixed up with the animal's legs; this feeling is soon replaced by one of implicit confidence when you get accustomed to the acrobatic performance, and find that no harm comes of it.

He inserts a charming drawing of a fish which particularly caught his eye. Durand describes him affectionately, though fishes with coats may seem unlikely ichthyological phenomena.

There are several sorts of fish in the fresh water. One with peculiar marking drew my attention. I have never seen him noticed. The dorsal fin is the centre of 3 circular or oval bands of dark colour, which show very plainly against the silver sides of the fish and present odd effect when he swims. The largest I saw was only probably a few ounces in weight. It would almost seem as if he had caught the colour of his coat from swimming constantly in these shallow crystal waters shaded by the long thin spikes of date palm but perhaps this is too Darwinian, as although fish do constantly take, and even change their colour from the sort of water they live in, they would scarcely take their marking in this manner.

Durand evidently kept abreast of current academic development as his reference to Darwin reveals. *The Origin of Species* had been published in 1859.

One of his most remarkable passages refers to his identification of a group of mounds near the village of 'Barboora' (modern Barbar) as of particular importance. He recognized that one large stone block on the surface had been worked; with remarkable perception he describes one square-cut hole having been made 'as if for a door-jamb'. The site was not excavated until more than seventy years after Durand's visit but the excavations then identified the block which he saw, which was still on the surface, as part of the entrance to the third of the temples which had been built at Barbar during the very late third and early second millennia.

Early on in his description of the fields of grave-mounds which were Bahrain's principal antiquarian interest in his day, he inserts a lengthy comment about the possibly Phoenician origin of Bahrain's antiquities and the Herodotean story about the origins of the Phoenicians themselves: the Phoenicians suggested that their origins lay in the Gulf, or, at any rate, the upper reaches of the Indian Ocean. Since he quotes 'Mr. Rawlinson' extensively (he presumably was unaware of Sir Henry's baronetcy) he may have been tactful to excise these comments in the *Journal* knowing that Rawlinson was indeed going to comment in print on the *Journal* extracts. However, one paragraph is worth quoting, if only for the very odd epithet employed for Alexander the Great, who sent his admirals to survey the Gulf and its islands towards the end of his life.

> It will however scarcely be called in question that these islands of Bahrain were in old days inhabited by a Phoenician race, and that they had here temples to their gods actually seen by Androsthenes, when he led the naval expedition under orders from the Macedonian boy-conquerer.

Herodotos may have been vindicated in his belief about Phoenician origins more than a century later, but Durand ascribed the origins of the remains on Bahrain to the Phoenicians quite erroneously. Durand's *Journal* extracts contain but one page of illustrations and that is devoted to his most important discovery, the inscription which is frequently referred to as 'the Durand stone', and which by its mention of the god Inzak, the tutelary divinity of Bahrain, suggested to Rawlinson the identification of Bahrain with Dilmun. The report describes its finding and the slightly deceitful way in which Durand persuaded the keepers of the mosque in whose wall it was imbedded to part with it. Then he says:

> I thought at first that it might be the prow or figurehead of some old ship, and I suppose this is possible. At any rate, however, we know that the Phoenicians above all worshipped the Phallus, and that the goddess Astarte, their particular favourite and the protectress of mariners, was worshipped by them under the form of a conical stone. Whether under this form she was even let into the prows of their ships I cannot say; as a figure-head I believe that her image was so used.

This, however, is a mere speculation, the writing will probably tell its own tale.

How he can have imagined a 60-cm (2-foot) long piece of basalt (if that is what it was) ever to have been the figurehead of a ship is difficult to imagine. It is less surprising that again he should drag in the Phoenicians, this time in a very nineteenth-century disguise as phallus-worshippers.

Durand then takes off for several paragraphs into a splendidly irrelevant and curious piece of historical fantasy, prompted by the inscription, which involves the legendary origins of the Arabs and their possible incursions into Europe in very early times. He writes of the inscription:

Here again is a puzzle to any but an adept. Some of the characters are evidently ordinary cuneiform, whether of Babylonian, Assyrian, or Achaemenian, the type seems much the same but some of the characters interspersed are hieroglyphic, as well as the tree or palm bough itself probably, that stands on the left of the inscription, a fact that might point to the stone having been engraved at a time when emblematic writing was being converted into alphabetical. This again is mere surmise. At any rate it is not of the real Phoenician type that Cadmus taught the Greeks, and from which their alphabet emanated, as the Phoenicians were supposed to have known this writing 1500 years BC.

Mr. Rawlinson would, I think, make Cadmus merely a mythical personage, under the form of Kedem the East, seeking Ereb the West, or Europe, but still he admits the cumulative force of the arguments that he enumerates, as very great towards the proof of a Phoenician settlement in Boeotia.

Going further than he does Mr. Forster says 'that this name of Cadmus can be traced through Kademah or Kadmas', which latter form, he states, to be a truly Arabic idiomatic one, and quotes it, through Melo, through Eusebius, and Alexander Polyhistor who gives the twelve sons of Abraham (Ishmael) by his Egyptian wife, and again that the only 'direct notice of the Arabs are among the early peoples of Europe to be found among the classic writers occurs in Strabo, who in his account of the peopling of Euboea off the coast of Boeotia reckons as the first inhabitants a colony of Arabs, who had accompanied Cadmus into Greece'. This statement carries within itself marks of its authenticity, since all the circumstances of the case attest the correctness of Strabo's information, &c. &c. He then continues that Cadmus is simply the Greek form of Kedemah, which is rendered Kedinah in the LXX, and Cadmos by Josephius, and the Ishmaelite tribe of Kedemah, we have already seen, was seated in the very locality assigned on independent grounds as the cradle of the Phoenician Cadmus, the namesake, and it may justly be inferred the youngest son of Ishmael.

He further goes on to clench his argument with an Arab tradition also proving the National consanguinity between the Peloponnesians and Boeotians and the Arabs (zebeydi Ishmaelites).

To return, however, without being sure that Cyrus rules these islands, we know that Darius did as they formed a part of his l4th satrapy, and were used by his as a penal settlement (the jockey King could scarcely have invented a better).

'Jockey King' is surely a peculiar epithet for Darius. It stems, no doubt, from a legend of Darius' origins and his unlikely election as Great King, in which one of his horses played a crucial, even a decisive, role. It is intriguing, by the way, that Durand should be speculating about the possibility of a Phoenician influence on Greece in early times, a reversal of the view which was gaining strength in his day, that Greece owed nothing either to Semitic (Phoenician) influences or to others which might have come from Africa (Egypt).

The stone may therefore well belong to this period of Persian rule, or again it may simply have found its way down from Assyria. The latter being the most likely, for the cuneiform seems to me to differ from the Achaemenian that I have seen, and the more so that no signs are used under that form of writing. Of course an expert would settle the question at once.

Durand's suggestion of the possibility of the stone having migrated from Assyria is not one which most scholars have followed, though it is by no means unreasonable. The question may well be asked why anyone should wish to transport a substantial piece of basalt from Assyria to the midst of the Gulf, and the improbability of such an action seems to have satisfied most commentators since Durand's day. But there is little doubt that the inscription which Durand reproduces belongs to the first half of the second millennium BC.

Durand's illustration of the inscription in the report is quite unlike the drawing of it which appears in the *Journal* extract. That in the report is drawn from a 'squeeze', a popular technique in the nineteenth century for the rapid copying of inscriptions of engravings in stone achieved by applying to the inscription a papier mâché or similar coating which, when it was removed, bore a negative impression of the subject. This is what Durand shows in the report. It must, one imagines, have puzzled the officials in the Viceroy's Foreign Department, for it is reproduced upside-down and in reverse.

Rawlinson translated the inscription for Durand, thus introducing his brilliant contribution to the archaeology of Dilmun. But this was not his first attempt. In a footnote to Paragraph 6 of the report, Rawlinson (now properly acknowledged as 'Sir H. Rawlinson', incidentally) is referred to gratefully by Durand, but the 'translation' is very much a first draft.

Figure 2.1 The burial mounds, as sketched by Durand.

At this point in the report Durand interposes two drawings of the great mounds at Aali in the northern part of Bahrain (or Ali, as he prefers it) which really form the focus of his report and of which he remarked earlier, though perhaps optimistically, 'with regard to the tumuli, we are standing on surer ground and cannot go far wrong.'

The drawings which Durand prepared for the report are really very handsome. They suggest vividly the commanding character of the Aali mounds before they were subject either to the archaeologist's spade or to the attention of the village potters, who have all but destroyed them in converting many of them into kilns. The drawings convey, as no other representation does, the massive size and extent of the mounds as they evidently appeared in Durand's day (Fig. 2.1). Certainly the quality of his illustrations varies considerably, ranging from what are plainly rapid sketches to more finished drawings; his plans are neat and informative, the first attempts accurately to depict any of the Bahrain tumuli and to plot the area in which they were to be found. His drawing of the fill in one of the entrance passages to one of the mounds is masterly, positively gothic, indeed.

Durand, both in the *Journal* extracts and in the report, speculates about the inhabitants of the islands who built these tremendous tombs. As he remarks, 'I have not heard of such another necropolis above ground in the world.' He believes, on balance, that Bahrain was a sepulchral island, a

Toteninsel, a holy place to which the dead were brought for burial from the mainland, perhaps, he suggests, from the lost city of Gerrha. He presumes that such inhabitants as the island possessed lived in simple houses built 'of the branches of the palm-tree, as do the poorer classes to the present day'. The type of indigenous building to which he refers is the *barasti*, which, until the setting up of Government-financed housing schemes, was the most common form of domestic dwelling in Bahrain.

Durand had a natural archaeologist's eye, still perhaps the most important professional tool that anyone who follows its practice can possess. The mounds at 'Barboora' to which he refers early in his comments are evidently those sited near the modern village of Barbar. The Danes lighted on these mounds early on in their work in Bahrain, and in excavations in the 1950s and 1960s uncovered a remarkable series of temples of a type which seems to link them with the successors of the Sumerians in southern Mesopotamia, possibly with the Sumerians themselves. Prominent among the structures which they excavated, the Danes found a magnificent stone well, which perhaps suggests that the temple was consecrated to Enki, the great god of the Apsu or the Abyss, to whom Rawlinson refers in his comments on Durand's report, under the name 'Hea'; an aspirated form of his Semitic (Akkadian) name, Ea. Given the excavation methods of the day and the fine artefacts which the Barbar mounds preserved, it is perhaps fortunate that Durand passed them by, though, as is evident from his notes, he did so with some regret.

Durand did not, of course, know of the settlements lying beneath the mound near which the Qala'at al-Bahrain now stands. Excavators who came after him, notably the Danes who found and dug the site, have shown that settlements were established there from the last quarter of the third millennium, and developed into a substantial city by about the year 2000 BC. It is now generally accepted that the island's population was quite capable of providing sufficient inhabitants for the great necropoleis which pit the surface of Bahrain's northern and central deserts. We know now, in part at least, the answer to Durand's question 'If these miles upon miles of crowded heaps are tombs, where did the inhabitants live?'

Durand's question, and his suspicion that Bahrain is an island of the dead, lead him again into another historical excursion which is full of entertainment, if it is a little thin on supportable fact. This time it is the Scythians in particular who attract him, with, again, a passing glance at the Phoenicians.

Causes, such as their fertility, their temples(?), their abundance in most beautiful water, may have caused these islands to have been regarded as holy ground.

Even at the present day the Hindoos look to be taken to the bosom of the Ganges, or the devout Mahomedan of these parts to be lain in the holy dust of Kerbela. May not some ancient tribe of Phoenicians on the mainland have looked to sleep their long sleep in the hallowed dust of these sacred islands? This may seem a far-fetched idea, but the vastness of the series of mounds must be my excuse. I have not heard of such another necropolis above ground in the world.

With regard to the distance as likely to negative this idea, compare the distance that the tribes of Royal Scythians are said to have carried their Kings before they laid them finally to rest in their appointed places of sepulture on the Borysthenes in the land of the Gerri.

The Thracians or Goths buried under tumuli, the Scythians, Lydians, and Libyans also, and indeed the custom appears to have been very generally adopted by the wandering Indo-European populations of the earth.

With regard to the bones of animals found, compare the Scythian customs. These gentlemen, when Kings at any rate, had a pet wife, a pet horse and other valued possessions buried with them. This was hard on the wives and attendants, as also on the body of 50 handsome youths and horses who were killed, stuffed and staked round the tomb as a mortuary body-guard – a ghastly sight.

Next Durand turns to speculations on the whereabouts of the great city of Gerrha, one of the most important emporia of late antiquity, located somewhere in eastern Arabia, to the west of the Bahrain islands. It is here that 'Dr. Anville' appears, suggesting that Gerrha might have been placed at 'Gram' (evidently a textual error for 'Grain', the early name for Kuwait).

Durand's excursions into the intricacies of Arabian place-names are inventive if not wholly convincing; he manages, improbably, to bring back the Scythinans into the discussions by positing a connection between Gerrha and the 'land of the Gerrhi'. He acknowledges however 'mere resemblances (between 'the likeness of names') which are so common and unreliable'.

To return, however, to Gerrha, as the first cause of these cemeteries, the correct site of which has been somewhat disputed, Dr. Anville would have placed it at Katif, Niebuhr at Koweit or Gram, and so on, but Forster places it, I think probably correctly, at the bottom of the bay behind Bahrain. Not content with his argument supported by Pliny and Strabo's accounts, whose descriptions, if they fail to apply here, will scarcely apply anywhere in the Gulf, Forster argues further that it is the received opinion that this country (the modern province of Haar or Bahrain) derived its scriptural name and primitive colonization from the Cushite Havileh.

The Pison of Genesis enclosed this land, which was the name for the branch of the Euphrates, that ran parallel to the Gulf and fell into the Bahrain Islands.

He contends that a direct proof of this region having borne the name of Havileh is supplied in Aval, a name retained for the larger island of Bahrain.

Ptolemy places Gerrha at the bottom of this same bay, and it is the precise site assigned by Abul Feda Nasir Ettarsi, and Ulug Beg to the city of Hagar, said by Strabo to have been founded by Chaldean exiles.

Forster says that the word Gerr'a is merely the anagram for Hagar, whose descendants he traces in the Agrai of the classics.

He would make the land of Hagar the birth place of the Chaldeans, the sons of Khalid (Ben Khali), intimately connected with the Ishmaelites and the founders of Babylon. He traces Khaled, Hkalid, Hkanlah, Khait, Huale, Huile, Hanilah, Aval and Havileh, as mere verbal forms of the same root.

The Chaldeans are, however, supposed to have had a Scythic or Turanian origin, and a large library and much study would be necessary before judging of the reliability of such derivations.

Is it possible that the forms of burial of different races were distinct enough to give some clue, and that further researches amongst the wilderness of tom[b]s in good preservation here may throw some light into a dark page of history?

I noticed above the Scythic customs of burials and transport of the dead to the land of the Gerrhi, to the point at which the Borysthenes becomes navigable.

Is it possible that there should be any ethnic affinity, to account for the likeness of names between Gerrhus and Gerrha, or is it one of those mere resemblances which are so common and unreliable?

Granting, however, that Gerrha was near here, what more likely than that these islands might have been used in the manner suggested above?

I have been told by Arabs that there are many large ruins on the mainland, and one man in particular told me that they found traces of building, stone and pillars at a place where salt is quarried. The bottom of the Gulf behind Bahrain has, I believe, never been carefully explored.

Durand's principal motive in visiting Bahrain was to investigate the island's immense fields of grave mounds which, in his day, were as the Gulf's sole relic of high antiquity of merit. In both versions Durand reports the opening of 'a small mound to the westward of the large group'. He inserts two small drawings in the report, respectively a plan and an elevation of the tomb. He then devotes a full page to a fine elevation and section drawing of one of the large mounds, the first such ever to be attempted (Fig 2.2). It is drawings of this quality and detail that make the reliance of archaeologists in the past on the edited *Journal* extracts, rather than the original report, somewhat to be regretted.

His entry into one of the mounds is the opportunity, yet again, for Durand to wander off, this time into charming reminiscence about his apprehensions on disturbing the long-dead and the antics of a favoured 'very nice bull pup'. What his masters in the Viceroy's office in Calcutta thought of all this is not recorded.

On creeping in under the huge slab above us I was sickened by a smell, which I cannot describe, and being new to the trade of body-snatching was assailed by some qualms of conscience as to the propriety of my conduct. On reflection, however, I came to the conclusion that the golden rule of life was, 'do unto others, &c' Applying this practically, and putting myself in the place of the defunct Phoenician, I thought that if I could think, under the circumstances, I should probably not mind being disturbed after being shut up for some thousands of years. So I went in bravely, 'Ce n'est que le premier pas,' and since then I have become hardened and keep several of the gentlemen's bones in a basket in my room. I was, however, disturbed, not to say distressed, at hearing them begin to rattle in the dark, but found on timid inspection that the noise proceeded from the intelligent researches of a very nice bull pup that I have. I remonstrated with him, as I thought that he might have drawn the line at such very innutritive substances, but the matter gave food for further reflection. I thought that such a subject

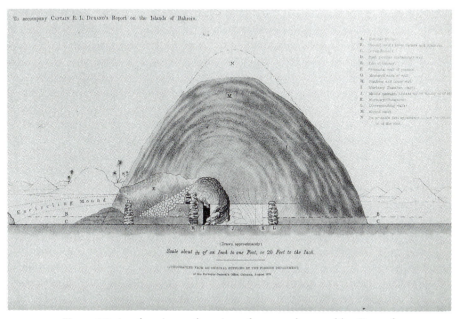

Figure 2.2 An elevation and section of a mound opened by Durand.

might almost have supplied Montaigne with a text for one of his humorous philosophical essays, and that treated by Artemus Ward or Mark Twain, the Castor and Pollux of modern wit and humour, it might also become ludicrous. Reverting, however, to my previous argument, I returned to bed.

Durand describes some of the material which he found in the mounds though, in the manner of most archaeologists of his day, very sketchily. However, he does refer to 'fragments of a vessel of coarse red earthenware'. This may well be the first record of the typical Barbar pottery which has been found in the Aali tombs and in the smaller tumuli of third millennium date. He goes on:

> In the small compartment facing the first we found the bones of some small animal, probably a gazelle or a sheep, and some remains of a rather delicate clay drinking vessel, whilst scattered here in the dust of the central passage were a lot of small shapeless pieces of oxidized metal, brass or copper, and some fragments of a vessel of coarse red earthenware.
>
> An intelligent Native remarked to me that these could no longer be made, as the colour of the earth had changed, he had found old bits before and always red, but now they can only make dirty white and light yellow. I suggested that age in the pots themselves might account for the change of colour, but he would not consent to the proposition.

Of course the 'intelligent Native' was quite right; the pottery for which Aali is renowned today is a pale biscuit to buff colour and, like the earlier wares, will keep its colour to the end of time. Durand, incidentally prefers the very nineteenth-century term 'crockery' for pottery. It should be noted that excavations nearly a hundred years later produced a handsome suite of three examples of the 'rather delicate clay drinking vessel' to which Durand refers (Fig 7.12).

Durand chose to describe in detail and to illustrate one of the large tumuli in both versions of his observations. In the report, however, he appends another of his small, marginal sketches and relates that 'he made use of my detachment of the 21st Native Infantry, working them in relays of a few men for a few hours, keeping them out of camp and of mischief'. These were sepoys of the Indian Army who were evidently in attendance on Durand.

Another drawing shows the mound (which he hoped 'might cover the ruins of a small temple') with steps cut in it from the top. From the report's description of Durand's penetration of this mound, the most detailed of any in either version, it is evident that he used gunpowder extensively, more than appears from the *Journal* extracts. In the report he notes, at one point:

> I picked my way along between these containing walls, removing the earth as I went, as also blowing down the mass of hard flint limestone,

and concrete soil from above us, thus gradually filling up the passage
behind us as we proceeded.

In the *Journal* extracts this has become: 'I picked my way between these
containing walls removing the earth as I went and then gradually clearing
out the passage behind as we proceeded.'

In both versions he goes on: 'This increased the labour enormously and
was I believe unnecessary from the compactness of the mass, the relative
small size of the gallery and the forward slope of the walls.'

But the report continues:

> . . . which gave a good sound thrust to the arch we left over us; but not
> being an engineer I could not risk it, and once having blown in a
> portion of our roof, it was *ipso facto* necessary to continue to do so, as
> the earth was thoroughly loosened and weakened by the shock of this
> first explosion. The necessity, however, might have become more
> apparent when we came to the inner wall, for here gunpowder had to
> be used.

It is the blocks in this passage which Durand draws so impressively.

Towards the end of Durand's report, when he speaks of the mound which
he would greatly have liked to excavate but now did not have the time, he
provides another marginal drawing showing what he describes as 'original
tombs'. A companion sketch shows the same mound 'present state
exaggerated'.

Durand's final comment is matter-of-fact: 'The whole subject may or may
not be worth investigation'; and, in a note in the margin, he adds: 'It is
astonishing that no scientific societies should have been sent out to examine
these coasts, where the climate is so perfectly adapted to preserve every thing
not attacked by man.'

It is stranger still that ten years were to pass before Durand's initiative was
to be matched by another intrepid traveller; the climate of the Bahrain
islands and the Gulf generally, sadly, does not support Durand's contention
that it preserves 'everything not attacked by man'. The exceptional summer
humidity is almost as powerful an agent for destruction as man himself.

Durand lived on to complete his life as a distinguished servant of the
Crown; like his mentor, Rawlinson, he was honoured by his country: he too
was created a baronet towards the end of his life. He returned to Britain with
the trophies of his excursions to Bahrain, including the basalt stone with the
precious inscription. It was not heard of for years. Then, in the 1970s, a sale
of effects of one member of Durand's family was held by the London
auctioneers, Christie's. An enquiry was put to them, for transmission to the
family, if anything was known of the 'basalt' stone which Durand had
brought back a century before. A member of the family recalled it; it had
lain in their house in Scotland for many years before being moved to the

family house in London. This, apparently, was destroyed by German bomb-
ing in the Second World War. The stone, presumably, lies buried still
beneath the buildings now erected on the site. And yet – it is just possible
that someone in those hectic days of the blitz recognized the stone as
something unusual and removed it. Perhaps the expression of Rimum's piety
still exists somewhere, even now.

Durand died in 1920. He is credited with two other excursions into
authorship, in addition to his seminal paper on Bahrain. One was on a
subject not entirely distant from the Gulf, a life of Cyrus the Great King
published in 1906. The other smacks very much of its period and of the
literary enterprises of imperial servants: its title was *Rifle, Rod and Spear in
the East.*

Durand's return to London from his visit to Bahrain was the occasion for
a lecture to the members of the Royal Asiatic Society, in the rooms of
Burlington House on an evening in the year 1880. The meeting was con-
vened under the direction of the remarkable Henry Creswick Rawlinson.

Rawlinson, a Major-General on the retired list, a Knight Commander of
the Most Honourable Order of the Bath, a Baronet, Fellow of the Royal
Society, President and Director of the Royal Asiatic Society, was one of
those nineteenth-century Englishmen of extraordinary drive, enthusiasm
and accomplishment in a variety of different vocations. As a young officer he
had spent his furloughs amongst the wild tribes of Persia and in immersing
himself in a bewildering variety of languages, ancient and modern. He had
achieved a perilous celebrity by climbing the face of the great trilingual
inscription of Behistun, the translation of which had led to the eventual
decipherment of cuneiform and the unlocking of all the immeasurable riches
of Sumerian and Babylonian literature, a process which continues to this
day. Rawlinson was a considerable historian, with a range and grasp of the
ebb and flow of events which would daunt any apprentice scholar in this age.
In his later years, rich in honours and in accomplishments, he became one of
the most visible luminaries in the London intellectual cosmos, forever
researching, leaping into areas not penetrated by others, constantly encour-
aging younger scholars, though jealous of his own achievements and the
recognition which they accorded him.

As the author of *Cuneiform Inscriptions of Western Asia*, in five folio
volumes, he had had a profound influence on successive generations of
historians and fledgeling practitioners of archaeology, the latter now emerging as a separate and discernible discipline. He knew the Gulf, at least from
the Persian side, though there is no evidence that he had ever visited the
Arabian littoral. Durand was fortunate that it was under Rawlinson's aegis at
the Royal Asiatic Society that his discoveries in Bahrain could be launched
on the intellectual London establishment, hovering on the brink of a new
decade, the 1880s.

Rawlinson's notes to Durand's report are, by any standards, a *tour de force*, though inevitably much of their scholarship would not be supported today. As much as any other consideration, too, the sheer enthusiasm and delight in his task, which seems to have possessed Rawlinson even in his eighth decade (he was 75 at the time when Durand's article was published in the Society's *Journal*), ring out of his text. This was the same quality of enthusiasm demonstrated by the great Sumerian god Enki, who was to be significant indeed in the early religions of the Gulf, when he was ordering the world, in one of these Sumerian myths of which Rawlinson was, as it were, one of the publishers to the modern age. Rawlinson demonstrates, in his notes to Durand's text, an ability to move with stunningly fluent ease from language to language, ancient and modern. Naturally he was immersed in the classics, the common currency of the educated man in the nineteenth, as in earlier centuries. Arabic, Persian and Hebrew are fluently commanded and that command extends to Assyrian, Babylonian and, though he does not use the term, the most ancient of all literary sources, Sumerian, of which he was one of the original translators.

Rawlinson sets Durand's comments into context by summarizing what was known, at that point, of the Gulf in antiquity. He begins with the story recorded by the Hellenistic writer Berossus in his great lost work, *Babyloniaca*,[5] the legend of the fish-man Oannes and his followers, swimming up the Gulf and bringing the arts of civilization to Mesopotamia. He accords the primacy of city establishment to Eridu, a fact supported by Sumerian belief and by archaeology; Eridu is Enki's city and the most ancient urban foundation in Mesopotamia.

Rawlinson occasionally has the most remarkable insights. Thus he attributes the origins of commerce to the early inhabitants of the Gulf, a perception which has largely been confirmed by more recent researches. His supreme achievement, in the present context, is his identification of the ancient paradisial land of the early texts, transliterated as Dilmun, with Bahrain. Before Rawlinson's attribution, this name, first used by the Sumerians 5,000 years ago, had not been in common currency for millennia.

Rawlinson was remarkably prescient in some of his opinions. His belief that the Gulf spread over a wider area of land surface in the past than it does today (though he was probably thinking mainly of the Tigris–Euphrates basin where the rivers debouch) has been borne out in studies of the shorelines of the Lower Gulf. As we know now, the sea in ancient times ran into the region known today as the Rub al-Khali and parts of the Gulf coast, as it is now, as well as much of eastern Arabia, were under water.

But no doubt much of what Rawlinson proposes looks fairly odd today. His mixture of philology, speculation and myth would make him an uneasy colleague for most modern scholars. He transliterates the cuneiform characters which spell the island's name, *NiTuk^{ki}*, a term which for a long time was used as an alternative to Dilmun. In fact cuneiform characters often have different values and the form *NiTuk^{ki}* ('ki' is a determinative for 'land' or 'mountain' and as such was not pronounced) is properly transliterated 'Dilmun'; it may have other values also.

Rawlinson writes well of the island of Icarus in the northern part of the Gulf; he did not know that Alexander's interest in the region which he records would be proved so notably by the discovery of the Alexander inscription (see Chapter 8) on Failaka island, which is now known to have been called Icarus in Hellenistic times. This island, in the Bay of Kuwait, also revealed considerable early second-millennium remains.

Rawlinson ranges cheerfully into Levantine studies, into cosmological speculation and star-lore. The distant Egyptians are grist to his mill and he, like others after him, speculates on the similarity of place-names in the Gulf and of cities on the eastern Mediterranean coast. He wonders at the possibility of the population movement on a large scale from the Gulf to the Mediterranean, though he does not feel, expressing a relatively sophisticated, indeed a quite modern view, that the mere coincidence of names is at all convincing. Anyone familiar with the similarity of place-names throughout the Arabic-speaking world today will agree with him.

Though he writes forcefully, even sometimes peremptorily (as befits, perhaps, a Victorian Major-General), he can mock himself in a most engaging manner. Thus, in writing of the identification of the planet Mercury with Dilmun (through Mercury's counterpart in Mesopotamian stellar myths, the god Nebo, and that divinity's involvement with the art of writing), he notes: 'A dissertation of some extent, if not of much interest, on Nebo's connexion with writing and learning will be found in my essay "On the Religion of the Babylonians and Assyrians".' An agreeable man, evidently.

Rawlinson's review of Durand's paper is highly allusive. He touches on ideas associated with the ancient Gulf, such as the fish-cults of Mesopotamia, for example, which have hardly been considered by later scholarship. He was a most creative antiquarian of profound scholarship and boundless interests. Above all, he was one of the first men who recalled Dilmun to the modern world and, through his analysis of Durand's notes, to the world of scholarship. In many ways Rawlinson's notes are the most significant contribution to Bahrain studies published anywhere until Danish archaeologists began their years of excavations in the 1950s.

The final note of Rawlinson's extraordinary and wide-ranging observations reminds us that two great institutions indicated their willingness to support future work in Bahrain, so impressed were they by Durand and, no doubt, by Rawlinson's review of his work. The British Museum, whose contribution to archaeology is unequalled, offered £100 for experimental excavation on the island. The Government of India had earlier offered a similar sum. Neither grant was, apparently, ever invoked by scholars interested in excavating in Bahrain, but Rawlinson's last words have the ring of prophecy about them: 'But the search, though suspended, has not been abandoned and important results may yet be looked for.' Those results were to come nearly a century after the words were written and were, indeed, important.

Ten years passed from Durand's visit. Queen Victoria held her Golden Jubilee, Disraeli was dead, Gladstone formed his last administration; the Gulf slumbered, its inhabitants getting on with the cultivation of the date palm plantations and the harvesting of pearls.

The next visitors to record their impressions of Bahrain and its antiquities were a husband-and-wife team of explorer-writers, Mr and Mrs J. Theodore Bent.[6] They represented a familiar phenomenon of the nineteenth century, very notable before the onset of visual media, the travel writers who wandered across the world recording their impressions of the life of peoples to whom the rise of the empire had given access.

The Bents arrived in Bahrain in 1889, equipped with cameras and some basic excavation techniques. During their stay they opened several of the grave mounds and recovered from them ivory, pottery and metal objects, of which the ivory was quite notable and served further to confirm the wholly erroneous belief that the mounds were Phoenician in origin.

Bent presented his findings to a meeting of the Royal Geographical Society on 25 November 1889, at the Society's rooms in Lowther House, Kensington. His talk was illustrated with slides taken from the photographs which they had secured during their stay. These are amongst the earliest recorded in Bahrain and are of some quality: in one of them Bent, looking like a gamekeeper who has strayed rather far from his customary beat, clad in deerstalker hat and tweeds, is revealed entertaining Bahraini dignitaries at the Aali mounds.

His paper is well structured and quite vivid in the impression which it gives of Bahrain; Bent was, after all, a professional. Many of his early comments, it will be evident, are drawn, largely unacknowledged, from Durand's extracts and Rawlinson's comments of ten years earlier. His own observation is sometimes slightly out of focus: thus he says that 'the merchants dwell in towers of certain architectural merit.' This is a reference evidently to the wind towers which were so typical a feature of domestic dwellings of the more substantial kind throughout the Gulf and eastern Arabia until the very recent past. The architecture he describes as 'strictly Saracenic', whatever that means.

Bent usefully summarizes the history of the region, with tolerable accuracy, from the sixteenth century, when the Portuguese landed. He is quite reliable on the ethnography of Bahrain in the late nineteenth century.

Although the stated purpose of the Bents' visit was to investigate the mounds, his paper deals with their excavation rather summarily. Like Durand, he and his wife concentrated on the Aali mounds, the most impressive in size of all the tumuli on the main island. The tombs which they opened are described concisely and the contents, such as they were, briefly reviewed. The material which they cleared from the tombs was handed over to the British Museum, where it remains.

In the discussion following Bent's paper, the happily named Admiral Lindsay Brine leapt to the defence of the Bahrainis' appearance, on which Bent was undeservedly harsh. Mr Cecil Smith reiterated the possibility of Phoenician origins in the Gulf and, as he represented the British Museum, gave it some canonical authority. His suggestion, that the Egyptian term for the land of Punt, 'To-Nefer', might mean 'the holy island' was especially interesting and deserved to be considered further.

The President wound up the meeting with what sounds suspiciously like faint praise of the Bents' journey, remarking that 'it proved that it was not necessary for a traveller who deserved to give the Society valuable information to go in all cases very far from the ordinary routes of commerce.'

In the years after his Bahrain enterprise Bent went on to do other valuable work, including a review of the ruins of Great Zimbabwe, an investigation of Axum in Ethiopia and travels in southern Arabia and the Red Sea. Another decade passed and Bent was dead, a victim of that scourge of western travellers in the East, malarial fever. His widow, however, who had accompanied him on his Arabian journeys, published in 1900 *Southern Arabia*, a popular record of their travels in Bahrain, Oman and the Yemen.[7] Mrs Bent's literary style, where her own hand is to be detected, is not generally to be commended, though she does manage to record the occasional illuminating titbit of information about life in Bahrain at the turn of the century. Thus paragraphs from her first chapter, describing Shaikh Isa bin Ali, the Ruler of Bahrain who brought a substantial degree of progress and stability to the state, will serve to show her at her best.

> We went to see him at Moharek, where he holds his court in the winter-time. We crossed over in a small baggala, and had to be poled for a great distance with our keel perpetually grating on the bottom. It was like driving in a carriage on a jolting road; the donkeys trotted independently across, their legs quite covered with water. We were glad when they came alongside, and we completed our journeys on their backs.
>
> The courtyard of the palace, which somewhat recalls the Alhambra in its architecture, was, when we arrived, crowded with Arab chiefs in all manner of quaint costumes. His Majesty's dress was exceedingly fine. He and his family are entitled to wear their camel-hair bands bound round with gold thread. These looked very regal over the red turban, and his long black coat, with his silver-studded sword by his side, made him look every inch a king.

The introduction to her second chapter, 'The mounds of Ali', shows her to less advantage, though in a declamatory posture no doubt typical of the time.

44

And now behold us excavators on the way to the scene of our labours. Six camels conveyed our tents, a seventh carried goat-skins full of water. Four asses groaned under our personal effects; hens for consumption rode in a sort of lobster-pot by the side of clattering pickaxes and chairs; six policemen, or peons, were in our train, each on a donkey. One carried a paraffin lamp, another a basket of eggs on the palm of his hand, and as there were no reins and no stirrups, the wonder is that these articles ever survived. As for ourselves, we, like everybody else, rode sideways, holding on like grim death before and behind, especially when the frisky Bahrein donkeys galloped at steeplechase pace across the desert.

'Southern Arabia', though suffering somewhat from Mrs Bent's effusive style, is valuable for the descriptions it contains, not only of Bahrain but also of Oman. In the case of the latter, it describes the landscape of Dhofar, one of the earliest descriptions to survive from a writer with an archaeological interest. Her descriptions of 'ruins', however, are imprecise, though it would appear that she and her husband visited the site of Sumharam, or Khor Rori.

These two records, Durand's and the Bents', of late Victorian excursions to what must have seemed a very distant and remote outpost of empire, were to set the scene for the archaeology of the region for many decades. For many years little interest was taken by foreigners; the British discouraged most of them, in any case, from penetrating a part of the world they were disposed to keep as far as possible to themselves. In consequence the earliest reports of an archaeological significance, as distinct from the records of travellers to the region or the occasional explorer on his way to more remote climes still, tend to focus on Bahrain to the exclusion of the rest of the Gulf. This situation persisted up to the 1930s, when the search for oil brought more people with leisure and relevant professional skills to the Arabian peninsula. The isolation of the Gulf and indeed of the peninsula itself from contact with scientific or academic interests, is, of course, the reason for the absence, otherwise inexplicable, of any reference to Arabia in works of historical or archaeological reference up to very recent times.

At the time of the publication of Durand's extracts in the Royal Asiatic Society's *Journal* both the Government of India and the British Museum had each, as we have seen, made available the sum of £100 for further research into the antiquity of the Bahrain island. No one, evidently, took advantage of these generous allocations at the time.

In 1904, however, something must have pricked the interest of the Government of India in renewing work in Bahrain, for we are told that in that year 'the Archaeological Department of the Government of India turned their attention to this ancient site, the Director General himself proposing to visit Bahrain with a view to settling if possible, the question of the origin of the necropolis.' These words were written by the next figure on the Gulf's archaeological scene, the incumbent Political Resident himself, Colonel F.B. Prideaux.

Colonel Prideaux's report, published in the *Archaeological Survey of India*, 1908–9,[8] is by far the most professional work of its kind to be published up to that point. Like others before and after him, Prideaux lifts observations from Durand's *Journal* article without acknowledgement, but he adds considerably to our knowledge about the immediate pre-Islamic period and the early Islamic centuries when Bahrain had acknowledged Islam, apostasized and then, again and finally, elected for the Faith.

For these times, generally obscure in the Gulf's history, he relies on Yaqut's *Mu'jam-al-Buldan*. He quotes, amongst others, as the origin of the name al-Bahrain ('the two seas'), the idea that it refers, on the one hand, to 'Buhaira', little sea, which received the surplus waters of the Hasa Springs (the great oasis on the mainland to the west of Bahrain) 'on the edge of the Oasis, and on the other hand to the Persian Gulf'.

Prideaux was a competent Arabist and he comments intelligently on the problem, which had perplexed some of his predecessors, of the similarities of the names of Bahrain with those in other, more distant, lands. He also provides a gazetteer of the names of villages and towns given by Yaqut as being in Bahrain and on the coast of eastern Arabia, and identifies them with sites of his own day. He also speculates, with considerable perception, that the ruin now known as the Qala'at al-Bahrain may conceal Babylonian levels. It does, and others earlier still.

But it is of course principally the grave mounds which attract Prideaux's eye. He writes of them sparely and with commendable precision. This is really the first report on the island's antiquities which can be considered as a scientific work.

In all, Prideaux examined sixty-seven of the mounds (Fig. 2.3). He made a number of minor but worthwhile finds, including more ivory. His photographs are clear and helpful, particularly for the collection of pottery which he is the first actually to record. He includes a map of the principal Aali mounds, which was frequently to be reprinted, and in it he identifies both the mounds opened by Durand and those on which the Bents had worked (Fig. 2.4). His map of the region shows the Eastern Province of Arabia, then largely divided amongst the various tribes of the Hasa, as 'Bahrain'. It was certainly not so called in his time but, unwittingly, it indicates the probable extent of the old Dilmun community of the third millennium BC.

It must be suspected that the Indian typesetters in Calcutta had some trouble with the Colonel's manuscript, as was similarly the case with Durand's text more than twenty years earlier. Thus in the third paragraph of the introductory notes on 'History' a reference, in parentheses, is made to '(Pihlical Ophir?)': presumably 'Biblical' is meant: throughout his text such vagaries appear and it is difficult to believe that he would have tolerated them for a moment had he been aware of them. Prideaux's report is

Figure 2.3 The burial mounds, photographed by Prideaux.

remarkable for the tone of deep exasperation in which much of it is written. He complains bitterly and frequently about the cost of excavation and of the excessive demands of his workforce.

Altogether Prideaux's report marks the real beginning of controlled observation of the Bahrain tumuli. The whereabouts of Prideaux's excavated material is now unknown, though it has been suggested that some of it may still be in India.

In 1925 a young archaeologist, Ernest Mackay, was directed to visit Bahrain by Sir Flinders Petrie and to examine the mounds. Petrie was a man of boundless energy, a genius at synthesizing evidence, much given to fearless and highly creative speculation. In 1914 he had earlier, in 1914, tried to interest T.E. Lawrence, another young archaeologist then working in the Levant and with Petrie in Egypt, in excavating in Bahrain on behalf of the British School. Writing to his friend D.G. Hogarth in February 1912 Lawrence relates

Prof. Petrie spoke to me two or three times in Egypt about the Persian Gulf and S. Arabia. He told me Bent had dug ivories (early) in Bahrain – and when we found some very curious Mesopotamian – like bull's legs on prehistoric beds (one I hope goes to Oxford – really good things) he declared that he believed the early dynasties came round by sea from Elam or thereabout to Egypt; and that Bahrain was a stage of their going. Finally in my last week with him he suggested my going down there to dig, say next year, as a preliminary season, to be followed by a second on a larger scale, if it seemed promising. He said he could provide the funds.

I told him I'd ask you about it. . . . I would like to dig in the Persian Gulf, and as Bahrain is nominally British, I suppose we might carry off the stuff. It all depends on what Bent found.[9]

Nothing came of this proposal and Lawrence was diverted towards other preoccupations; in the process he was handed over to history, even to legend. Archaeology concerned him no more.

In the midst of all his other labours, Petrie found time to publish a remarkable magazine, *Ancient Egypt*. One number, produced during the Great War, dealt with the evidence of Mesopotamian influence or connections in late Predynastic Egypt. Writing on the art of the period Petrie observes:

The strong Mesopotamian suggestions of the designs have, as we noted before, no exact parallels in the East. They seem rather to belong to a people of Elamite or Tigrian origin and ideas, who had progressed on their own lines. The presence of shipping as an important factor would

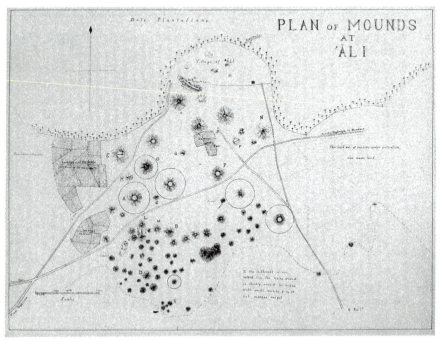

Figure 2.4 Prideaux's map of the Aali grave mounds – the 'Royal Tombs'.

48

be against their having come to Egypt across the Arabian desert. The probability seems that they had branched off to some settlement in the Persian Gulf (such as the Bahreyn Islands) or on the South Arabian coast, and from their second home brought its style and ideas into Egypt.[10]

It is not clear what planted this idea in Petrie's mind, nor do we know what he knew of the 'Bahreyn Islands' that led him to this remarkable perception. But he returned to it again, in *The Making of Egypt*, published just before the Second World War, in 1939. The book is an extraordinary *mélange* of information, culled from nearly sixty years of work in the Nile Valley; it attempts to explain what went into the creation of the society which emerged around the end of the fourth millennium BC (though Petrie believed the date to be earlier) and which led to the splendours of the Egyptian kingship, marked by the long succession of the dynasties. In the course of a chapter entitled 'The Dynastic people', Petrie develops his concept of an invasion from the east, as one of the essential elements in the development of the distinctive culture which was to flourish for so long.

The distinctive character of the lst Dynasty, which separates it from all that went before, is the conquest and union of the whole land of Egypt. It became thus subject to the falcon-bearing tribe of Horus, which was the natural enemy of the Aumu, the Set-bearing tribe. This falcon tribe had certainly originated in Elam, as indicated by the hero and lions on the Araq Knife handle XXXXV. They went down the Persian Gulf and settled in the 'Horn of Africa'. There they named the 'Land of Punt', sacred to later Egyptians as the source of the race. . . . Those who went up the Red Sea formed the dynastic invaders of Egypt, entering by the Qoceir–Koptos road. Others went on to Syria and founded Tyre, Sidon and Aradus named after their home islands in the Persian Gulf (Strabo XVI, iii, 4).[11]

It is now generally accepted that there are distinct traces of Mesopotamian influence in the late Predynastic cultures of Egypt, though how these were transmitted in the Nile Valley is not clear. Certainly one possibility is that merchants, or at any rate seafarers who used or knew of Mesopotamian boats, reached Egypt from the Red Sea. This is suggested particularly by the rock carvings of such boats in the eastern Egyptian desert and by their appearance on works of art of late Predynastic times. However, a route overland, crossing the Arabian peninsula, is also a possibility.

Ernest Mackay was Petrie's later nominee and substitute for Lawrence in exploring the antiquity of Bahrain. He had worked in Palestinian archaeology in the years immediately after the Great War and was later to make a considerable name in India, where he instituted a programme of archaeological activity, inherited and extensively developed subsequently by the late Sir

Mortimer Wheeler, who was himself to play a small part in the later history of the archaeology of Bahrain.

Mackay's work in India was eventually to have considerable pertinence to the understanding of the past of the Gulf and, in particular, of Bahrain. As the evidence unearthed by the Danes at the Qala'at al-Bahrain in the 1950s and 1960s came to be examined, it was evident that close affinities existed between Bahrain and the Indus Valley cities, the result of the Gulf's far-ranging trade in the third millennium BC. In 1925, Mackay set out for Bahrain to ascertain 'the nature of the tombs and their contents'. His report is published in the series instituted by the Egypt Exploration Society, which was founded by the remarkable Amelia Edwards, author of *One Thousand Miles up the Nile*, a minor masterpiece of archaeological and travel literature. The Society which she founded maintained a policy of swift and detailed publication of its expeditions; to this procedure Mackay responded readily.

The volume in which his report appears is entitled *Bahrein and Hamamieh*; it is uncommonly rare.[12] Hamamieh is a mixed Predynastic and later Egyptian site, which is reported in the same volume. Presumably it was decided by the editors that Bahrain alone did not warrant its own volume (Hamamieh, incidentally, is notable in Egyptian archaeology in that it is the only stratified Predynastic site yet published).

Mackay's report is a careful and expert summary of his work. He describes briefly that of his predecessors and then proceeds straight into a detailed description of the mounds. He is really the first person to analyse professionally the different methods of construction which Bahrain's tumuli reveal.

Although he was most careful about his work, Mackay went somewhat off-course in some of his conclusions. He thought that Bahrain could not have supported so large a population as the fields of mounds imply and that most of the burials were brought to the island, though he knew of the existence of similar mounds on the Arabian mainland. He does not commit himself to the matter of the Phoenician provenance of the burials, contenting himself with repeating the British Museum's assertion that the material shown to that institution by Bent proved the Phoenician origins of the tombs and their occupants.

He did, however, deliver himself of one firm opinion, to the effect that, despite the admirable quality of its dates, Bahrain could not be Dilmun. This, he says, is proved since the ancient records show that copper was to be found in Dilmun; he did not apparently understand the island's role as an entrepôt, though some of his predecessors seemed to have had an inkling that this was part of Dilmun-Bahrain's story. In the work of later scholars the copper trade is recognized as a profoundly important element in Bahrain's history and in its identification with Dilmun.

Mackay's illustrations are excellent and he is the first to give careful plans of the tombs and their construction. He includes a page of pottery drawings, though he does not show any vessels that can be recognized as the third-millennium wares distinctive to Bahrain and known as 'Barbar' and 'chain-ridge' wares. He uses Prideaux's map and acknowledges his debt to his report very properly.

Shortly after Mackay's visit to Bahrain there appeared what is perhaps the most singular of the documents in the record of the progress of archaeology in Bahrain over the past century: *Bahrain, Tilmun, Paradise*, published in 1928 in the august papers of the Biblical Pontifical Institute of Rome.[13] Its author was a Jesuit, remarkable in his erudition even for that learned body of subtle scholars and propagandists for the Roman faith. His name was Edward Burrows.

Burrows worked on several of the excavations carried out by British and other teams in the south of Iraq, in the land which had been Sumer. He was present at the epoch-making excavations of Sir Leonard Woolley at Ur; he was responsible for the deciphering of a number of the early texts, preserved on the familiar baked clay tablets of the archives of the city-states in the Land of the Two Rivers.

It was presumably in the course of this work that Burrows' interest in the Sumerian Paradise Land was stimulated. Several scholars, including German and American specialists in ancient texts had identified references to Dilmun (or, in the Semitic form of the name, Tilmun) in them. These had prompted some diverse speculations about the nature of this archetypal Holy Land, its origins and even the origins of the Sumerian people themselves.

Burrows' interest might be expected to be engaged on two scores: on the one hand, his scholarly concern as an epigrapher and philologist, who would quite properly analyse a place-name from the ancient texts; on the other, the Christian priest who might, however uneasily, recognize the source of some of the powerful myths that he was himself concerned to promote in the discharge of his sacerdotal functions.

At all events Burrows approached the study of the paradisial nature of Dilmun-Bahrain and the meaning that might be concealed with its name, with committed and persistent application, even, it might be said, with an attention approaching the obsessive. Obsessionality, too, seems to be demonstrated in the actual presentation of the Burrows' paper, for every word, including the references in all the several languages in which Burrows was supremely competent, is written by hand with differing forms of epigraphy denoting italic or other variations. He also uses different-coloured inks for still greater distinction or emphasis. Burrows was an ingenious and patient cleric; he produced a report which, though it may be considered distinctly odd, yet deserves to be remembered. If for no other reason, its concern with the etymology of the name 'Dilmun' (which is still unsolved) may repay study.

Essentially, Burrows' concern is to penetrate the meaning of the ancient name of Bahrain. He begins, logically enough, with the Sumerian version, pointing out that the cuneiform characters *NiTuk* (with *ki* added as an unarticulated determinative to demonstrate that the word is the name of a country) can also spell Dilmun. He notes that Tilmun is frequently identified as a source of dates. (He tends to use the Semiticized *Tilmun* more frequently than the Sumerian *Dilmun*.) Then he suggests that *NiTuk* could also be pronounced 'Dugud' in Sumerian. He proposed that the signs have the meanings 'terrible' or 'majestic' and, in the case of Dugud, 'great one'. He believed that Dugud would be an appropriate name for a sacred island like Dilmun: in this context it would suggest 'venerable', to which he would add the nuance 'dark', relating this in turn to the name of Bahrain's central massif, the Jebel Dukhan, the Mountain of Smoke, the name by which it is still known.

With the surefootedness of an ibex or a mountain goat he leaps from linguistic rock to rock, ranging across a dazzling selection of ancient tongues. He even identifies Dilmun-Bahrain's concern with the smelting of copper, linking that trade in antiquity with Bahrain's and eastern Arabia's later reputation for the manufacture and export of brass and copper goods.

One piece of negative evidence is particularly telling in his criticism. Burrows remarks that one objection which might be advanced against the equation Bahrain = Dilmun was the absence of any connection with pearls in ancient times. He notes that there had been an attempt to derive *NiTtuk* from a word for 'pearl' in Old Turkish and Hungarian, but this he dismisses as he is unaware of any connection between the Gulf island and the trade in pearls. Later archaeology has proved such a trade to have been flourishing in Bahrain and eastern Arabia for at least 5,000 years.

He plunges into the Epic of Gilgamesh, breasting the glittering phosphorescent seas around Bahrain and identifying Siduri's magic garden and its jewel trees (see Chapter 10) with the glow which the phosphorescence gives. He locates Siduri's isle in the Gulf and reminds us that ultimately she became the Erythraean Sibyl and, more remarkable still, the daughter of Berossos. He was the Chaldaean historian of the Seleucid King Antiochos' time, who recorded the story of Oannes, the strange amphibian creature, part-man, part-fish, that brought the arts of mankind to the ancestors of the Sumerians and each night returned to the waters of the Gulf.

Hebrew and Arabic are at Burrows' command and he researches skilfully amongst the Arab geographers for support of his attributions. He brings all this evidence together in a splendid coda in which he identifies Tilmun, Bahrain and Paradise. The land is Enki's garden.

The meaning of the island's name has always perplexed and intrigued scholars. 'Bahrain' itself means 'the two seas': an episode in the Quran involving Moses and the mysterious figure El Khidr is stated to occur at the place of 'the two seas' (see Chapter 10). Earlier commentators assumed that this meant the vicinity of Suez where the Red Sea and the Mediterranean come into close proximity. Nowadays, however, most opinion places the meeting in the Gulf and agrees that 'the two seas' are the salt waters and the sweet, the latter bubbling so surprisingly out of the very seabed, to the north of the Bahrain islands.

Some commentators have suggested that Dilmun in its Sumerian form (*NiTuk*) means, almost unbelievably, 'the place of the bringing of oil',[14] a name which was certainly justified after oil had indeed been discovered in Bahrain in 1932; Deimer, a distinguished German scholar, writing in the 1920s, proposed that in archaic times the ideogram *NiTuk* meant 'oil-ship'.[15] The oil to which this refers is, of course, bitumen, the surface deposits of which were well known to the Sumerians. Bitumen has, indeed, a modern part to play in the development of the Gulf's archaeology.

Not all scholars would go all the way with Burrows today. But one thing is certain: the work which he so painstakingly initiated and in which few scholars would have either the application or the skills to follow him, would certainly repay revision and a fresh view.

The last of the archaeologists who preceded the Danish expeditions of the 1950s onwards, was a young American scholar, Peter Bruce Cornwall. 'On the location of Dilmun' was published in October 1946.[16] This article, though it is quite short, neatly summarizes much of the work of earlier scholars, pulls it together and presents the whole as a convincing demonstration of the equation that Bahrain equals ancient Dilmun.

Cornwall visited Bahrain and the Eastern Province of Saudi Arabia in the winter of 1940–1. His contribution to Dilmun studies was to be considerable. He excavated extensively in the islands – and to a more limited extent on the mainland – and uncovered some telling evidence. Most remarkable perhaps was an enigmatic structure which he discovered in Manama and illustrated in his article, which he suggested might represent a council chamber, probably of pre-Islamic date. It was found below street level in the town and is now lost.

Cornwall had, some years before the publication of the *BASOR* article, submitted a doctoral thesis to Harvard University entitled 'The history of Bahrain before Cyrus'.[17] Evidently, he expected his thesis to be published; unhappily for the wider promulgation of Bahrain's ancient importance, it never was. It is a remarkable and perceptive synthesis of all the historical and textual references to Dilmun in the ancient sources, with a careful analysis of the evidence; in its extent and sensitivity it has hardly been bettered. It remains a mine of fascinating and significant material for the assiduous Dilmunologist.

Cornwall's article of 1946 was written in reply to one published by the distinguished American Sumerologist, Samuel Noah Kramer, who, almost alone amongst his colleagues, stood out against the acceptance of the identification of Bahrain and Dilmun.[18] In later years Kramer remained silent on this question and most authorities would consider that Cornwall provides a convincing counter to his arguments.

Cornwall made another important contribution to Dilmun studies when he published two letters from a Kassite official based, in all probability, on the mainland, to his colleague in Babylon.[19] He complains about the depredations of the Amorite nomads on the dates waiting shipment back to Babylon. He also refers to a mysterious woman, in Cornwall's view perhaps a Sutean priestess, who had crossed over from the mainland to Bahrain (see Chapter 7).

Cornwall brings Dilmun-Bahrain into a clear association with Sumer. Though it is a small matter, his discovery in some of the mounds of hairpins of the type with which the Sumerians used to fix their characteristic buns, gives special life to his evidence. He is wrong in two particulars of chronology: the Durand stone dates to the early centuries of the second millennium and the grave mounds fall broadly into two periods, the second half of the third millennium to the early part of the second and the closing centuries of the first millennium BC.

The Second World War was not a propitious time for any sort of serious archaeological work to be carried out in so remote a theatre as the Arabian Gulf. The importance of the Gulf, however, came increasingly to be recognized as the Powers realized their dependence upon sources of supply of petroleum for industry and the machines of war. Bahrain, to its surprise, was bombed by the Italians, presumably by mistake, but it could not be said that the war greatly affected life in the region as a whole. However, its future importance was being determined in those days and its people were, unknown to themselves, shortly to experience an astonishing transformation of their lives as the focus of world energy needs swung towards the Arabian deserts.

In 1953, some seventy years of occasional and fragmentary research came to an end with the true beginning of serious archaeology in the Gulf. Such work as there had been up to that point was largely the consequence of individual initiative, essentially spasmodic and largely uncoordinated. Despite the attention which the various reports of work carried out, especially in Bahrain, had gained, rather surprisingly they led to no planned or sustained programmes by serious institutions. But in 1953 the first Danish Expedition arrived in Bahrain and began work. Over the next seventeen years they were to transform the state of knowledge of the Gulf's antiquity and to recall to the world a civilization which had been forgotten for millennia.[20]

The story of the Danish Expedition has been agreeably told by Geoffrey Bibby in his popular book *Looking for Dilmun*.[21] Bibby – and the expedition's original leader, P.V. Glob – deserve to be remembered not only as notable originators and the men largely to be credited with recalling to the world a forgotten and important part of its heritage, but also as amongst the century's most fortunate archaeologists: luck is a quality, in archaeology at least, as important as technical competence. Between them and their colleagues they wrote a new chapter in the world's history and showed that 4,000 years and more ago a civilization flourished in the Gulf which bore comparison with its great contemporaries in Mesopotamia, Egypt, Iran and the Indus Valley.

The way in which the Danes first received permission to work in Bahrain demonstrates the importance of having fortunate stars to guide the destinies of archaeologists. The British adviser to the Ruler of Bahrain, Sir Charles Belgrave, a man of some modest scholarly interests but with little experience of archaeologists, received, to his evident surprise, two applications for permission to excavate Bahrain's antiquities in the same week: one was from the Danish Expedition based at the University of Aarhus at Moesgaard in the north of Jutland, the other from the considerably more influential and very much richer University of Pennsylvania. Feeling himself unable to make an informed judgement as to the professional merits of either bidder, Belgrave decided that the most equitable means of reaching a decision would be on the toss of a coin. The coin was tossed and Denmark was free to resume an association with the Gulf which had begun with an expedition some 200 years before undertaken, under quite appalling circumstances, by a team sent to explore the peninsula by the Danish king, Frederick, and of which only a young naval officer, Carsten Niebhur, survived. Of such random circumstances is archaeological history made, but it is difficult not to wonder what the much more richly endowed Pennsylvanians might have made of it.[22]

In the past twenty years it is particularly the contribution of the various Departments of Antiquities, established by the various governments in the region, which has transformed both the nature and extent of Arabian archaeology. At the same time, also, there has been an increasing awareness by the governments which have charge of this part of the world's heritage, of the importance of what is in their keeping. Most of the states have established Departments of Antiquities and have introduced laws protecting archaeological and historic sites both from uncontrolled development and from plunder.

An achievement of several of the states is the creation of learned journals charting the progress of the scholarship of the past in the country concerned. Two in particular should be noted: first, *Atlal, the Journal of Saudi Arabian Archaeology*, which has been published regularly since 1977 and which has recorded the progress of the very remarkable land survey of the Kingdom undertaken from 1976 onwards.[23] In the course of the survey an immense catalogue of sites has been compiled from every part of the kingdom, which must be one of the most inhospitable for such work as well as having been amongst the largest unsurveyed areas of the ancient world, until the Saudi Department of Antiquities and Museums commenced its ambitious programme.

The second publication concerned with archaeology which was established in the peninsula is the *Journal of Oman Studies*, the first number of which appeared in 1975.[24] This, too, has provided valuable coverage of the course of Oman's distinctive archaeological heritage.

Another important undertaking instigated by the various governments in their attempts to bring an understanding of the past of the peninsula to its present-day inhabitants has been the creation of museums, designed to conserve and present the region's ethnographical and archaeological heritage. This has become a particularly creative and innovative aspect of the work of the Antiquities' Departments (and others) in the states concerned.

The first attempt at a museum which set out to employ contemporary communications and exhibition techniques was in Bahrain in 1970. It was opened on the occasion of the Third International Conference in Asian Archaeology which was held in the state during March of that year.[25] The museum, though it was quite a modest installation, excited both warm comment and considerable interest in Bahrain and in the Gulf. It was essentially archaeological in character, though it attempted also to communicate some of the elements of the many ancient myths and legends associated with Dilmun-Bahrain to its visitors as well as something of its rich and varied ethnography. Bahrain has now built and equipped a splendid new museum, part of a complex of buildings on the corniche in Manama. It contains what is beyond question the most important collection of archaeological material from the Gulf. It also houses extensive ethnographic collections, and examples of modern Bahraini art.

The next important museum development was in Bahrain's neighbouring state of Qatar. There the Amir, Shaikh Khalifa bin Hamed Al-Thani, made the creation of a museum one of his first publicly announced priorities when he assumed the rule of his country in February 1972. The Qatar National Museum was set up on an abandoned and derelict site belonging to the Amir's family, on the sea-front at Doha, the capital. It was a particularly fortunate circumstance as the site contained a number of ruined but still beautiful traditional houses, in one of which the Amir had been born. They were restored and formed an integral part of the museum, together with a new building, known as the Museum of the State, which contained the principal archaeological and ethnographical collections (probably the most important in eastern Arabia), a marine museum and a lagoon on which were moored examples of typical Gulf sailing-craft.[26]

The Sultanate of Oman has also shared in the Gulf's programme of museum development. Its first museum was opened at Seeb, to provide an introduction for visitors to the country, which is large, complex and rich both in its environment and its history. Later, one of the fine eighteenth-century 'great houses' in Muscat, Bait Nader, was restored to provide a museum for the capital.

Oman's most notable museum however, the Museum of the Sultan's Armed Forces, was also to be housed in a restored eighteenth-century house, this time a fortified country house, at Bait al-Falaj, in the Ruwi Valley, which guards the approach to the capital city. The house, a particularly fine example of Oman's architecture of the period, was carefully restored and now contains a historical survey of the Sultanate's important military past.

The United Arab Emirates has come relatively late into the conservation of its heritage but it now has several museums, or similar installations, established within its territory. A museum has been set up in the fort at Dubai; a fine coastal fort has also been restored at Ras Al Khaima and contains a museum for the state. Both contain locally recovered archaeological material, drawn from the several expeditions which have been conducted in the UAE in recent years.

Kuwait maintained a small museum on Failaka island, the scene of a large-scale engagement during the Iraqi withdrawal from the territory which it invaded in 1990. The collections of early second-millennium material from the island's sites are irreplaceable. The collection of Islamic art, formed by Shaikh Nasser Al Sabah, which was seized by the Iraqis, was removed to Baghdad but is reported to be intact.

The Kingdom of Saudi Arabia has embarked upon the most elaborate and imaginative museum programme of all the peninsula states. The first museum project of the newly constituted Department of Antiquities in 1974 was the creation of the Museum of Archaeology and Ethnography in Riyadh.[27] The planning of the historical profile for the museum provided the opportunity to set the chronology of Arabia into a firmly established sequence for the first time, ranging from Lower Palaeolithic times in western Arabia, to the Revelation of Islam and the foundation of the Kingdom by King Abdul Aziz bin Abdul Rahman Al-Saud, in the early decades of the present century.

Plans have now been developed for a national museum to be built on one of the most important sites in the city of Riyadh, which incorporates the Murabba Palace, one of the principal residencies of King Abdul Aziz. At the same time the planning of the restoration of the Masmak fortress, which was captured by the then Amir Abdul Aziz at the outset of his campaign to recover his patrimony in January 1902, has been completed. The Masmak is to be installed as a museum for the city of Riyadh, with the themes of the relationship of the oasis to the city – one of the essential paradigms of the development of Arabia's history – and of the unification of Arabia which began with the capture of the Fortress.

The most ambitious project of the Department of Antiquities and its advisers was the creation of a network of regional museums throughout the country. Thus far, six have been completed, at Jizan, Najran, Al-Ula, Taima, Jawf and Hofuf; two more are planned, at Khamasin and between Buraida and Anaiza.

The regional museums are designed primarily to serve archaeological and historical sites within a 200-kilometre (125-mile) radius. They comprise conservation, records, photographic and draughting facilities, storage, accommodation for visiting archaeologists and others and exhibition halls for the display of archaeological and other material from the region served. Each museum contains displays, common to all the museums, which relate to the history of the Kingdom and identify the relationship of the region represented by the museum in the larger sequence of Saudi Arabia's history.

The creation of the site or regional museums throughout Saudi Arabia has provided the opportunity further to extend and to refine the archaeological and historical sequences first set down in the more restricted compass of the Museum of Archaeology and Ethnography in Riyadh. Each of the six so far completed has a double purpose: to act as the centre for a local archaeological region, expressing the essential, historical character of that region, and second, to provide a national framework for the history of Saudi Arabia, into which each museum may be placed, defining the contribution of the region to the Kingdom's history and archaeology overall.

The museums are built to two basic plans, varied to suit the local terrain and its physical conditions. Taken together, the museums will constitute a powerful influence in bringing about a unity of policy and activity in a country as diverse and as large as Saudi Arabia.

Plans are also in hand for the restoration and conservation of the monuments in the important north-western site of Mada' in Saleh, or Higr. This consists of a rock-enclosed, approximately circular area in which are contained over 130 superb rock-cut tombs built by the Nabataeans, the builders also of Petra, further to the north.

The rapid, even spectacular, advances which the Danes made in Bahrain in the first ten or so seasons of their work inevitably – and quite properly – prompted them to look at the larger context in which Dilmun had established itself and in which its strange mixture, of the mercantile and the mystical, flourished. At the same time word of the Danes' success began to filter into other parts of the area, with the consequence that they began to look at, and later to commence work in, various of the states around Bahrain.

Their exploration of these areas was rewarding; they began to lay down the archaeological profile of the whole region, from Kuwait in the north to Oman. Each state made, as it were, its own distinctive contribution to the story of the Gulf's ancient prosperity. The results of that work are set out in these pages.

Some misgivings, understandably, were expressed, though in the mildest terms, by the Bahraini authorities, who felt that their hospitality, generously given, was becoming a trifle strained by these excursions into the lands of their neighbours. However, as the Danes' work in the adjacent states tended to prove Bahrain's ancient paramountcy for so much of the period when the

Gulf culture was at its most productive, they stifled any reservations that they might otherwise have felt.

The Danes had the field largely to themselves throughout the first twenty years of their work from 1953 onwards. Then, in 1970 a decision to hold the Third International Conference in Asian Archaeology in Bahrain drew the attention of the worldwide archaeological community to what was contained in the Gulf's islands and the mainland contiguous to them.

The conference, which was also the occasion for the inauguration of the first Bahrain Museum, which brought into existence a whole generation of museums in the Gulf, was attended by archaeologists of many nationalities. They included two of the most distinguished living scholars, Sir Mortimer Wheeler and Dame Kathleen Kenyon. Sir Mortimer was representative not only of the British Academy of which he was the Secretary, but also of the archaeology of India, of which he was one of the innovators. Dame Kathleen had excavated extensively in Jordan, particularly at Jericho, the site which will always be associated with her name.

During the conference a total of seven papers was presented which bore directly on the Gulf in antiquity. The scholars who attended the conference, the guests of the unfailingly generous government of Bahrain, were able to visit all of the island's principal archaeological sites.

The years which followed the 1970 Conference saw foreign teams beginning to challenge the virtual monopoly which the Danes had enjoyed. Representatives of the most advanced disciplines being developed in archaeological technology were drawn to the Gulf states from the United States, Britain, France, Italy, from Jordan and Iraq. The rate of publication, often supported by the local Departments of Antiquities, escalated significantly; more and more books on the region's antiquity began to appear in the bookshops and on the shelves of learned institutions.

One of the principal causes of the advancement of the study of the Gulf's archaeology occurred in 1983 when the Government of Bahrain held a large-scale conference entitled 'Bahrain through the Ages' in Manama in December of that year. The 200th anniversary of the foundation of the ruling Bahraini dynasty, the Al Khalifa, fell at this time. With typical modesty and maturity the Government of Bahrain, eschewing military parades and the spectacle which might have appealed to a less enlightened regime, chose to commemorate the event by convening a conference which would lay down the historical profile of the State of Bahrain over its nearly 5,000 years of recorded existence.

The 1983 Conference was in marked contrast in scale to its 1970 precursor. Over 120 scholars attended it at the invitation of the Government of Bahrain, from all over the world. Over eighty papers were presented to the conference, dealing with Bahrain in all its historical manifestations, from the earliest times to the beginning of the twentieth century.

The Proceedings of the conference are published under the general title

Bahrain through the Ages in two substantial volumes.[28] The first, *The Archaeology*, extends approximately to the period immediately before the coming of Islam; the second, *The History*, deals with the period from the Revelation of Islam to the beginnings of Bahrain's modern history.

Since the Bahrain Conference the rate of publication of serious work on the archaeology of the Gulf has further increased. Today it may be said with reasonable confidence that the Gulf is beginning to be represented in academic bibliographies to an extent appropriate to the importance and variety of its historical experience, making it comparable with some of its more established peers.

The 1970 Conference in Bahrain acted as an important stimulus to archaeology in the Gulf as a whole. It came at the right time: considerable political and social changes in the Gulf states were bringing new leaders to the fore who recognized the importance of the past, the need to present its records and its physical evidence, in laying down a sound basis for a contemporary society. At the same time upheavals in the Middle East meant that it became increasingly difficult for foreign teams to work in many of the countries which had traditionally formed the foundation of much of the western world's foreign archaeological activity. The relative freedom of working in the Gulf states and, in many cases their evident concern to encourage the establishment of a proper archaeological structure, gave the opportunity for many foreign institutions to mount expeditions to various of the states.

The French proved to be particularly active in this regard. French teams were responsible for important work being carried out in Failaka (which they virtually took over from the Danes) in Qatar, where they changed radically the chronology which hitherto the Danes had attributed to the stone tools which are so much a feature of the scoured landscape of the Qatar peninsula, in Bahrain, where they have worked extensively on the post-Dilmun levels at the Qala'at al-Bahrain, in the UAE and in Oman.

A British committee, intended to promote the participation of British institutions in the archaeology of the Gulf, had been formed after the 1970 Conference. It has similarly been active throughout the ensuing years. Its earliest work was in Qatar, at the time of the preparation of the National Museum, when it was necessary to undertake an archaeological survey of the country. Amongst other notable discoveries (described further in Chapter 8) the committee's expeditions found the first evidence of the connections with makers of Ubaid pottery from early Mesopotamian sites in the lower Gulf, at several Qatari sites.

Later the same committee despatched an expedition, over several seasons, to Bahrain. This also found important Ubaid traces (at Al Markh, initially) and excavated a remarkable late third millennium 'temple' structure at Diraz (see Chapter 7).

The Americans too were much engaged, especially in Saudi Arabia, where they had been involved in the Kingdom-wide survey conducted throughout the 1970s by the Department of Antiquities. Several of the early expeditions mounted by the Saudi Arabian Department were conducted with the participation of American institutions and scholars.

More generally, the British have been active in the UAE, conducting extensive excavations at ed-Dur, for example. The French have also made important contributions to the archaeology of the Emirates, in Sharjah and, particularly, in Abu Dhabi where they have worked on a number of early and later third-millennium sites, at Hili and Al Ain. German activity in the Gulf has not, thus far, been extensive but teams from Göttingen have worked in Shimal in the UAE. The Danes have sustained their interest throughout the years, though inevitably on a somewhat reduced scale. The Italians have been active in the Sultanate of Oman, especially at the important, very early fishing settlement at Ras al-Hadd.

The Arab states have also contributed to the latest phases of the Gulf's archaeology. In the Sultanate of Oman Moroccan teams of conservators have been engaged in the restoration of several of the sumptuously decorated fortified palaces which were built by the country's rulers in the seventeenth century. In this work they were preceded by the Italians, who were responsible for several of the original programmes of conservation in the Sultanate.

Arab archaeologists have made important contributions to the understanding of Bahrain's archaeology. Several seasons' work by Jordanian teams, working with Bahraini and American specialists, carried out valuable work on the grave mounds, particularly those at Sar. Two important publications resulted from this activity (Ibrahim, 1983; Mughal, 1983).

Throughout this period the national Departments of Antiquities have been growing in size, confidence and skills. More and more the work of uncovering the past of the Gulf region will be carried out by Gulf nationals. However, the scope is so substantial and the areas involved so large that it is probable that foreign expeditions will be welcomed in the area for a long time to come.

Over the period of the last century or so during which archaeological activity – of one sort or another – has been pursued in the Gulf the outlines of the study of the region's ancient past have remained remarkably consistent. Durand, the pioneer of Gulf archaeology, recognized the importance of the fields of burial mounds and saw them as the evidence of a long-vanished civilization. He apprehended the importance of sites such as Barbar and was able to see a place in the archaeology of the central Gulf for the Mesopotamians and for Alexander the Great. The Phoenicians tended to intrude into many of the early studies of the region, witnesses to the significance which the early history of the Levant occupied in the consciousness of European scholarship in the latter part of the nineteenth and the beginning of the twentieth centuries.

Apart from Petrie's inspired intervention, when he seems, almost by instinct, to have detected a connection between the Gulf and archaic Egypt, an intuition which was not, at the time, pursued, the grave mounds were the dominating theme of such studies as there were. Cornwall, following Mackay, recognized that the dominion of Dilmun extended to the Arabian mainland, evidenced by the presence of grave-mound fields there which were comparable with those in Bahrain.

At the heart of the history of the Gulf's archaeology lie the extraordinary perceptions of Rawlinson's review of Durand's notes on his 1878/9 expedition to Bahrain. The implications of Rawlinson's analysis of the importance of the Gulf's ancient culture are so profound and so perceptive that it is a further wonder that the Gulf had to wait until relatively late in the twentieth century for the archaeological community to pay it the attention that it so manifestly deserved.

3

CLIMATE, SEA-LEVELS, MAN AND HIS COMPANIONS

It is not only man who has been profoundly affected by the often dramatic climate of Arabia. He shares the land and, so far as he is able, the sea, with a rich and varied fauna, many of which have adapted with extraordinary ingenuity to life in so apparently bleak an environment. Thus it is a pleasing thought that the unicorn, that fabulous and magical beast, may still be alive, well adapted and living in eastern Arabia.

Like the phoenix, the unicorn is a creature of the desert as much as it is of fantasy, the product of who knows what tales ancient travellers brought back with them from the further limits of the known world. Yet the probability is that the unicorn is the oryx, a creature which combines massiveness with elegance, and power with seeming tranquillity. The unicorn is an inhabitant of that misty land which divides legend from reality; at one moment he is visible and he is gone the next. He is notable for his susceptibility to virgins; indeed, so susceptible is he that he will surrender himself to human captors if a virgin is available in whose lap he may lay his head.

There is no evidence that the oryx, if he is indeed the unicorn's prototype, shares this unusual propensity. But there is no doubt that overhunting of the poor beast contributed to his imminent extinction. It is estimated that there are probably no more than a few dozen head of oryx left in the wild in Arabia. It is greatly to the credit of governments in the peninsula that efforts to save the species have now been rewarded with success.

In their preserves the oryx maintain a watchful, dignified existence. To go among them is disconcerting: they turn on newcomers a long look of cool appraisal and then, thoughtfully, lower their massive heads on which grow two long, thin, black, razor-sharp horns. The young of the breed are pretty and delicate creatures; but power, not prettiness or delicacy, is the character-istic of the adults, particularly of the bulls. Their long, slender horns, which look as though they could be deadly, are the cause of the oryx's identifi-cation with the unicorn: seen in profile their two horns become one and the equation is exact. Both Aristotle and Pliny held the view that the oryx was the unicorn's prototype.

But another factor, other than the depredations of man, has contributed to bringing this rare and beautiful antelope to the very edge of extinction. This is the fact that in all probability the oryx is a relic of an earlier climatic period, in popular terms, a living fossil. It belongs to the fauna of the Plio-Pleistocene, a division of geological time which ended around 2 million years before the present. Then the climate of eastern Arabia was somewhat more generous than it is today; it could support, in what was probably a savannah-type environment, herds of animals larger and more dependent on supplies of food and water than are those creatures which survive in the desert today, when the climate is, truly, hyper-arid.[1] The oryx is said never to drink water in the wild; this, however, sounds more like a traveller's tale than an observation of strict scientific fact, though the animal is known to have a phenomenal ability to detect small quantities of atmospheric moisture. It also feeds at night when, in desert conditions, plants contain more moisture than they do during the day.

Arabia presents conditions as harsh as anywhere in the world for the survival of animals. These extreme conditions – scorching heat, occasional bitter cold, and sparsity of vegetation – have meant that species have had to adapt in order to survive. However, the vegetation and abundant water of the Al Hasa oasis, one of the largest in the world, provides a powerful attraction for birds and desert animals.

In order to survive in deserts, animals have adapted both their behaviour patterns and their physiology. Their overriding need is to minimize water loss in the face of high daytime temperatures and extreme aridity. Lack of water also means scarcity of food, shortages of prey and a scarcity of other members of the same species. In consequence sharp hearing, mobility and an ability to store food are crucial in many desert-dwelling species. The lack of cover also means that camouflage colouration is often found.

The oryx serves to illustrate one of the characteristics of the climate of eastern Arabia and the fauna which the region sustains: the climate of the Gulf region is liable to quite marked changes which have often been rapid and sometimes very substantial. It has long been recognized that climate and the geophysical factors which attend his habitation have profoundly influenced the life and development of man. But just how profound such influences are and how fine the tolerances may be which can divide abundance from devastation are only now being apprehended by scholars; they have always been very clearly apprehended, let it be said, by people such as the desert-dwellers, living at the whim of nature for millennia.

The margin, taking temperature for example, or the effects of prolonged rainfall or of drought, is fine indeed; a few degrees' change overall, either way, could bring in its train another ice age or spread the deserts across lands which are now rich and fertile. Man clings precipitously to the edges of the inhabitable world; but he is the most malign influence in effecting ecological change and has been so throughout the millennia.

64

The climate of the last 10,000 years or so, during which the whole of the history of modern, city-dwelling man is compressed, has been especially benevolent. Because our planet has been enjoying a phase of exceptionally favourable climate, cities have been built, empires have arisen, art has flourished and man has stepped on to the moon. A degree or two away from the global mean and the development of mankind would have been irreversibly blighted. It could still be.

GEOLOGIC ORIGINS

The extreme nature of the climate in eastern Arabia on the one hand demonstrates the effects which can so easily occur in consequence of climate shifts and, on the other, the extraordinary ability of man to adapt even to the most improbable climatic circumstances. Geomorphologically, Arabia is still a relatively volatile part of the earth's land surface. It is moving, drifting inexorably in a north-easterly direction, thus separating itself still further from its original union with Africa and pushing steadily against Iran. The Red Sea was flooded in early Pliocene times (c. 12 million years ago) when the final rupture with Africa was effected and the land bridge which had joined east Africa with south-west Arabia was broken.[2]

Before the Gulf came into existence, what is today eastern Arabia and Iraq were covered by warm shallow seas. Between 12 and 2 million years ago, during the Pliocene age, the Arabian peninsula continued to move north-east as a result of continental drift, reducing the size of the sea, and creating the Gulf. The Zagros mountains of Iran were thrown up by the collision of the peninsula with Iran. This movement is still continuing.

For much of this period the Eastern Province is known to have been dry land; but later, between 2 and 3 million years ago, research has shown that the sea-level was up to 150 metres higher than today. This meant that much of the Eastern Province and the Rub' al-Khali was under water. The coastline lay in the vicinity of al-Hufuf, along the edge of the al-Summan plateau, while Jabal al-Qara was an island, and the beating of the waves formed caves.

The sands of the Rub' al-Khali, the Empty Quarter in the south-east quadrant of the peninsula, came into being at this time, composed of sediment washed down from the Hijaz and Yemen mountains into a shallow sea.

The extent to which the Gulf is still in motion can be demonstrated at both its extremities and in the centre. Thus the Kuwaiti part of the delta at the head of the Gulf has been shown to have subsided by more than 30 metres over the past 5,000 years,[3] whilst at its south-east limit the Musandam peninsula in Oman has subsided by approximately 60 metres during the past 10,000 years. On the other hand the Bahrain Ridge, in the centre of the Gulf, is thought still to be rising.[4]

The Gulf is a product of the Tertiary period; it was formed as a consequence of tectonic movement, of the great plates of the earth's surface grinding further away from each other. It is a roughly rectangular depression, approximately 1,000 kilometres (600 miles) in length from its head, where the Tigris and Euphrates debouch, to the Straits of Hormuz, guarded on the western littoral by the towering walls of Ras Musandam; it is 230 to 250 kilometres (150 miles) wide. The seabed slopes quite sharply; the Arabian coastline is fairly shallow whilst the deep water is all on its Iranian side. Its mean depth is 35 metres whilst its maximum is approximately 165 metres. The circulation of the Gulf is believed to be a counter-clockwise motion, with its waters moving up the Iranian coast, crossing the head of the Gulf and then flowing down the Arabian littoral. Temperatures range between 15° and 33°; in the shallow waters the temperature can reach as high as 40°.[5]

Although the physical profile of the Gulf was laid down long ago (though relatively not so long ago in terms of the geological age of the Earth), it is really only in comparatively recent times that it has assumed the character and appearance with which we are familiar today. The environment of eastern Arabia has been affected by marked fluctuations in the conditions which permit more or less permanent settlement. Some of these fluctuations have continued well into the historic lifetime of man.

CLIMATE

The question of the extent of climate change, and its effect upon a region as climatically extreme as eastern Arabia and the Gulf now are, is difficult of analysis or solution. Whatever may have been the true effect of changes in seawater stands, of the different levels in the water-table and the apparent variations in the rate of precipitation, one influence on the environment is definitely to be identified – man. If ever the present generation, with its laudable concern for the protection of the environment of our beleaguered planet, needs to call evidence from the past, that of eastern Arabia will stand as a sufficiently awful warning for even the direst prophet of the impending destruction of our species.

One factor alone may be cited to demonstrate the extreme fragility of the conditions under which we live and the hazards which, all unthinking, we inflict on ourselves and our descendants. Much of the wealth of eastern Arabia in antiquity was drawn from the discovery of the uses to which copper could be put; indeed, a neat equation of copper, spice and oil can stand for the last 5,000 years of Arabian history and its sum, the acquisitiveness of the world outside the peninsula. But copper, before it can be manipulated by the smiths, must be smelted: smelting demands high temperatures and heat requires fuel. It is thus far speculation, but it is surely not unwarranted to suppose that in Oman, on the terraces perhaps of the

Jebel Akhdar (the Green Mountain), in north-west Arabia and Sinai, where extensive fourth- and third-millennium copper mining sites abound, and even on Bahrain itself, millions of trees were sacrificed to the needs of the copper industry. The stripping of the hillsides in Oman, for instance, would immediately reduce precipitation: the value of trees as wind-breaks would be lost and the fertile earth would be swiftly eroded.

How much, therefore, the needs of the ancient copper industry may be the cause of much of today's deserts is a moot question. Certainly it seems not unreasonable to think that some of their most extreme aspects may be quite recent in origin and at least in part are the consequence of man's own inability to maintain his environment properly.

The degree of tolerance in these matters is very slight and the extent of change, either of climate or of the environment, and the level of precipitation in a particular region due to the loss of an ancient stand of trees, needs only be marginal to bring about a catastrophic alteration in the balance of nature. Tinkering with the environment is one of the more dismal inheritances of the ancient world.

Man is not entirely unaided in his depredations on the world around him. In this malignant process he possessed a most industrious assistant who played a notable part in denuding landscapes; this was the goat, whose domestication was distinctly an equivocal benefit.

There is some disagreement about the extent to which Arabia was affected by the great glaciations which so dominated the last million years or so in the northern hemisphere (Fig. 3.1). However, glacier wasting in the north raised sea-levels throughout the world between 20,000 and 10,000 years ago. To whatever degree Arabia shared in these larger climatic changes, the volatility of its own was such that climate patterns were subject often to quite short-term changes: for example making part of the coast for a period capable of supporting a larger population than before, in consequence of a short 'wet phase'. There is evidence of several 'wet phases' in eastern Arabia; of the most recent, the first ended about 10,000 years ago, whilst another began 1,000 years ago and lasted for 300 or 400 years.[6] This coincides, for example, with the growth and decline of the little fishing settlements at Murwab and Huwailah in Qatar recorded and published by the British Expedition in 1978, following the successful survey in Qatar from October 1973 to January 1974.[7]

THE FAUNAL RECORD

The discovery of Dryopithecine remains in north-eastern Arabia[8] demonstrates the extent to which the climate 15–12 million years ago differed from that of its present profoundly desert, hyper-arid character. Dryopithecines are arboreal creatures, tree-haunting and flourishing in a broad savannah-type environment; they may or may not be on the line of ancestors which

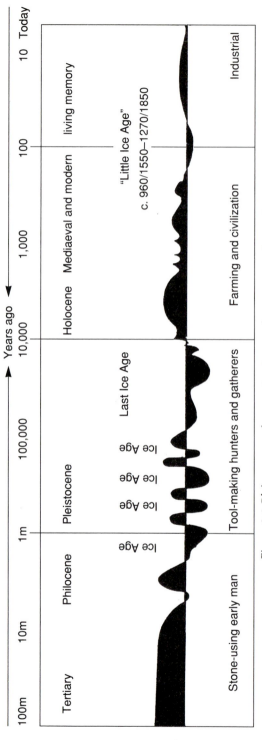

Figure 3.1 Pleistocene and recent Ice Ages and temperature fluctuations.

68

ultimately produced man. In their heyday Arabia probably would have looked much like East Africa now, with plenty of cover for larger game.

During the Miocene period, 17–15 million years ago, a shallow sea covered much of eastern Arabia and what is today the Gulf.[9] Swamp and marshland would have been part of the rich environment, the consequence of the prevailing hot and humid climate.

The savannah-like terrain would have supported gazelle, giraffe, pig, rodents and rabbit (Fig. 3.2). In the denser woodlands and the mangrove running down to the lagoon's edge would have been found elephant, rhinoceros and dryopithecus. Around 12 million years ago the climate became more arid and the trend towards still greater aridity continued into the Pliocene.[10]

There is evidence that from Pliocene times (from c. 3.5 million to c. 1.2 million years ago) Arabia underwent a protracted 'wet phase' when in all probability it enjoyed a warm, moist climate. Its vegetation then would have been lush and tropical. During this long wet phase it is possible that hominids, like those that flourished in East Africa at the same time, were present in Arabia. At this time the great wadi systems (dried-up river or flash flood courses) of Arabia, Wadis al-Rima and al-Batn, and Wadis al-Dawasir and al-Sahba came into being in a period of much greater rainfall than today. Extensive erosion of the upper reaches of the wadis was matched by the deposition of fans of gravel and silt washed down in the lower reaches. Much sand was washed down into a sea covering the Rub' al-Khali in the south. This sand, since dried out, has been shifted and sorted by the wind to form the sand deserts of today. During the Pleistocene period the level of the Gulf's waters fluctuated, as did many of the world's seas, the result, doubtless, of the advance and retreat of glaciers during the successive Ice Ages.[11] After this time arid conditions supervened, reaching a level similar to that prevailing now, around 17,000 years ago. Since then the climate has varied erratically and recent evidence has distinguished a sort of climatic antiphon, with an arid phase being followed by a moist one, in at least eight periods over the past seventeen millennia (Fig. 3.3).

The faunal record in ancient Arabia is still very far from being complete. However, the presence of large beasts, such as mastodon in Abu Dhabi (at Jebel Baraka)[12] and in the eastern region of Saudi Arabia,[13] testify to a marked degree of environmental change over the millennia. In recent years a number of significant palaeontological finds at a site near Jebel Dhanna in Abu Dhabi have been reported.[14] A group of Miocene-period rocks, the Bainuna Formation, has revealed a considerable concentration of Miocene fauna. This discovery is of importance in contributing to the mapping of faunal distribution worldwide during the Miocene. At this period a land bridge joined Africa and Asia; many species therefore, which originated in Africa, reached Asia through Arabia.

The fossil-bearing rocks of the Bainuna Formation are remarkable for the quantity and accessibility of the faunal evidence which they preserve. So far

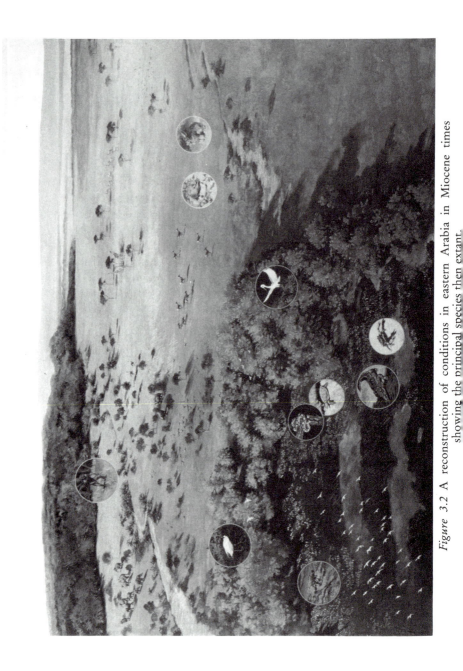

Figure 3.2 A reconstruction of conditions in eastern Arabia in Miocene times showing the principal species then extant.

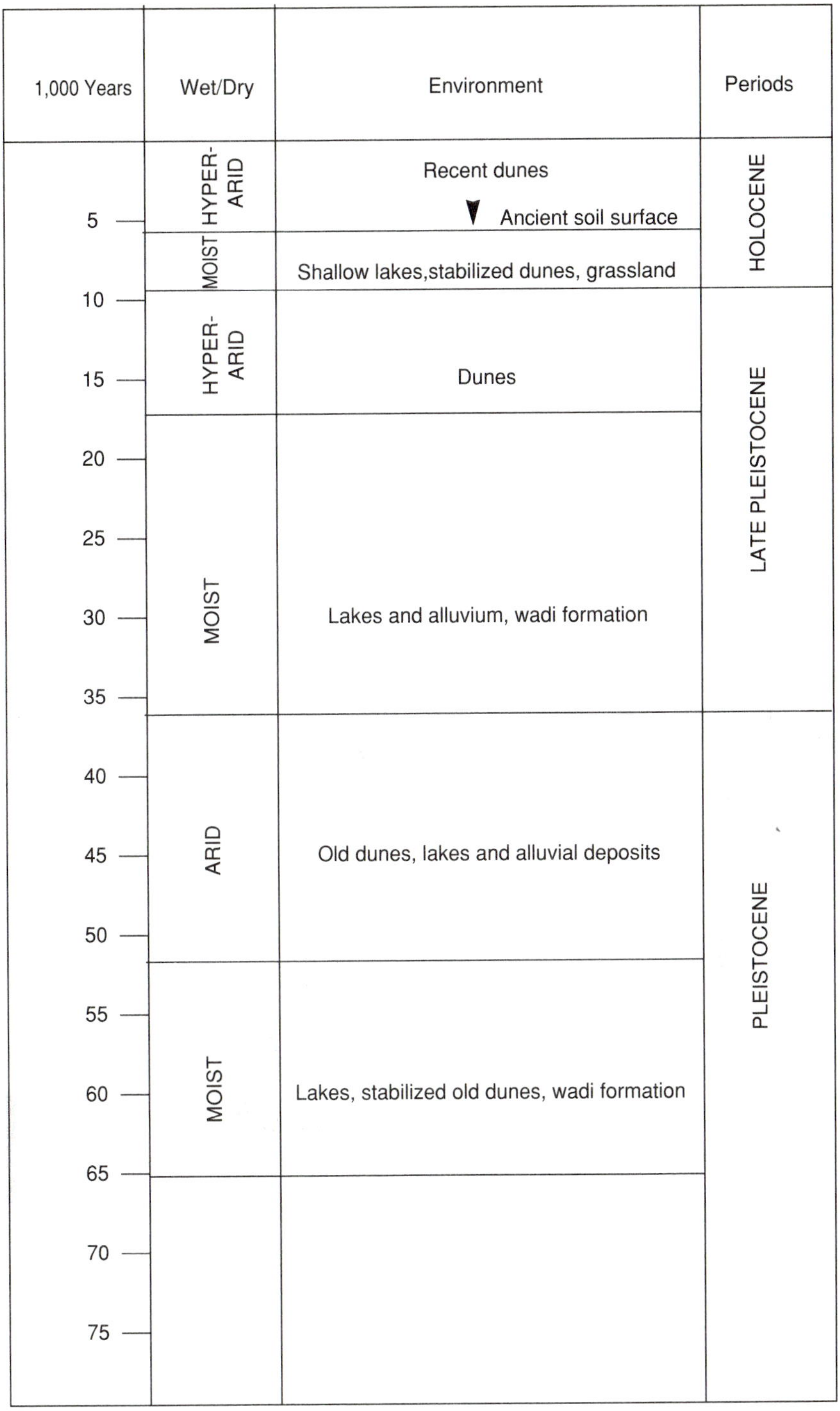

1,000 Years	Wet/Dry	Environment	Periods
5	HYPER-ARID / MOIST	Recent dunes ▼ Ancient soil surface	HOLOCENE
10		Shallow lakes, stabilized dunes, grassland	
15	HYPER-ARID	Dunes	LATE PLEISTOCENE
20			
25			
30	MOIST	Lakes and alluvium, wadi formation	
35			
40			PLEISTOCENE
45	ARID	Old dunes, lakes and alluvial deposits	
50			
55			
60	MOIST	Lakes, stabilized old dunes, wadi formation	
65			
70			
75			

Figure 3.3 Arid and relatively moist phases in Arabia during the last 7,500 years.

the remains of late Miocene fauna, including *Deinotheres* (distantly related to the modern elephant), hippopotamus, crocodile and turtles are amongst those identified. Remains of a macaque-like monkey and of the three-toed *Hipparion*, an ancestor of the horse, have also been found; evidence has been recovered from the same formations of what may have been an archaic canid. These fauna are characteristically Ethiopian; when they existed in Arabia the environment would have looked more like the landscape of East Africa today: savannah, woodland, lakes and swamp.

To judge from the rock carvings which are found in other parts of Arabia (the eastern region does not seem to have encouraged the development of that most characteristic and ubiquitous art form as did other parts of the peninsula), lion, baboon, ostrich and water buffalo, all creatures of the savannah, were common in later times.[15] It is from this sort of ecological environment that the oryx probably descends and, by chance, survives.

It is in the region of the Rub' al-Khali, the Empty Quarter of south-eastern Arabia, so often the focus of all manner of traveller's tales, that the change in eastern Arabia's capacity to support life is shown at its most dramatic. Both at the edge of this tremendous sand-sea, whose arid dunes and sandy wastes stretch from horizon to horizon, and deep into areas which are virtually impervious to sustained human access, are to be found many small Neolithic hunting and fishing encampments, perhaps even some more permanent settlements.[16] The presence of the Neolithic Arabians, who lived here 6,000–5,000 years ago, is marked by the scatters of the fine and elegant tools they made, some of the most beautifully crafted artefacts to have survived from Stone Age Arabia, or, indeed, from anywhere else. Here have been found the remains of hippopotami, which once lived in the swampy margins of what was a series of lakes and inland waters, reaching deep into the desert.

Generally speaking, however, in the period during which man has inhabited the region, the fauna, some members of which would have contributed to his diet, has probably not changed greatly. The desert hare, the fennec fox, the gazelle, the ibex and the diminishing oryx have all been present, then as now. The onegar, a form of wild ass, was probably once indigenous and has now disappeared; the camel is domesticated now, but that is a relatively recent development. In the third millennium and for much of the second it was probably known but as a relatively rare and certainly wild beast; it did, however, make some contribution to the inhabitants' diet.[17] Some enterprising fisher folk varied this diet significantly by the addition of large aquatic mammals like the dugong or sea-cow hunted by the early settlers at Umm an-Nar in Abu Dhabi.[18]

The richness of Arabia's fauna in the relatively recent past is demonstrated by evidence from the region to the south and west of the peninsula. In the south-west Rub' al-Khali, the evidence of the presence of large bodies of standing water well within the lifetime of man is also supported in a rich and varied faunal register. This includes the Asiatic wild ass (a relative of the onegar), *Bos primigenius*, the great archaic bovine which once also roamed the forest lands of Europe, *Hippopotamus antiquus*, the water buffalo and the ostrich.[19] Since the hippopotamus inhabited the east, it is possible that at least some of the others were once present there. The probability is that increasing desiccation and the lowering of the water-table drove the animals further and further south and west, until ultimately they encountered in man a scourge probably more dangerous than even the most inhospitable climate.

When the Rub' al-Khali was lacustrine, the coast of eastern Arabia would have had the appearance of a string of little islands with deep inlets reaching into the desert, rather like the creek around which Dubai has developed. This would have affected parts of Qatar and the northern coast of the Oman peninsula where the United Arab Emirates is now located; it also affected Bahrain, for the small al-Ubaid pottery-bearing site at Al-Markh was a little island at the time of the occasional fishing expeditions which landed there.[20] It is now part of the principal island of the Bahrain archipelago. In Oman, evidence from Umm as-Samman[21] shows that an arm of the sea once reached there. Today it is many miles distant from the coast, stretching indeed up to and beyond the border with Saudi Arabia.

SEA-LEVELS

During the middle and later Pleistocene, from about 80,000 years ago, the level of the waters in the Gulf fluctuated, as indeed was the case worldwide. In many places along the western (Arabian) shore of the Gulf it is possible to see old shorelines from times when the sea-level was a few metres higher than today; others have also been detected underwater in the Gulf. Such changes in sea-levels were the consequence of the advance and retreat of the glaciers during the succession of glaciations and interglacials. The formation of these ice-sheets locked up vast quantities of water, leading to a lowering of the sea-level worldwide.

The level of the Gulf appears to have risen and fallen fairly sharply over the past 100,000 years (Fig. 3.4(a)).[22] There is considerable evidence that between 120,000 and 10,000 years ago the sea receded, leaving the sandy floor of the Gulf exposed. It would then have been a broad plain, watered probably by an extension of the Shatt al-Arab, which may have reached the shelf margin of the Gulf of Oman, representing a fall of some 110 metres below the present level.[23] The most marked regression of the Gulf waters happened between 70,000 and 17,000 years ago: then the sea withdrew beyond the Straits of Hormuz.

Whilst there is evidence of marked changes in the sea levels in the Gulf, such changes are far less dramatic in the Gulf's sister, the Red Sea, to the west of the Arabian peninsula. This would appear to be contradictory and the dilemma which it produces has not yet been resolved.

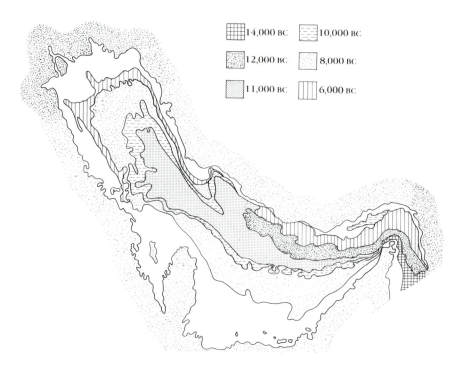

Figure 3.4 (a) Sea-levels in the Arabian Gulf from *c.* 14,000 BC to *c.* 6000 BC.

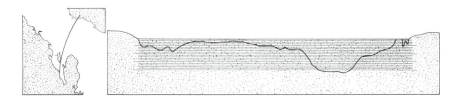

Figure 3.4 (b) Bathymetric profile of the Gulf.

During the latest cold peak in the last Ice Age, 18,000 years ago, the sea-level fell to 110 metres below today's. In only a small area inside the Strait of Hormuz was the sea present. The exposed seabed consisted of a pattern of wadis and sand-dunes, much like Arabia today. The Tigris and Euphrates rivers, which today empty into the Gulf, may not have reached the sea but have run into the sand.

The sea began to return around 17,000 years ago. An acceleration in the process took place about 11,000 years ago, perhaps by as much as 2 to 4 cm per annum. Bahrain Island became separated from the mainland between 6,000 and 7,000 years ago;[24] previously it had simply been a dome-shaped prominence inland.

The sea reached its maximum transgression (that is, its highest level) between 7,000 and 4,000 years before the present. Then it was perhaps some 2 metres higher than it is today.[25] Along the low coastline which characterizes so much of the Arabian littoral of the Gulf even so relatively small a rise in sea-level would result in the flooding of large areas.

An aspect of the Gulf's tendency to acute climatic variation was of crucial importance in influencing the course of human settlements in the area and, in consequence, the development of the societies which lay around its shores and on its several islands. This was what is generally known as the 'Neolithic Wet (or Moist) Phase'.[26]

Over the past 36,000 years or thereabouts the climate of the Gulf has veered between relatively moist periods, in which there was a notable increase in precipitation, and periods of aridity, some of which, like the one which persists today, were of considerable ferocity. Thus the period 7000–4000 BC saw the appearance of active springs and shallow lakes with a consequent, if slight, increase in rainfall. Even the most minor variation will permit – or prevent – settlement and the raising of crops and herds. During this time there is clear evidence in eastern Arabia of the creation of small, probably seasonal, settlements of people who may, from the evidence of their tools, have been the forerunners of the Gulf's most enduring industry, the harvesting of pearls.[27]

Another climatically hospitable period is detectable between 3000 and 2000 BC. This coincides with the formation and early flowering of the Gulf's most important cultural and social phenomena, the prosperous mercantile communities associated with the Dilmun culture.

CHART OF MOIST AND ARID PHASES

Moist	34,000–15,000 BC
Arid	15,000–13,000 BC
Moist	13,000–9500 BC
Arid	9500–7000 BC
Moist	7000–4000 BC (the 'Neolithic Moist Phase')
Arid	4000–3000 BC

Moist	3000–2000 BC
Arid	2000–800 BC
Moist	c. 800 BC–AD 200
Arid	c. AD 200–c. AD 900

Evidence for fluctuating conditions also comes from Saudi Arabian locations including lake deposits at Jubba in the Nafud, throughout eastern Arabia and on the outskirts of the Rub' al Khali. Such evidence can be supported by that from locations in the Saharo-Arabian desert belt which has always been climatically a homogeneous unit due to similar latitude, elevation and topography.

One of the features of the physical landscape which are particularly evident throughout all the Gulf seaboard states are the *sabkha*, the surface salt-pans which are found around the coast and inland where the sea has once transgressed. Essentially, the *sabkha* are formed by the action of the sun on sea-water held in shallow pools on the surface of the desert. The water evaporates as a consequence of the sun's heat and a salt-encrusted layer is formed, the salt being drawn up, as it were, to the surface by the effects of evaporation.

Many of the Gulf *sabkha* are relatively recent in origin. Those in the Abu Dhabi coastal area have been dated by the Carbon-14 process to approximately 4,000 years before the present.[28] However, whilst inland *sabkha* tend to be lacustrine in origin, some of them are relics of the marine transgressions; thus some of the *sabkha* inland in Saudi Arabia represent a sea-level approximately 150 metres higher than at present and in Oman the *sabkha* of Umm as-Samman is thought to have been one such relic.

The importance of the water-table, that is, the artesian or other potable waters that lie below the surface of the land, is obviously supreme. In Arabia the water-table slopes eastwards, rising as it does so. The aquifers are fed by the winter rains and melting snows of the Syrian and Jordanian mountains; much of the water in the aquifers is fossil water, put down in some cases 20,000 years and more ago. The fact that the water-table rises as it slopes towards the east accounts for the remarkable phenomenon of the freshwater (or at least brackish) springs which bubble up from the sea-floor around Bahrain and which must have contributed considerably to the island's ancient reputation for sanctity and special selection by the gods. It may also account for the name by which the region has been known, at least since Islamic times: Bahrain, the 'Two Seas'.

Six thousand years ago the early urban civilization in southern Iraq was already undertaking large-scale irrigation projects; transportation by land was effected by the domestication of the donkey.[29] In eastern Arabia small semi-pastoral communities depended upon domesticated goats, sheep and cattle as early as 5000 BC.[30] The first domestication of these animals and of wheat and barley appears to have taken place in the Fertile Crescent, Anatolia and the Zagros mountains between 9000 and 6000 BC.[31]

Although in geographical terms it is outside the limits of this study, it may be appropriate to record, in this context, one of the least anticipated results of recent archaeological survey in Saudi Arabia, the discovery of the widespread and large-scale domestication of cattle.[32] This is apparent in the western region of the peninsula and in the north. Large herds of bovines could only be supported by climatic conditions much more hospitable than is the case today. The cattle herds were evidently numerous and the people who herded them created an elaborate form of art which celebrated the animals; on what seems to be every available rock surface in northern and parts of western Arabia representations of cattle, of divinities associated with them and of the men and women who kept and guarded them, are pecked or engraved on the rock surfaces.

In the earliest stages of domestication wild goats and gazelles may have been captured and coralled for meat. The need to provide fodder for them may have led, first, to the collection and then the cultivation of cereals about 10,000–9,000 years ago. Barley and two types of wheat are found wild in the Fertile Crescent. Herding and cultivation led to domestication and then to physical changes in the various species brought about by many successive choices of the most suitable individual animals and plants for human use. The Gulf was to benefit from the increased activity of settled, urban living which allowed the people of southern Iraq to develop all manner of specializations which, because of their land's lack of natural resources, encouraged them to seek new lands and new sources of supply for the raw materials they needed, to the south.

It is one thing to excavate the evidence of man's past from the sites where he has lived and to analyse them, extrapolating from them such assumptions as we may be able to make about the way he lived and the motivations which moved him: it is quite another to investigate the history of the earth which bore him. The evidence of climate in eastern Arabia is complex and often obscure but the very lack of research in the region, compared with other parts of the Near East, prompts scholars to consider recovering such evidence as they can about the factors of climate and the physical environment before social and industrial development, which are now sweeping across the region furiously, obliterate it forever.

4

DILMUN, THE ANCIENT
CULTURE OF THE GULF

To set the Gulf, its islands and the coastal lands of eastern Arabia into a coherent historical and cultural perspective it is helpful to look first at the structures and mores of the societies which are immediately contiguous to them, and which exercised a notable influence on the region throughout the course of its history. Of these lands by far the most important and influential was Mesopotamia, the Land of the Two Rivers. Iran, Inner Arabia, the Indus Valley and Oman were all, to varying degrees, to exert an influence on the character of ancient Bahrain and the Gulf, but none of these seems to have approached Mesopotamia in the depth of its impact and its enduring quality.

This is especially true in the earlier periods, when Dilmun was presumably located in eastern Arabia. Then the natural contact was with Mesopotamia, as much by land as by water. Certainly the gods of Sumer were always identified with Dilmun (see Chapter 5). The myths which associate Dilmun as the place of origins, the birthplace of the gods, were Sumerian.[1] Later it is clear that influences from the Indus Valley began to predominate in many of the aspects of the society which evolved in the Gulf. But these tended to be at a firmly pragmatic level – a common system of weights for example – which obviously are derived from considerations of commerce rather than belief in the gods. Philosophically and intellectually, so far as the evidence can be interpreted, Mesopotamia continued to exercise the most profound influence on the Gulf, even though it evolved its own typical forms and no doubt its own ideas, maintaining its independent connections with other peoples far distant from the Land of the Two Rivers.

Mesopotamia is today principally contained within the borders of the Republic of Iraq and divides naturally into two geographical regions, north and south; its other divisions are ethnic and religious and do not concern us here. In the early centuries the south was incomparably the more important of the two, though a northern Mesopotamian influence can frequently be discerned, even in the earliest times, until ultimately, in the second millennium BC, it became dominant. Then it imposed its character on the whole extent of the Land between the Two Rivers.

The essential quality of Mesopotamian culture was its extraordinary capacity for invention, the product of the genius of the land's first and most notable inhabitants, the Sumerians. Whilst the progress achieved in the scientific cultivation of crops and the management of herds owed much of its origins to northern Mesopotamian farmers, it is as city-dwellers that the Mesopotamian people are most significant, and the emergence and growth of the city is to be observed particularly in the south. It was because of the Sumerians' dependence on the city as the basic structural element in their society that their influence spread far beyond their own borders, affecting the patterns of life in lands and times far distant from their own.

THE FIRST CITIES

It is clearly significant that in Egypt and Iraq, and later in India and China, the first great urban civilizations grew up in the river valleys. The siting of settlements on the banks of fast-running and capricious rivers and the consequent invention of irrigation permitted the development of sophisticated agricultural techniques. These, in turn, led to the conditions in which a highly developed political organization became necessary, to ensure that the manpower of the community was marshalled in good order, and that the canals and the lands which depended upon them were efficiently maintained and protected in the interests of the community at large. The emergence of the warrior caste and ultimately of kingship itself resulted in all probability from techniques associated with the management of rivers and canals. Thus it may be said that technology played a critical part in the establishment of early societies and the hierarchies and social structures which grew up within their boundaries. As the communities grew and as the more skilful, charismatic or more powerful leader would begin to assert a form of hegemony over more widely dispersed groups, so kingship would be, in the Sumerian expression, 'handed down'.[2] The principle of government under an autocratic ruler was early on found to be essential to control the resources that the societies had at their disposal and so to produce what was required for the needs of an increasing population. This in turn led to the emergence of a class structure and the fostering of specializations and individual skills by members of the societies, the early artist-craftsmen whose work expanded the horizons of their contemporaries and made it possible for the corporate life of the state, in the person and way of life of the ruler or in the service of the gods, to find expression. Through the invention of writing and of monumental inscriptions it also became possible for one generation to communicate with others over long periods of time and to eliminnate the total dependence on oral tradition which characterized all earlier attempts at formulating the corporate beliefs and intellectual inheritance of the community.

Building in stone and brick led to permanence not only in architecture but in beliefs and social structures; however, the use of long-lasting materials in architecture was not, it is now known, an original invention of Near Eastern societies. Carbon-14 datings from some western European megalithic structures suggest that they are earlier in construction than all monumental buildings in the Near East thus far known. But so far as we know, the societies in northern France, Britain and Malta which produced these remarkable monuments did not develop structurally as did their Near Eastern peers. It was the invention of writing which made still greater controls in the society possible and led to entirely new dimensions of experience.

From the ability to retain ideas in a permanent form came man's discovery of still further potentials, hitherto only dimly realized, within himself. The ability to make permanent records which were capable of comprehension by any with the necessary skills (which, unlike other forms of craftsmanship, required only a normal intelligence and application for the acquisition of proficiency) was arguably the most important single advance ever made by man. It is one with a special relevance to the future of the societies in the region with which we are concerned. Equally, by the better organization of his resources man discovered the means to produce more than he needed of both the necessities and the luxuries of his world. Gradually he found the leisure in which to produce more and better things and in which to enjoy them. From this last discovery, the creation of surplus, the confines of his world expanded dramatically, for now trade and the peaceful intercourse of different peoples became familiar aspects of his everyday life.

In Mesopotamia special conditions prevailed, for man had settled there relatively late in his dispersion over the surface of the inhabited world, although Lower Palaeolithic sites have been found in the north, as have the remains of Neanderthals.[3] The Neanderthal was once the prototype of the half-human, half-ape, a creature of nightmare whose brutish existence was liable to abrupt termination by his equally brutish neighbour. But discoveries at Shanidar, in northern Iraq, and the analysis of other remains have begun to present a different picture of a creature who cared for and protected the old and infirm in his group and who, at their death, went out on to the hillside to gather flowers to bury with them. The discovery, too, that the cranial capacity of Neanderthals is on average somewhat larger than modern man's has also begun to qualify the unflattering picture which Neanderthal's modern descendants (if such we are, in part at least) were pleased to draw of him. Instead of the loping brute of earlier belief, Neanderthal is rapidly acquiring an air of pensive and gentle melancholy – a generalization which, though more kindly, may be as specious as the earlier one.

MESOPOTAMIAN ORIGINS

In Mesopotamia, the contrast between north and south is most marked in the earliest periods. In the north, around the tenth millennium BP, the beginnings of agriculture and the controlled breeding of herd animals appear for the first time anywhere in the world. But the southern part of the land offered little inducement for settlers, since it was virtually bereft of minerals, stone or trees. Only when man had learned to control his environment, in particular to manage the rivers and lagoons which formed so much of the southern landscape, and so himself to create the conditions in which his needs could be satisfied, did a settled existence become possible in the southern part of the Land of the Two Rivers.

Over millennia small groups of migrants had drifted into Mesopotamia from the south and the west, where the deserts of Arabia lay, from the mountain lands of Iran in the east, and from Syria and Anatolia in the north. In the north the little settlements flourished and, incidentally, very early on began to produce pottery of an extraordinary fineness and elegance. It is remarkable that some of the earliest pottery in the world is also some of the most beautiful: that which is identified with Hassouna and Halaf is of quite exceptional, indeed superlative, quality.[4]

THE ARABIAN NEOLITHIC

The early Arabian Neolithic was affected by the agricultural and pastoral revolution in the Fertile Crescent as a whole. However, the lack of permanent settlement and the differences which are apparent in the stone tool assemblages imply rather a transition by a hunting and gathering society towards an early pastoralism but one with a strong reliance on hunting. The particular influences and the constraints of Arabia's environment produced special cultural developments distinct from those of other settled societies in neighbouring regions.[5] Tools from this period – blade-type tools with projectile points and scrapers – have been found in eastern Arabia in the lower levels at Ain Qannas, south of the Hasa oasis and in the Yabrin oasis area, near extinct sources of water, in areas where water collected, and in the valley bottoms.[6]

The Neolithic brought a great diversification of stone tool types, both through advances in manufacturing techniques and by the recognition of a wider range both of needs and of possibilities. In these toolmakers we can perhaps recognize the first 'experts' or craft specialists; it is still possible to identify 'workshop' sites where tools were fabricated, sometimes 'roughed-out' and prepared for final shaping by another 'specialist'.[7] The immense range of Neolithic tools is well demonstrated from northern and southern sites in eastern Arabia and from the Qatar peninsula.[8] In these processes the marginally more benign climate undoubtedly assisted in occupation of regions which otherwise, and later, would be inhospitable to peoples still reliant to a substantial degree on hunting and gathering.

THE UBAID

By the end of the fifth millennium another culture of comparatively high development had spread both to the north and south of Mesopotamia. It is from the south, from a small *tel* not far from Ur, that its archaeological site name of al-Ubaid derives.[9] Little is known of the social structures of the people who lived there, other than through the traces which were left in succeeding cultures and their most distinctive pottery, which is found over an immensely widespread area, fanning out from Mesopotamia to the Levant, Iran and, most significantly in this present context, to east Arabian and Gulf sites. As for evidence of religious cults, in the oldest pre-Sumerian settlement, Jarmo in northern Iraq, a goddess figurine has been discovered, but no representations of gods of comparable antiquity are known. In the Ubaid region in the south it is a fair guess that the priesthoods must have been exceptionally powerful. The size of many Ubaid period temples is formidable.

The Ubaid pottery levels are followed on southern Mesopotamian sites by the more sombre Uruk pottery and then by that which is typed by its find-site, Jemdet Nasr. In terms of absolute chronology Uruk spans the middle centuries of the fourth millennium and Jemdet Nasr continues until the beginning of the third.[10] It is thus equivalent in Egyptian chronology to Naqada II or the Gerzean period, immediately prior to the First Dynasty of kings.[11] In Sumer (to use the term which by the beginning of the third millennium is appropriate) these pottery sequences are followed by the Early Dynastic period, which, divided archaeologically into three phases, continues until the appearance of Sargon the Great in the twenty-fourth century BC.[12]

THE SUMERIANS

By the end of the fourth millennium southern Mesopotamian society has become recognizably Sumerian, in language, custom and in the development of that most Sumerian of institutions, the city. The Ubaid culture disappears, subsumed into the predominantly Sumerian mass. However, the transition from Ubaid to Sumerian is virtually unmarked and, whilst it was once thought that the Sumerians were a 'new people' who arrived at some unspecified point in the first half of the fourth millennium, this view is today much less firmly held. Rather, scholars believe that Ubaid society evolved into the Sumerian, perhaps with the leavening of some alien elements but with no evidence of a major population change having taken place. The evidence of a long pottery sequence from Ubaid to early Sumerian forms is one of the more convincing arguments in favour of a cultural continuity in the south over the thousand years or so which anticipate the first certain appearance of the Sumerians as a distinct and identifiable group around

3500 BC.[13] The evidence of language is less clear, however; whilst the first pictographic tablets to be found in Sumer are thought to be written in Sumerian, many of the place-names which were adopted as the names of the cities and shrines of Sumer are not themselves Sumerian words.

They appear to be the inheritance of some pre-Sumerian strain which once was thought to be the remnants of the language of the Ubaid people – Proto-Euphratean, as it was sometimes called. It is by no means certain, however, that such a separate language ever existed and the issue is yet another of the perplexing elements still unresolved in the history of this distant epoch.[14]

The problem of the origins of the Sumerians themselves is one of the most tantalizing of the unresolved mysteries of the ancient world. At one time or another, practically every possible origin (and a variety of quite impossible ones) has been suggested for them, but still the question must, for the present, end in uncertainty. Their language, usually one of the surest means of pinpointing an ethnic group's origins, bears absolutely no relationship to any other language, living or dead. Sumerian is agglutinative, that is to say its clauses are built up by adding syllabic elements to the original root. In this it is similar to Finnish, Turkish, Hungarian and Basque, but it is connected with none of these nor with any other known tongue.

Sumerian was a rich and flexible language and it soon became one of the most powerful media for the expression of the Sumerians' exceptional creative genius. Sumerian literature, with its amazing repertory of epic poems, of the sagas of heroes, 'wisdom' literature, hymns and songs, love poetry, proverbs and laws is immensely rich;[15] it boasts the oldest surviving corpus of literary texts in the history of the world and, in many ways, one of the most noble, full of humanity and with a deep concern for the human condition. No account of Sumerian ways can ignore the literature of the Sumerian people and in the present context extensive use will be made of extracts from that part of the literature which bears upon the Holy Land of Dilmun, a particular theme of these early epic writers.[16]

THE INVENTION OF WRITING

The most important single contribution which the Sumerians made to the progress of mankind was the invention of sophisticated writing systems. It is difficult, maybe even impossible, to think of any invention which has contributed more to the fulfilment of man's destiny, nor one which has added more to his enjoyment of the world in which he found himself placed by the whim of the gods.

It is not certain that the Sumerians were the first to invent the concept of writing. In Upper Palaeolithic times, it has been suggested, some form of calendrical notations may have been employed to keep track of the seasons and the passage of the days.[17]

A group of tablets excavated at Tartaria in Rumania, has been thought by some observers to bear some resemblance to early Sumerian forms and to be ancestral to them. If this was the case, it would hint at yet another point of origin for the Sumerian people themselves; however, the Tartaria tablets may be later than first thought or, at best, may simply represent another direction from which some powerful, contributing influence travelled.[18]

Recent research has opened up another remarkable and exciting vista on the origins of writing. For many years past, workers on sites in the Near East have been turning up quantities of small baked clay objects in a variety of seemingly arbitrary shapes, spheres, half-spheres, cones, tetrahedrons and the like. These have been variously described – as toys or ritual objects – or dismissed outright as inexplicable.

These tokens are found on sites dating back as far as the ninth millennium BC. This is astonishingly early, coinciding virtually with the first appearance of agriculture in the Near East, one of the most momentous of all changes which man has experienced since Upper Palaeolithic times.

These various shapes seem to have been used over the many thousands of years which separate their first appearance from that of the first tablets from Sumer to carry what may properly be called 'writing'. What makes the discovery so momentous, however, is the recognition that they are the earliest device for recording the numbers and species of animals possessed by a temple, for example, and that the scribes of several thousand years after their introduction used the same symbols, incised on stone or clay, as were represented by the clay tokens.[19]

Frequently the tokens were contained in hollow clay containers, roughly the size of tennis balls. On the outside of the container the number and type of tokens which it enclosed would be incised, to prevent fraud or the passing of incorrect information. The only example so far known to have come from an east Arabian site is stated to have been 'an isolated surface find near Dhahran in Saudi Arabia'. Sadly, it was removed from Saudi Arabia and is now in the United States.[20] However, such precedents as the 'tokens' in use before the Sumerians' introduction of writing do not in any way diminish the splendour of the Sumerian achievement; the Sumerians were the first to devise a technique of making permanent records which was also flexible enough to be capable of expressing concepts and ideas and of recording for ever the very speech of the people.

The earliest known examples of Sumerian writing come from Kish[21] and Uruk,[22] two of the most ancient antediluvian cities in Sumer; those from Kish are marginally the earlier but both sets of tablets are dated to the Uruk period. On these small, cushion-like clay tablets, excavated from levels c. 3500 BC, were found pictographs, representations of the object about which it was required to record quantities. From this point the technique developed rapidly, with the pictographs becoming more extensive as the records became more complex. It was soon realized that the simple representation of an object by drawing a picture of it was both cumbersome and limited. Then the great leap forward was taken in synthesizing the pictographs with abstractions which would represent the object on one level but also the sound of the word or syllable concerned on another. By this means it was possible to develop a form of writing which could itself record observations without being wholly dependent on the representation of objects alone. The actual script devised for this purpose is known as cuneiform, for the characters are wedge-shaped, the product of Sumerian 'pens': sharpened reeds whose angled writing points most easily produced the combination of lines and wedges ·which made up the Sumerian script. Ultimately there were some 2,000 standard signs of which 600–700 were in general and relatively frequent use. To learn them and to inscribe them competently must have demanded a formidable standard of education for the boys who attended the schools specially set up for the purpose of training scribes. The scribal profession was one which was greatly to be envied, a situation which also prevailed in Egypt.

The sophistication of the Sumerian intellectual establishment even in the fourth millennium BC was quite extraordinary. This is demonstrated by the fact that, like many early languages, Sumerian originally had an extremely complex and cumbersome vocabulary. Thus it was particularly rich in nouns with many words for objects which would more conveniently be qualified by adjectives. At some point in the latter part of the fourth millennium, the language was reformed and instead of there being, say, twenty-six words for various types of sheep, the number was drastically reduced and qualifying adjectives (or their equivalent) employed. This was surely one of the most remarkable and momentous intellectual decisions ever taken in the history of man.

The cuneiform script itself went through some six stages of adaptation[23] before it was finally stabilized into what might be called its classical form around 1800 BC. When the Semitic-speaking hordes from the Arabian and western deserts began to move into the Sumerians' lands, since they were of course illiterate, they adopted cuneiform as their own form of writing though it is ill suited to a Semitic language. As a consequence, however, of the tribes' adoption of it, its use spread to other Semitic language-speaking states around the Near East, so that by the middle of the second millennium BC, 2,000 years after the Sumerians had invented it, cuneiform was widespread in use throughout the ancient world, though Sumerian itself had become purely a liturgical language by then. Typically, since they believed that nothing of theirs could ever be improved upon, only the Egyptians did not employ cuneiform characters (except under diplomatic duress), preferring their own system of hieroglyphic and hieratic scripts, the first of which is surely the most elegant yet invented by man.

It has been suggested that the Egyptians must have borrowed the idea of writing from the Sumerians as the chances of both peoples independently making the same revolutionary invention at roughly the same time (the earliest examples of Egyptian writing appear shortly after the Sumerian) is stretching the theory of independent development too far. However, the Egyptian system bears little relationship to Sumerian forms, and it seems strange that this should be so if the Egyptians did borrow the idea originally. In the later centuries of the second millennium, when all the kingdoms in the Levant and Mesopotamia were using cuneiform, even the scribes of the Egyptian foreign office, who maintained an extensive correspondence on the Pharaoh's behalf with his contemporaries, were obliged to conduct this part of their correspondence in cuneiform. With the Egyptian conviction that their ways were so unreservedly superior to all others, this necessity of writing in another people's orthography must have been a trying experience.

The texts which have survived from Sumer, and which are to be reckoned in tens of thousands at least, are preserved on clay tablets, the most convenient and accessible substance which the scribe could procure on which to write. Following the same cushion-shape of the earliest stone tablets, the clay tablets were first smoothed, the characters swiftly incised on them with the wedge-shaped reeds and then baked, in which form they are virtually indestructible. Often they were sealed in envelopes and then (like the earlier tokens from which, in a sense, they may descend) neatly filed away in archive rooms which have become familiar and important elements in the excavation of many a Near Eastern palace or city site.

The consequences of the Sumerian preoccupation with writing – and they were an almost compulsively literate people – was to be of profound importance to the people of the Gulf settlements. The Sumerians did not invent writing primarily to record their folk epics or the proverbs which show them to have been a worldly-wise people with a nicely ironic cast of mind. Their purpose was, some might think, a less elevated one; they were concerned to maintain accurate records of their trading activities. These activities were to become perhaps their greatest single preoccupation and trade accounted in no small part for the diffusion of Sumerian and Mesopotamian influences over a wide area of the known world. In this aspect of their life the Gulf islands and settlements played a particularly significant part.

THE SUMERIANS AND TRADE

The Sumerians were the first people to organize trade as a corporate function of the community, to a large extent making it the very basis of their societies. Southern Mesopotamia is an odd part of the world; it is now, as it was in the days of the Sumerians themselves, a land of harsh, windswept desert, of fast-running rivers that lay down rich silt and mud fields which are capable of exceptionally high yields when managed carefully, of lagoons stretching from horizon to horizon, teeming with fish and game, but virtually without any other natural resources whatsoever. There is hardly any stone in Sumer and the few trees, such as they are, with the exception of the ubiquitous palm tree, are of little value to the craftsman or builder.

Because of the nature of their land the Sumerians, in the latter part of the fourth millennium, were faced with a singular dilemma: a burning creative enterprise which was prevented from finding expression in the conversion of the products of nature into the artefacts of man. To obtain the raw materials their craftsmen needed, therefore, the city and temple administrators were forced to search for sources of supply far distant from their own ungenerous land. From early times we read of trading expeditions reaching out to far distant lands, of treaties between Sumerian states and foreign powers for the supply of Sumer's needs and the mounting of military expeditions to keep open the caravan routes or to subdue brigands and the other barbarians whose activities might prejudice the free flow of trade to and from the ports of Sumer's cities.

In the course of developing a trade which ultimately stretched from Anatolia to the Indus Valley, from the Levant and the islands of the Mediterranean to central Asia and north and south through Bahrain and the east Arabian towns, the Sumerians devised a complex series of techniques to facilitate the exchange of goods on an international scale and to finance the activities of their professional merchants.[24] In the course of doing so they invented banking, the concept of capital and equity holding, mortgaging and the advancing of working or risk capital against securities, indeed much of the paraphernalia of international finance which sustains world-wide commerce to this day. Later this study will examine the surviving correspondence of an Old Babylonian merchant who, in immediately post-Sumerian times, operated a trading enterprise of some scale but of doubtful probity between the city of Ur and the city of Dilmun, located on the north shore of Bahrain's principal island.[25]

Sumerian trade operated in two ways: first by establishing sources of supply of the raw materials which were so much needed and, second, by creating export markets for the surplus goods the cities made, as a result of their enterprise and their skilful management of people and resources. The actual processes of manufacture were industrialized and highly organized. Factories were operated, turning out a particular product range, with a well-organized and generally well-cared-for labour force. Sumer's manufactures included textiles, furniture, jewellery, copper and bronze objects, and fine inlays; in addition she exported her surplus agricultural products. Her imports were first and foremost copper, and all sorts of timber and stone for her lapidaries, sculptors and architects. Timber came from Indian forests and from Oman; stone from Persia, perhaps from Oman and, in the case of the precious lapis lazuli much appreciated by the gods, from distant Badakhshan. Gold was mined in Elam (south-western Persia) and in Syria.

The staple of Sumerian trade was copper; its conversion by man is very ancient and there is evidence of its being smelted in Anatolia in the seventh millennium.[26] Indeed, some scholars have suggested that the Anatolian sources were lost to the Sumerians in the fourth millennium BC;[27] in consequence, they were forced to look for other sources of supply, which they found, it is suggested, to the south: Oman may have been one of the principal sources discovered in this search. But the idea of Sumer's discovery of the Gulf being the consequence of her search for copper is improbable. No doubt the need to prospect the Gulf lands for this vital element in her economy added greatly to Sumer's knowledge of the region but there is really nothing to suggest that Anatolian copper was so significant in the early history of the people. However, it is certain Bahrain played an important role as an entrepôt in the movement of copper from its sources, notably in Oman, to Mesopotamia. There is evidence of a considerable quantity of copper being handled in Bahrain, through the quays of the successive cities at the Qala'at al-Bahrain site.[28]

Trade was conducted, as will be seen from the correspondence which survives, by barter in part but also by the much more sophisticated technique of expressing equivalent values in a standard of currency, in the Sumerians' and Babylonians' case in silver. They did not, however, find it necessary to take the conclusive step of introducing a coinage.

THE GULF AND SUMERIAN ORIGINS

It has often been suggested that the immigrants into southern Mesopotamia, who were to become the Sumerians, came to the land from the south, travelling up the Gulf or along the Arabian coast.[29] The presence of Ubaid pottery in southern Mesopotamia has already been observed, and it has been found, in very recent years, on many east Arabian and Gulf sites. However, there is as yet no evidence that the Ubaid culture progressed, as it were, from south to north; indeed the pottery seems to suggest that the earliest examples are to be found in the north, whilst the analyses of Ubaid sherds which have been carried out on the Gulf examples connect them with potteries at Ur.[30] But the fact remains that the Sumerians believed that the arts of civilization had been brought to them from the Gulf by the fish-man Oannes, who may be a manifestation of Enki, the benign creator-god of whom much more will be heard before this present work is done.[31] One cycle of legend makes Dilmun, which features in the Sumerian consciousness both as a commercial trading centre and as an idealized Paradise Land, the place of creation, from which concept undoubtedly the Biblical story of the Garden of Eden is derived.[32] Thus it would be unwise to dismiss absolutely the possibility that the people who became the Sumerians, or perhaps other immigrants who influenced them considerably, did come up the Gulf from some as yet unknown southern point of origin.

The centre of the land of Dilmun, which exercised so powerful an appeal to the Sumerians, was the principal Bahrain island. However, its borders were never immutably fixed; at certain periods it was known to include the eastern Arabian coastline up to present-day Kuwait and to include Failaka island on which important early second-millennium remains have been found. Dilmun was not only the Place where the Sun Rises; it was also the Land of the Living, in Sumerian *Kirlu Ti-La*.[33]

There has been considerable speculation whether the Gulf in Sumerian times reached significantly further north than it does today. The view was widely held, until fairly recently, that it did, this opinion being strengthened by the historical record of such cities as Eridu and Ur which boasted of a sea trade and which now lie up to 450 kilometres (150 miles) from the Gulf. At one time it was thought that the shorelines of the Gulf had not much changed since relatively early times, certainly since the lifetime of man. However, some doubt is now being cast on this view.[34] It may be that the region of southern Iraq, now inhabited by the Marsh Arabs, a people who could well be the last survivors of the Sumerian (even pre-Sumerian) way of life, was then, even more than it is today, an area of lagoons, reaching far into the Sumerian hinterland. Thus some of the principal Sumerian ports in the south would have been situated on the shores of a lagoon and linked by a chain of them, each opening into another, down to the Gulf.

ERIDU

Eridu, the most southerly of all the Sumerian cities, was also the most ancient. It was one of the great antediluvian cities, for the Sumerians reckoned historic time from the legendary ages before the Flood. Archaeology has borne out this tradition of Erudu's antiquity and suggests that it is a fact: so far, no city has been found that is of earlier date. A long series of temples was excavated at Eridu; the four oldest, reaching ultimately down to the virgin sand, are the earliest identifiable as buildings of the Ubaid period.[35]

In the context of the Gulf, this fact of the antiquity of Eridu is extremely important, for Eridu was sacred to Enki, the god of the sweet waters. Throughout Sumerian history Eridu was the cult centre of the one Sumerian divinity who was well disposed towards humanity.

According to the evidence of legend, Dilmun and Enki were closely identified in Sumerian belief; the worship of the god, it has been argued, might have originated in Dilmun.[36] Enki is sometimes conflated with Oannes, the amphibious monster who swam up the Gulf, accompanied by a train of outlandish marine creatures. Oannes' epiphany has been cited as evidence that the Sumerians came from the south: it has been suggested that Oannes was a sort of abstraction of the people themselves and also, more pertinent to this story, that on their northward journey they had settled for a time on Bahrain island. This, it was supposed, accounted for the tenderness with which they looked back to Dilmun and for the sanctity with which they invested the island, making it in truth the island of blessedness and innocence.

The exceptional antiquity of Eridu has further been called in support of the contention that it was the first true Sumerian settlement, the landfall as it were of the immigrants, who commemorated their seaborne journey by consecrating their first mainland city to the water-god Enki. In this context, too, it has been noted that in the second half of the fourth millennium, Uruk, the city which was to give birth to the greatest of Sumerian heroic kings, Gilgamesh, shows a marked and sudden increase of population.[37] It has been suggested that this increase might have been the consequence of a migration of people from the Gulf region. If such a migration took place (for which, at present, there is no archaeological evidence), it would account for the infusion of myths and legends which are centred on Bahrain–Dilmun, revered as the original home of gods and men.

It has been noted already that most authorities see an uninterrupted sequence of occupation in southern Mesopotamia from early Ubaid times through to the first appearance of writing, and hence to the first appearance of the Sumerians when it was possible to put a name to them, in the latter part of the fourth millennium.[38] The most compelling evidence for this view comes from the Eridu temple itself: the earliest humble shrine, which underlies the great, late third-millennium ziggurat (which was consecrated to Enki and thus honoured the god of fish and the deep waters), displays a startling continuity from the days of Mesopotamia's earliest occupation, around 5000 BC, down to the lifetime of the mighty ziggurat some 3,000 years later. The evidence of pottery too, is quite clear. From the products of the Ubaid people, through the types associated with the Uruk and Jemdet Nasr periods, the succession of each type from its predecessor is evident. Pottery is a certain marker in these matters and its evidence is unequivocal. Thus, if the Ubaid or the Sumerians, or any part of them, came from the south then they must have moved along the Arabian shore; but such Ubaid pottery evidence as there is at present, which has now been found at sites in eastern Arabia, Bahrain, Qatar and the United Arab Emirates, in the south of the Gulf, indicates connections with the later Ubaid and, in all probability, with established communities in Mesopotamia.[39]

One of the most significant artefacts from the very beginnings of the Sumerian period comes from Eridu in the late Ubaid period, the oldest model of a sailing-boat yet found anywhere in the world.[40] With a little modification, this type of vessel continued to sail the waters of the Gulf and, where they were navigable, the rivers of Mesopotamia, far into historic times. The Eridu boat would have been seaworthy and further supports the belief that the Gulf could easily have been explored by men in prehistoric times. It was on the Gulf's tricky waters, or on the waters of southern Mesopotamia's marsh-bound lagoons, that man first developed the art of harnessing the winds to his service and using their power to drive the early sailing craft of which the Eridu boat is the prototype. How far these early voyages reached is yet a matter of speculation but the presence of shells which can only have originated in India, in a very early grave at Tepe Gawra far to the north in Mesopotamia, could be taken as evidence, even this early, of a route to India through the Gulf. A land route cannot be completely ruled out, however, though the experience of historic times makes it less likely. Shells from the Gulf have also been found in Egyptian graves of the Naqada I period, equivalent to the Uruk period in Sumerian chronology. Similarly, lapis lazuli has been found in Predynastic Egyptian contexts and can only have reached the Valley from the east.[41] Whilst again a land route cannot be dismissed, the possibility of these materials having reached Egypt by sea cannot be discounted.

The most notable characteristics of Sumerian society grew out of the land and the conditions necessary to organize it in such a way that it could support a rapidly growing population with increasingly sophisticated needs. There is some evidence that the earliest Sumerian political unit was an assembly of free men who, under the leadership of the elders, together openly debated issues affecting the community.[42] Some commentators have, perhaps a little optimistically, seen in this institution the earliest recorded example of democratic, even of parliamentary, government. In the event, however, this phenomenon is much more likely to demonstrate the lingering vestiges of the old tribal assemblies of Neolithic times, possibly an inheritance from the Ubaid communities, and one which clearly proved to be unworkable in the earliest phases of the true Sumerian period. However, the Sumerians remained throughout their history a fiercely independent and individualistic people. It would certainly not have been out of keeping with their nature if the citizens had demanded a share in their own government. The most inspired of Sumerian rulers, Gilgamesh, is, albeit in a purely literary context, shown consulting the elders of the state – and then going against their advice.[43]

THE SUMERIAN TEMPLE

There is evidence that the earliest centre of administration and authority in the fledgeling Sumerian cities was the temple: this is logical enough, for the city is merely the central point of the earthly domain of the god to whom the city was consecrated. In the early centuries the city, and the state which depended on it, was, literally, a theocracy, god-directed and god-ruled. All land was owned corporately on the god's behalf and managed by his vicars, the stewards of his estate who in early times no doubt formed a powerful confraternity of priests under the rule of the *En*, the high priest. The title was sometimes also used in a purely political context, divorced from any cultic role; in such cases *en* may reasonably be rendered 'lord'.

To these practical priesthoods the world may owe much. In the early centuries, trade, that essential aspect of Sumerian society, was in the hands of the temple authorities; merchants bought and sold on the temple's behalf and all the goods involved were the temple's property. The practice of writing was invented, so far as we may judge, principally to effect a system of accounting for the temple's treasure; the earliest pictographic texts are inventories of goods and animals in all likelihood belonging to the temple.

One of the puzzles, and a most intriguing one, about the process of disseminating an invention like writing is how, in so fragmented a political society as the Sumerian cities undoubtedly were in the historic period, they managed to develop a writing system which rapidly became accepted throughout the land, paying no apparent regard to the distinctions which one city-state might vaunt over another or the pretensions which the adherents of one divinity might advance against the other gods. It seems that the sort of freemasonry which the priesthoods represented must have been powerful enough and sufficiently organized throughout the country to make the decisions of some central college outweigh local differences or preferences. It is perhaps the first historic example of a bureaucracy at work, maintaining its own larger interests at the expense of any short-term policies which might otherwise have supervened.

But, though their states were governed either corporately or autocratically, the Sumerians nonetheless retained throughout their existence a respect for the individual and for the rule of law applied equally to all citizens, to a degree remarkable in antiquity. In most ancient societies it is generally the state, perhaps personified by the king, which is all-powerful and all-pervasive, private interests being liable to be sacrificed to a frequently arbitrary judgement of what was represented as the general or national interest. The Sumerians were the first people to attempt to define the role of the individual in society and to establish a formal, written code governing behaviour and defining responsibilities between one citizen and another and between the citizen and the state. In doing so, they invented law and rightly prided themselves on the fact.[44]

THE CITY-STATE

The Sumerians thought of themselves as one people, and as quite distinct from their neighbours, but they early on fragmented into a constantly changing mosaic of little states, competing noisily with each other, though their frontiers sometimes barely stretched beyond the city walls. One after another claimed the paramountcy over the others, to be overtaken quickly by a marginally more powerful or politically more agile neighbour. Only rarely was the land harnessed under one leadership for longer than a lifetime and in general terms Sumerian political history is made up of the records of the mass of little cities constantly squabbling amongst themselves like puppies in a basket.

Sumer was thus never a unitary state for longer than a few decades at a time, the individual cities often maintaining much of their autonomous character meanwhile. When the distribution of cities, built perhaps on earlier Ubaid settlements, was established in the pattern which was to persist throughout the historic Sumerian period, Sumer could be said to stretch from just below modern Baghdad in the north to the sealands of the Gulf in the south, bordered by the Arabian desert in the west and the foothills of the Iranian plateau in the east; it was only some 10,000 square miles in extent, a tiny portion of the world's surface when measured against the influence its people exerted. Amongst the earliest cities, in addition to Eridu, were Ur, which provides much of the best known archaeological material from Sumer,[45] Uruk, the city of which Gilgamesh was king, and Nippur, which was always the most sacred of Sumerian cities, consecrated to Enlil; Kish, Badtibira and Lagash were other cities of immense antiquity. By Early Dynastic times, in the first centuries of the third millennium there were some twenty city-states which made up the polity of Sumer.[46]

Each of them followed a similar if not identical political pattern: there would be a king or governor, a *lugal* or *ensi*, a temple to the principal god of the city and other lesser fanes consecrated to his or her coadjutors. Built around and beyond the sacred enclosure of the temple which formed the heart of any Sumerian city (and which was indeed the city's reason for existence, for the city was the personal property and domain of the divinity to which it was consecrated and the temple his or her dwelling-place) were the citizens' houses of baked mud-brick. The city's roads criss-crossed with blank walled alleys from which opened gates into the houses. These might be little more than one- or two-roomed huts, or in the case of the more prosperous craftsmen, merchants or administrators, spacious buildings on two floors, with pleasant courtyards and loggias elegantly decorated,[47] but like all well-designed Near Eastern dwellings to this day, looking inwards to the household and the family which it enveloped. None of the cities covered very large acreages; the most famous, Ur, covered about half a square mile. Uruk, the city of Gilgamesh, was much bigger, however, ranging over almost 2 square miles.

As Sumerian society developed and expanded, shops, factories, schools and barracks for the enlisted men became conventional landmarks in any Sumerian town. As, almost beyond anything else, the Sumerians believed in trade, the rivers' quayside market-places, where far-ranging ships would disgorge the merchandise of many lands, became more and more important in the life of the cities and central to the experience of its people.

A busy, prosperous, creative and largely cheerful people, the Sumerians had, by the beginning of the third millennium, established themselves securely upon their land. In essence, the cities which they built, the clothes that were worn in their market-places, and the buzz of many tongues would have made their society seem little different from that of any Middle Eastern country up to the beginning of the twentieth century AD.

The racial origins of the people of Sumer, it has already been observed, are unknown. They have not helped the matter by tending, throughout their history, to portray themselves as rather tubby, short-necked, round-headed people. In fact, the evidence of their skeletons indicates that their grasp of morphology was slight, but nonetheless many early commentators were led to believe that they were racially entirely distinct from the desert peoples to the west of them, who were Semitic-speaking and who constantly pressed upon the established urban communities which the Sumerians developed. But linguistic distinctions do not reveal themselves in skeletal remains: a Sumerian urban skeleton is indistinguishable from one of a Semitic-speaking desert-dweller.

The successors of the Sumerians – the Akkadians, Babylonians and Assyrians – were Semites and the language and culture of the land became progressively Semiticized over the centuries to the extent that Sumerian was totally lost as a living language. However, from evidence so far available, it is impossible to argue anything conclusive about the Sumerian race. Certainly all the peoples of southern Mesopotamia intermarried freely and Semitic names in early Sumerian times are almost as frequent as Sumerian names surviving into the early Old Babylonian period. Within the present limits of knowledge, the terms 'Sumerian' and 'Semitic' are to be understood simply as cultural and linguistic divisions rather than as indications of distinct racial groupings.

The recorded history of man-the-dweller-in-cities opens with the Sumerians having established themselves on their land and with the transformation of what were perhaps tribal or clan settlements, small villages which felt the need for some sort of 'central place' either for exchange or for ritual observance and so gradually led to the beginnings of city life. The earliest settlements of the Near East, which had developed erratically in Iraq itself, in Iran, Palestine, Syria and Turkey, rapidly grew in Sumer into what modern man would consider properly organized cities. By the end of the fourth millennium a sizeable proportion of the Sumerian population spent its life within the boundaries of a city. Unhappily, what may have been one of the primary considerations in drawing man to urban life, security, proved illusory in Mesopotamia, for the nomadic desert and mountain tribes, which hedged the cities about, quickly decided that they were prizes worth devouring and their riches worth seizing. Further, in moving to the city man had put himself at one remove from nature and the stress of city life began to weigh heavily upon him.

It was an entirely new experience for mankind, this living together permanently in highly organized, usually tightly walled, settlements. Economic pressures and the need for firm political controls in a powerfully developing economy were added to the hope of limiting the depressing cycle of onslaught and invasion which marred the enjoyment of life (or even its continuation) in post-Neolithic societies, newly awakening to the prospects which that life had to offer. The evidence available and the interpretations, particularly those which are influenced by modern psychological analysis, suggest that the transformation from Neolithic village communities to urban settlements and the development of political structures and technology brought in train a series of acute and radical changes and attendant tensions. The most profound of these were experienced, first, in the emergence of art as a formal discipline, which both in its origins and in its later practice was concerned with the unseen world as much as the real one; and, second, in the change from magic to religion, and consequently the organization of belief and the responsibility of man to the gods in terms which the modern world could comprehend. Art and religion were as inextricably intertwined in Sumer as indeed they have always been, practically everywhere else.

THE ART OF SUMER

There is little trace in early Sumerian art of the propitiatory role which religion often fulfilled in hunter-gatherer societies. It is much more concerned with the declared worship of the gods, the decoration of their temples and with binding them to care for the world of men. The cults which the people developed were, in the manner of religious observance ever afterwards, a method of catharsis, of the release of tensions and the assuaging of fear and apprehension. The uncertainty of their environment, the constant menace of the desert tribes and, eventually, the rivalries of the little cities themselves, all created a degree of uncertainty amongst those early city-dwellers which some may see manifested in the works of art which they produced. Monstrous shapes, reflecting man's deepest fears, began to emerge into tangible, artefactual form and so lost some of their terror.

Although the judgement is necessarily a highly subjective one, much early Sumerian art often seems to be pathological in origin and demonstrates a neurotic, tense, introverted quality which can still be deeply disturbing. As man tried to accustom himself to living in the mass, these monster forms seem to betray the Sumerian's anxiety and uncertainty about coping success-fully with the tensions which this communal life provoked. However, it is essentially this quality which makes the art of early Sumer so especially interesting: it is the first produced by a predominantly and consciously urban society.

Although Sumerian art softened over the centuries and reduced many of the bleak and fearful qualities it early manifested, it never wholly lost this characteristic undercurrent of disquiet. It must also be admitted that, with important exceptions, the early art of Sumer is often notable, when compared for example with that of contemporary Egypt, for its technical incompetence. The Sumerians may be partly worsted in the comparison by the strict discipline displayed by Egyptian artists from the earliest times; but in any event they were better with words and ideas than with plastic materials, the result perhaps of living in a land bare of wood and stone. This peculiar blend of the neurotic and the incompetent did not, however, reduce the marvellous quality of Sumerian seal-cutting, in which perhaps the black-headed people achieved their highest and happiest artistic skills. Sumerian unhandiness, in any case, is rather endearing.

ELAM

The Sumerians were not entirely alone in developing that corner of south-western Asia which they occupied. To the west development was erratic, but to the east and south, in what is today south-western Iran, another talented people was establishing its place in the world.

One of the imponderables of the archaeology of the Gulf in early times, in the late prehistoric period for instance, is the extent to which its culture and way of life were influenced by this people, one of the more mysterious of the Sumerians' neighbours, the Elamites. Elam broadly occupied the Iranian province known historically as Khuzistan, centred on the great and enduring city of Susa which, in turn, has led to the region sometimes being referred to as Susiana. By whatever name it is called, Elam was a powerful and influential western-Asiatic state, in many ways the peer of Sumer itself; it was also an important Gulf power, with a long reach of the eastern coastline under its control.[48]

The origins of Elam are as obscure as Sumer's. Their frontiers marched together in the region of the southern Zagros foothills. In historic times they were frequently in conflict with each other. Elam seems to have been a more integrated state than Sumer usually was, except on the infrequent occasions when a dynast in one of the little states emerged with sufficient power or charisma to impose his hegemony over the whole land. Cities in Elam, it has been suggested, were the consequence of the need for staging and exchange posts to be established to serve the search for raw materials and resources.

Elam shared with Sumer the early use of sophisticated writing systems. The system the Elamites employed is an adaptation of Sumerian cuneiform; the paramountcy in its use is still Sumer's. Unfortunately nothing is known of ancient Elamite; at present it remains indecipherable and consequently far less is known about the early Elamite kingdom than would otherwise be the case.

The Elamites early on adopted the practice of seal-making, a skill they shared with their Sumerian contemporaries. Elamite seals are exceptionally rich in design themes and in the skill which the seal-cutters demonstrate in achieving their often very complex effects. Even more than their Sumerian colleagues, Elamite seal-cutters were remarkably able at bringing about positively monumental effects in a tiny compass.[49]

Many Elamite themes and designs were incorporated into Gulf seal forms, and Elamite influence was at least as considerable as Sumerian. But no one equalled the Elamites in making pictorial seals which show monumental buildings or scenes of ritual or of palace life.

Many Gulf and east Arabian sites, of the third and second millennia in particular, yield quantities of a soft, easily carved stone which is frequently identified as soapstone or steatite but which is more accurately called chlorite. This is a dense, rather plastic-looking stone which varies in colour from brilliant green, through blue to grey and black. Its ease of handling meant that it was ideal for the manufacture of everyday containers, ones that, as it were, required mass-production because of the ubiquity of their use.[50] It has been demonstrated that much of the raw material required for this trade came from southern Persia and was traded through cities like those at Shahr-i Sokta and Tepe Yahya; there were also steatite mines in western Arabia and another source was near Yabrin.[51] The variety of forms and designs used by the chlorite craftsmen is very extensive but certain themes repeat themselves with remarkable persistence. The vessels used range from tiny household jars, many with side-lugs allowing them to be suspended, to huge ritual vessels with designs of complex and often extravagant pictorial detail.

To what extent, if at all, there was contact directly between Elam in the east and Bahrain and the western Gulf littoral is uncertain. On the face of it there would certainly not seem to have been as much as with Sumer in the north and with the Indus Valley cities to the south and east. But with the amount of traffic which the Gulf must have borne, certainly in the second half of the third millennium and in the beginning of the second, it is difficult not to conclude that there must have been some regular and familiar contact. There are evidences of influences percolating into the Gulf from even further east and north (from the Caucasus and Transoxiana for example) and in all probability running through Elam. There was a temple at Susa, Elam's principal city, consecrated to Enshag, the tutelary divinity of Dilmun.[52] There may perhaps have been a colony of Dilmunites resident there.

It has often been proposed that many of the western-Asiatic influences which become apparent in Egypt in late Predynastic times came in fact from Elam. The pear-shaped maces, whose changing form seemed to some commentators to mark the invasion of a new people in the Nile Valley, may be Elamite in origin; some of the elaborate ceremonial carving on votive palettes and knives may also come ultimately from the same inspiration.[53]

The extent of Elam's influence on the history of the societies of late fourth- and early third-millennium western Asia is still awaiting study and quantification. When this is done the degree to which that influence extended westwards to Egypt, if at all, will be better known, as will its contribution to Dilmun. It may be recalled that it was suggested by no less a figure than Sir Flinders Petrie that the islanders of the Gulf may have been the carriers of Elamite and Mesopotamian influences to Egypt in the late Gerzean (Naqada II) period.[54] It was Petrie's view, one followed by several of his successors,[55] that the 'dynastic race' entered Egypt and imposed its will over the Valley by force. The pear-shaped maces were, it was proposed, the weapons of the conquest. It seems very much more likely to the scholars of today that such influences as were transmitted entered Egypt peacefully, more probably brought by merchants than by warriors.[56]

The achievements of the people of Sumer were extraordinary: it is one of the injustices of history that they are still generally deprived of the credit for them. Their exceptional antiquity, reaching back to the very invention of history, has of course not helped them. The fact that, in a sense, they invented the means of history itself, by inventing writing, merely piles irony on unwarranted neglect.

5

THE POLITY OF
THE ANCIENT GULF

The one Sumerian sovereign of whom most people will have heard is Gilgamesh.[1] By his appearance in the story of Dilmun in an episode in the Epic story identified with him, which describes his quest for the flower of restored youth, he highlights the essentially mystical nature which that land enjoyed in the minds of the people of Sumer who lived during and after Gilgamesh's time. More than this, in the person of Gilgamesh of Uruk, Sumerian legend and historical reality come into conjunction. To the people of the land he remained one of the greatest of heroes throughout their existence and indeed beyond it, for he was a potent symbol to their Babylonian and Assyrian successors. His appeal, apart from the universal characteristics of his legend, seems to have rested upon the real achievements of his reign and the memory which the people retained of its glories. The exploits of later kings may also have contributed to it by being absorbed into the older legend.

URUK

The kings of Uruk are some of the better-documented of the earliest rulers of the Sumerian states.[2] The historical existence of Gilgamesh has been proven by the discovery of the records of temple-building in his name at Uruk and by the confrontation between himself and an historical king of Kish, Agga; he reigned *c.* 2700 BC.[3] Gilgamesh was preceded on the Uruk throne by his father, Lugalbanda, by Dummuzi-Tammuz (subsequently a god) and by Enmerkar, who seems to have been the first of the hero figures to catch the imagination of subsequent generations. It is, incidentally, likely that the Sumerians were the first people to have developed the concept of an heroic age, the time of these early kings, in much the way made familiar by the legends of the Mycenean age in Greece, the Northern sagas and the Vedas of India, many hundreds of years later.

Uruk has provided some of the earliest surviving Sumerian documents referring to Dilmun and dating from well back into the fourth millennium. One of the earliest such references comes from a tablet, *c.* 3000 BC,[4] and appears to refer to a tax official. It is likely that at this time Dilmun meant eastern Arabia.

THE KINGSHIP

In the surviving texts relating to the reign of Gilgamesh, the record of a number of the characteristics associated with Sumerian kingship may be found. Kingship was an essentially practical function in Sumer and seems, in its early days at least, not to have been overlaid with any specifically mystical significance. Kings emerged comparatively late in the early period of Sumerian history. The king ruled but he did so by consent and frequently had to persuade his men of the rightness of the course of action which he proposed. He probably descended from the war-band leader, appointed by the city or state in times of emergency. The levies of warriors which he led were always ready themselves to urge a policy on their sovereign and, clearly, he was obliged to take their representations into account, though not necessarily to accept them. The Sumerians were an independently minded people and were not usually prepared to abdicate absolute power to their kings, other than in times of crisis.

The succession to the kingship seems generally to have been by the hereditary principle but most of the dynasties were short-lived, rarely lasting for much more than a century or so. The kingship could be assumed by humble citizens who, doubtless by the process of assassination or other political device, might be seen to manifest the favour of the city divinity, in whose hands the gift of kingship rested. A gardener is listed amongst the kings, as is a woman tavern-keeper.

The Egyptians neatly solved the problem of the evident contradictions of monarchic rule as a political system by an absolute identification of king and god. It is difficult to argue with the administrative decisions of an immanent and divine ruler: treason and blasphemy become identical. Indeed, happy is the society which may see its god in the flesh every time he chooses to show himself, discharging his divine role in public. Much of the permanence and apparent changelessness of Egypt came from the sense of security which the king's divinity brought to the Two Lands: there, all was patently for the best in the best of all possible human situations. The Sumerians, who did not possess the same innocence of view which often typified the Egyptians at much the same time, did not have the comfort of knowing that God was living in a handsomely furnished white-walled building, only, as it were, a short distance down the road. Such was the happy case of the people of Memphis and of others of the early royal centres of Egypt.

To the Sumerians, the concept of kingship was more significant than the person of the king. In the Sumerian phrase, 'kingship was handed down' from heaven, mirroring the system by which the divine world was organized: 'As above, so below.' The king was originally conceived as little more than the overseer of the labour force required to farm the god's land. The gods recognized that their workers needed overseers and, therefore, kingship was delegated from heaven to earth: the king became, in the first place, the steward of a divine master. But in Sumer kingship seems also to have had its darker side.

UR AND THE 'ROYAL TOMBS'

Of all the cities of Sumer the most celebrated is Ur, first by reason of its Biblical celebrity and then because of the extraordinary discoveries of Sir Leonard Woolley.[5] Until the 1920s the mention of the city of Ur was inevitably followed by the Biblical epithet 'of the Chaldees' and it was pigeon-holed as the putative birthplace of Abraham, the Friend of God. This ancestor of the Semitic-speaking peoples of the Syro-Arabian desert, would have been a desert shaikh whose immediate forebears had migrated to the city probably at the beginning of the second millennium, amongst the waves of Semitic incursions which characterized all phases of Sumerian history. Ur, however, had been great long before Abraham, and the discovery of what may have been the tombs of the Sumerian kings in the city by Sir Leonard Woolley in 1922 revealed its greatness in a startling, indeed in a chilling, manner.[6]

In the twelfth tablet of the series from which the most complete version of the Epic of Gilgamesh is drawn, there appears to be the description, in part, of the burial rites of a Sumerian king.[7] From this is seems that, sometimes at least, servants, courtiers and members of the royal family may have gone into the Underworld with the king, sacrificed to his royal eternity. Whilst this tablet does not really constitute a part of the Epic proper, it is particularly interesting in the light of Woolley's quite exceptional discoveries.

After working in the ruins of Mesopotamian cities for many years, during which he greatly advanced the knowledge of Sumer's contribution to the world that succeeded it, Woolley discovered a number of complete burials of the Early Dynastic period at Ur, now dated to the middle of the third millennium BC, probably within a century or so of the reign of Gilgamesh, and just after the great pyramids were built at Gizeh in Egypt. One grave was contained in a deeply sunk pit and was very richly furnished with gold, silver, bronze, ivory and copper artefacts of a singular beauty and high craftsmanship. Goblets, cups, jewellery, regalia and the rich trappings of a powerful and luxurious court were released from their four and a half thousand years of entombment. What was even more remarkable was the discovery of the court itself, or at least some seventy-four members of it, who had been sacrificed and laid in orderly rows to wait upon the eternity of their sovereigns.

The practice of such ritual sacrifice, by which individuals were put to death to accompany their chieftains into the darkness, is of great antiquity. It is a practice which is to be found in all historical periods over most areas of the world. It is still not unknown in Africa where, for example, thirty-two members of the court of Asantehene, the somewhat more than mortal paramount chief of the splendid Ashanti people of Ghana and the guardian of its collective soul, were clubbed to death in the tribal capital, Kumasi, only a little more than half a century ago on the death of the last but one holder of the office. Naturally, to the modern world which reckons the numbers of its sacrifices in millions, there is something particularly frightful in finding evidence of the deliberate slaying of seventy-odd courtiers, whose deaths were occasioned solely by religious belief and not by the demands of politics.

The rationale of the practice is, of course, not difficult to see; usually the king so served also exercised a priestly function as the mediator between his people and their gods, and in this capacity he would be required to carry out complex and extended rituals to achieve the prosperity of the folk. Ceremonies invoking the gods, rites connected with the fecundity of herds, the fertility of the crops or the averting of natural disasters needed many participants and acolytes to the principal celebrant. Obviously any such ceremonies would be vastly more effective if they were performed in the presence of the gods whom they sought to influence; therefore, the king's closest assistants would be required to attend upon him and to assist him when he carried out the sacrifices in the afterlife.

The contents of the great tombs at Ur inevitably came to be compared with Tutankhamun's, which was discovered earlier in the same decade. But the elegant daggers, the slender cups of gold, the great electrum helmet of Prince Meskalamdug, are so superlative in their simplicity and restraint of design, brilliantly compounded with the costliest materials, that they make the glitter of many of the sad little boy-pharaoh's often weirdly designed death-gifts seem more meretricious even than some of them really are. The contents of the Ur tombs are simply extraordinary, the most sumptuous ever made by any people. They are quite untypical of the general run of Sumerian work, even of the finest. Nothing that has survived from Sumer encourages the expectation of works of such quality. Only the art of the seals, some of which have the quality of jewels, has something of the same brilliance of form and design. But the objects in the tomb are really unparalleled and are witnesses to what must have been a culture of the most remarkable material splendour. It is difficult, however, to suppress the suspicion that the contents of the Ur tombs were not the sole unaided work of Sumerian craftsmen, though whence they may have come is quite beyond speculation. There is something altogether very un-Sumerian about the entire Ur experience.

The Ur burials are mirrored by others in China, south of Peking, dating from the Shang dynasty, several centuries later. There is one important difference between the two, apart from the differences which ought to be expected to exist between two cultures so disparate in time and place. The attendants in the Shang tombs have all been violently killed and the grave is in effect an execution site, a Bronze Age shambles. The tomb in Ur is at first sight even more chilling, and yet reflection may suggest otherwise; the members of the court who went to their deaths evidently did so willingly, without force being used upon them and without regret at leaving the world. There is evidence that they laid themselves down in the pit and that each one took a drug, presumably a narcotic or soporific, witnessed by the many small cups found in the tomb, which would ease their passing. When they were dead or unconscious, their bodies were neatly laid out to remove any evidence of the convulsions of death which they might experience; then the earth was brought down upon them, as they thought, for ever. One woman, it appears, was nearly late for her own funeral and lay down hastily amongst her companions.

Altogether Woolley found sixteen 'Royal Tombs'. In one of them seventy-four courtiers were buried; in another, known as Pur Abi's (for a long time she was mistakenly called Shub-ad), there were seventeen. In the so-called 'King's Tomb' (there is actually no evidence that the principal occupant was a king) there were fifty-nine bodies; Meskalamdug, he of the magnificent helmet, had forty companions. It would appear that the practice ran out after the examples in Ur. It is no more clear why it should have ceased than why the practice began in the first place or who introduced it. It must always be remembered that archaeology can only base its assumptions on the evidence before it. We do not know whether these ritual holocausts were practised in earlier times because there is no evidence yet found to indicate it. However, the references in the Gilgamesh Epic may suggest that they were part of Sumerian custom at an earlier date.

It has been suggested that the persons who occupy the principal places in the Ur tombs may have been surrogates for the living princes, sacrificed at the end of the celebration of the *hieros gamos*, the sacred marriage of god and goddess enacted in Sumer on the upper platform of the ziggurat, the sacred mountain, to ensure the fertility and prosperity of the land.[8] There is no positive evidence to support this suggestion, but it does seem that the practice of the killing of a mock-king was known at other periods in Mesopotamian history.

The ready acceptance of death by those who went with the main figures in the drama was warranted by the certainty of immortality as they waited upon their king in the eternal exercise of his office. It was a comforting doctrine to a people to whom the afterlife was a matter of deep uncertainty and it suggests a modification, at least for the period during which the practice was current, of the traditional Sumerian disbelief in any satisfactory afterlife at all. Generally speaking, the Sumerians, like their Semitic successors, believed that whatever fate awaited man after death, it offered little attraction. The souls of the dead were conceived as huddled together in dusty windswept corridors of some unamiable underworld where they were battered by the scaly wings of predatory birds.

It may well be that the custom of the sacrifice of attendants on the principal occupants of the tomb, which seems to have been practised only for a short time, was foreign to Sumer and may therefore have been introduced by an alien dynasty. With all the rationalization in the world, however, it is still disturbing to think about the large and handsomely accoutred procession of men and women with the pack animals who would die with them, their harnesses and trappings jangling, winding its way down through Ur to the place of ceremonial death, one bright Sumerian morning.

The kings of these early Sumerian states are shadowy figures and little is really known of them. Compared with their Egyptian contemporaries of the Archaic period and the early Old Kingdom, they are obscure indeed. Occasionally the record of a campaign, of a benefaction to a temple or the conclusion of a successful merchanting venture survives.

The material and intellectual heritage of Sumer is so immense, however, whether in practical invention or in the creation of the world's first great literature, that we may presume that life in the little cities was, at this time, especially vibrant. In many respects the virility of the Sumerian experience at this time resembles that of the Italian cities of the Renaissance, with which, in political character as well, the Sumerian cities may to some degree be compared.

However, conflicts between the little city-states and the resulting tensions continued unabated and eventually became insupportable; first one, then another enjoyed a brief spell of the paramountcy of Sumer, and dynasty followed insecure dynasty in the palaces of the land. The black-headed folk had always been a disputatious people. As the temple and city lands of one state became insufficient to support its people, or as the possessions of one divinity seemed disproportionately greater than another whose adherents coveted the riches of their neighbour, or as a palace servant seized the 'lugal-ship' from a failing master, so the pressures began to mount which eventually would lead to the collapse of the Sumerian state.

Now another problem, though already a familiar one to all the cities, obtruded itself still more urgently into the consciousness of the people: the threat, ever present but now increasing, posed by the barbarous tribes which surrounded them. These were nomads of the desert or wild hillmen with no understanding of the fragile culture which the little cities had so patiently built up over the centuries, but with an unthinking envy of their material wealth. From all directions these restless and destructive hordes menaced Sumer, but the cities were unable to produce a common policy even to protect themselves.

SARGON OF AKKAD

In the twenty-fourth century BC, the beginning of the end came for Sumer, and it was heralded by the emergence into history of one of the most remarkable men of the ancient world. But for the poverty of the surviving information about him, he would deserve to rank with the greatest political leaders of any era. Whilst he preserved for a time the fabric of the Sumerian way of life, he also introduced elements into the society which eventually made its destruction certain. For a century or so he created an empire which was wholly Sumerian in its manners and customs, although he himself was a civilized member of one of the barbarous desert hordes which pressed upon Sumer. He was a Semite, of those people who were to make so profound a contribution to the end of the Sumerian period.

In the palace of Kish, the king Ur-Zababa had in his service as his cup-bearer (an office of importance in the state and evidently not possessing the equivocal overtones associated with the same appointment, whose duties were discharged as frequently in a horizontal as in a vertical mode, in later, Greek monarchies) a young man who was to be known to history as Sharrukin, or Sargon. He was to prove a man of exceptional military ability, an outstanding administrator and a political innovator of genius.

A fascinating legend about the birth and early life of Sargon has survived and it bears a remarkable resemblance to the legendary origins of another, later, and historically even more shadowy Semitic leader, Moses. In the text it is Sargon himself who is speaking:

Sargon the Mighty King, King of Agade, am I.
My mother was a changeling, my father I knew not.
The brothers of my father loved the hills.
My city is Azupiranu, which is situated on the banks of the Euphrates.
My changeling mother conceived me, in secret she bore me.
She set me in a basket of rushes, with bitumen she sealed my lid.
The river bore me up and carried me to Akki, the drawer of water.
Akki, the drawer of water, lifted me out as he dipped his ewer.
Akki, the drawer of water, took me as his son and reared me.
Akki, the drawer of water, appointed me as his gardener.
While I was a gardener, Ishtar granted me her love.
And for four and forty years I exercised kingship.
The black-headed people I ruled, I governed.
Mighty mountains with chip-axes of bronze I conquered.
The upper ranges I scaled.
The lower ranges I traversed.
The sea lands three times I circled.
Dilmun my hand captured. . . .

Whatever king may come after me

Let him rule, let him govern the black-headed people.
Let him conquer mighty mountains with chip-axes of bronze.
Let him scale the upper ranges.
Let him traverse the lower ranges.
Let him circle the sea lands three times.
Dilmun let his hand capture
. . . from my city, Agade.[9]

There is more than bombast in these last lines; narrow-eyed menace seems to hiss down the more than forty centuries which separate Sargon from our own day. By this time (approximately 2370 BC) Dilmun was evidently so significant to anyone seeking the kingship of the land that its capture was a matter for pride, even for the man who was to be the mightiest conqueror of his time. But the inscription above was written at the end of his long and tempestuous reign and much was to be accomplished before he could boast that his hand had captured Dilmun.

Sargon's master, Ur-Zababa, was attacked and evidently killed by the ambitious ruler of Umma, Lugalzaggesi, who had marched on Kish after razing to the ground the holy places of Lagash. Lugalzaggesi claimed the kingship of all Sumer, the first occasion on which a formal claim in terms of the 'Kingship of the Land' was made to the paramountcy; having evidently taken power in his own city, Sargon set out to avenge Ur-Zababa, and to destroy the usurper. He gathered an army together and attacked Uruk, where Lugalzaggesi had established himself; despite a powerful confederation brought in to defend the city, Sargon was victorious and Uruk fell. Lugalzaggesi apparently escaped when Sargon attacked, for the next we hear is of a pitched battle between the king's host and Sargon. Again, the Semite was totally victorious: he destroyed Lugalzaggesi's army and this time captured him. Nothing more is heard of Lugalzaggesi except that he was led before Sargon by the neck, 'haltered like a dog', and it may be assumed that his end came swiftly.

Sargon now assumed the highest power and swept through Sumer, eliminating any pockets of resistance that were still loyal to Lugalzaggesi. Eventually he subdued not only the cities of Sumer but many of the lands which bordered it; he was forced to this course in order to check for a time the further incursion of the tribes from which he had himself come, and which menaced what had now become his extensive empire. After the subjugation of the Sumerian states, Sargon 'washed his weapons' in the waters of the Gulf, by this act perhaps demonstrating his claim to sovereignty over them and the lands which bordered them. It was now that he could set out on the conquest of the Holy Land of Dilmun.

In the ruins of one of the principal sites of this period on Bahrain island, the Qala'at al-Bahrain, there is evidence of the abrupt destruction of the earliest settlement, here identified as City I, though, in fact, it was little more than a village (see Chapter 7).[10] It has been speculated that its apparently insufficient defences were overthrown during Sargon's conquests and that it was his troops which carried the evidence of his power even to the sacred land of Dilmun. The next occupation level shows extensive ramparts around the new complex of buildings (City II), presumably to ensure that Sargon's governor or vassal prince was not so easily conquered as his predecessor in Dilmun's rule (see Chapter 7).[11]

Sargon's accession to the kingship of Sumer marks a fundamental change in the political organization of southern Mesopotamia. Hitherto each little state has been the be-all and end-all of its inhabitants' lives. Sargon was evidently an altogether more sophisticated politician than his predecessors in the Sumerian kingship, with the Semitic sense of race and kinship which he strongly evinced; he swept away, for the period of his empire, the little loyalties of each city and imposed instead the absolute sovereignty of the king. He moved closer to the concept of kingship that was characteristic of Egypt (although at this time without the direct identity between god and king which the Two Lands so successfully developed), making the office a manifestation of his own personal power, rather than the more metaphysical concept of a responsibility delegated from the gods. The Sumerians conceived kingship as transcending the human vicars who might temporarily exercise its power on behalf of their divine principals; Sargon made kingship a political reality and in doing so inaugurated the long line of oriental autocracies which ended with the deposition of the last Ottoman sultan.

The empire which Sargon created, the first political entity in world history to warrant being so called, now entered upon a phase of unexampled splendour and power. As if to mark the fact that a new period of Near Eastern history had been inaugurated, Sargon decided to build a new capital, away from the traditional cities of Sumer. The place he chose came to be known as Agade (the Akkad of the Bible) and whilst its exact site is now unknown it was located somewhere in the vicinity of Kish, near the neck of the two rivers, strategically one of the most important positions in all Mesopotamia, as the cities built there by successive rulers after Sargon testify. It would be pleasant to think that this choice of site for his new city might demonstrate a streak of sentiment in Sargon, that he should decide to build his own magnificent city within the sight of the lesser one from which, as a relatively minor official, he had started out on his great chain of conquests: more likely it was evidence of his powerful command of the site's strategic potential. In any event, its selection represents the first evidence in Sumer's history of the movement towards the north which was to influence both the political and economic directions of the Middle East from the later centuries of the third millennium onwards, and which was to result in the axis of world communications being shifted away from the Gulf to the Mediterranean.

Soon Agade was the most powerful and gorgeous city of the time, and into its harbours sailed ships bearing tribute and merchandise from the four corners of the world, of which Sargon claimed the sovereignty amongst his titles. An inscription survives in which Sargon speaks proudly of the ships of Dilmun riding fearlessly at anchor in the harbour of Agade, some measure evidently of the power that now he exercised and of the peace which he had brought to the Near Eastern world:

> Sargon, King of Kish, was victorious in thirty-four campaigns and dismantled all the cities as far as the shore of the sea. At the wharf of Agade he made moor ships from Meluhha, ships from Magan and ships from Dilmun. . . . Enlil did not let anyone oppose Sargon the King. 5,400 soldiers ate daily in his palace.[12]

This extract is from an inscription on a statue, probably from the period following Sargon's reign.

Though he came from the desert Sargon evidently understood the importance of trade to the Sumerian nation and to the prosperity of the cities. The emperor (Sargon is the first historical figure who perhaps justifies that title) was always sharp-eyed in the protection of his merchants' trade routes and was quick to punish any marauders or those jealous princes who might menace the free movement of trade across the wide sweep of lands that came under his *imperium*.

Sargon was, by all reports, a devout follower of the gods of Sumer and, like other *arriviste* conquerors after him, he saw as his destiny the honourable preservation of the wonders of the world he had inherited and of the worship of its gods. Sargon's empire preserved much of the best of Sumer but at the price of its becoming virtually entirely Semitic in language, administration and influence, thus paving the way for the later Babylonian and Assyrian empires, which were its eventual successors. These, too, were Semitic states, though they preserved, like Sargon, much of the essential qualities of Sumerian culture, manners and beliefs.

Sargon appointed his own relations and members of the Semitic tribes to many of the most powerful positions in the state. There was, no doubt, an element of policy as well as nepotism in this, for Sargon probably recognized that in the long term it would be hopeless to try to hold back the growing involvement of the tribes in the affairs of Sumer; he may have persuaded himself that a policy of involving the desert peoples in the management of the state would prepare more of them for the responsibilities of empire and subdue their destructive and unthinking envy of Sumerian culture. On the other hand, he may simply have liked to have his relations around him.

It may be that this policy worked, for when the reckoning with the tribes came it was not the Semites who overwhelmed his empire but the Guti, a tribe of equal barbarity and even greater ferocity, who surged down on Sargon's state, probably from the Zagros mountains in the east. The Guti were a people 'which brooks no control'. They came from the region that was later to nourish the Kassites, another of the successor nations to Sumer's greatness and, later still, in the first millennium BC, the centre of the remarkable metal-working and horse-loving people of Luristan. Anarchy and desolation followed the Guti invasion, which had apparently been brought down on the land to avenge some dreadful but unspecified sacrilege perpetrated by Sargon's grandson, Naram-Sin. It was Enlil himself, the ruler of the High Gods, who called the Guti, 'the Mountain Dragon', down upon Agade. The once glorious city was utterly destroyed and over its ruins the gods in their wrath uttered a terrifying curse.[13] The people who once slaughtered animals for sacrifice are willed to 'murder their wives instead of slaying sheep'; the hope is expressed that they may slaughter their children and, in the case of the poor, specifically to drown them. 'Agade,' the curse proclaims, 'may your palace built with a joyful hand be turned into a depressing ruin.' It concludes on a baleful note: 'Who says "I will lie down in Agade" will not find a good sleeping place.'

The curse seems to have worked, for to this day the site of the golden city so proudly built by Sargon the Great King, the King of the World, is undiscovered, buried beneath the debris of the Mesopotamian plain and the anger of the gods.

UR-NANSHE AND GUDEA OF LAGASH

With the exception of Ur, the Sumerian city-state which is perhaps most generally remembered today is Lagash, in the south-eastern part of the land. Its modern celebrity derives from the many statues, scattered over the world's museums, of one of its rulers, known to us as Gudea, who reigned at the end of the third millennium.[14]

Lagash, however, emerged into prominence several centuries before Gudea, at the time when Sumer was still powerful. It would seem that the city was not one of those which bore a special mystical significance to the peoples of the time, as many cities did, for a record of its sovereigns does not appear in the surviving king-lists. One of the early rulers of Lagash was Ur-Nanshe, who governed the city in the middle of the twenty-sixth century before our era. His inscriptions, of which many survive, are particularly interesting in the present context in that they record the bringing of tribute from far distant countries to him, borne to Lagash 'by the ships of Dilmun'. Ur-Nanshe's inscription is now some 4,500 years old. It is apparent that 'the ships of Dilmun' had, in his time, become a symbol of a wide-ranging maritime power, rather like the 'hearts of oak' in the popular English ballad.

Later, when Sargon's empire was destroyed by the barbarous Guti, Lagash became for a time the most important Mesopotamian city-state, for the conquerors seem to have favoured its rulers, an early example perhaps of the fruits of collaboration with the occupying forces. The dynasty which came to power, by accommodating itself with the wild men who were now in command of Sumer's destiny, is largely memorable because of Gudea, its second king. If the dynasty is to be judged by Gudea's many surviving portraits, it was a worthy, solid family, rather bourgeois in appearance, with a firm approach to the business of managing the splendid heritage which the capricious gods of Sumer and the intervention of the Guti had handed to them.

Gudea would not have felt out of place at the Tudor courts, even if he was, to his credit, substantially less shifty-eyed than so many of the members of those dubious assemblies. Certainly, as for the Tudor kings, trade was a principal concern for Gudea; quite properly so, since much of Sumer's splendour depended upon the importation of the raw materials and merchandise that were needed to embellish the court and the temples of the gods.

Gudea listed proudly the merchandise which flowed into his city, recording that much of it was trans-shipped from Dilmun, where it was brought from many lands. The ships brought to him gold from Egypt and Anatolia, silver from the Amanus, copper from the Zagros, ironite from Egypt, carnelian from Ethiopia, and from Dilmun itself, timber.

In the reigns of his successors, there are reports that copper utensils, lapis lazuli, tables inlaid with ivory and other ivory objects, combs, breastplates and boxes, ornaments for furniture and semi-precious stones were commonly to be found in Dilmun's market-places. Then there are reports of other imports from Dilmun, no less essential than gold and ivory to the life of a rich and prosperous city: the island's onions and dates which were famous throughout the ancient Near East, and what the Sumerian texts refer to as 'fish-eyes'.[15] It is generally agreed that this term signifies pearls. Pearling was, until recently, an important industry in Bahrain and the Gulf, although it is now in decline. Oyster middens, mounds of discarded oyster shells, have been found on the island which date back beyond historic times.[16]

THE FALL OF SUMER

Gudea's dynasty was eventually overthrown by a brilliant usurper of the throne of Ur, whose previous ruler had broken the power of the Guti. Without the invaders' support, the Lagashite dynasty fell to the newcomer, Ur-Nammu, who ushers in the last of the great periods of Sumerian history, the third and final dynasty of Ur.

Ur-Nammu was one of the outstanding rulers of Sumer, a capable administrator and military leader, a builder and, perhaps more important than any of these, the promoter of a legal code which regulated man's conduct to his fellows and the state, and anticipated the more famous code of Hammurabi by several hundred years.[17] In law, as in so many other departments of life which today are taken for granted, the Sumerians seem to have been the innovators. But despite its brilliance, his reign was a short one: Ur-Nammu seems to have possessed the kingship for only nine years; he was then killed in one of the battles that Sumerian leaders had constantly to face. The portrait which survives of him shows him as delicate of feature, sensitive in appearance.

One of the most splendid sequences in Sumer's history began with the accession to the kingship of Sumer and Akkad of Ur-Nammu's son, Shulgi, in the year 2095 BC. His reign was to be long and glorious; when he died in 2048 BC he had created an empire as extensive as Sargon's and, in many ways, more integrated and coherent. It was a time of great ziggurat building, the remains of some of them, built in Shulgi's time, standing to this day.

Shulgi, like his father, was a notable law giver, always one of the most creditable activities of Sumerian sovereigns, and a distinguished soldier who extended far afield the influence of his empire and of his capital city. His family seems to have been of a strong religious bent, manifested both by their extensive programme of temple building and by the thoroughly un-Sumerian practice of proclaiming themselves to be divine. A state cult, involving offerings to the statues of the king and the naming of one of the months of the calendar in his honour, was introduced and is reminiscent of Roman practices under the Principate. Shulgi is commemorated in one of the principal texts to survive from this time: it describes the sacred marriage (the *hieros gamos*) and contains passages reminiscent of the Song of Solomon, that ecstatic invocation of the splendours of the beloved. In it Shulgi is addressed in terms of the most passionate longing by the priestess, with whom he was to enact one of the most important of Sumerian religious festivals, ensuring the fertility of the year.

An inscription of Shulgi's reign records the king having sent a royal messenger to Dilmun, Ur-Dumuzi, to bring home two invalid officials, a perhaps not altogether usual example of royal concern at so early a time.[18] At his death, the venerable Shulgi was succeeded first by one son and then by another, Shu-sin (2038–2030 BC). In common with the other members of his family, Shu-sin was divine but he had rather more problems to test both his divinity and his statesmanship than his predecessors had. The nomads of the Syrian desert on the western borders of the empire were once more stirring and for the rest of the dynasty's rule, and indeed for more than a thousand years afterwards, constant incursions of fierce Semitic tribesmen (amongst whom may have been Abraham and his followers) continued to harry the foundations of the Sumerian state and those of its successors. Dilmun once more appears in the archives of this time, when one of Shu-sin's officials, Arad-Nanna, lists amongst his titles 'Prefect (*gir-nita*) of Dilmun',[19] the first of the elements in his name prefigures one of Dilmun-Bahrain's own later names. It was around this time that the richest period of Dilmun's trading empire flourished with Ur as its headquarters.

A peculiarity of the house of Ur-Nammu was its burial customs which are unlike those of other Sumerian dynasts. Large, richly furnished tomb chambers built deep in the ground contained the bodies of the kings of this time which recall the royal burials of Early Dynastic Egypt and of the Royal Tombs at Ur, though without the human sacrifices which attended those interments. It is possible that the Third Dynasty burials were associated with the rites of Dumuzi, the Sumerian god of vegetation and rebirth who, as a dying god ruling over the Underworld, has many parallels with the Egyptian Osiris, with whom later Pharaohs were identified in death.

Like most of the dynasties founded on the rule of the agglomeration of city-states with its constant round of intrigue, power politics and decline, that created by Ur-Nammu was not destined to last for very long. With its fall, and apart from one or two uneasy and temporary survivals, the end of Sumer must be recorded, after a period of nearly 2,000 years during which time its peoples had given more of importance to the world than ever did any nation of antiquity other than Egypt. But by now the land of Sumer was exhausted.

For too long the society had sought to withstand the friction of the different cities, the unpredictability of the two rivers between which they had first tried to build a nation, and the constant onslaught of barbaric and envious tribes on every frontier. Unlike Egypt, for which some of its most splendid times were just dawning and which would take another 1,500 years to exhaust its strength, Sumer had too volatile and fragile a structure to withstand the pressures which were mounting within and around it. The world, however, was fortunate that a ruler of the northern city of Babylon, a Semitic prince named Hammurabi, with something of Sargon about him, succeeded eventually to Sumer's empire. At his accession, around 1750 BC, the history of Sumer ends and that of Babylon begins. It is the peculiar glory of Babylon that she conserved much of Sumer's legacy to the world, which still draws a handsome dividend from it to this day. It is from this period, c. 1740 BC, that the last mention of Dilmun appears in the records, in the context of the copper industry.

With the absorption of Mesopotamian culture by the Semitic speaking peoples who had incorporated the immense legacy which the Sumerians (and then the Semitic Akkadians) had bequeathed, the Sumerians themselves now pass from history, their very existence eventually to be forgotten. But this gentle people, energetic, often bewildered, perpetually creative, inventive seemingly beyond even the customary boundaries of genius, often fearful but never wholly despairing, may seem closer to us than most ancient peoples, precisely because they display so intense a quality of humanity. The monuments which they left behind were not only, or even principally, of stone or precious metals, but were words, images, concepts and ideas which have deeply influenced the life of every civilized man who ever lived in the lands which draw their intellectual origins from western Asia. The magnitude of the achievements of Sumer, like those of its contemporary, Egypt, down to the end of the third millennium, can only be measured when it is realized that, when their high and elegant cultures were flourishing, the rest of the world was virtually empty of anything even remotely approaching civilization.

Although Sumer's days were over and her name survived only as an archaic formula in the titularies of some of the more antiquarian-minded sovereigns of the later Mesopotamian states, her influence was never wholly lost, for the successor states retained much of her heritage. But before examining the outline of Mesopotamia's post-Sumerian history it may be pertinent to take a view of the world as it was at the end of the Sumerian period when, as we reckon historical time, the second millennium before the present era was beginning.

THE SECOND MILLENNIUM

The processes of change once again began to accelerate, as they had done so remarkably at the end of the fourth millennium. Even Egypt, seemingly imperturbable if not eternal, experienced the shock of a brutal disruption of her tranquil way of life. The first and greatest period of her dynastic history ended with a collapse into chaos and anarchy after the nearly interminable reign of Pepi II, who doddered on into the ninety-fourth year of his kingship, having been proclaimed Lord of the Two Lands when he was 6 years old. The rule of god-kings works admirably when they are in possession of their faculties; a senile divinity is both politically and philo-sophically an appalling concept. The long years of Pepi's reign, when the great-grandsons of the men who watched his coronation were old before its end, must have made some of his more conscientious courtiers long for the days when the god had been sent back to rule other gods, before the decline of his powers could prejudice his rule of men.

After a long and harrowing period in which famine, anarchy and a total disregard for all the most respected Egyptian values stalked the banks of the Nile, order was painfully restored by the austere and dedicated Pharaohs of the early Middle Kingdom. Peace returned to the Valley; Egypt regained her soul and the successive Montuhotpes, Amenemhets and Senwosrets added new splendour to the majesty of the Two Lands. Then new pressures began to bear upon Egypt and a weak, increasingly decentralized monarchy in the shadowy Thirteenth Dynasty let power and resources ebb away and, an unheard-of calamity, Egypt was invaded by a Semitic people related to those who had already assumed the sovereignty in Mesopotamia. The 'Hyksos' princes (who used to be called, charmingly but as it happens quite inaccur-ately, the Shepherd Kings) seem never to have been entirely happy ruling this mysterious and, to foreigners, bewildering land. They tried anxiously to adopt Egyptian ways and to gain the acceptance of the people, but settling self-consciously in the Delta, where they could feel that their ancestral

Syrian and Arabian deserts were not so very far away, they never wholly penetrated Egyptian life. Probably undeservedly, they were cursed with unparalleled vituperation and hatred when finally they were expelled by a family of Theban nobles whose chief was exasperated by the presence of aliens upon the throne of the sacred land. Rising against the usurping kings, he restored the rule of the gods and the prosperity of his house. The long late summer of Egyptian greatness now began with the creation of her magnificent, luxurious and paradoxical empire – for, deep in her heart, Egypt still distrusted all that lay beyond her frontiers – which exalted the throne of the Pharaohs of the New Kingdom high above all other thrones in the world.

In other lands, the wheel of change was revolving irresistibly. In the west, Crete was inaugurating her domination of the Mediterranean and a distinctive if, later, somewhat neurotic culture, many elements of which were probably Asiatic in origin. Far to the north, the early cities of Troy were built to guard the route which linked the Aegean with the Black Sea, on whose shores wild savages with discouraging habits roamed in search of human prey. Across the mass of European lands, as far as the islands in the North Sea which, shrouded in mist and fog, were known if at all only by legend and the discounted reports of occasional travellers, new people were moving, seeking new pastures or the protection of new gods. In Greece, a new race came down from the north with different gods and broad, handsome faces, whose gold-masked chiefs were buried on the windswept and menacing hill at Mycenae. The great ports of the Syrian coast sent argosies to Egypt and Crete and wherever a profit might be made.

In Mesopotamia, too, profound changes were in train. The final disappearance of the old Sumerian states and the dominance of the Semitic rulers meant a shift away from the south and the creation of northern kingdoms, first in Babylon and then Assyria, which looked to the Mediterranean lands, those of the Upper Sea, as their natural outlet for conquest and trade. In time the southern cities of Sumer, once the most important in the world, declined to the level of simple village settlements and so most of them have remained to this day. Occasionally a ruler with a taste for history or in the hope of pleasing the almost forgotten gods, would build a temple or repair a ziggurat. But most of the cities disappeared, buried beneath the mounds of dust and sand which, wind-blown, piled over them and hid them until the modern world, happily more careful of its ancestry than were its own ancestors, painstakingly uncovered them.

In the middle of the second millennium a series of spectacular cataclysms overwhelmed much of the ancient world. In the Mediterranean the eruption, as it is now believed, of Santorini brought down the cities of Crete, admitting both the harsh Achaeans to the island's splendid palaces and, in all probability, the myth of Atlantis into the modern world. Somewhat earlier, in what is today the state of Pakistan, the mighty civilization of the Indus

Valley, including the powerful cities of Harappa and Moenjo-Daro, collapsed, from whatever cause. The impact of these events was brutal and absolute. In what had once been Sumer the poet lamented piteously: 'Who was King? Who was *not* King?'

As the political and economic axis of the world began to shift to the north, so the Gulf too declined in importance. Bereft of its main market by the destruction of the Indus Valley cities and with the establishment of caravan routes more reliable and better policed than in the early days, the Lower Sea became, literally, a backwater.

Dilmun had witnessed many changes of political control in Mesopotamia and always her religious and commercial appeal, then as now an irresistible combination, ensured her prosperity. Now, however, it was different, for her commercial significance seems to have been destroyed by the collapse of the great Indus Valley cities which were the outlet for much of Sumer's merchandise and the decline of the southern Mesopotamian cities. From this time onwards, Dilmun ceases to be important; only occasionally does a mention of it appear in the ancient sources and then it sinks into an obscurity from which Bahrain and the other Gulf states have only tentatively emerged in this century. Certainly, never again would it occupy the special place that it did for the Sumerians and their immediate successors. Already the world had begun to change and the decline of Dilmun's commercial significance even produced a decline in her legendary status as the island of the gods. Soon the Sumerians themselves were forgotten and only occasionally was Dilmun noticed, for now it was merely a distant province of whatever power ruled Mesopotamia.

THE AHLAMU STEAL THE DATES

In the fourteenth century BC, during the reign of Burnaburriyas, a contemporary of that odd-looking religious innovator Akhenaton of Egypt, two letters were sent by the incumbent governor of Dilmun, Ili-ippasra, to his colleague in Babylonia, then ruled by the Kassites, of which the island was a province.[20] Ili-ippasra was evidently a man of substance: his daughter was at school in Nippur, one of the ancient centres of Sumerian learning and the study of the gods which, even in these relatively late times, was clearly the place to send one's children to be educated, girls as much as boys. The school was evidently reserved for the children of the aristocracy. Ili-ippasra's daughter was suffering from an inflamed nostril and the headmaster wrote to him in Dilmun to assure him that she was well on the way to recovery. This correspondence is especially interesting for it throws a light on a number of characteristics which had come to be identified with Dilmun historically and which confirm its association at this time with the principal Bahrain island. Extensive evidence has been discovered in the Al-Hajjar graves in Bahrain[21] of the period during which the island was under Kassite domination; it suggests that circumstances in the islands were much more prosperous than had appeared to be the case.

It is apparent from the text of the first letter (Ni615) that the writer is awaiting a 'Sutean woman' to cross the water and visit him. From this it may be deduced that the writer is living on the mainland of Arabia, which, at this as at other times, was included in the term 'Dilmun', which thus becomes the name of a substantial region, far exceeding the confines of the island itself. However, it is reasonably certain, from the evidence of City III at the Qala'at al-Bahrain, where the remains of the Kassite occupation have produced quantities of their rather unattractive pottery as well as some as yet unpublished cuneiform tablets, that Bahrain was the capital of what might be thought of as the Dilmun province in Kassite times. The writer knows that the Sutean woman has reached Dilmun proper, in other words, Bahrain, but has not yet crossed the straits to the mainland. The Sutean woman is a mysterious figure but it is known that in many of the north-east Arabian tribal groups of this and later times women were powerful, often as priestesses, even as queens.

> To Ililiya speak! This is what Ili-ippasra thy brother said: Unto thee be well-being! May Inzag and Meskilak, the gods of Tilmun, guard thy life!
>
> Iltam who will arrive, I have met. Also the Sutean woman has crossed the sea and she will arrive. Of the coming of this Sutean woman I am not so sure. Now I have directed her to Babil. Before the month of Epuly draws to a close she will reach there. Around me the Ahlamu have carried away the dates, thus with me there is nothing I can do. But a single town must not be allowed to be pillaged. In the town which I am living in when from Sin-nun I heard and the temple I heard about is the old house of Nin [. . .] the house was old and had collapsed. Now he has done nothing at all he let it go. And from that day on they keep on seeing dreams and the destruction of the palace has been indicated for the fifth time.[22]

The writer complains that the Ahlamu have carried off the dates, evidently stored ready for shipment back to Mesopotamia. The dates of Dilmun were always specially favoured in ancient times and probably the best of them came from the oases of Qatif and Hofuf in Saudi Arabia, another indication of the likely extent of Dilmun's territories in this period. In the ruins of Qala'at al-Bahrain (City III) extensive storerooms have been found which suggest that they were used for the warehousing of dates before they were shipped and also for the pressing of date juice, which, when fermented, produced an agreeable and very intoxicating drink.

In both letters the texts are preceded by a benediction in which Inzak (the Sumerian Enshag), the guardian god of Dilmun, is invoked with a goddess,

Meskilak, the Lady of Pure Decrees. She was a divinity most appropriate for Dilmun, for one of its epithets was the Land of Pure Decrees.

The first letter contains a reference to the antiquity of certain temples in Dilmun and to their deplorable state of disrepair. Where the text mentions 'the house of Nin . . .' it is tempting to restore the missing word to read 'Ninkhursag' or 'Ninsikilla', both of them patrons of the island. Prophecies about the destruction of the 'palace' are also reported in conjunction with the unruly behaviour of the thieving Ahlamu and indicate the generally anarchic situation which prevailed in the Gulf at this time as a result of the depredations of the Badu tribes.

The second letter is less informative than the first, but still complains of the difficulties which the Kassite administration was experiencing at the hands of the Ahlamu.

> To Ililiya speak! This is what Ili-ippasra, thy brother said: Unto thee be well-being! May Inzag and Meskilak, the deities of Tilmun, guard thy life! The Ahlamu certainly talk to me only of violence and plunder: of conciliation they do not talk with me. The lord put it upon me to ask them, but they did not comply.[23]

These two letters are important for their references to two peoples, the Suteans and the Ahlamu, whose descendants are in all probability the Arab tribes of the Gulf and Saudi Arabia today.[24]

Both groups were nomadic Badu who constantly harassed the settled communities on the shores of the Gulf and in the nearby oases, like those from which Dilmun's dates came. The Suteans were originally drawn from the area between Mari and Qatna, well to the north of Mesopotamia in Syria, a region in which the Semitic and Sumerian strains in Mesopotamian culture possibly were first integrated. Contact was established but frequently the tribes got out of hand and had to be put down severely. At the end of the fifteenth century BC the king of Babylon gave instructions for the extermination of the Suteans, but they survived, no doubt by withdrawing into the desert, which was always a hopeless obstacle to town-bred soldiers.

The pressures of the desert peoples, the Badu as they would be called today, were a constant problem to the cities and settled people of the Gulf, as they were to the cities of Mesopotamia. It is altogether likely that the original decision to move the centre of Dilmun from the mainland in the middle of the third millennium to the Bahrain islands was forced on the Dilmunites by the activities of the Bedu. At least with 30 kilometres (20 miles) or so of water separating Bahrain from the mainland the people, their gods and the merchandise which they traded could be safe.

The Ahlamu were a long-established tribal group, formed originally perhaps by the occasional confederation of those nomads who constantly disturbed the peace of states from Syria to the Gulf. They were, in all probability, ancestral to the Aramaeans, who secured a powerful place for themselves in the later history of the region and who, by the eighth century BC, formed an important linguistic family, to the extent that Aramaic became eventually the common language of much of the Near East. The Arabs themselves, another linguistic family closely related to the groups already mentioned, are first recorded in the Assyrian annals of the ninth century BC. The Semitic elements which, throughout Sumer's history, alternately menaced and, by adopting so many of its institutions, sustained the land came out of the Syro-Arabian deserts, like the nomads who still, though in diminishing numbers, live in the desert to this day.

Surveys in central Arabia have identified numerous rudimentary sites which may be attributed to a 'proto-Bedouin' period. By the ninth to seventh centuries BC the Assyrian records of campaigns in northern Arabia show that fully developed camel-herding Arab tribes were already in existence. These tribes were probably the direct descendants of the earlier 'Ahlamu'.[25]

The correspondence addressed to Ililiya in Babylon is one of the few evidences of a concern with the affairs of the south to survive from the troubled centuries which followed the collapse of Hammurabi's dynasty in Mesopotamia. From this time onwards, Dilmun's history becomes increasingly obscure. The world had expanded enormously since the days of the Sumerians and there were more rewarding markets and richer civilizations to conquer than small islands and barren tracts of desert on the coast along the Gulf.

DILMUN'S LATER HISTORY

Occasionally Dilmun (or, more accurately, Tilmun, since the languages which speak of it were Semitic) is mentioned in the dismal recital of conquest and repression which characterizes the history of the kings of later Babylonia and Assyria, the latter being arguably the most repellent of all the princes of the ancient Near East. Thus Tukulti-Ninurta I, one of the greatest warrior-kings of Assyria, who reigned from 1242 to 1206 BC, conquered Babylon, dragged its king in chains to his capital at Assur and went on to absorb the whole of the land that had been Sumer. Dilmun became subject to him and he proclaimed himself 'King of Sippur and Babylon, King of Dilmun and the country Melukhkha, King of the Upper and Lower Seas, King of all mountain regions and the deserts'.[26] Tukulti-Ninurta's barbaric reign ended appropriately when he was assassinated by his own son.

In the annals of Sargon II, the king of Assyria who reigned from 721 to 705 BC, nearly 2,000 years after his namesake, the great Emperor of Agade, there is mention of one of the few kings of Dilmun whose name is known: 'Uperi, who lives like a fish in the midst of the sea of the rising sun'.[27] This reference to the Sea of the Rising Sun echoes the similar terms which were used of the Gulf and Dilmun in some of the earliest references in the epic works of the Sumerians.

Islands were often said to be, reasonably enough, 'in the midst of the sea'; it was an expression commonly used by Assyrian monarchs of island nations which they conquered in the Mediterranean or in the Gulf. Uperi may seem to be dismissed rather contemptuously by his self-proclaimed suzerain, though 'like a fish' could, just possibly, recall a fish cult which was associated with Dilmun and its earliest divinity, Enki. Dilmun, in Sargon II's time, as in the days of Burnaburiyas, probably covered much of the eastern Arabian coast, possibly including Kuwait. One of the names of Bahrain in pre-Islamic times was *Samak* which, curiously, means 'fish' in Arabic: it may be that the principal island's shape, a roughly extended oval, suggested the form of a fish.

In 694 BC Sennacherib was king of Assyria and renowned – at least in Byron's recension – for his attack upon Jerusalem. He also conquered Elam in the south-west of Persia; like many of his forebears, he attacked and overthrew Babylon and it is reported that the debris from the sacking of the city floated down the Gulf to the shores of Dilmun.[28] This improbable circumstance so intimidated the island's inhabitants that they quickly swore allegiance to the Great King.

The king of Dilmun of the day, whose name is unknown, evidently considered it politic to demonstrate his adherence to Sennacherib's interest more positively than by the mere expression of loyalty. He sent a team of labourers to assist in the razing of Babylon after the city had fallen to the Assyrians. They brought with them the tools which are described as typical of their country, 'bronze spades and bronze pikes'. Metal-working, even at this late date, was evidently still one of the most readily recognized characteristics of Dilmun, as it had been in Sumerian times when Dilmun was the centre of the copper trade.

From late Assyrian times comes a most curious text, which was published originally in a study of Chaldaean astrology. This purports to be an astrological prediction which forecasts a disaster for an unnamed king of Dilmun.[29] The prediction links the fate of various kings to eclipses of the moon in different months. The relevant parts of the prediction read:

> Contemplate its eclipse, a decision will be given for the King of Dilmun. Someone will kill the King of Dilmun during an uprising, a stranger will ascend the throne. If the eclipse takes place on the 15th day someone will kill the King of Dilmun during an uprising, a stranger will ascend the throne.
>
> If the eclipse takes place on the 16th day then the King will be killed during his procession, a fool will ascend the throne.

No date is known for the origin of this mysterious piece of astrological forecasting. One commentator[30] has suggested that some of the other events with which it seems to deal relate to the troubled and dangerous times when the Guti, the wild tribes from the mountains dividing Sumer from Iran, swarmed down on Sumer and wrought such devastation.

The brutal and relentless Assyrians tore up the established order in the Near East and imposed their harsh absolutism upon all the lands that came under their influence. The inscriptions of the Assyrian kings are catalogues of terror and oppression. In the early years of the seventh century, Sennacherib's son Esarhaddon lists Dilmun high amongst his conquests and supplies us with the name of another Dilmunite king.

> Upon Qanaia, King of Tilmun, I imposed tribute, due to me as his lord.[31]

Later still, Assurbanipal (668–631 BC) proclaims his power by assuming some of the most ancient royal titles which recall the titulary of Sargon the Great, from nearly 2,000 years earlier. Now Tilmun appears as one of the boundaries of his empire and is used by him to demonstrate the extent of the world that he ruled. Interestingly, he mentions Tilmun and Tyre in the same context, identifying them as comparable entities, the one in the Upper Sea (the Mediterranean) and the other in the Lower (the Gulf).

> Assurbanipal, the Great King, the legitimate King, the King of the world, King of Assyria, King of all the four rims of the earth, King of Kings, prince without rival, who rules from the Upper Sea to the Lower Sea, had made bow to his feet all the other rulers and who has laid the yoke of his overlordship upon them from Tyre which is an island in the Upper Sea as far as Tilmun which is an island in the Lower Sea – and they pulled the straps of his yoke.[32]

Another of the shadowy kings of Dilmun is mentioned in the annals of Assurbanipal. The Assyrian king's general, Bel-ibai, launched a campaign against southern Mesopotamia to consolidate the northerner's rule over it. He conquered Bit-iakin, possibly the region of Kuwait in the north-eastern corner of the Gulf, and Elam in the south-western part of Persia. In his correspondence from the field, Bel-ibai mentions 'Hundaru, King of Dilmun'.[33] The king of Assyria seems to have thought it expedient to deal with the Dilmunite ruler by diplomacy rather than by attempting force of arms and in a letter he offers to confirm Hundaru's rule in exchange for an acceptance of Assurbanipal's suzerainty and for support in his war against Babylon. This the lesser king evidently thought was a prudent course and a Dilmunite ambassador, I'idm, is reported as being accredited to the Assyrian court. At this same period, the arrival of what is tribute, booty, or an exchange of gifts between two rulers – the point is not clear and probably depends on whether it is Assurbanipal's or Hundaru's point of view that is considered – is recorded as arriving at the Assyrian capital from Dilmun. Whatever it was, it was a rich consignment of merchandise; it included twenty-six talents of bronze, goods manufactured from that metal and from copper, and sticks of precious woods, testifying convincingly to the wealth that Dilmun evidently still enjoyed. The excavations at the Qala'at al-Bahrain of this neo-Babylonian period (c. 700 BC) reveal an extensive town with handsome public buildings.[34]

ALEXANDER THE GREAT AND THE GULF

The ancient world reached its climax and its end in the colossal figure of Alexander the Macedonian. Perhaps the only man so far born of woman (in his case the appalling Olympias) who was entitled to suspect that he was a god, Alexander bridges the ancient and modern worlds, the West and the East. In many parts of western Asia he is still a living presence; there is much in the intellectual heritage of the West that can be traced back to Alexander's unleashing of the flood of knowledge, ideas and technology which the Near Eastern states possessed and which, pouring over the intellectually barren lands of Europe, made them flourish.

In the last year of his life, shattered by the death of Hephaestion, his companion from boyhood, Alexander's never wholly stable personality toppled over into what was, in all probability, acute mania. With the memory of the appalling march through Gedrosia (Makran) on the south-eastern side of the Gulf still vivid in his mind and in the minds of his unfortunate commanders and men, he turned his eyes towards Arabia.

He was, it is alleged, angered at the refusal of the Arabians to allow him the homage which, as the world conqueror whose dominions were vaster than those of any emperor who preceded him, he felt entitled to demand. Already the stark and matter-of-fact sense of total independence of spirit, so characteristic of the desert-dwellers, made the prospect of acknowledging even Alexander's sovereignty unthinkable to the people of the peninsula. Alexander had hopes, similarly unfulfilled, that he might be recognized as divine by the Arabians who, he was given to understand, only worshipped two gods, who were identified by the Greeks with Uranus and Dionysos. It was not, Alexander considered, unreasonable that he should be regarded as worthy of divine honour since his achievements surpassed even those of Dionysos; Uranus was, of course, far too old a divinity to be considered as an Alexander.

All of this we learn from Arrian, a Bithynian civil servant in the service of the Roman Empire, who flourished in the second century AD and who wrote the most monumental surviving history of Alexander's lifetime. Though he lived several hundred years after his subject's own career, it is evident that he was able to draw on sources contemporary with Alexander himself. Amongst these were the logs of several of Alexander's sea captains, including his most celebrated admiral, Nearchos the Cretan. Arrian lived in the days of Hadrian, perhaps the most agreeable and certainly the most civilized of

Roman emperors, himself a worthy successor to Alexander, whom he held in deep admiration.

Arrian gives a detailed description of their voyages, particularly Nearchos'; it is appropriate now to turn to his words:

> Alexander had ideas of settling the seaboard of the Persian Gulf and the off-shore islands; for he fancied it might become as prosperous a country as Phoenicia. The naval preparations were directed against the Arabs of the coast, ostensibly because they were the only people in that part of the country who had sent no delegation to wait upon him, or shown their respect by any other normal act of courtesy; actually, however, the reason for the preparations was, in my opinion, Alexander's insatiable thirst for extending his possessions.
>
> Report has it that Alexander had heard that the Arabs worshipped only two gods, Uranus and Dionysus, the former because he is seen to contain within himself not only the stars but the sun too, the greatest and clearest source of blessing to mankind in all their affairs, and the latter, Dionysus, because of the fame of his journey to India. Alexander accordingly felt it would not be beyond his merits to be regarded by the Arabs as a third god, in view of the fact that his achievements surpassed those of Dionysus; or at least he would deserve this honour if he conquered the Arabs and allowed them, as he had allowed the Indians, to retain their ancient institutions. Moreover, the wealth of their country was an additional incitement – the cassia in the oases, the trees which bore frankincense and myrrh, the shrubs which yielded cinnamon, the meadows where nard grew wild: of all this report had told him. Arabia was a large country, its coast (it was said) no less in extent than the coast of India; many islands lay off it, and there were harbours everywhere fit for his fleet to ride in and to provide sites for new settlements likely to grow to great wealth and prosperity.
>
> He was further informed of the existence of two islands off the mouth of the Euphrates. One of them lay fairly close, at a distance of, perhaps, fifteen miles from that point on the shore where the river joins the sea. This, the smaller of the two, was densely wooded, and contained a temple of Artemis the regular service of which was performed by the islanders themselves. Deer and wild goats found pasture there, and as they were held sacred to the goddess it was unlawful to hunt them except for the purpose of sacrifice. For this reason only was the ban upon taking them removed. Aristobulus tells us that Alexander decreed that this island should be called Icarus after the Aegean island of that name.
>
> The second of the two islands, called Tylus, lay off the mouth of the Euphrates at about the distance a running ship can cover in a day and a

night. It was of some size, most of it neither wild nor wooded, but fit to produce all sorts of cultivated crops in their proper seasons. Some of this information Alexander got from Archias, who was sent out in a galley to reconnoitre the coast for the proposed expedition against the Arabs. Archias reached Tylus, but did not venture beyond; Androsthenes, who went in command of another galley, got further, sailing round a part of the Arabian peninsula, and Hiero, the ship-master from Soli, made greater progress than either. Alexander put him in charge of a third galley and gave him instructions to circumnavigate the whole peninsula as far as the Egyptian town of Heroopolis on the Red Sea. But even he found his courage fail him, though he had sailed round the greater part of the Arabian coast; he turned back, and stated in his report to Alexander that the peninsula was of immense size, nearly as big as India, and that a great headland ran far out into the ocean. This headland had, indeed, been sighted at no great distance by Nearchus' men on their voyage from India, before they altered course for the Persian Gulf.[35]

This passage is of considerable interest for the light which it throws on the Gulf in antiquity. It may be worth pausing for a moment to consider it in greater detail.

Arrian draws on Aristobulus for some parts of his account and Aristobulus was a contemporary of Alexander. However, most of his analysis of Nearchos' voyage depends upon the admiral's own authority; it appears in the form of *The Indica* which Arrian based on Nearchos' journals.

The first point to observe is that Alexander had ideas of settling the seaboard of the Gulf and the offshore islands; he fancied it might become as prosperous a country as Phoenicia. If nothing else, Alexander demonstrates here a remarkable foresight, for after his death colonies of Greeks established themselves along the Arabian shore and inland in Arabia.[36] The colonies flourished greatly for they lay athwart the spice routes from the south which, even in Alexander's time, were already bringing great riches to the peninsula, a point which Arrian himself records.

It is in his geographical observations, however, that the greatest interest in Arrian's narrative lies. He describes 'two islands off the mouth of the Euphrates'; one of them, densely wooded and rich in game, was sacred to a goddess whom the Greeks identified with their own Artemis. Alexander decreed that the island should be called Ikaros, a curious choice despite the explanation which the text provides. Ikaros in the Gulf puzzled commentators greatly until the discovery of a substantial temple, also of the Hellenistic period, unmistakably Greek in architecture and attributes, made it clear that Failaka is Ikaros (see also Chapter 8).[37]

The second island is called Tylos; this is Bahrain, and it features in most of the records left by ancient historians and geographers. Indeed it has a quite unique recorded history for the first literary reference to it was more remote from Arrian's day than his time is from our own.

The seriousness of Alexander's intentions towards the exploration, if not the conquest of Arabia, is manifested by the fact that other senior officers of his staff, beside Nearchos, carried out voyages of exploration in the Gulf. These were Archias, Androsthenes and Hiero, the last having evidently sailed beyond the Gulf and begun the formidable task of sailing round the Arabian coast, through the Red Sea to Egypt. He did not complete it.

According to Nearchos, Alexander sought intelligence about the people along the coast of the peninsula, their habitations and in particular the distribution of safe anchorages, sources of fresh water and of game or other victuals. It has been speculated that one of the most extraordinary acts of Alexander's life was connected with his interest in Arabia and the unexplored regions to the south and west of his dominions.[38] In his later years, seized compellingly with the idea of his divinity, Alexander saw himself fulfilling a destiny which had never before fallen to the lot of any man, divine or merely mortal. He became subject to one of the strangest and most persistent preoccupations of his lifetime. This seems, in essence, to have consisted of a deliberate attempt to sweep away, or at least to symbolize the sweeping away, of the barriers which had divided the east and west of his dominions, the Greeks and those others who inhabited European lands from their brothers in the Persian lands which had been brought under his hegemony. The remarkable and spectacular marriage of 10,000 at Susa, when Greeks and Persians were mingled in what seems to have been a consciously sacramental, if somewhat Hollywood-styled, occasion, was the most remarkable manifestation of this idea. As he moved towards his death Alexander became more and more exalted; a sort of transcendental quality seized him, manifested in his conviction (one which indeed it is difficult perhaps entirely to disregard) that his destiny was different in kind from those of other men. The control of the Gulf and of its western littoral (he already held the eastern shore by his subjugation of the Persian Empire) would have enabled him to bring all of his wide dominions into coherent and mutual contact, to unite the two great divisions of the world under his divine sovereignty. Then, no doubt, he would have turned towards the west and to a destiny which is, alas, beyond speculation.

His death in Babylon, which he entered in defiance of the Chaldaean soothsayers (who were amongst the most skilled in what must have been a generally difficult and often risky profession) ended any prospects of the universal brotherhood of man being introduced in this early dawn. If the King had lived out a more generous lifespan, the bleak 2,000 years which ultimately succeeded his time might have been suffused by a kinder light, had the precepts of the Academy prevailed, rather than those of the synagogue and the several Romes.

Unawed by Alexander's claims of divinity, the people of Arabia and the Gulf, accustomed perhaps to less equivocal godheads, ignored his tremendous presence and were thus never brought into his short-lived empire. But for a region which for 3,000 years before Alexander's day had the reputation of being the meeting-place of an entire and formidable pantheon, a slight, obsessive Macedonian, divine or not, did not perhaps mean very much. The gods of Sumer assembled in Dilmun were certainly more elemental than Alexander and, as gods, more practised in inspiring awe amongst their followers. However, even they did not achieve his extraordinary reputation.

Whatever may have been Alexander's role as a divinity, we are on firmer ground with the inscription which he caused to be set up on Failaka island in the Bay of Kuwait, preserving it as a sanctuary. The stone is now to be seen in the Failaka Museum.[39]

One of the many remarkable discoveries which have resulted from the past years of excavation in the Gulf and eastern Arabia has been the hitherto entirely unexpected penetration of the region by Greek influences. Alexander's interest in Arabia was, of course, well known and his determination to conquer it among his last recorded acts of policy. What had not been expected was the extent to which settlements quite unmistakably Greek had been established in Arabia in the years following his death.

The involvement of the Greeks in the region marks one of the high points of its history. All over the area, in Bahrain and in eastern Arabia as well as on Failaka, even far down into the Arabian desert, Greek influence indicates a degree of prosperity and importance for the region which it had hardly enjoyed since Old Babylonian times. The evidence of the grave fields in Bahrain is notable in this regard: no accurate count has been made, but, whilst a substantial percentage of the tens of thousands date from the late third and early second millennia, a large number can be traced to Hellenistic times. It is, indeed, curious how the inhabitants of Bahrain and the nearby mainland in the third and second centuries BC reverted to the practice of mound burial employed by their predecessors. Not all the bearers of Greek traditions, however, favoured (or perhaps could afford) interment in a family or individual grave mound. A Greek burial ground, in which the graves are simple shafts, though set beneath one large mound, was found by chance in Bahrain's capital during a construction project.[40] No doubt the inhabitants of the graves were modest people, seamen perhaps, who lived in or were connected with the fourth city level at the Qala'at al-Bahrain, which is associated with the times immediately succeeding Alexander's lifetime. Two skeletons were found intermingled in the same grave. From Sar, a most important site in the earlier periods of Bahrain's prosperity, the graves of the Hellenistic period have yielded, amongst other objects, an appealing little pottery horse and rider, perhaps a votive object, perhaps a toy.

In Failaka, Greek influences were of great significance. Whether this was because of Alexander's interest in the island or whether the Greek involvement was of longer standing is unknown, but a substantial Greek settlement has been identified. One of its buildings was evidently a factory for the manufacture of pottery figures;[41] since most of these seem to be cultic, it may be presumed that they served the sacred nature of the island, perhaps indicating the presence of pilgrims who would make use of the products of the factory.

The Greek presence is also to be detected deep into the Arabian desert. At Fau, about 600 kilometres (370 miles) south of Riyadh, a market-town with considerable evidence of Greek influences has been excavated by the King Saud University, Riyadh.[42] A whole chain of settlements was strung out across the desert, linking the spice-producing regions in the south with the Gulf coast in the east. From the cities on the eastern seaboard, including Bahrain, Arabian spices were exported to the Greeks of Persia and as far away as those who settled, in the wake of Alexander, in India.

But the most significant remains of the Hellenitic period on Failaka, other than the Alexander proclamation, are those of a small Greek temple, excavated on the island.[43] It is a handsome construction, though modest in scale; it is, in fact, a very pretty miniature Greek fane. The quality of its architecture, however, shows nothing provincial about it; indeed, it would seem likely that its construction was supervised by a Greek-trained architect, perhaps using craftsmen imported for the project. The temple was built after Alexander's death and perhaps its quality is a consequence of the importance which his decree gave to this distant outpost of the Greek world.

According to another inscription, dedicated by one Soteles, a citizen of Athens, Artemis in Failaka bore the surname Suteria and is hailed as 'Sarconices'.[44] The Greek presence on Failaka was not only religious, however. Presumably to defend the little temple, the factory and the township from marauders, a fort was built. The inscription left by Soteles joins 'the soldiers' with him in its dedication; it is difficult not to feel some sympathy for Greek soldiers so far from their homeland in so very remote and distant a place as Failaka must have seemed, far from the customary entertainments and civilities of Greek life.

6

THE MYTHS OF SUMER AND DILMUN

Like most of mankind before or after them, the Sumerians were puzzled by the world and felt keenly the need to explain it to themselves. Through the medium of their language they created splendid images and stories to link the worlds of gods and men, with the facility with which the Egyptians carved in stone to the same purpose. They wondered at the world and took, on balance, a rather humble view of their place in it. Their gods, an unappealing and generally disagreeable race, were, with few exceptions, largely ill-disposed or at best indifferent to man.

The Sumerians saw all life as vain and man as the powerless creature of a capricious and often malevolent destiny; they are a people with whom it is easy to find much in common. It may be that their dispiriting view of the world was in part the result of their geographical location; in part it may have been the inheritance of the generally pessimistic religious ideas of the Semitic-speaking component in their society. Their land lay between two powerful and unpredictable rivers, which, despite all the controls they might exercise, in one year could bring abundance and in the next ruin. In considering this sense of impending catastrophe – the apparently basic Sumerian belief that something dreadful was always about to happen – it must be remembered that the Biblical story of the Flood is the record of a Sumerian cataclysm, dimly recalled by the descendants of the nomadic tribes which wandered the deserts beyond the cities' limits. The social and political structure of their society was weighted against permanence and tranquillity and, as in Greece 2,000 years later, constantly led to war and the destruction of one little state by another.

Nor did they find any consolation in creating comforting fantasies about an afterlife, which on the one hand might redress the pain and suffering of the earthly existence, or, on the other, would be an idealized extension of life on earth. To the frankly rather complacent Egyptians, for example, no more perfect life could be imagined than a perpetual sunlit existence in the Nile Valley. But the Sumerians, anticipating alike Freud and the doctrine of original sin, said 'Never has a sinless child been born to its mother'[1] and in some of their moods (though fortunately not their most characteristic) they bore a frightening load of quiet despondency around with them, which manifested itself most strongly when they considered their likely fate after death. Forlornly, they described a state in which the souls of the dead crouched twittering, hungry and thirsty, beaten by the scaly wings of dreadful birds in the dusty, windswept corridors of an underworld[2] which has many features, if so they may be termed, of the Christian or Muslim Hell and the Greek Hades; indeed the whole dispiriting idea of the place of eternal punishment and suffering may well descend from this dismal Mesopotamian concept.

THE GODS OF SUMER

The gods of Sumer were responsible for many, if not all, of the problems which beset mankind. The Sumerians invented a splendid and colourful theogony but it was one in which the gods are rarely seen to advantage for, in the Sumerian view, there was little good that might be said for them.

The dispassionate view which many of the ancients took of divinity is in sharp contrast to the more respectful attitudes of later ages. Everyone is familiar with the discreditable antics of the Greek pantheon, whose members, obsessed by alternating waves of greed, lust and ill-temper, mirrored only too exactly the character of humanity itself. The Hebrews, influenced by the harshness of desert life and apparently responding to the darker aspects of Sumerian beliefs (though *their* ancestors may have been responsible for the blacker sides of Sumerian convictions), created the jealous and temperamental Yahweh, who only emerged as the sole god, hidden on his Jerusalem mountain-top, after his adherents had disposed of those other deities whom once the Hebrews worshipped and of whom they long sustained nostalgic memories. Only the Egyptians, typically insulated alike by their desert boundaries and the high opinion they held of themselves, blessed the gods unreservedly, feeling compassion towards those less happy races of mankind which had the misfortune not to be born Egyptian. If there was one thing of which, for example, a Memphite landowner living in the early centuries of the third millennium could be certain, looking out contentedly over his estate as evening came on, it was that God was an Egyptian; there was no comparable comfort to sustain the Sumerians.

In the Sumerian canon of belief the greater and the lesser gods, the latter often the servants of the former, were brought into existence first; and the world (by which was really meant the land of Sumer and the Gulf, the sea whose waters washed its southernmost shore) was made ready for them. Every major divinity received a plot of land which was to be his or hers, and the elements and all visible and hidden things were each apportioned to the charge of one of them. All the great gods, collectively known as the Annunaki, were given households of lesser gods who, in addition to serving their divine masters, also served the useful purpose of interceding between mankind and the gods, when men had been created. They were, it has been suggested, the spiritual ancestors of the Christian 'guardian angels', and every Sumerian family head had his personal divinity to whom he would address his prayers, begging him to take a petition to the High Gods, for they were too awful for man directly to approach.

When, in the beginning, the world was made and parcelled out to the various gods and goddesses, all was admirably conceived, but the divinities felt that their world lacked something: it needed docile and obedient creatures who might cultivate the earth and harvest it, and maintain order amongst the other animals. Indeed, the first recorded strike took place when the lesser Sumerian divinities, the Igigi-gods, downed tools and, glowering at the Annunaki, the High Gods, intimidated them into accepting their just demands for leisure and their belief that largely agricultural pursuits were unsuitable occupations even for minor deities.[3] The ruling divinities were thus forced to take action and to improve the conditions of their junior colleagues. Clearly the work had to be done by someone, and so man was created for the purpose of carrying out such menial and ungodly tasks. Having made man, the gods also decided it would be both pleasant and useful for a system of worship to be introduced, thus showing that from the earliest times they suffered from that curious and recurring sense of insecurity to which divinities seem much to be subject, an insecurity which needed to be assuaged by their constantly being told, by legions of believers, how sublime they were. For these humble purposes, therefore, was mankind created, to be the creatures of each god and the workers on his estate. This was the time of primaeval innocence, when, dutifully,

> The whole universe, the people in unison,
> to Enlil with one tongue, gave praise.[4]

The Sumerians' concept of the trappings and attributes of divinity still, in some respects at least, haunt contemporary man. When the gods manifest themselves they are fully realized in what might be described as the classic divine mould. They are superhuman, invisible, unbound by time and space, rulers of the elements and hungry for worship. They are represented in human form but are gigantic, with distinctive clothing and, in the case of the male gods, with rather alarming hats, apparently a sort of horned turban with which they are invariably portrayed on, for example, the seals which are one of the glories of Sumerian (and later, Akkadian) culture. The horns would appear to be those of bulls, probably *Bos primigenius*.[5]

Male divinities predominated in Sumer; the Mother, known by many names but in her most potent form called Ninhursag, is a great one, but never supreme. Unlike Egypt, where in the case of ancient gods like Ptah, Horus and even Osiris, it is possible to speculate about dimly observed human originals, mighty heroes who left the memory of their rule so vivid in the people's consciousness that they raised them to the most honoured rank they could conceive, Sumer's gods are far more elemental and harshly absolute. They never achieved the numinous quality of that most mysterious of Egyptian gods 'Him whose name is hidden', the nobility of the later 'unknown' Amon, or even the philosophically rather tepid beneficence of Akhnaton's Aten.

The Sumerian cosmology held that in the beginning was the primaeval sea, represented as female; her oceanic form possibly again commemorates the Sumerians' own preoccupation with the sea, in this case the waters of the Gulf. From the chaos of the waters, the cosmic mountain was begotten, in which form heaven and earth were united in the persons of two great divinities, An, the god of Heaven, and Ki, the goddess of Earth. From their union sprang Enlil, the Lord of Air, who then became the executive leader of the Annunaki, the assembly of the High Gods, and the recipient of the chorus of praise offered by all the people.

An and Enlil were associated with two other major divinities: Enki, Lord of the Abyss, the water god, one of the most popular in the pantheon, and Ninhursag, the Lady of the Mountain, the Great Goddess. Other important members of the divine family included Utu, god of the Sun (whose Akkadian name Shamash survives in the Arabic word for sun, *shams*); Nanna, god of the Moon, later to be known as Sin; and Inanna the Ishtar-Aphrodite goddess of love and lust. Inanna was a highly equivocal goddess. She softened when she became the Semitic Ishtar under the Babylonians, but, as will be seen from the Gilgamesh epic later in this story, the Sumerians themselves were very much in two minds about her. Inanna has part of her legendary connections linked with Dilmun and hence to the subject of this study. She says of herself: 'I am Inanna of the place where the sun rises.'[6] She is also reported to have 'washed her head in the fountain of Dilmun',[7] a reference perhaps to the many freshwater springs which may be found in the north of the island, and, more surprisingly, in the sea itself which divides Bahrain from the mainland of Arabia. The subterranean waters of eastern Arabia and the central Gulf were a particularly powerful element in giving the region its reputation for sanctity and the special favour of the gods.

ENKI

Enlil and Enki were the most important of all the gods to the Sumerians. Enlil was thought of as a sort of divine Chief Executive, stern but usually just. Enki was the most beloved of the gods of Sumer, for he is the friend of man who brought knowledge of the arts and sciences to the black-headed folk, riding up the Gulf accompanied by rejoicing fishes. Enki's epiphany is marvellously described:

When Enki arose the fishes rose and adored him,
He stood, a marvel unto the Apsu,
Brought joy to the Enqu,
To the sea it seemed that Anu was upon him,
To the Great River it seemed that terror hovered about him,
While at the same time the South Wind stirred the depths of the
    Euphrates.[8]

Although Dilmun had its own tutelary divinity, Enshag or Inzak, who will be revealed further in the legend of Enki and Ninhursag, where he is spoken of as 'Lord of Dilmun', Enki was possibly the land's first and most important god. It has been suggested, indeed, that the veneration of Enki, Lord of the Abyss, and patron of the fishes, may have originated in Dilmun and from there have moved north to the Sumerian lands.[9] If this were so, and if Enki was the original tribal god of the Sumerians, it could well be the reason for the belief that he brought the arts of civilization to Sumer from Dilmun. It would also be another reason for the reverence and affection in which the black-headed people held Dilmun as the Terrestrial Paradise.

Enki was beloved by the Sumerians for the sympathy he displayed towards humanity and the kindly interest he seemed to take in the well-being of the race of men. He was less remote and terrible than most of his colleagues, more inclined to behave predictably and with goodwill towards man. He is among the most frequently portrayed of all the great gods in the vibrant and revealing glyptic art of the time. He appears in countless seals in various manifestations, on the water, in his reed house (which bears a close resemblance to the houses built by the Marsh Arabs to this day), amiably wrestling with wild beasts, receiving petitions. He is also represented in one of the most important activities of Sumerian gods, the sacred marriage, the *hieros gamos* which was celebrated down to Ninevite times, with the king enacting the god's role, partnered by one of the sacred temple women playing the part of the goddess. In many of his appearances, two streams of crystal water cascade from Enki's shoulders, in which his creatures, the fishes, disport themselves joyfully. Water is Enki's special element, in particular the sweet waters hidden beneath the earth whose management was essential to the Sumerians. In their rather confused view Enki rode the waters of the Gulf and, by thus agitating them, filled the Tigris and Euphrates with their overflow, so bringing prosperity and abundance to his people.

Enki is a chthonic divinity, his dwelling-place the Abyss, far from the haunts of man. His name means Lord of Earth, and by it his original sovereignty over the world is suggested. At some time, however, Enki's supremacy was challenged by Enlil, the Lord of Air, who then became the head of the Annunaki, under the kingship of the distant An. An was, incidentally, conceived of as some sort of demiurge who, having created the world, largely withdrew from its affairs to the higher heavens.

The reason why Enki lost his primacy is uncertain: it may be that once the Sumerians had settled down to an existence on land and no longer depended so exclusively on the sea (as evidently they did originally, in witness of which are the offerings of fishes which were piled on Enki's altars at Eridu and the nets which were hung about them) they became more conscious of the mysterious powers of wind, storm and rain which whipped to fury the rivers and lagoons on which they had established themselves. The more kindly god of the sweet waters and the fishes was replaced by an elemental and implacable divinity whose officers were the bringers of storm and deluge. But it is likely that Enki is the most ancient male divinity whose name we know. Certainly the little shrine at his city, Eridu, piled high with the offerings of his creatures, the fishes, is the earliest of all temples that can be identified as such for certain. Enki, incidentally, was the god who was responsible for marking out the ground plans of temples.

ENKI AND THE WORLD ORDER

An early text describes Enki as the father of Enlil, suggesting that, as was repeated again in Babylonian times with Marduk, and with the triple sequence of Uranus, Kronos and Zeus, the son could become greater than the father. Another legend survives which shows Enki, here described as the son of An, to have been the original creator-god, displaying a brisk and cheerful attention to all the needs of the earth. A long and complex myth, *Enki and the World Order*,[10] describes his joyful bringing of order and all its blessings to mankind, to animals and to the land and cities of Sumer. Responsibilities are allotted by Enki to all the smaller divinities who have power over specific functions, elements or sections of the economy.

The myth gives the impression of bubbling enthusiasm on Enki's part and it emphasizes his joy in the work which he had wrought.

Enki proclaims his divine titles:

I am the first son of An. . . . I am the Lord of the Land
I am the father of all lands
I am the 'Big Brother' of the gods
I am the record keeper of heaven and earth
I am the leader of the Annunaki.

Enki turns to the organization of the earth and amongst the first lands to be blessed are Magan and Dilmun:

The lands of Magan and Dilmun
Looked up to me, Enki,
Moved the Dilmun-boat to the ground
Loaded the Magan-boat sky-high.

In Sumerian times Magan was in all probability located on the coast of Oman and also perhaps on the Makran coast across the Gulf.

Sumer itself next received Enki's blessing and he proclaims its glories. Ur, the city whose fate has been decreed by Enlil, and Melukhkha, probably the coastal regions of modern Pakistan, together with the cities of the Indus Valley are celebrated by the god; then back to Dilmun:

> He cleansed, purified the land Dilmun,
> Placed Ninsikil in charge of it.
> . . . he eats fish. . . . he eats its dates.

Enki's blessing of Dilmun is especially generous and gives it a strong identification with the sea, emphasizing the land's dependence on the fruits of the sea as well as on the products of agriculture:

> May the sea bring you its abundance,
> The city – its dwellings are good dwellings,
> Dilmun – its dwellings are good dwellings,
> Its barley is very small barley,
> Its dates are very large dates.

Even late in the second millennium BC, long after the Sumerians had disappeared for ever, Dilmun's dates were still greatly sought after by the rulers of Mesopotamia. They were also responsible for a notably high rate of caries in the teeth of the early inhabitants of Bahrain.

Amongst those whose power is called up by Enki is Utu, the sun-god, whose home is in Dilmun. One of the Paradise Land's epithets may be recalled in the following passage in which he identifies Dilmun in the same terms as the goddess Inanna, quoted earlier:

> The hero, the bull who comes forth out of the forest,
> Who roars lion-like,
> The valiant Utu, the bull who stands secure,
> Who proudly displays his power,
> The father of the great city, *the place where the sun rises*,
> The great herald of holy An,
> The judge, the decision maker of the gods,
> Who wears a lapis lazuli beard,
> Who comes forth from the holy heaven,
> Utu, the Son born of Ningal,
> Enki placed in charge of the entire universe.

In some of the legends which survive and recount the doings of the fish-god, Enki presents a slightly disreputable, even a faintly absurd figure. But the Sumerians seemed to have loved him, whilst the other divinities they feared. In one of the most important and complete of the early legends, Enki comes into full conjunction with Dilmun, for the story begins in that land, before time was. Dilmun is already Enki's home.

ENKI AND NINHURSAG

The myth concerns the rather fraught and complicated relationship of Enki and Ninhursag, one of the manifestations of the great and terrible primaeval goddess who survived into Sumerian times, her supreme authority then being subjected to that of the male gods.[11] Dilmun is splendidly described, a land of joy and peace, whose creation has been an unreserved success. Ninsikil is a tutelary goddess of Dilmun: her name means 'the pure queen'.

> The land Dilmun is a pure place, the land Dilmun is a clean place;
> The land Dilmun is a clean place, the land Dilmun is a bright place;
> He who is all alone laid himself down in Dilmun,
> The place after Enki had laid himself by his wife,
> That place is clean, that place is bright,
> He who is all alone laid himself down in Dilmun,
> The place, after Enki had laid himself by Ninsikil,
> That place is clean, that place is bright,
> In Dilmun the raven uttered no cries,
> The kite uttered not the cry of the kite,
> The lion killed not,
> The wolf snatched not the lamb,
> Unknown was the kid-killing dog,
> Unknown was the grain-devouring boar,
> The bird on high . . . not its young,
> The dove . . . not the head,
> The sick-eyed says not 'I am sick-eyed',
> The sick-headed says not 'I am sick-headed',
> Its old woman says not 'I am an old woman',
> Its old man says not 'I am an old man',
> Its unwashed maid is not . . . in the city,
> He who crosses the river utters no . . .
> The overseer does not . . .
> The singer utters no wail,
> By the side of the city he utters no lament.

Only one thing apparently mars life in this happy land, the lack of sweet water, but the cohabitation of Ninsikil and Enki soon overcomes this deficiency. Ninsikil, a practical if somewhat opportunistic goddess, prevails upon the relaxed and good-tempered Enki, evidently in a state of post-coital euphoria, to provide the island with the water it needs. He at once calls upon Utu the sun-god, to make the sweet waters flow. Utu does so, and all that is possible for the enjoyment of men is realized in Dilmun. Even the economy is transformed.

> Her city drinks the water of abundance,
> Dilmun drinks the water of abundance,
> Her wells of bitter water, behold they are become wells of good water,
> Her fields and farms produce good grain,
> Her city, behold it is become the house of the banks and quays of the
>   land.

An alternative translation[12] of the last line would have Dilmun as the place of assembly of the gods, their meeting-place and, so far as the Sumerians were concerned, the place of their origin. A fragment of a cuneiform tablet found at Asshur, the capital of the later bloodstained Assyrian Kingdom, indicates that e-karra, 'the House of the Quay', was the name of a temple in Dilmun.[13] It may be recalled in the last line of the extract above and it is entirely in keeping with the Sumerians' commercial preoccupations that the quays of mercantile Dilmun should be so commemorated, even in the context of a hymn of praise to the most lofty of the gods.

Now, however, the story takes another turn, and a strange and slightly sinister element enters it. Clearly no place so well endowed as Dilmun should be without plants and the benefits of cultivation. Enki proceeds to deal with this by inducing a complex and cumbersome series of pregnancies on successive generations of plant-goddesses, brought into being for that purpose.

The process starts with the Great Mother herself, Ninhursag, whose nine months of pregnancy are equivalent to nine human days. Their daughter is Ninsar; Enki rapidly lies with her too and in nine days her daughter Ninhur is born. Enki, indefatigable and undeterred by the fact that he is now dealing with his granddaughter, fathers Uttu, the plant-goddess, on Ninhur.

Ninhursag, who apparently has been absent during this succession of pregnancies, now returns to the goddess-littered island and takes an ill-fortuned hand in the affair. She offers Uttu some helpful advice on the predictable course of her relations with the still tumescent Enki. What she proposes is, unhappily, lost from the tablet which contains the legend but Uttu, like a dutiful great-granddaughter, takes Ninhursag's advice seriously and, as a result, promptly if unexpectedly, gives birth to eight plants, unaided by Enki.

The god, despite his divine nature, is now apparently exhausted by the efforts which he has so urgently been making in the cause of agriculture, and is lying 'stretched out in the swamp-land'. With him is his attendant, Isimud, and from him he learns the names of each of the eight plants which Uttu has mothered. As Isimud pronounces its name, Enki eats the plant concerned. Are there portents here of other myths reaching us from this Sumerian Eden: the Hebrew legend of the forbidden fruit and the Greek story of the ingestation by Kronos of his children?[14] It is also remarkable that when Enki is lying alone in the marshes, he masturbates, like Atum[15] the Egyptian creator-god, who, in one of the Egyptians' explanations for the process of creation, since he is the unique being, is obliged to resort to this procedure to start off the sequence of divine births which ultimately leads to the making of the earlier generations of the gods.

When Enki has eaten all the plants, Ninhursag returns again, this time in a wild and angry epiphany. In a swirling rage she curses Enki for having eaten the plants: 'Until thou art dead, I shall not look upon thee with the eye of life.' Full of anger she disappears and Enki is stricken with a mortal sickness which affects eight parts of his body, each plant that he had eaten taking its revenge on a different organ. It is also possible (if confusing) that Enki is impregnated by his own semen in this phase of the story, again recalling an Egyptian parallel, the story of the conflict of Horus and Seth, where something not dissimilar occurs.[16]

A peculiar characteristic of the gods of Sumer seems to have been a tendency to fall to pieces in times of stress. The Deluge myth will demonstrate how badly they could behave when things became really difficult for them. The High Gods become discouraged: seeing the powerful Enki himself brought down by Ninhursag, they fall into a deep despondency and sit hopelessly in the dust. The peace and happiness of Dilmun is clouded by their distress and lack of resource.

A new element is introduced at this point into the legend. The Sumerians, seemingly, were fond of animals and were the first people to record stories in which animals play a human role, like those to which Aesop later gave his name, and of the same order as those in the engaging animal cartoons which survive from Egypt and for which, indeed, there are also many Sumerian parallels. In this case it is the fox, not a creature normally noted for his sagacity and resource in Sumerian fable, who takes the initiative in the matter of Enki's sickness.

Finding the miserable gods hopelessly watching their divine comrade sinking into what looks suspiciously like mortality, the fox offers to bring back Ninhursag so that she may heal Enki. As Enlil, the Lord of Air and prince of the gods, can think of nothing better himself, he accepts the fox's offer swiftly.

At this point the text is indecipherable and we do not know by what means the fox persuades Ninhursag to return. But return she does and she agrees to heal the hapless Enki by means of the facility (a routine matter apparently to Sumerian goddesses) of giving birth to a succession of deities, each of whom acts as an antidote to one of Enki's ailments. Abu, Nintul, Ninul, Ninsutu, Ninkasi, Nazi, Dazimira, Ninti and Enshag are successively sprung from the goddess' fecund womb and each, having healed the appropriate part of Enki, is either appointed the tutelary of certain lands or married to another. Ninhursag then places Enki by her vulva and speeds his healing. Enki is restored to his full godly powers and the poem ends with a paean of praise to him.

The two last-named gods in the sequence brought to birth by Ninhursag to heal Enki, Ninti and Enshag are of special interest in the present context. Kramer has suggested that Ninti may be the original of the legend of Eve, the 'first mother' of the Genesis creation myth and thus, possibly, a remote link with the two Paradise myths.[17]

Enshag is not one of the great gods of Sumer but he has a vital role to play in the identification of Dilmun and Bahrain. The discovery of the island's principal cuneiform text with its mention of this god has its place in a later section of this study.

A text was found on Cythera, in the distant Aegean far away from the islands of the Gulf, which also refers to Enshag.[18] It is written in an archaic cuneiform and appears to refer to the god Enshag and the goddess Lakhamun, the gods of Tilmun, to whom it said 'The king of Tilmun Naram-Sin, son of Ibiq-Adad, king of Tilmun, for his life has made an offering.'

Naram-Sin is not the king of Sumer and Akkad who was the grandson of Sargon the Great but was evidently a ruler of Esnunna c. 1830 BC. Ibiq-Adad seems to be unknown. What an inscription of this comparative obscurity was doing on an Aegean island so far from its own supposed island of origin is totally mysterious.

ENKI AND OANNES

Enki was a fish-god; the charming readiness of the fishes to adore him has already been recorded. One of the more remarkable and certainly one of the most ancient legends associated with the Gulf and the origins of knowledge concerns Enki in a curious manifestation of a creature, part-fish, part-man called Oannes, a Hellenized form of his Semitic name, Ea.

Enki is almost invariably shown in human form in Mesopotamian art. Fishes were sacred to him and so was the ibex, a creature which features frequently on the seals which are so notable a product of the societies flourishing in the Gulf in antiquity; sometimes, indeed, Enki is manifested in the ibex, and his boat, in which he is often portrayed, was called *Ibex of the Absu*. The story of Oannes is contained in the work of Berossus,[19] who was a contemporary of Alexander the Great; he was Priest of Bel in the great temple of Babylon. He seems not to have been a very remarkable man nor, to judge by the parts of his *Babyloniaca* which have survived in extracts quoted in other men's work, a particularly gifted one. He was given a somewhat more exalted posthumous biography by the hand of legend, however, including fathering the Erythraean Sibyl.

Berossus was a Hellenized Babylonian. He was an admirer of things Greek and he sought to reconcile the history of his own people with that of the new masters of the world. He wrote for Antiochos I, one of Alexander's successors, and set out to make available, in the Greek language, books of stupendous and quite unbelievable antiquity preserved at Babylon which contained the origins of his people, the transmission of the arts of civilization to them by the bizarre amphibious creatures which manifested themselves in the Gulf, and a list of kings, from before the Flood to Alexander. The books, suggested Berossus, contained 'the histories of heaven [and earth] and sea and the first birth and the Kings and their deeds'.

The weird and mysterious creatures of which he tells suddenly appear and attach themselves to the race of men, proceeding to teach them all knowledge. The leader of the team of didactic monsters is 'a beast named Oannes' which

> appeared from the Erythraean Sea in a place adjacent to Babylonia. Its entire body was that of a fish but a human head had grown beneath the head of the fish and human feet had grown from the fish's tail. It also had a human voice. A picture of it is still preserved today. . . . This beast spent the days with the men but ate no food. It gave to men the knowledge of letters and sciences and crafts of all types. It also taught them how to found cities, establish temples, introduce laws and measure land. It also revealed to them seeds and the gathering of fruits and in general it gave men everything which is connected with the civilized life. From the time of that beast nothing further has been discovered. But when the sun set this beast Oannes plunged back into the sea and spent the nights in the deep, for it was amphibious. Later other beasts also appeared. He [Berossus] says that he will discuss these in the book of the Kings. Oannes wrote about birth and government and gave the following account to men.[20]

Oannes, himself, then describes the 'time when everything was darkness and water'. Strange monsters appeared; all manner of creatures came forth, to be ruled by a woman called Omorka. Then Bel, the great god, arose, split the woman in two, destroyed the monster forms and created men and beasts able to endure the air.

The second of Berossus' books was *The Book of Kings*. He records in it the names of the kings of Babylon from the beginning of things. The earliest kings ruled for many thousands of years. They were attended or advised by other creatures, like Oannes, who came up from the Gulf; Berossus gives the names of these creatures, which were known collectively as *apkallu*, a term which may mean something like 'sages'. They were all of them mixtures of men and fish.

The 'kings' are the legendary sovereigns who reigned before the Flood. The last of them is Xisouthros, a figure from Greek myth whose name is a Hellenized form of Ziusudra, the Sumerian hero of the flood myth in the Epic of Gilgamesh.

Berossus describes the Flood. The warning of its impending approach is given to Xisouthros by Kronos, the Greek equivalent of Enki. He includes a curious little story which purports to describe the birth of Gilgamesh, his being saved from an early death by an eagle and his upbringing, like Sargon the Great, by a gardener.

The events which Berossus charts are, he says, based on records reaching back more than 400,000 years. This can safely be discounted, but his description of the fish-men *apkallu*, coming up to Babylonia from the Gulf is, if nothing else, a charming legend which enshrines the belief of the Babylonians and their Sumerian predecessors that their civilization origi-nated from the Lower Sea, the place where the sun rises.

Oannes and his attendants are clearly Enki and his familiars. Even in relatively late times priests of Enki/Ea were depicted wearing fish costumes, with fish head-dresses above their own features, thus impersonating quite convincingly the form of the *apkallu* described by Berossus.

As to the *apkallu* themselves, none of the representations (so far as we know) to which Berossus refers, survives. However, there is a group of strange little figures, of uncertain provenance, which appear to come from early levels in south-western Iranian city sites.[21] These are in the form of men, covered with fish scales (though otherwise human in form) and each with a deep scar running down his face. These little figurines are made in segments: they are remarkably powerful and quite unlike anything else from Sumer or from early Elam. Whether they actually represent *apkallu* only Enki knows.

The earliest of all temples discovered in Mesopotamia is at Eridu and was consecrated to Enki. It dates from Ubaid times, a simple sanctuary built on the virgin sand; it is the ancestor of all Sumerian temples. It was overlaid by seventeen successive buildings, each one more elaborate than its predecessor, culminating in a great third-millennium ziggurat, a splendid structure raised to the glory of Enki, more than 2,000 years after the little Ubaid shrine had introduced his worship to the land.

In the first sanctuary was an altar piled with offerings 15 cm (6 inches) deep in fish bones, the relics of sacrifices placed there more than 5,000 years ago. The fish were sea-perch, creatures of the brackish lagoon waters. Enki was also much honoured, understandably, by sailors who courted his favour and goodwill in launching themselves upon the uncertain mercy of his kingdom's waters. If it is possible that Enshag-Inzak may be a manifestation of Enki himself, the suggestion that his worship in Bahrain may have preceded his cult in Sumer is wholly tenable. According to Rawlinson, the Babylonians acknowledged having received all their knowledge from 'the mysterious islanders of the Persian Gulf'[22] – which, as the Babylonians were the direct cultural successors of the innovating Sumerians, they patently did not. It is another matter, however, with the Sumerians themselves.

The gods of Sumer are to be seen at their best perhaps in the context of their place of assembly, the land of crossing, which was Dilmun. After the disaster of the Flood, they were said to cluster around the sacrifices provided for them by the prototypical survivor, Ziusudra, 'like flies',[23] a somewhat distasteful metaphor but one which reveals the consistently down-to-earth view of their gods which the Sumerians maintained. But they also clustered around the sacred land of Dilmun, the original Holy Land, from the legends of which all the others in the western world actually descend. In these legends they are revealed as a tremendous presence, great if intangible forms which were to exercise a profound influence on the world; so profound as to endure over the five or six thousand years since the people who invented them first began to fill their world with the stories of their intervention in the affairs of men. The modern world, when it takes account of such matters, draws its inspiration of the divine from the great monotheistic faiths which have moulded society over the last 2,000 years. Hebrew, Christian and Muslim religious beliefs have all drawn their inspiration from a common, though of course not from an exclusive, source. That source had its beginnings in the people of southern Mesopotamia; to those people Dilmun was a magical land, a faery place, half realized, half a place of myth. This was the Garden of Eden, the place of origins; there was no Fall there, though. In Dilmun all was pure and enduring. It is not surprising perhaps that its very existence was forgotten for so long, but the fact remains that, without this island and the legends which it bore, the world would not be quite the place that it is, nor would people, for at least the past 3,000 formative years, have believed quite what they came to believe.

7

BAHRAIN
The Blessed Island

When Captain Durand visited Bahrain in the winter of 1878/9 he opened several of the tumulus burial mounds which dominate the Aali district, near the village of the same name. He reported to his government enthusiastically on his findings. In one of the tombs he appears to have come up against a wall, inconveniently sited for his further exploration; with disarming succinctness he observes: 'We blew this out.'[1]

However, the practice of dynamiting tombs is not a fair measure of Captain Durand's contribution to the uncovering of the early history of the Bahrain islands, for one discovery which he made in the casual manner of those days was to be of crucial significance in establishing the part that Bahrain had played in the early history of south-west Asia and, indeed, in the developing awareness of the extent of man's history. He found a black basalt stone which had engraved on it a plaque of cuneiform script, one of the few examples of early epigraphy yet discovered in Bahrain, and incontestably the most important.

The inscription was embedded in the wall of a mosque in the Bilad ed Kadim, the ancient capital of Bahrain. Of this the Suq al-Khamis mosque is the only substantial building surviving, now much restored. Durand's stone was about 65 cm (26 inches) in length and its discoverer described it as being like the prow of a boat or an animal's tongue: it has also been said to look like a foot. Towards the narrower end of the stone an upright palm branch was inscribed. Beside the branch a rectangular 'box' contained four lines of inscription in the style of cuneiform script which prevailed during the eighteenth century BC, at the time of the first Babylonian Empire, roughly contemporary with Hammurabi, the great law-giver. 'Old Babylonian' cuneiform had by then become the customary script for most Near Eastern countries' official and business correspondence and for the literary productions of the Babylonian and Assyrian heirs of the civilization of Sumer (Fig. 7.1).

**I. SKETCH OF STONE DISCOVERED BY CAPT DURAND.
(2 FT. 2 IN. LONG).**

2. PALM BRANCH OVER INSCRIPTION.

4. THE SAME IN ASSYRIAN.

Figure 7.1 (a) The 'Durand inscription' written in the cuneiform script in general use in the eighteenth century BC.

142

THE DURAND INSCRIPTION

In the report to the Foreign Secretary's Department of the Viceroy's Administration in Calcutta, Durand reproduced the inscribed stone from a 'squeeze' which he had made on the spot. Rawlinson attempted a translation in the Calcutta version: it is not, however, satisfactory and he evidently was able to revise it.

It can be accepted with reasonable certainty that the stone is from Bahrain itself, perhaps the last fragment to survive of a palace of one of the island's merchant princes. Who 'Rimum' was will perhaps never be known, but at least his act of piety in invoking his god has assured him some small immortality. The text reads:

e-gal ri - mu - um eri din - za - ak LU a - ga - rum.

The Palace of Rimum, the Servant of Inzak, of the tribe of Agarum.

The mention of Rimum's tribe, the Agarum, provides an example of the quite extraordinary continuity which may be found amongst peoples whose way of life remained traditional and predominantly tribal. It has been proposed that 'Agarum' is perpetuated in 'Hagar', as the Hasa Province of eastern Arabia and Bahrain itself were collectively called in mediaeval times. A tribe of nomads called the Beni Hagar still occupies land in the Hasa province of what is now Saudi Arabia and may, therefore, be related to Rimum's tribe. The Beni Hagar are an interesting phenomenon, incidentally, with a knack of appearing at significant moments of history. They seem to have been one of the Christianized Arab tribes in late pre-Islamic times and, having moved up to the north, to have been present at the fall of Jerusalem when it was captured in the seventh century AD by the Caliph Omar.

THE GOD ENSHAG-INZAK

'Inzak' was the Akkadian form of the name of the Sumerian god Enshag who features in the last stage of the chain of births which took place in Dilmun and is described in the legend of Enki and Ninhursag (Chapter 6). He was one of the principal divinities of the ancient inhabitants of Bahrain and in the legend referred to is proclaimed 'Lord of Dilmun'; he is said to control reason and wisdom, an area of concern which clearly he inherited from his father Enki. Temples were dedicated to him in Sumerian and Elamite[2] cities and he was worshipped in Babylonian times, under the name Nabu; later he became an influential member of the pantheon. He is, according to Rawlinson, the god represented in the sky by the planet Mercury, the sun's closest attendant and a divinity of considerable power and mystery in the ancient world.[3] The planets, incidentally, were called by the Sumerians 'the big ones that walk about', distinguishing them from the stars, 'the little ones which are scattered about like grain': both are pretty concepts.

Enshag-Inzak-Nabu-Mercury was the 'dark' god, a wise and supple deity. His name has been interpreted (again by Rawlinson) as meaning 'the nearest Lord', referring perhaps to his position as Mercury in the solar system. There is some evidence that one of Enshag-Inzak's symbols was the palm-tree; it is displayed prominently on the Durand stone where it is given particular importance. It is also very frequently represented on the Gulf seals (see Chapter 9) and it may be that it was an ideogram signifying the god's name. After all, according to the legend quoted earlier, the cultivation of the palm-tree was said to have originated in the Gulf. Rawlinson further sugges-ted that the ancient name of Bahrain might mean 'the Blessed Island', an intriguing and pleasing suggestion in the light of its significance to the Sumerians.

Rawlinson referred to the fact that in his *History* Herodotos reported Phoenician legends of their origins in which they ascribed their beginnings to the islands in the Gulf. If there is any truth in this myth at all, the far-famed ability of the Phoenicians in the arts of commerce and of navigation might reasonably have been attributed to their island origins. For if the Gulf islands did see their beginnings, they made their eventual home in Syria/Lebanon, one of the most important centres of trade of the ancient world.

It would perhaps be unwise to base any firm conviction on an Herodotean report alone. But it cannot be said too often that peoples in ancient times did cover extraordinary distances and, seemingly quite cheerfully, under-took great migrations. The founding of the Greek colonies around the Mediterranean and far into Arabia demonstrated this procedure in compara-tively late times: the Phoenicians themselves were renowned for the practice in earlier times still. It now appears not wholly improbable that the report recorded by Herodotos was based on some historical reality.[4]

The theory of 'wave-migration' has demonstrated that groups, a tribe (whatever that may be) or a congeries of more or less related families or clans, can cover vast distances over a few generations simply by advancing almost imperceptibly year by year across grazing lands or territory other than that which requires settled cultivation. If, as seems quite probable, there was a deterioration in climatic conditions in the Gulf area during the early second millennium, its people may have started to move westwards until, in a comparatively few decades, they found themselves moving up or down the Levantine coast.

DILMUN 'THE HOLY LAND'

It may be appropriate to turn aside for a moment and consider further the identification of Dilmun with Bahrain and the island with the idea of the Terrestrial Paradise. It should be said that the Sumerians did not, so far as we know, suggest that Dilmun was a place to which the spirits of the dead were translated. They had only the haziest and, as has already been demonstrated, generally pessimistic views of an afterlife. Paradise meant for them the place of origins, the site of the original and benevolent creation. The original concept of the Garden of Eden has something of the same idea.

Dilmun is the archetypal Holy Land, the first land in the world to be accorded this sacred character. Dilmun was holy ground and the legends which grew up around it all emphasize its sacred nature.

Burrows (the philologist and epigrapher who speculated so compellingly about the possible meanings of many of the toponyms associated with the study; see Chapter 2) thought that the name 'Dilmun' may be Semitic in origin, not Sumerian. He suggested that it was a 'native proto-Arab name', an interesting suggestion indeed, but one which perhaps would not attract a great deal of support today. The speculation about a pre-Sumerian language, proposed in particular by the American Sumerologist, Samuel Noah Kramer, is a consideration which has arisen since Burrows' day. Kramer believed that certain words – the names of the two great rivers of Sumer, many place names in Mesopotamia, and some of the most common terms in use in Sumerian times – were inherited from an earlier people who occupied the land before the Sumerians entered it. This language has been variously called 'proto-Euphratean' and 'Ubaidian'; however, though the words concerned do not appear to be either semitic in origin *or* Sumerian, most authorities are satisfied that the Sumerians and the people who made Ubaid pottery are one and there is no evidence of an earlier people occupying southern Iraq before the Sumerians entered it. It is puzzling, nonetheless, this intrusion of what appear to be wholly alien names, particularly those which apply to places and which we know persist over very long periods of currency and time. Whether Dilmun may be one of these pre-Sumerian names is not certain, but certainly the name is of immense antiquity.

THE EARLIEST RECORDS OF DILMUN

The first recorded mention of Dilmun, *c.* 3000 BC, appears in tablets from Uruk,[5] the city of which, some 300 or 400 years later, the great hero Gilgamesh was to be king and from which he set out on his immortal quest. A large number of tablets was recovered from the centre of the ancient city, from the ruins of the archaic temple district of Eanna. The excavations began in 1928 but it is only in recent years that some of the tablets have been recognized as mentioning Dilmun. These are the earliest written texts yet known from anywhere in the world, and it is an attestation of the importance that Dilmun represented to the Sumerians that even at this early date it appears in the city's records.

All of the references in the Uruk tablets to Dilmun seem to have a bearing, perhaps not surprisingly, on trade. One seems to refer to a tax- or, possibly,

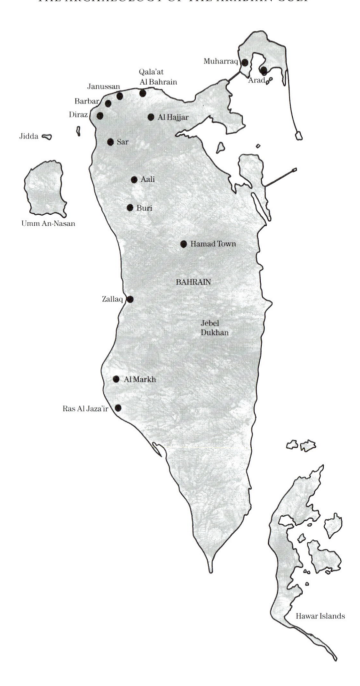

Map 2 Principal archaeological sites in Bahrain and adjacent islands.

a rent-collector – a reminder, if one were needed, of the antiquity of such professions. This is contained in one of the literary forms much favoured by the Sumerians when they were still experimenting with writing, the making of lists. The tax-collector appears in a list of the professions. There are also lists of metal objects, in which a 'Dilmun axe' is noted. Dilmun occurs in a geographical list, which would be especially interesting if it were possible to read the text more completely; it would be valuable to know, for example, the sequence in which Dilmun was listed with other places, for the Sumerians later on tidily listed places in a coherent order, according to their distance from Sumer, for example. The state of preservation of the particular tablet on which this reference appears, however, is such that it does not permit precise decipherment.

There is another mention of Dilmun which associates it with textiles, later to be one of the staple exports from Sumer in that Gulf-wide trade which Dilmun was to dominate throughout much of the third millennium and into the beginning of the second. Similarly, reference is made there to various foodstuffs, in the context of one of which there appears a somewhat mysterious figure, who seems to be 'the prince of the good Dilmun-temple'.

The exceptional antiquity of these tablets from Uruk makes them of supreme importance in the history of writing and, hence, of communication. It is especially significant therefore that the Gulf, through the medium of its most important political construct, Dilmun, should already at this early date feature in so many different contexts, suggesting that already it was a diverse, multilevelled society. These early texts provide an opportunity for observing the method of writing the sign for 'Dilmun' from the earliest, at the end of the fourth millennium BC, to the beginning of the second millennium, over a thousand years later, by which time the conventional cuneiform system was fully evolved (Fig. 7.1b, see note p. 202).

Figure 7.1b

By the time that Dilmun first appears in the records, the Sumerians had already begun to set out on extensive voyages. They used the considerable waterways which existed naturally in southern Iraq. They also sailed the waters of the Gulf and established the unusual culture which was to flourish there. In doing so, they were the inheritors of a long tradition. At some time, in the very distant past, man took to the water. No doubt his early excursions on it were involuntary, but no amount of speculation will ever disclose to us how seamanship began. All we can reasonably assume is that the real breakthrough may have come when the making of reed-boats was adopted by the people living on the banks of the Tigris and Euphrates and the lakes and marshes which were connected with them, and by those who lived in similar though more favoured circumstances on the Nile. How this remarkable discovery was made is not known, but the building of reed-boats which

147

depended on the 'wash-through' principle for their buoyancy and which would carry very considerable loads was one of the key discoveries of ancient technology. Reed-boats built to this principle also had the merit of being virtually unsinkable.[6]

Even when the Sumerians had perfected the construction of sea-going vessels of timber, the reed-boat was still the form they preferred, certainly when it came to depicting water or sea-borne voyagers. It was invariably associated with their gods, who were determined travellers. Unlike their Egyptian colleagues, however, who used boats principally for their journeys across the stars, the Sumerian gods were more inclined to use the river system for their visits to one another's cities and in the course of their godly activities.

Islands, such as Bahrain, have always been invested with a mysterious and numinous quality. Early seamen must always have recognized gratefully their presence in the middle of an otherwise hostile element; often they have been consecrated to the great goddesses who, in remote antiquity, ruled the assemblies of gods which were later to be dominated by male divinities. To the Egyptians an island was the place of beginnings: the Divine Emerging Island that first rose out of the chaos of waters forming the Abyss in which the original creator-god lay inert.[7]

All islands, if they are to fulfil their mystical character, tend to be filled with a sense of presence, of something half-glimpsed out of the corner of the eye, of sounds heard in dream, uncertainly recollected on awakening, of groves stirring with unseen and elemental forces, of Apollo or Dionysos. Though Bahrain is essentially a desert island (some four-fifths of its land surface is stark and barren desert), it nonetheless possesses this mystical quality in generous measure. There are parts of the island, near the shore at Zallaq for instance, where the mangrove and palm grew lushly, densely indeed, like primaeval jungle. It is not difficult to believe that this is what the world was like, once upon a time. To the early voyagers a landfall near these groves must have seemed like evidence of the protection of a powerful god, whose presence might be manifested at any moment.

The shoreline of Bahrain, in common with other parts of the Gulf, has advanced over the past 4,000 to 6,000 years as the level of the Gulf's waters fell. Many Neolithic sites originally on the seashore are now inland. Bahrain's main Ubaid site, at Al-Markh south of Zallaq, where sherds of Ubaid pottery have been found was, during the time it was used as an occasional camping area for small fishing expeditions, a little islet, separated from the main island of which, with the fall in the level of the Gulf, it is now a part.[8]

Bahrain is the only safe harbour between the head of the Gulf, where Sumer's seamen would have left the relative safety of their rivers and marshes, and Oman, the source of the copper which they so eagerly sought. In this voyage of some 1,000 kilometres (620 miles), Bahrain must have been singularly well-omened for them.

Bahrain has probably changed little in physical character, other than in its buildings, road systems and all the appurtenances of modernity, since the time of its first settlers. Then, as now, only the northern part of the island was fertile. Roughly in the centre of the island is its most striking natural feature, the Jebal Dukhan, the Mountain of Smoke. It could only be described as a mountain in a land which is otherwise almost wholly flat: the Jebal Dukhan may be said to tower modestly, to a height of 130 metres. In the white heat of midday it does shimmer in haze and thus may have earned its 'smoky' epithet.

On and around the mountain some of the earliest remains of Bahrain's history have been found. Here, and at sites on the coast, the hunters of the late Stone Age chipped their flints, making tools often beautiful as well as efficient.

These once-coastal sites have yielded one of the most significant of Bahrain's archaeological finds: they are the only sites in the lower Gulf from which sickle-blades have been reported.[9] This suggests that Bahrain participated in early agricultural experiments and practices with which such sickles are associated, although it may be that they were used simply for the harvesting of wild cereals and do not imply their domestication. These sickles, though they must have been somewhat inefficient, for the teeth were set in highly friable materials including earthenware, were used for gathering corn. This is demonstrated by the glitter on the sickles' teeth caused by the silica in cornstalks. Sickles of this and similar types are known from Egypt, Mesopotamia and early Palestinian settlements.

THE ARCHITECTURE OF DILMUN

Amongst the many archaeological sites of importance on Bahrain there are two outstanding ones which demonstrate undoubted links with Sumer (as indeed they do with other cultures to the south and east); one is this large and complex *tel* known as the Qala'at al-Bahrain, whilst the other lies about 6 kilometres (4 miles) further along the coast at Barbar. Many similarities in building technique, architectural detail and evident purpose proclaim their Sumerian connections, but with an important difference. Whereas in Sumer itself stone building was comparatively rare, due, reasonably enough, to the absence of local materials, the Bahrain remains are all stone-built and thus preserve more faithfully than many in Mesopotamia the format of buildings from early times. For this reason alone the Bahrain remains should warrant a reputation as some of the more important survivals from the ancient Near East. When the age of some of the Bahrain structures is considered, they deserve to be credited as amongst the most ancient of buildings indeed, for the earliest of them, particularly those at the temple site of Barbar, must have been erected not long after the first centuries of the invention of stone architecture itself.

Both sites demonstrate the importance which Bahrain must have held in the minds of the Sumerians and their successors. An interesting light is thrown by the stone-built Bahrain temples on the origins of that most familiar of Sumerian structures, the ziggurat, the stepped temple platform from which the legend of the Tower of Babel originates. The idea of the ziggurat seems to have originated in the need to keep sacred buildings clear of the flood-plain and in the very ancient Sumerian practice of regarding certain areas as irrevocably sacred.

A building erected on a sacred site was thought of as being consecrated for all time. When the mud-brick structures needed major repair or when a larger place of worship was called for, the Sumerians simply filled in the courts and chapels of the original temple, raised a mound over it and erected another building on top of it. This procedure produced a stepped effect after the second of such rebuildings. Then the idea grew until the form itself became holy and, all over Sumer and the later Babylonian and Assyrian empires, stepped and terraced ziggurats were built, on the topmost level of which was built the god's most sacred shrine. The essential, if rather obvious, fact that produced this sequence may well have been the realization that mud-brick walls cannot be reused. The destruction of the original temple was thus rationalized by preserving it for ever under the mound raised above it.

In Bahrain this did not happen, except perhaps vestigially at Barbar, because the buildings were of stone which, once it was cut and shaped, required a more intensely developed religious sense than the pragmatic Sumerians possessed, to resist reusing it.

QALA'AT AL-BAHRAIN – THE 'CITY' OF DILMUN

The mound which covers the city remains at Qala'at al-Bahrain is some 400 by 800 metres east to west, rising to a height of 15 metres. This is a very substantial area and compares favourably in scale with the *tels* of Mesopotamia which cover some of Sumer's greatest cities. Only a tiny fraction of the site – some 5 per cent of the total – has been excavated and it is possible that if the whole area were cleared an entire archaic city would be revealed. Despite the modesty of the extent of the excavations so far undertaken, assumptions about the nature of the Qala'at al-Bahrain site have not been expressed with reservation; rather, the most generous conclusions have been drawn on really very little evidence. If the site were to be properly excavated, there is no telling what might be discovered. The first 'city' located at this site was little more than a small village settlement, used principally by seamen coming, in all probability, from further to the south. Having used the shore for occasional visits and for taking on supplies, they perhaps began to put down roots, to establish families there and, eventually, to produce a settlement. Such a sequence has happened in other

Gulf sites, sometimes as the consequence of imperceptible changes in precipitation or climate.

From its position near the shore and from the visible stoneworks which lie out in the shallow water, the second of the cities on the site is probably that from which the Dilmun merchants conducted their wide-ranging trade at the beginning of the second millennium, thus perpetuating a commercial tradition already centuries old.

Five ancient (pre-Islamic) levels were established at the Qala'at al-Bahrain site by the Danish expeditions working there since 1953:[10]

1 City I, probably contemporary with immediately pre-Akkadian times (late Early Dynastic III in Sumerian terminology) c. 2400 BC.
2 City II, perhaps founded in the period following the reign of Sargon the Great, King of Sumer and Akkad, c. 2370 BC, and flourishing particularly at the end of the third and the beginning of the second millennia, c. 2000 to c. 1750 BC.
3 City III, corresponding to the Kassite period in Mesopotamia, c. 1600 BC.
4 City IV, corresponding to the Neo-Babylonian period, c. 650 BC.
5 City V, the Greek period, c. 300 BC, continuing into the early centuries of the Christian era, before the Revelation of Islam.

The second city is clearly the most important of those identified on the site. The list of settlements at the Qala'at also shows that there is little significant occupation to be detected in Bahrain before the closing centuries of the third millennium. One solitary Umm an-Nar sherd was found in the lower levels of the foundations, suggesting connections with a culture originating in Oman, whence Dilmun probably obtained the bulk of her copper.[11]

Traces of copper fragments have been found on the beach close to Qala'at al-Bahrain, lending material support to the record of Dilmun's trade, in which copper played so considerable a part.[12] Within the ruins have been found the remains of a metalsmith's forge, including a double bellows. It seems likely that Bahrain's exceptional fertility and the fact that the island was well wooded contributed to her value as a metal-working centre. Only with abundant timber could the fires have been kindled to smelt the raw copper into ingots.

The distillation of liquor also played a part in the early Dilmun economy and rooms specially designed for the pressing of date juice demonstrate the antiquity of a process which may still be seen in use in parts of Arabia. Pottery was manufactured there and inside the ruins was uncovered the workshop of a maker of the distinctive Bahrain stamp seals, the discovery of which has added a new dimension to the Gulf's archaeology and to the minor arts of the ancient world.

The walls of Qala'at al-Bahrain have survived the long ages since they were built remarkably well. In the area still uncovered today the buildings that remain date, in the most part, from the seventh century BC and, like many others in the island, are built with limestone cut from Bahrain's little neighbouring island, Jidda. Broad stairways and high gates also survive and still show the finely carved semi-circular hinge stones designed to bear the weight of massive doors. But Qala'at al-Bahrain has a history which reaches back nearly 2,000 years before this city flourished, at the very end of Dilmun's history.

The first city at Qala'at al-Bahrain was built late in the second half of the third millennium and endured until it was destroyed, probably during the twenty-fourth century BC and maybe by the conquering armies of Sargon the Great who, it will be recalled, proudly claimed Dilmun as part of his empire. When he 'washed his spears in the waters of the Gulf' he may have referred to his conquest and pillaging of the sacred island, whose ruler had presumably displayed some reluctance at being drawn into the Akkadian's empire.

This period has yielded one of the characteristic pottery types, particular to the island. These vessels are large, with a highly distinctive chain ridge decoration; a number of early seals and a handsome steatite *pyxis* engraved with geometric designs and whorls, of which other examples have been found at Barbar, were also found in the first city levels. The steatite (or, more strictly, chlorite) vessel is typical of a product found extensively in other eastern Arabian contexts, dating from earlier in the third millennium (see Chapter 8). One of the steatite vessels is intact and of fine workmanship. It had three lugs, which suggest that it may have been suspended. This, with its slightly curving sides and outline, gives it the appearance of the alabaster vessels from the Cyclades, with which it may be approximately contemporary.

Chlorite, as well as being the most popular and the most practical material for the fashioning of the Dilmun seals, was also favoured by Sumerian and Elamite craftsmen for making all kinds of vessels.[13] Its use continued for over 2,000 years with the same general profile and decoration being turned out throughout that time. One steatite pot from Bahrain has a cross engraved on it as well as the typical dotted circle which frequently runs round the rims of the pots.

From the Qala'at al-Bahrain City I, a fragmentary inscription was recovered, impressed on the inner rim of a large clay jar so that it could easily be read by tilting the pot; it gives a measure of capacity. The amount is expressed as:

2 pani 4 sar 7 qa

and has been equated to *c*. 118.8 pints.[14]

After its supposed Sargonid destruction, the city was rebuilt, but this time with a high stone rampart, presumably in the hope that its people would be secure against a second attack. At various places around the perimeter of the mound the city wall of the second foundation can be seen. Recently French excavations on the site have uncovered buildings from City II, some of them substantial in scale.

This second city probably survived until well after the turn of the third millennium and was the southern location of the *Alik Tilmun*, the guild of energetic merchants from Ur who were responsible for so much of Bahrain's ancient prosperity. More seals were found on this level as well as Indus Valley weights, which reflect the close commercial relations which existed between Bahrain and the cities of Harappa and Moenjo-Daro. There is evidence that a sophisticated customs system existed in the city. City II is thought to be contemporary with the first temples at Barbar.[15] There is no doubt that the time during which it flourished was the highest point of Bahrain's ancient prosperity and influence. Excavations have revealed what appears to be the actual harbour, dredged from the shore, which allowed ships to run close into the city.

Recent estimates of the number of burials represented by the Bahrain mound fields have also produced an estimation of the likely population of City II at the Qala'at al-Bahrain. The latest informed figure of 6,700 is based on the area occupied within the city walls; setting this figure against the population of the island as a whole, indicated by the number of burials, would suggest a total population of upwards of 60,000 inhabitants.[16] Such a population would be considerable for a small island in the third millennium.

The extensive and perplexing necropoleis of Bahrain will be described later and the point made that little enough is known of the people who were laid in the mound-tombs; however, there can be little doubt that they were the people who lived and flourished at the various cities at Qala'at al-Bahrain and at other settlements on the island. Ivory ornaments were often placed in the tombs and ivory was worked at the Qala'at al-Bahrain, for a tusk prepared for further working by an ancient craftsman has been found there.[17] In all probability the ivory came from Melukhkha, the Indus Valley region where the elephant was indigenous and much venerated, though it is possible that it was taken from the dugong, the sea-cow indigenous to the waters around Bahrain.

The next level at Qala'at al-Bahrain, the third city, appears to be contemporary with the period when the Kassites, a people from the mountains of Iran, ruled Mesopotamia. They were a rather barbarous people whose art was certainly not as distinguished as that of others among the ruling peoples of the land; however, they left their traces in Bahrain: tall, slender, roughly made pots and some of the very few cuneiform tablets yet to be found there, which are, as yet, unpublished.

A Carbon-14 date sets the destruction of City III at a median of 1190 BC ± 60 years. This reading was obtained from date stones found in the ruins, a witness to the produce (the *Sum Dilmun* in Sumerian) whose excellence identified Dilmun in the minds of the ancients as strongly as its role as the Holy Land. The 'Kassite' city was clearly handsome, with a large, rectangular palace with parallel rooms on either side of it as one of its principal monuments. It is from the later years of the Kassite period that the correspondence survives between Ili-ippasra and Ililiya (Chapter 5), who was resident in Dilmun. It may be that Ililiya's letters were sent from this place, around 1370 BC.

The fourth city was rich in finds, dating from the neo-Babylonian period. From this time, much later than the great days of Dilmun, came a hoard of silver dated, by means of a fine silver signet-ring bearing an Egyptian-style cartouche,[18] from the seventh century BC. This hoard was first thought to demonstrate links between Bahrain and the great civilization of the Nile Valley, which existed despite the two seas and the immense Arabian desert which separate them. However, later research suggests that the ring is Egyptianized Phoenician work (one of the few positive Phoenician links with Bahrain actually to be identified) and probably indicates a connection with that other great emporium of the ancient world, Byblos in the Lebanon. It was thought that the hoard had been buried deliberately, probably by a silversmith to whom it belonged, during the time of the invasions and wars in the Near East which the records of the period reveal. However, recent research has proposed that much of the silver may be an early evidence of 'money', the tokens and silver pieces that were used before the introduction of coinage.

It is this city which is open to the sky, and is approximately contemporary with Uperi, a king of Dilmun known from the Assyrian records.[19] One of the most readily identifiable remains is a large, almost square, white lime-stone pillar base, near the bottom of a flight of broad, shallow steps. Behind the pillar base a female skeleton was found in one of the terracotta, bitumen-coated 'bath-tub' coffins, reminiscent of, but in no sense connected with, the Mycenaean *larnax*. Scattered around this area other burials were discovered, including one which yielded some finely made bronze objects, including a bowl and a wine-dipper. Some of the burials were of children, their small bodies placed in simple pots.[20] Others, however, were such that a new light was cast on the beliefs and cult practices of the people of Dilmun *c.* 700 BC and on their continuity over a very long time. The cult also revealed much more ancient connections.

Sunk in the floor of the buildings were several small pits, seven of which contained the coiled skeletons of serpents. Beads were also found in close proximity to the snake burials. The discovery was made in 1957 and it set up echoes of one of the incidents in the Gilgamesh Epic (see Chapter 10), when the serpent steals from the King of Uruk the flower of eternal youth which he had wrested from the seabed after many long and perilous adventures.

In Zallaq, a small town in the centre of Bahrain's western coast, so-called 'phallic' stone pillars were discovered in 1956; they have been removed from their original location.[21] Phallic objects, like beauty, tend often to be in the eye of the beholder. Whatever these are, one now stands at Barbar, whilst the others are in Denmark waiting to be returned to Bahrain. Though they date from a much earlier period than the snake burials (probably from the third millennium or the early second) and their allegedly phallic character depends upon an entirely subjective judgement, it is tempting to associate Gilgamesh-Serpent-Fertility-Phalloi-Snake Burials all in one neat equation and postulate the existence on the island of a snake cult of great antiquity. To many of the ancients, the serpent embodied the mysterious, hidden powers of the life-giving earth. An architectural fragment from Abu Dhabi, down the Gulf from Bahrain, whose archaeology is closely linked with it, demonstrates this strongly since snake and phallus have become one[22] (see Chapter 8). French archaeologists are now excavating the neo-Babylonian city at Qala'at al-Bahrain. It is already clear that much new information will be recovered from the site in consequence.

The last level of Qala'at al-Bahrain in the pre-Islamic period, the fifth city, testifies to the extent of Bahrain's trade at the time with the Hellenistic world, for extensive finds of Attic pottery have been made there. This was the city which followed Alexander's blazing career but it has also yielded artefacts which suggest that once again the trade to India was open, demonstrated in particular by an attractive pottery figure of a girl of unmistakably Indian type.

Throughout the early history of Bahrain there is evidence, as might well be expected, of connections with cultures on the mainland of Saudi Arabia. The fifth Qala'at al-Bahrain city has, for example, produced a number of miniature altars in pottery and a fragment of a steatopygous (with abnormally fat buttocks and thighs) pottery figure which make it clear that the island shared, to some degree at least, the goddess cult then prevailing in Saudi Arabia. This was perhaps centred around Thaj, where similar material has been recovered from surface sites in the vicinity of that extensive desert city.

After this period, the Qala'at al-Bahrain site appears to have been abandoned until Islamic times. On the face of it, this long time gap seems improbable and merely points again to the importance of further excavation in the area. But, as with the written records of the island, it is Alexander and his times that close the Qala'at's record in antiquity.

Just outside the gateway of the fifth city was found a pottery jar, buried in the ground, presumably to hide it either from its owner or from potential robbers. Inside the vessel were found some 300 silver coins dating from the reign of one of the Antiochid kings, of the same house as the one for whom Berossus wrote his *Babyloniaca*.[23] The coins are magnificent, most of them seemingly uncirculated tetradrachms. They bear a portrait of Alexander himself, wearing the horned head-dress in which he is identified as Herakles, that over-muscular hero whose legend seems to have absorbed incidents from the much earlier, if also substantially legendary career of the noble Sumerian king Gilgamesh. Alexander assumed the horns after he had been recognized by the priests of Siwa as the son of the ram-headed god Amon and hence true Pharaoh of Egypt. The Alexander hoard makes a splendid terminus to the record of the cities which had been established on the island's northern shore and which had flourished there at least 2,000 years before the Macedonian's lifetime.

THE TEMPLE COMPLEX AT BARBAR

About 6 kilometres (4 miles) to the west of the Qala'at al-Bahrain lies the island's other principal site, this time one with still more striking Sumerian connections, the great temple complex of Barbar.[24] Barbar lies on the northern shore of Bahrain facing up the Gulf to Sumer; its probable significance was first suggested by Durand on his pioneering survey of the island in 1878–9, a tribute indeed to his perception.[25] The Barbar mound is just under 2 hectares in extent and at once demonstrates the size of the complex of buildings it conceals. It is now encircled by palm plantations; the second and third temples are each superimposed upon its predecessor (Fig. 7.2).

The earliest temple was built on a rectangular platform approximately 24 metres (80 feet) long and 15 metres (50–55 feet) wide which may have been enlarged at a later stage (Fig. 7.3(a)). It was surrounded by a stone wall and there were a number of small stone-built rooms on its summit surrounding an open courtyard. The temple appears to have been built on a carefully laid layer of clean sand, above which, in turn, a layer of blue clay had been put down. A further layer of sand was then piled over the mound, presumably to ensure its ritual cleanliness before building actually began. Even in its first phase, the element of water which, as will be seen, was probably the most important factor in the rituals enacted at Barbar, already appears. In the south-western corner of this early complex two staircases led down to a square-built well.

It has been suggested already that the Barbar temples have marked Sumerian connotations, though with notable differences which may well be the consequence of local Dilmunite influence. Two essentially Sumerian characteristics in relation to their sacred buildings may, however, be noted here: first, the buildings of the Barbar temples followed the practice of building over temples and shrines which had outlived their purpose or which required renewing, thus demonstrating the belief in the inalienably sacred character of a place once it had been consecrated to the service of the gods. This custom was observed when Temple II came to be built (Fig. 7.4). Temple I was largely dismantled but the central cult complex was allowed to stand and the new altars raised above it, showing this aspect of Sumerian influence at work over a period of 500 years (Fig. 7.3(b)).

The other Sumerian practice which is represented at Barbar is to be seen in the burying of 'foundation deposits', quantities of pottery and metal objects ceremonially laid in the earth at the time of building, presumably as votive

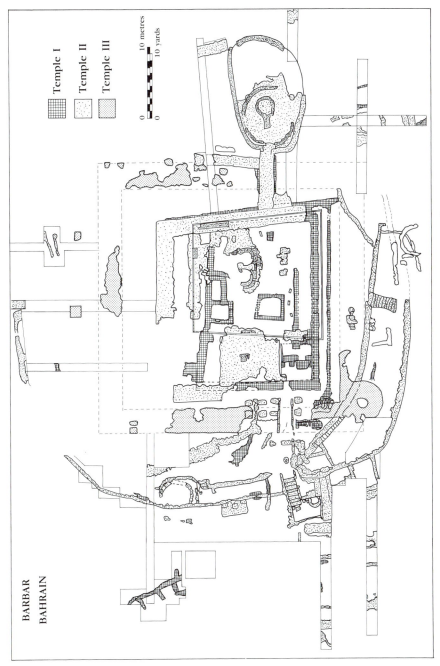

BARBAR
BAHRAIN

Temple I
Temple II
Temple III

0 ——— 10 metres
0 ——— 10 yards

Figure 7.2 A plan of the principal temple site at Barbar. The three temples date from c. 2100 BC to c.1700 BC.

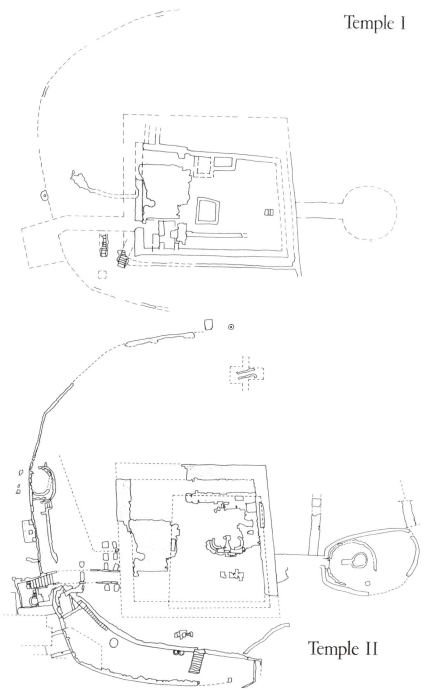

Temple I

Temple II

Figure 7.3 (a), (b) Plans of Temples I and II.

Temple III

Figure 7.3 (c) Plan of Temple III.

offerings to the chthonic gods. At Barbar the excavators found nearly a hundred conical clay beakers, all ritually broken, in the fill of the temple platform.[26] These beakers were perhaps used in a ritual feast at the time when the temple was first inaugurated. A small cylinder-shaped jar of limestone was also found under the ramp leading up to the temple.

The second temple was an extension and enlargement of the first, but it broadly followed the same design. The central platform was retained though it was raised. It marked the sacred area but it was surrounded by a lower terrace, confined by an oval wall, some 66 metres (220 feet) in length; about 27 metres (90 feet) of the outer wall still remains. To the south of the temple a wide staircase, which is still standing, led up to the oval terrace. The foot of the staircase, incidentally, marks the ground level as it then was, showing how the land has risen over the ensuing forty centuries: this area around the temple is still largely unexcavated.

An additional feature, the 'sacrificial area', was added to the complex at this time. It is to be seen to the east of the site: an oval courtyard, lying somewhat below the level of the principal terrace and reached by a gradually descending ramp. In this area was found a thick layer of ash (still indeed to be seen towards the end of the oval, to the right), which contained the burnt bones of sacrificial animals.

The most notable feature of the second temple was the sacred well, or spring, perhaps the 'Apsu' (the Abyss of subterranean waters) of Enki, which lies to the west of the platform on which the temple stands. A long staircase, now partly destroyed, led from the terrace to the well, the stone steps actually reaching down into the water (Fig. 7.5). The well, like so much of Barbar, is constructed from finely cut stone blocks, from stone brought from Bahrain's nearby island, Jidda; Temple I, on the other hand, was built from a local Bahraini stone.

That the temples, given their apparent Sumerian connections, are built largely of stone is itself of great interest: the Sumerians built in baked mud-bricks, their land being entirely bereft of stone, which in Bahrain was plentiful. Evidently the island even then possessed skilled craftsmen who could handle the fine-grained limestone, working to the designs and instructions of some unknown architect who, if not a Dilmunite (though he may well have been), knew much about the techniques of building in a material which must largely have been strange to the people who apparently inspired the temple's construction.

The second temple in use during the early centuries of the second millennium BC was larger again than its predecessors. In the centre of the site a square platform was enclosed by a massive stone wall of finely cut masonry (Fig. 7.6). Along the wall towards the west and north are remains of a room, whilst the platform itself was paved with limestone slabs. Two circular

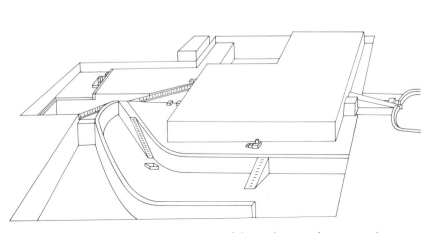

Figure 7.4 An isometric drawing of the Barbar temple construction.

Figure 7.5 The sacred well or 'Apsu' at the Barbar temple complex.

offering-tables of finely cut stone with a low altar between them still stand in the middle of the courtyard. East of the offering-tables three stone altars once stood. To the south-west, three stone blocks are standing, each pierced with a round hole. It was suggested that these were used for tethering the sacrificial animals; however, it now seems more likely that they have their nearest parallels in the stone anchors, of the type associated, for example, with the Sixth Dynasty mastaba of Mereruka, far away to the west in Saqqara, Egypt.[27]

In the north-eastern corner of the courtyard was a square pit containing rich foundation deposits, all of copper.[28] This is appropriate, since the mercantile Dilmun, the secular counterpart of Dilmun the sacred land, depended on the copper trade for its exceptional prosperity.

The third temple's terrace probably covered an area some 15 square metres (50 square feet) in extent and faced to the north (Fig. 7.3(c)). It is not known for certain whether the sacred well, and the handsome processional staircase that led to it from the temple platform built for the second temple, were incorporated into the new structure. Standing high above the surrounding buildings, which probably clustered around its walls and the landscape in which the whole complex was set, the temple, gleaming white, would have been impressive indeed.

One curious survival from the third temple may still be seen in the gypsum mortar or *juss* which was used to bond the stones in the wall foundations on the west side of the upper terrace and on the floor of another building to the north-west of the main temple. The print of a large naked foot is clearly impressed in the mortar.[29] A number of footprints and some handprints have been found in the temple area; there are also the paw-marks of a dog, showing that even in such remote times, where men were, dogs were close by. The foot was one of the most frequently employed symbols in the iconography of the Dilmun seals which are described later in this survey. However, there is no evidence of whether the footprints at Barbar are deliberate or merely the consequence of chance, the footsteps of a workman on the site, perhaps preserved by accident for the past 4,000 years. The connection between the Bahraini temples and springs of fresh water is clear. In the case of Barbar three conduits provide outflows, perhaps, to the rather Shakespearian idea of 'the three corners of the world'. It may be that the building of temples over important springs relates also to the management of water resources which, in various forms, has long been a preoccupation of the people of the peninsula and the Gulf. The *falaj*, the stone-built

Figure 7.6 The platform on which the second temple at Barbar stood.

water conduit, probably originally of Iranian origin, is familiar to anyone who has known the Gulf in the recent past. In Bahrain water conduits were called qanats; the qanats were generally subterranean. In Oman, where it is still to be found, the *falaj* conduit runs above the surface. In Oman, too, in the country districts the auctioning of water still takes place. In antiquity it would be entirely consistent with the view of how the world was managed for the distribution of water to be in the hands of the priests, supported by the temple administrations. It would certainly give support to the clearly very important position which Enki, the god of the sweet, subterranean waters, occupied in the minds of the Sumerians and, in all probability, of the people of the Gulf too.

Many of the objects which have been recovered from Barbar are of very fine quality indeed and testify eloquently to the high standard of culture which flourished in Bahrain in the third millennium BC. Barbar produced a very distinctive type of pottery (now known as 'Barbar ware'), which was first identified on the site. It can be recognized easily by its marked horizontal ridging.

The Sumerians respected the tools of the trades which the people practised. Gods were placed in charge of them and poems celebrated their qualities. It is not surprising therefore to find at Barbar, in the second temple deposit, a copper axe and a copper adze, the one concerned with building, the other with agriculture.[30]

Copper 'models' of spearheads and crescent-shaped shaft-hole axes were found in the fill of the central platform, as well as beads of marble, lapis lazuli and carnelian. Lapis was one of the products frequently identified with Dilmun; it was traded as far as Egypt but its only known source is away to the east at Badakhshan, in Afghanistan. A small strip of gold was also found in the deposit.[31]

Some of the most attractive products of ancient Bahrain recovered from the Barbar site are examples of the stamp seals which are so specially identified with Bahrain and the Gulf at this time. Several seals were found at Barbar, including a group from the sacred well itself. It has been suggested[32] that these were thrown into the well in some sort of ritual act, presumably to draw to the attention of the resident divinity, Enki himself no doubt or Enshag his son, the needs and aspirations of the seals' owners.

The seals all come from the second temple levels. They are of the developed type characteristic of Bahrain and Failaka at the end of the third millennium and the early years of the second.[33] This was the time of Dilmun's commercial greatness and the seals, in all probability, are the 'trade marks' of merchant companies and families based in Bahrain but trading with Sumer in the north, Oman in the south and, to the east, the great Indus Valley cities such as Moenjo-Daro and Harappa (see Chapter 8) (Fig. 7.7).

A particularly fine pottery sherd also survives which shows the impression of a Dilmun seal very clearly (Fig. 7.8).[34] This was found in the well

Figure 7.7 A group of the characteristic seals from Bahrain at the beginning of the second millennium, recovered from the sacred well at Barbar.

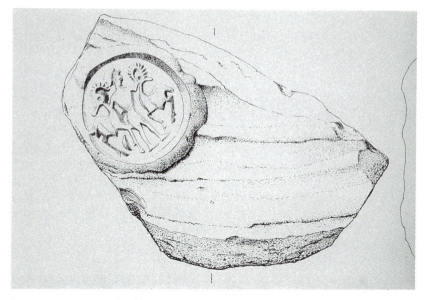

Figure 7.8 A pottery sherd bearing the impression of a Dilmun seal. The design is of great antiquity; versions of it are found throughout Mesopotamia, Elam and from as far away as Egypt.

at Barbar, and shows a heroic figure grasping two animals by their necks, exercising his will over them.

This design is of great antiquity. It is known from late fourth-millennium Sumer, from south-western Iran, where some authorities believed it originated and, far away to the east, from Egypt.[35] There its presence in late Predynastic times, at the end of the fourth millennium, has prompted speculation about the extent of influences from the Gulf and Mesopotamia which Egypt experienced at the time immediately before the unification of the two Kingdoms of the Nile Valley, under the first kings of Egypt. It was remarked earlier that some authorities, including Petrie, have believed that Mesopotamian influences came to Egypt by the intervention of 'the islanders of the Persian Gulf'.[36]

Another Gulf seal shows a heroic figure dominating, in the same manner, two huge scorpions. The use of this same motif in this unlikely context suggests that it was of great significance in early antiquity.

Music was a notable feature of all Sumerian religious ceremonies. Many representations of musical performance have come down to us, including some pleasing scenes featuring animals as the musicians. But in the temple ceremonies at Barbar we must assume that solemn and sonorous melodies would have risen from the courtyards, to charm the gods. The chanting of the priests was no doubt matched by the sound of pipes, harps, flutes and percussion instruments, including drums, rattles and something very like modern castanets.

This concern of Sumerian ritual with music is hinted at in Barbar. Amongst the deposits of the second temple was a small copper rattle, perhaps from the percussion department of an ancient orchestra; it was associated with the most important and handsome find of all, a majestic bull's head, finely cast in copper.[37] Though it is supposition, it is possible that this fine piece ornamented the sounding-box of a Sumerian lyre, of the type which was found in the great death-pit at Ur and so miraculously preserved by Sir Leonard Woolley. Stringed instruments bearing richly adorned animal heads were characteristic of Sumerian temple and royal ceremonies and it is certainly possible that the Barbar bull-head served this pleasant purpose. A Dilmun seal from Failaka, which from the beginning of the second millennium was part, in all probability, of Dilmun's 'empire', shows a bull-headed lyre of just this sort (Fig. 7.9).[38]

The artefacts recovered from Barbar are among the most important to be found anywhere in the Gulf; they contribute much to an understanding of the religious practices and beliefs of the Dilmunites of 4,000 years and more ago. Within the precincts of the first and most ancient temple was a double line of cut stone blocks, eight in all, set by the temple's western side. Cut into the blocks' upper surfaces were two square holes (in one case, three holes) which were originally lined with a copper sheeting, bonded to the

Figure 7.9 A Dilmun seal (from Failaka island) which shows a bull-headed lyre and an enigmatic scene which may be of the sacrifice of a second bull.

stone with bitumen. Through the copper, nails had been driven, their points inwards and in some cases with wood still adhering to them. It seems likely that they were either the supports for wooden columns or for the bases of wooden statues: the third hole in one of the blocks could be explained as having secured a staff or wand carried by one of the figures. On the side of one of the blocks two figures of men are roughly carved, one with down-turned arms, the other with his arms raised, the fingers of each hand splayed out.[39] This particular block seems now to have left the site; it was not found when the temples were re-excavated in 1983.

Though the remains of the second temple are much the best preserved and extensive on the site, the third temple at Barbar was probably architecturally the most complex and sophisticated. By the time it was built the consecrated area, the main sanctuary, was raised high above the surrounding landscape. A double circular stone plinth supported the temple's principal altars with, facing them, a stone seat or throne with a libation altar before it. A pit of offerings, stone-lined and thus deliberately built as an integral part of the temple, like its Sumerian parallels, was found beyond this altar and in it were alabaster vases, the copper figures of a naked worshipper, perhaps a priest (which may originally have served as a handle of a mirror) and of a bird. Three of the alabaster vases were virtually in perfect condition, the others in fragments: similar ones have been discovered at Ur and can be ascribed to the end of the third millennium.[40] A large well, associated with the third temple, has not yet been excavated.

An extensive collection of the horizontally ridged type of pottery, which is now known as Barbar after its find-site, has been recovered; the other most distinctive Bahraini pottery is the 'chain-ridge' ware. Some of this pottery would seem to have been exported to Sumer, for examples have been found in Early Dynastic tombs in Ur. A stone vessel decorated with concentric circles is also similar to others found in Ur burials of the same period.[41]

As would be expected in what appears to have been the most important sanctuary on an island whose ancient economy was derived, to a significant degree, from the copper trade, a considerable number of copper (and later, bronze) artefacts has been recovered from Barbar. Among them were numerous arrowheads of a type which once again recalls similar examples from Ur, and a quantity of copper axeheads. Many of the axes recovered from Bahraini sites are purely votive and could never have been functional. The 'Dilmun axe', it will be remembered, appeared in the earliest inscription relating to the land at the end of the fourth millennium.[42]

The presence at Barbar of the fine bull- or ox-head mentioned earlier, with its great upcurving horns, provides an echo of that remote time when the predecessors of the Sumerians were beginning to develop the most important characteristics of their splendid and beneficent culture. The bull- or ox-head, the 'bucranium', is one of the earliest pictographs and was used to symbolize, reasonably enough, an ox. This sign appears on the earliest tablets of what was to develop into formal writing: the early pictographs developed successively through abstractions of the original ox-head shape to the final cuneiform characters.[43] The ox-head is also the ancestor of the *aleph* and the *alpha* and, ultimately, of the Roman *a*.

The bucranium was a powerful symbol from as early as the Anatolian settlement of Çatal Hüyük on the Konya plain. There, bull-heads were set up as elements in the design of the shrines which were so important a feature of this little proto-'city'.[44] Similarly, Egypt honoured the bull-head; in one of the First Dynasty royal tombs at Saqqarah a number of bulls' skulls were placed on a low platform at the sides of the tomb of a great noble of the reign of King Den.[45] Queen Her-Neith, again of the First Dynasty, was also buried in a tomb decorated with the skulls of bulls.[46]

In the Gulf the bucranium appears frequently as a motif on the seals which are peculiar to the culture of the region. The bucranium was, from the very earliest period, a favoured motif in Mesopotamian design, where it underwent many refinements and adaptations, moving from the naturalistic to a more and more abstract interpretation, a development which was repeated in its progress from pictograph to cuneiform. It is particularly striking in the beautiful, very early pottery from Halafian sites in northern Mesopotamian sites: in a stylized form it is also found in the repertory of Ubaid potters and painters.

THE DIVINITIES OF BARBAR

It is possible only to speculate about the god or gods who were worshipped at Barbar. Although the most important divinity to be worshipped in Dilmun was probably Enki, other Sumerian deities were identified with the island. Thus, Inanna was worshipped in a temple at Ur called E-Dilmun-na, commemorating her links with the island.[47] Dilmun was a land of the gods, and it is not surprising, therefore, that majestic temples should have been set up there in their honour, though the sheer number of them in so small and remote an island is deeply puzzling. The kings of Sumer congratulated themselves on their piety in restoring the temples when they fell into decay. Warad-Sin (second half of the nineteenth century BC), in a long inscription in Ur which refers to E-Dilmun-na, says:

> For Inanna the lady clad in great splendour wielding all the powers, eldest daughter of Sin, his lady: Warad-Sin, the prince who favours Nippur, nourisher of Ur, who takes thought for Girsu with Lagash, who reverences E-barra, King of Larsa, King of Sumer and Akkad, the strong one who seeks out the [divine] oracles and executes their purpose, who builds anew the house of the gods, am I: on whom Enki

bestowed a wide understanding to perform the duties of the City. Because of this, for Inanna my lady, with my prayer [I restored] E-Dilmun-na her dwelling of rest and of heart's delight. That the eye might see and its interior might be liked I enlarged its area more than before. Unto days to come for my life I built it: its head I raised and made like a mountain. Over my works may Inanna my lady rejoice. Length of days, years of abundance, a throne securely based, a sceptre to subdue the people as a gift may she grant me.[48]

E-Dilmun-na seems always to have been of special significance to the Sumerians, again perhaps because of the nature of Dilmun itself. If it was 'the place of assembly' of the people, and not only of their gods, on their journey to Sumer, this is understandable enough. The cult centre of Sin-Nanna was at Ur, at the edge of the desert out of which poured perpetually floods of wild nomads who variously threatened and were absorbed by the Sumerian cities, eventually enriching them immeasurably but at the expense of their survival. Sin-Nanna was one of the greatest of the gods and many cities other than Ur honoured him with temples and shrines. The successive levels of Sin temples found at Khafajah show that, from the earliest times, the moon-god was a divinity to whom worship was elaborately given. It has been observed that the moon is the prototype of the universal god to desert people and that the Semitic tribes followed this belief. Moon temples were built by the pre-Islamic Arabs who, like their ancestors, considered the planet mild and beneficent, an understandable view for a people who had to endure the daily torments of the sun at its height. Thus, it is argued, Sin-Nanna would naturally be a god of special significance and affection to the people of the desert as they first settled in the city of Ur, on the desert's fringe.

TEMPLE OVALS

In the light of the discovery of a temple at Barbar in Bahrain, which is very similar in at least one important respect to the temple built to the glory of Sin in Khafajah, it is interesting that a fragment from a hymn to the moon-god speaks of 'the temple [Sagnamsar] which is the mount of Dilmun'. It seems wholly possible that this refers to a temple complex in Dilmun, perhaps that at Barbar itself. Whilst the hymn is addressed to Sin-Nanna, some commentators have seen the divinity being celebrated as the ubiquitous Enki. This view is strengthened by one interpretation of Sagnamsar as meaning that it is consecrated to the Benefactor of Writing, an appropriate epithet for the god of wisdom.[49]

However, it is not only in Mesopotamia that oval-terraced temple structures are to be found. In Upper Egypt, at Hierakonpolis, an oval revetment contains a roughly square temple enclosure, a combination of features strikingly un-Egyptian; indeed, the Hierakonpolis temple is unparalleled in the whole of Egypt.[50]

Hierakonpolis was the original capital of the line of princes which was credited, throughout Egyptian history, with the unification of the Nile Valley Kingdoms. It was the location of the richly endowed 'Main Deposit', which contained such artefacts as the Nar-mer Palette (on which there are iconographic elements like the powerful man mastering lions which is also to be found in the Gulf and which originated in Western Asia) and a superb golden falcon-head. It was also at Hierakonpolis that the celebrated painted tomb 'Tomb 100' was found; its walls were plastered and painted with a sequence of vignettes, many of which are echoed in the design compendium of the Gulf, though a millennium later.[51]

There is too great a gap between the accepted date of the Hierakonpolis examples (c. 2800 BC at the generally accepted latest estimate) and the Gulf examples (c. 2000 BC at the earliest) for the conclusion to be reached that they are in some direct way associated. Their appearance in both cultures is, however, puzzling and highly suggestive, given their very distinctive character and their precise duplication.

Two recent studies on the meaning of the name 'Barbar' are of interest in that, whilst both of them point to quite different conclusions, each suggests that the origin of the name may reach back to the time when the temples themselves were flourishing. 'Barbar' is not an Arabic word: its meaning must therefore be sought elsewhere.

One study[52] suggests that 'Barbar' may convey the meaning 'foreigners': this would imply that the builders of the temples were not indigenous to Bahrain and were identified by the local Dilmunites as such. However, the same authority goes on to note that Samaš, the sun-god, a significant divinity in Sumer and, like Enki, generally well disposed to man, was worshipped in the Sumerian city of Larsa in temples called *e-babbar*, which, he notes, is usually translated as the 'White House'. In Sumerian *bab bar* also meant 'sunrise' and Dilmun was celebrated as the Land of Sunrise.

Several of the Bahraini sites known to date, which have as their most prominent element a temple or important shrine, prompt questions about the sacred and particular character of the island in Sumerian times. All Sumerian cities were built around the temple, which, in most cases, was the original reason for their being brought into existence. The process of city-making is complex and various: in the case of the Sumerian proto-cities it seems likely that they began as cult centres, serving the needs of a group of villages and settlements of which the city in its beginnings formed the nucleus. The city was consecrated to one or several of the gods; it belonged to them. No city was ever built without its temple.

In the city built at the site of the Qala'at al-Bahrain, all the buildings so far excavated there are secular, consecrated to trade rather than to the honour of the gods, with the exception of one large hall which bears some resemblance to the style of temple structures. Yet Dilmun was a land of temples; such areas in the north of the island that have as yet been surveyed confirm the presence of many large structures and each site that has been excavated, other than the tomb fields, has produced a crop of sacred buildings. In the region of Barbar, for example, there is little doubt that further excavations will produce more temples.

The explanation, of course, may lie in the reputation for exceptional sanctity that the entire island enjoyed.[53] It was the whole island, perhaps, that was the cult centre, consecrated for ever to the High Gods. The waters encompassed it instead of the walls of other, land-locked centres. Within its sea-girded walls everything would have been sacred, the equivalent of the *temenos*, the sacred enclosure in every Sumerian city. If the main temple was located at Barbar (and indeed if it does not still await discovery) 6 kilometres (4 miles) or so from the city, this would not have been a material consideration; city and temples alike would all have been contained within the island's own holy precincts. In truth Dilmun was the first, the archetypal Holy Land, the place of assembly not only of the people but of the gods.

THE ARCHITECTURE OF BARBAR

The architecture of Barbar temples reveals a high standard of technical competence, particularly in the careful shaping of the ashlar blocks from which the structures and the great well or bath were built. The area of sacrifice contained a number of blocks which, when assembled, formed two circular structures; around the temples a wall was built which also curved gently at its corners. Parts of the ashlar walls demonstrate one interesting characteristic: an irregular shaping of the stone courses which fit into each other, a technique of strengthening stone walls more typical of Egypt in the third millennium than of Sumer. Indeed, the assurance with which stone is handled both at Qala'at al-Bahrain and at Barbar is reminiscent more of the authority with which Egyptians built than of the work of Sumerian architects. However, the technique of stone-building at Barbar and some of the other early second-millennium sites also recalls the methods of using relatively small, cut stones in the earlier architecture from Umm an-Nar and it is very probably from this direction that Bahrain's architectural traditions came.

The ashlar stonework, large and finely cut blocks, at Barbar is characteristic of the later temples; in the first structure the stones are small, packed together tightly. They suggest an unfamiliarity with the properties of stone on a large scale: indeed, they have prompted speculation whether they may not represent the work of craftsmen who were only beginning to find their way in its use, in contrast with the assurance with which the later monumental courses are handled.[54]

The site at Barbar is certainly the most important in the Arabian Gulf yet to be discovered. It was first uncovered by the Danes between 1955 and 1963;[55] after its first clearance the site was backfilled for its protection. It was then decided, in 1983, to clear its previously excavated areas and to conserve the remains as a monument, so that visitors could comprehend something of its extent and significance. This has now been achieved, under the control of Bahrain's Department of Antiquities.[56]

OTHER BAHRAIN SITES

There are many other sites of archaeological importance in Bahrain. There is an increasing awareness of their significance amongst the archaeological community, alerted originally by the Danish excavations.

One such site, at Umm es-Sejour, 1.5 kilometres (a mile) to the west of Diraz, has produced some unexpected finds, which may bear upon the question of the religious character of the island. The site is a small well-temple which achieved a later celebrity when, according to legend, the Caliph Abdul Malik Ibn Marwan, incensed at the Bahrainis' reversion to their ancient gods in the early years of Islam, invaded the island and destroyed the well as a punishment for the people's heterodoxy.[57] However, long before this, there was a sacred building here and in its ruins were found the headless statues of two stone animals. They were probably the ornaments of a portal or the decoration of a shrine built in the high days of Dilmun's influence, in the late third millennium before our era; carved in limestone, the animals have been decapitated by some zealot who, presumably, disapproved enough of them to wish to ensure their ritual 'killing'.

Considerable interest had been kindled in 1971 in archaeological circles by the identification of Ubaid pottery on eastern Arabian sites principally at Ain Qannas, Dosariyah and Abu Khamis.[58] The Arabian sites had been expertly and professionally excavated: Ubaid pottery had been found at Al-Da'asa, at Ras Abaruk, Dukhan and in the region of Bir Zikrit in Qatar.[59] Up to this point no such very early pottery had been found in Bahrain.

In 1973 a small British team was sent to Bahrain to work on three sites which had previously been identified as being likely to repay effort. These were Al-Markh, Diraz East, near the 'Well of the Bulls' dug by the Danes in the 1950s, and a later site at Jannusan North. The initiative for this expedition was taken by the committee formed in the aftermath of the 1970 Conference (see Chapter 2). The British worked in Bahrain from 1973 until 1978.[60]

AL MARKH

The British team selected Al-Markh as a consequence of some sherds having been found on the surface of the site and identified as Ubaid in 1971.[61] Al-Markh lies inland from the west coast, south of the village of Zallaq. It is a low, sand-covered mound and north and east of it are *sabkha*, the treacherous flats where evaporation has produced a fragile crust of impacted sand. There are considerable quantities of flint and of fish and other animal bones scattered about.

The expedition found and excavated a number of what they believed to be fire pits used for the preparation of food. They detected two phases on the site, the earlier one when fish were predominantly represented in the remains and a later one when mammal bones became significant and when meat evidently formed an important part of the diet of the site's occupants. The animals represented included the Bahrain hare, which still lives around the site, the dugong, the sea-cow which breeds in the bay between Bahrain and Qatar, and, most frequently, the goat. A change in the technique of catching fish was suggested to the excavators by the fact that in the earlier levels the fish species tended to be small whilst in the later ones they were generally larger and 'included more carnivorous fish'. It was suggested that these 'may have been caught by hook and line, by harpoon or by bow and arrow'. A greater density of flints would have been needed to butcher the larger mammals and larger fish than would have been required for the small species.[62]

A statistical analysis of the pottery sherds found at Al-Markh led to the conclusion, at first sight surprising, that only in the earlier occupations of the site had pottery been used. The sherds are painted and are dated to *c.* 3800 BC.[63]

It seems most likely that there was no permanent settlement at Al-Markh at this early fourth-millennium date, but rather that it was occupied seasonally by hunters or fishermen coming from some other place, possibly from southern Mesopotamia and from the contemporary Arabian sites which also had access to Ubaid pottery. The somewhat higher level of the Gulf at the time would have meant that Al-Markh would have been a small island. It would be interesting to know more about the people who used the site then and, particularly, of how and by what means they sailed to the island, presumably from the Arabian shore, some 20 kilometres away. But of this sort of information, not surprisingly, the little site at Al-Markh, sparse even by the most austere standards of desert archaeology, communicates nothing.

DIRAZ EAST

Diraz East, the other important site to be dug by the British expedition,[64] is part of a substantial third-millennium settlement in the fertile northern sector of the island. It has always been fertile and has been inhabited consistently at least since the Barbar period. An isolated Ubaid sherd was found there.

What appear to be the remains of an important building was described by its excavators as 'a temple'; since a partly destroyed altar was

Figure 7.10 A small, evidently sacred building at Diraz East, notable for the large columns which presumably supported some substantial upper storey.

found in the remains of the building, this seems reasonable enough (Fig. 7.10). The building itself is notable for the rows of large columns which originally stood inside it. There was a large stone and mortar basin adjacent to the building, though this was suspected of being later in date than the building itself, perhaps of the Late Babylonian period. Sherds from pottery of this time were found and in one of the rooms the burials of at least five persons, dating from Late Babylonian times, were discovered. A 'snake bowl', like the ones from the Qala'at al-Bahrain, was found but it was empty. Two crude stamp seals were also found.[65]

Because of its value as an agricultural area, many of Diraz's ancient sites have been disturbed. The discovery of the temple at Diraz East is significant, however, for if it is third millennium in origin, then it is quite unlike any other building of the period known from Bahraini sites. Interestingly, if only because of the frequency with which the creature is portrayed on Dilmun seals, Diraz is notorious for the number of scorpions which abound there and which, even now, make excavation difficult.[66] To this day the scorpion, so often shown circling the seals and in the designs they display, seems to guard Diraz from intruders.

A brief excavation was conducted by the British Expedition at Aali East which uncovered a double-chambered tomb of the seventh century BC.

Though the tomb had been conscientiously robbed in antiquity, three seals have been overlooked. A cylinder seal, dating to c. 650 BC, is of neo-Babylonian form. A stamp seal with the round boss on the reverse is obviously derived from the much earlier Dilmun seals and may, the excavators suggest, have been an heirloom or a treasured possession of whoever took it with them into the tomb.

THE BURIAL MOUNDS

Little has yet been said about the people who lived on the island during the long centuries of its most expansive period. This is for the simple reason that little is known of them: very few remains have been found outside the principal sites, and little evidence of how the people lived. From examinations of their skeletal remains, it seems probable that they were a healthy people, somewhat taller than their present-day successors, and relatively long-lived, a quality entirely appropriate for the island of the gods, where all had once been perfection.[67]

Remarkably, the Dilmunites of the third and second millennia appear to have practised dentistry of a quite sophisticated order.[68] A number of skulls have produced evidence of carious teeth extracted in life. Only the Egyptians could claim a comparable clinical technology so early: Hesy-re, a Third Dynasty nobleman buried at Saqqarah, was, amongst his other attainments, a dentist, as recorded in his tomb.[69] The early Dilmunites had a diet high in carbohydrates, notably the dates for which Dilmun was famous, and in consequence suffered from caries. All the early inhabitants, on the evidence of their skulls, were Caucasoid.

Whilst it may be said that there is comparatively little known of how men lived in Bahrain, there is abundant evidence of how they were treated after death. The last of Bahrain's major archaeological phases, which at its earliest probably overlapped with the later centuries of the Sumerian period, is represented by its gigantic graveyards.

The earliest mound burials in Bahrain appear to be of the same architectural design as those built in Umm an-Nar, in Abu Dhabi (Fig. 7.11). These date from the middle of the third millennium and may represent the burials of the first settlers in Bahrain.

To judge from the Ziusudra episode in the Epic of Gilgamesh (Chapter 10), it would not be unreasonable to suppose that, in addition to its sacred and mercantile characters, Dilmun was conceived as an island of the dead, a prototype of that strange and evocative concept of the mortuary isle which looms, shrouded in mist and lapped by the water of death, in so many later mythologies. Whilst there is no doubt that the island's city could provide a substantial number of candidates for the tombs over the centuries, it is only very recently that anyone has attempted to compute the likely numbers buried in the island and from that to extrapolate the inhabitants of the city.[70]

From these studies it appears that a population of 4,500 people will, over a period of 1,000 years, account for 128,000 dead. The figure of 4,500 is probably low as the mean for the Dilmunite population during the time of its greatest prosperity; the island could thus easily provide the numbers required to fill the grave mounds.

Whilst it may be tempting to think that Dilmun may have been like Abydos in Egypt or, more recently, Kerbala in Iraq (as Durand proposed), widely recognized as a desirable place in which to be buried, there is no evidence of the dead being brought to Dilmun for burial. It must in consequence be assumed that most of those buried there are native to the island. But the presence of similar tombs on the mainland suggests that there must have been some sort of mortuary cult in Dilmun as a whole. There is, of course, nothing to prevent the island and mainland Dilmun serving both as a place to which the dead were brought and as a flourishing mercantile kingdom with a substantial population who lived on the profits of its many-faceted trade. Indeed, it has been suggested that some of the prosperity which was so evident a feature of life in Dilmun may have been the consequence of the stream of visitors who came to the island to bring their dead to its holy shores.[71] There are, after all, plenty of parallels for such practical benefits from the exercise of religion. Nothing, however, has ever been found in the mound burials in Bahrain to suggest that the occupants of the tombs were foreigners to Dilmun.

It has now been calculated that there may be at least 170,000 tombs in the Bahrain deserts.[72] The fields of tumuli create a curious undulating effect in the desert, stretching on and on to the horizon. So closely packed are they that it would now often be difficult to build a new one between the ancient mounds. Many today are broken hillocks of rubble and sand collapsed on their stone-lined chambers, and are sometimes difficult to recognize. Others still rise to more dramatic heights, their contours firm but with their sepulchral chambers empty; in one group, at Aali village, some of the mounds still stand over 12 metres (40 feet) high with a diameter of more than 30 metres (100 feet). There is still some debate on the structure of the mounds in antiquity. Some authorities have it that they show today the general shape in which they were built, rounded mounds of sand and rubble raised over a stone-built interior.[73] Others take the view, which is gaining support, that the mounds were enclosed within high ring-walls;[74] in some cases a form of terracing has been identified, recalling both the Mesopotamian ziggurat and the earliest mastaba tombs and pyramids in Egypt, which were stepped or terraced. If the mounds were enclosed with stone walls rising to the substantial height which the diameter of the mounds as they exist today would suggest, they would have been formidable monuments.

The great tombs at Aali, which are further described below, are generally thought to have conformed to this architectural form, which is otherwise unknown from any other Near Eastern site. Interestingly, Mackay, when he visited Bahrain in 1926[75] and surveyed the Aali mounds, came to the conclusion both that they were originally of a considerable height and that terracing was a feature of the smaller mounds which were contemporary with them. They were, in effect, funerary towers.

There seems to have been something of a preoccupation with towers amongst the architects of monumental buildings in the Gulf in antiquity. The Aali tombs are towers, and towers were built, for defensive purposes, from very early times in Oman. At the other end of the Gulf, on Failaka island, a high tower near the shore would have been visible to seamen approaching the island from far off (see Chapter 8).[76]

The tumulus fields of Bahrain are of immense proportions, extending over 3 square kilometres (2 or more square miles); they are widely scattered over the island, even extending down to the desert lands of the south. The larger proportion of the mounds comes from the time of Dilmun's height of prosperity, from the end of the third millennium and the beginning of the second. Two principal types have been identified: the earlier without capstones, the later with them. Some underground burials have also been found and there seems to have been a return to mound building in Hellenistic times. Various forms of structure have been identified: the earliest small

Figure 7.11 The occupant of a grave of Umm an-Nar type at Medinet Hamed; third millennium BC.

and compact with corbelled roofs a metre (3 feet) in height, and the later, much larger tumuli with provision for multiple burials, probably, in effect, family mausolea, or the resting-places of people linked by clan ties.[77]

The doorways of the tombs, high and strongly built, tend to be turned towards the west, looking towards the region where the sun dies. The dead generally lie with their heads towards the north-east; often the hands of the dead are placed in front of the face. Perhaps the occupants of the tombs were, like the Egyptians, able thus to enjoy the sunset when, gathering at the doorways of the tombs, their spirits could daily watch the sun set out upon the journey which they had already taken. The westerly orientation of the tombs suggests elements of a solar faith and the recognition of the sun's divinity, and it will be recalled that Utu, the sun-god of the Sumerians, lived in Dilmun. It has also been suggested[78] that the entrances to the tombs are aligned to Venus at sunset, recalling the supposed stellar orientation of the shafts of the pyramids at Giza, where, when they were built, the light of the Pole Star may have shone directly down them.

It is curious that tumulus or mound burials are found in a great arc from the Near East to Ireland, and in parts of northern Europe the mounds heaped up over the graves of chieftains assumed a size and splendour equalled only by the tholos tombs of the Mycenaeans, the pyramids of the Kings of Egypt or the huge mound-towers of the Dilmunite rulers. The tholos itself may have originated in Western Asia, where houses in the forms of tholoi are known from northern Iraq, though the evidence comes from so early a period that it must be uncertain.

The mound burials also recall the great structures of the European Early and Middle Bronze Ages, the megaliths, the groups of standing-stones which, often following the meander or the circle, are said to represent the Mother Goddess. Stonehenge is the most celebrated of them, whilst Avebury and Carnac are almost of comparable significance and power; with them earth burials are invariably associated. Even the pyramids, those most titanic of all funerary monuments, may have originated, in the opinion of some scholars, in the little mounds of sand heaped over the modest graves of Predynastic chieftains.[79]

The Bahrain tumuli are generally stone-lined, with well-cut blocks, and are designed to make a secure resting-place for the dead. Behind the building of such permanent burial places lies the belief in the continued survival of the individual after death, although this is not a belief typical of all early Semitic peoples, many of whom seem rather to have believed in the extinction of all personality once death had ended the earthly existence.

Until recent years only a few of the Bahrain mounds had been opened professionally, except by that long-established group, the robbers of tombs. It would be very unlikely that many (if indeed any) of such obvious monuments, built with no attempt to conceal them, could have escaped depredation. But from the fragmentary remains that have been found scattered in the tombs it is possible to reconstruct some idea of what they originally contained.

Usually the body was placed either on its side in the attitude of sleep or seated, facing the tomb's entrance. The extreme humidity of the Bahrain climate has not allowed the survival of human remains other than bones and skulls, usually fragmented and scattered – the work of the small desert creatures which live among and inside the tombs.

There are few hints of the riches the tombs might once have contained. Certainly much pottery has been recovered, indicating a ritual of placing offerings or providing the means of sustaining the spirit after death. Copper and bronze artefacts, swords, daggers and dress ornaments have all left their traces in the tombs. A fairly high degree of material luxury is indicated by the ivory which has sometimes been found amongst the debris of the tombs, suggesting in at least one case that the corpse was laid upon a bed decorated with ivory carvings and ornaments. One little ivory figurine, itself fragmentary, has been found: a girl, slender-waisted and wide-hipped, her latter feature recalling, though in a greatly refined degree, the steatopygous figures of the goddess from early times, which were carved with monstrously enlarged thighs and buttocks.[80] It seems likely that many such small statues were placed in the tombs: the torso of another was found by one of the early excavators in Bahrain. They may have been representations of the dead, guardian divinities, or servants.

In one Bahraini tomb, excavated by Mackay in 1925, some very curious ivory objects were found. They appeared to be wands or sceptres which seemed to have been broken deliberately and cast into the tomb.[81] What significance the broken wands held is unknown: perhaps their destruction marked the dead man's final break with this world. Similar ivory wands have been found in the Indus Valley.

In several of the tombs the remains of what appeared to be ivory caskets were discovered amongst other ivory fragments, including spindle-whorls, so decayed, however, that it was virtually impossible to reconstruct them, or to guess what they once contained.[82]

The examination of the ivories found in the Bahraini tombs originally produced the view, which was frequently asserted, that they were of Phoenician workmanship. However, the Phoenicians flourished much later than the time when the Bahraini tumuli were built; it is likely that the ivories are simply another link with the cities of Sumer for, whilst little has remained, due to the climate of southern Mesopotamia, it is known that ivory was widely used in the cities and that it was recorded as one of the important goods trans-shipped through Dilmun. It must be remembered, too, that much ivory was imported through Dilmun from the Indus Valley. Another possibly Sumerian connection has been provided by the quantity of bronze pins found in the tombs, similar to those with which the

Mesopotamians fixed their characteristic 'buns', the most common coiffure favoured by them in the latter centuries of their existence.[83]

THE 'ROYAL TOMBS' AT AALI

At Aali village, now the centre of a local pottery industry, is the most remarkable group of tombs in Bahrain, concentrated together within a relatively compact area (Fig. 7.12). There are some twenty of them, all exceptionally large, and many of them still rise to impressive heights. It seems likely, from their size and certain other evidence described below, that these are the tombs of ancient chiefs, perhaps even of the kings of Dilmun. They conform, except in their great size, to the general pattern of the islands' graves of the Early Bronze Age period: a central shaft, stone-lined, with two niches at the head of the shaft forming a T-section. These, it is assumed, were for offerings placed by the head of the corpse. A peculiar feature of these tombs is that, after the sand and rubble had been heaped up high over the burial, a high circular surrounding wall was built to enclose the tumulus. Thus the tombs would have looked like gigantic, up-ended cylinders crowned by a dome of sand – very strange monuments indeed. They may, however, have perpetuated the tradition of the building of towers which seem to have been one of the most typical architectural forms to have originated in the Gulf. Towers were elements in most of the settlements,

Figure 7.12 The 'Royal Tombs' at Aali

Figure 7.13 Three fine goblets, assembled from fragments recovered from a grave mound at Aali, late third millennium BC.

from Oman to Failaka; the kings of Dilmun (if it is they who were buried in the tombs at Aali) may have chosen, hopefully, to spend eternity in still greater towers.

Durand, as earlier reported, had surveyed this part of Bahrain during his 1878–9 visit and had recorded his impressions of Aali.[84] He left behind some notable drawings of the village as it was then, showing a far greater density of mounds than is evident today.[85] The Danish Expedition, in the early 1950s, recognized the importance of the site and mounted their largest-scale excavation there.

In the 1961–2 season the Danes recovered some striking pottery vessels from one of the Aali tumuli.[86] The tomb had been robbed at an unknown date, but a trail of potsherds, found in the tunnel cut by the robbers into the tomb chamber, enabled the archaeologists to reassemble them and so present a 'suite' consisting of two handsome goblets, elegantly proportioned and painted with a geometric decoration in black on a red slip, and three slender-walled cups (Fig. 7.13). In type the goblets recall an early design found in Iran and Pakistan and can be dated to the second half of the third millennium. It is known that ostrich eggs made to serve as drinking-vessels were also placed in the tombs, recalling a particularly Sumerian practice; similar deposits were found in the burials of Early Dynastic Ur and Kish.[87]

But one object in particular from the Aali tombs testified to links more distant still and to connections even with remote and legendary Troy. The object, slightly smaller than a man's thumbnail, is a gold quatrefoil meander, the four spiral shapes being linked by a central bar.[88] It is extremely finely made and indicates a very high degree of metal-working craftsmanship to which the princes of Dilmun had access. The shape is a familiar one, associated throughout the Near East and right across Europe with Early Bronze Age burials. It is particularly identified with the practice of mound burial and examples very similar to the Aali fragment have been found as far west as Greece, as well as at Troy.[89] Further west still, the same spiral or meander shape, cut into massive stones, is the most frequent motif on the large barrow tombs of Ireland.[90] Two recently published examples, which appear to be identical with that from Aali, come from the hoard of Aegean gold acquired by the Boston Museum, which, from the gold cylinder seal bearing the cartouches of two Egyptian kings, can be dated to the twenty-fifth century BC.[91] This corresponds well with the upper limits of the estimated age of the principal Aali tumuli.

These gold ornaments seem to have been identified throughout the ancient world with royal burials. That one should have been discovered as far south as Bahrain is quite unexpected and it suggests a much closer connection with the burial practices of the great civilizations of the ancient world in the third millennium than could ever have been reasonably anticipated. It also suggests a high degree of sophistication and luxury and, sadly, confirms the view that the original contents of the tombs must have been well worth the plundering. This one tiny gold object is, in all probability, a proof of the rich and splendid treasures originally buried with the kings, as splendid perhaps as anything buried with the great magnates of Egypt or, nearer Bahrain still, the persons, royalty or victims, who lay in the Royal Tombs at Ur.

It has long been suggested that the Aali tombs represent royal burials through successive generations, beginning around the middle of the third millennium (though this would now seem to be rather too early an estimate) and continuing into the early centuries of the second. In several of the tombs, the bones of rams and sheep may be the remains of sacrifices, performed at the threshold before the tomb was sealed. Some of the tombs show that they have been reused at various periods since their construction: material of much later times has been found in one or two of them. In one tomb, opened by Prideaux during his visits to Bahrain in 1905–6 and again in 1908, two pottery jars were found in each of which was a handful of dates, recalling the significance which the date had for so long in the economy of Dilmun.[92]

Many more of the tumuli have been destroyed over the years by villagers using the stones to build their own houses and, in recent times, by the demands of the Aali pottery. In recent years, road building and other phases of Bahrain's modern development programmes have added to the destruction of the tombs. However, they can still produce splendid objects: a very fine copper drinking-cup was excavated in recent years by the Department of Antiquities (Fig. 7.14).

Grave mounds similar to those most characteristic of Bahrain have been found directly to the west in Saudi Arabia, at Abqaiq near Hofuf, at

Dhahran and at other mainland sites.[93] Relatively little work has been done on these tumuli, compared with those in Bahrain but their methods of construction and the similarity of the pottery which they have yielded suggest the same origins as the Bahraini burials. To judge by the similarity of the mounds and their contents, the populations of the Bahrain island and those on the mainland to the west of them were very similar, in all essential respects, a situation which after all persists to this day. It is probable that the people of the settlements in eastern Arabia were the residue from which it is presumed the Bahrain islands were populated after the middle of the third millennium.

AN EARLY SETTLEMENT AT SAR

Work is continuous on the Bahraini tomb-fields, for they are so immense that, inevitably, modern development is constantly requiring the destruction of many areas of them annually. The archaeologists try, at best, to keep ahead of the bulldozers. Near the village of Sar, where the mounds are particularly densely concentrated,[94] extending over many acres, several types of tomb, different from others on the island, have been identified; one rises high above the plain and is ringed by smaller subsidiary burials, for all the world like the burials of retainers around the great mastabas of the early kings of Egypt.[95] But this cannot be, for the dates of the Sar tombs are from early in the second millennium, nearly a thousand years after the practice was discontinued in Egypt. The tomb at Sar may merely be that of some great man or a particularly revered or patriarchal figure around whom others chose to be buried, in the hope that this propinquity would bring dividends in the afterlife.

Figure 7.14 A copper goblet from a grave at Aali.

Figure 7.15 Burials were densely congregated at Sar.

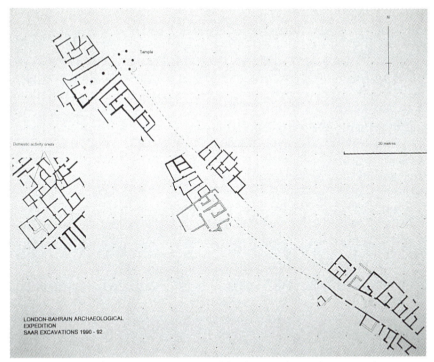

Figure 7.16 The area at Sar, excavated by the London-Bahrain expedition.

In the same part of the island a group of burials of children has been found (Fig. 7.15).[96] Since the ancients were not generally particularly sentimental about children, infant mortality being a common hazard, the presence of this group of tombs apparently reserved for children is arresting. Perhaps it is a tribute to Dilmun's reputation as a 'pure and clean place' in which disease was the exception. The apparent relative longevity of the Dilmunites, suggested earlier, may have been a factor in creating this reputation.

Sar is the location for some of the most extensive and densely packed grave fields in Bahrain. In some cases it must be assumed that these are the resting-places of the less prosperous, those unable to afford the cost of building one of the large and often complex mounds.

Now the site of a new township for the inhabitants of Bahrain, Sar is also the location for a remarkable late third-, early second-millennium complex of buildings connected by alleys and a road, situated on a ridge looking out across sparsely cultivated land which at this point is unusually contoured, close to the road which now connects Bahrain with Saudi Arabia by the King Fahd Causeway. The buildings were first discovered (though not apparently recorded) by a Jordanian team carrying out rescue archaeology in the area, which excavated a number of the burial mounds. The complex consists of a small settlement lying at the foot of the ridge, which climbs up the little wadi in which the buildings lie (Fig. 7.16). A road rises towards a structure which seems to be a temple, or other monumental building (Fig. 7.17).

The buildings near the temple and below it seem mostly to be private dwellings (the first such houses to be identified in Bahrain) and are currently being excavated by a British team sponsored by the Institute of Archaeology.[97]

The earliest levels of the site probably correspond with City I at the Qala'at al-Bahrain, dating perhaps from around 2300 BC.[98] The site's principal feature is the 'main street' which runs from the settlement almost to the temple's portal. The houses are small but well constructed, generally to a common plan, an L-shaped room, with another, inner rectangular chamber.

The settlement lies on the edge of a limestone outcrop in one of the most densely populated areas of the principal island throughout its history. It is within easy reach of the 'City' site at Qala'at al-Bahrain and of the temples at Barbar and Diraz.[99] The temple lies on the highest part of the site, on an escarpment which looks out across the fertile plain which lies below it.

The façade of the temple looked on to three round columns, similar to

Figure 7.17 The site of Sar, early second millennium BC. The temple is in the centre of the complex in the foreground.

Figure 7.18 The temple at Sar contains some unusual architectural elements, notably pilasters which articulate the walls and these crescent-shaped 'altars', which recall strongly the 'Horns of Consecration' from a later period in Crete. They also suggest the very much earlier horned altars at Neolithic Çatal Hüyük in Anatolia.

those found at the supposed temple at Diraz which was excavated by an earlier British expedition (Fig. 7.10).[100] The temple itself contained further substantial columns, one round, one square and another square, subsequently covered with a circular skin of stones, thus altering it to a rounded shape and suggesting that square columns pre-date round ones.[101] The temple seems to have undergone a number of rebuildings and contains some perplexing architectural features which, at first sight, do not seem to derive from any of the cultures with which Dilmun was in touch; in this respect, of course, they may prove to be indigenous to Bahrain. Thus, a number of the temple walls are articulated with pilasters, a technique not recorded in other Bahraini sites of the period, though evidently present on Failaka island. There are also several raised platforms with, at the rear abutting the wall, crescent-shaped structures standing proud from the wall to which they are attached (Fig. 7.18). These are reminiscent of the so-called 'horns of consecration' which are features of monumental buildings in second-millennium Crete, but are several hundred years earlier than the Cretan examples. Crescent-shaped altars are illustrated on several seals from the Gulf, especially from Failaka, where they seem to be associated with rituals at which the attendants are sometimes masked as bull-men (see Chapter 8).

The crescent altars themselves are most reminiscent of the horns of the wild bull, the aurochs, which were set up against pillars abutting the walls of the shrines at Çatal Hüyük. But these date from 4,000 years before the examples at Sar and so any apparent correspondence must surely be discounted. Burnt deposits containing fish vertebrae were found at the base of one of the crescent-shaped altars.[102] The temple also produced some plaster fragments which appeared to have fallen from its walls. The temple at Sar, though it is somewhat rustic in character, is especially well preserved, with its walls standing over a metre high. It appears that an earlier structure lies beneath the building which stands above ground level (Fig. 7.19).

Six houses have been excavated to date. A variety of domestic objects, including a net-sinker, weights, pounders and a wide range of Dilmun seals and sealings, has been recovered. Several of the houses contained plaster basins. One of the houses was more substantial than the others, with five rooms[103] and probably accommodated the town's principal inhabitant, perhaps connected with the temple.

Pottery from the site is principally of the Barbar type and the excavators date it to around 1900 BC, the time of particular prosperity for the island.[104] One jar, it has been suggested, may have been used for the brewing of beer.

Sar has provided some evidence of what appears to have been a significant change of diet by the inhabitants. In more than one of the houses a bread oven was discovered *in situ* and comparisons with similar period material from Failaka and the Qala'at al-Bahrain suggests that Sar flourished at a time when bread was disappearing from the people's diet, to be replaced by a 'boiled staple'.[105]

The Sar settlement has produced a substantial crop of seals and sealings, suggesting that the town was involved with Dilmun's international trade (Figs. 7.20–7.23).[106] The seals are similar to those recovered from Failaka and date to the same period, at the beginning of the second millennium.[107] The scenes depicted on the seals are generally comparable with those from other sites in Bahrain and the Gulf. Two of them are particularly attractive: one (Fig. 7.23a) has two sets of three caprid heads on either side of an elongated 'chequer-board', laid out in two lines; the other (Fig. 7.23b) has a central figure holding two ibexes, one by a horn, the other by the neck.

A number of sealings or bullae has been recovered, rather more, it would appear, than from other Bahraini sites. These suggest that merchandise either sent from another destination or prepared for dispatch, was handled at Sar. The designs, again, show familiar motifs from the seals found on the island and elsewhere (Fig. 7.23c).[108]

An intriguing aspect of the Sar site is the fact that the houses of the settlement have all of their entrances blocked up. It is clear that this was done deliberately and that the site was abandoned in an orderly fashion,

Figure 7.19 The temple site after excavation by the London–Bahrain Expedition.

Figure 7.20 A Dilmun seal from Sar, of an unparalleled and very striking design.

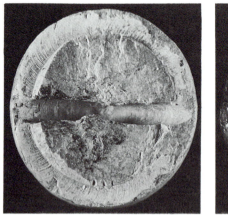

Figure 7.21 A Dilmun seal from Sar.

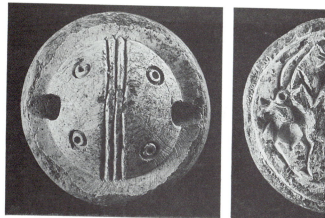

Figure 7.22 A Dilmun seal from Sar.

Figure 7.23 (a), (b), (c) Sealings recovered from the houses at Sar.

Figure 7.24 A fine chlorite circular vessel with a temple-façade design. This type of vessel is a characteristic product of the Gulf in the late third millennium.

Figure 7.25 Baskets coated in bitumen have been found in eastern Arabian sites as well as these from Sar.

though for what reason is not known. What is by far the finest chlorite vessel excavated in Bahrain has been found in one of the graves at Sar. This is circular in form and is lavishly decorated with carved motifs. One of these is of a Sumerian form, which is also found in Elam and shows the front of a temple or shrine, an appropriate theme to be found in the archetypal Holy Land (Fig. 7.24). There are also examples from Sar of a most distinctive product, baskets coated in bitumen forming substantial but quite lightweight containers (Fig. 7.25a). Similar bitumen baskets have been found in eastern Arabia and it may be remembered that Cornwall suggested that there may have been a source of bitumen on Bahrain in antiquity. He thought that it might have provided the reason for the remarkable linkage between what *may* have been the meaning of Bahrain's ancient name, composed of the Sumerian characters which were to be transliterated as 'NiTuk^{ki}', 'the oil-ship'.

Both Sar and Medinet Hamed have produced quantities of well-made chlorite vessels (Fig 7.26). It does appear that this material, also known, more accurately, as chlorite, was one of the principal media used for the manufacture of containers. No doubt these were regarded as more important or more valuable than, for example, the bitumen baskets which have been recovered from several sites, here and in Arabia.

Altogether, Sar seems likely to prove one of the most important sites in Bahrain. It adds another entry in the remarkable catalogue of temple buildings dating from this period which so evidently was the high point of Dilmun's ancient prosperity and importance. Near the third-millennium remains there is a small Hellenistic temple, indicating, as in so many other cases, that sites in Bahrain remained sacred over many hundred of years. The Hellenistic phase in the Gulf, when the successors of Alexander established colonies there, as well as in mainland Arabia, is well represented at Sar. Graves of the period suggest a prosperous Hellenized population; from one of the graves an engaging figure of a rider and his horse, perhaps a toy, was recovered (Fig 7.27).

MEDINAT HAMED

A quite distinctive group of mounds has been excavated at Medinat Hamed by the Department of Antiquities of Bahrain. The Medinat Hamed mounds are important in that several of them seem to be unplundered and they are, it would seem, particularly early. Their special interest lies in the fact that they are similar in construction and layout to the tombs on Umm an-Nar in Abu Dhabi.[109] Umm an-Nar was probably the port from which raw copper was exported to Dilmun for smelting and onward shipment to Sumer. There is also another tomb which looks as though it may have Umm an-Nar connections on the Budaiya road; these connections are of great importance in attempting to establish the likely origin of the Dilmun culture and the

Figure 7.26 Chlorite vessels from graves at Sar; similar vessels have also been recovered from burials at Medinet Hamed.

Figure 7.27 A terracotta horseman from a grave at Sar, from the Hellenistic period.

Figure 7.28 The burials at Al-Hajjar.

direction from which came the civilizing influences found in the Gulf in the mid-third millennium. Pottery from the Medinat Hamed graves also appears to sustain the Umm an-Nar connection.

AL-HAJJAR

A further indication of the archaeological riches which seem still to lie everywhere in Bahrain, just below the surface, was provided in 1970 by two large mounds at Al-Hajjar.[110] These were originally penetrated by that frequent enemy and occasional friend of archaeology, the bulldozer. Subsequent excavation, by the Bahrain Department of Antiquities, revealed a complex and extensive cemetery containing burials from c. 3000 BC, the earliest period of the island's history, down to Hellenistic times (Fig. 7.28). Some of the graves were unplundered, their inhabitants still comfortably reposing in them; most of them had been efficiently pillaged. Many of the graves were rock-cut, several were compartmented and some of the early ones were sealed with a type of small portcullis. Several produced features new to the repertory of Bahrain's ancient burial practices. One third-millennium tomb at Al-Hajjar revealed the burial of a dog, evidently sent to spend the afterlife with its master (Fig. 7.29). There are also examples of dogs found in early graves in Sumer; in one particularly early burial of a boy, a dog was laid with him and thoughtfully provided with a bone to take with him to the afterlife.[111]

Al-Hajjar has produced a considerable quantity of high-quality artefacts from all the periods represented. It was the first site to yield a Dilmun seal in direct relationship to a burial; from its position it would appear, as might be expected, that the seal was worn around the neck (Fig. 7.30).[112] Another of the graves produced a Jemdet Nasr seal which, it has been suggested, may have been ancient when it was imported into Bahrain. It had probably been re-cut and may have been a family heirloom (Fig. 7.31).[113] Indeed, seals of all periods were found at Al-Hajjar including an unusual concentration of cylinder seals, attesting the continuation of some degree of commercial or official activity in Bahrain during the otherwise relatively obscure period in the later second millennium.

A baby buried in a round pot, its skull still clearly recognizable, recalled similar burials from the Qala'at al-Bahrain, a few miles away. One grave, from the Assyrian period in the eighth century, produced a fine painted goblet.

From all the wide range of graves extending over a timescale of more than 2,000 years, one of the most notable elements of the Al-Hajjar burials was the presence of fine steatite or chlorite vessels from all periods. The quality of manufacture and the consistency of design over an extended period of time are remarkable.

Figure 7.29 A dog was buried in one of the Al-Hajjar tombs, a practice known from Mesopotamia and Egypt.

ON THE SANCTITY OF DILMUN

One of the determining marks of the Dilmun civilization was that the principal island of Bahrain was regarded as especially and specifically *holy*; this indeed was its most enduring quality, particularly for the people of Mesopotamia. It was matched, of course, and to some degree offset, by its commercial status. However, the island's sacred character does have implications for the development of Dilmun's society which are as significant as its function as a major commercial centre. The remarkable concentration of temples in the northern part of the principal Bahrain island – Barbar (at least two) Sar, Umm es Sejour, Diraz, East and West, implies an extensive administration and, presumably, a priestly hierarchy to service them. If Dilmun's temples were to any extent associated with Sumer's, then it is likely that the round of temple ceremonies was frequent and elaborate. However, the temples of Dilmun were also quite distinctly Dilmunite and seem to have developed largely independently of any of the island's larger neighbours.

A high degree of specialization, which was presumably associated with the cults which were conducted in Dilmun, is demonstrated by what was clearly one of its principal industries, the construction of large and substantially built tombs. The various types of tomb developed in Bahrain (and to a lesser extent on the mainland) each represent many thousands of actual examples, built over 600 to 800 years. This predicates a system of planning and design control which is truly formidable.

The tombs themselves are considerable structures, with stone courses carefully laid, capstones cut and fitted and, in most cases, with ring-walls of well-cut stones. They are not hastily thrown up or randomly built. They were built to common patterns over an extensive geographical area, in eastern Arabia as well as in Bahrain. Oman and its coast had its own distinctive style of monument.

Whilst few scholars today would argue strongly in favour of Bahrain having been a funerary island, a puzzling feature of the mounds is that quite a significant percentage of those which have been excavated appear never to have contained an actual burial.[114] This has produced the rather fanciful – but engaging – idea that the empty tombs were perhaps cenotaphs, built to commemorate Dilmunites who had died away from the island, perhaps in the course of travel on business.

However, if, as it seems must surely have been the case, the building of burial mounds in Bahrain in particular was managed on an industrial basis then it is likely that they would have been built industrially, that is to say

Figure 7.30 Al-Hajjar was the first site in Bahrain to produce a Dilmun seal buried with its owner; it would appear to have been worn around the neck.

Figure 7.31 A stamp seal of the Jemdet Nasr period, *c.* 3000 BC, originating in Sumer and perhaps a family heirloom, was recovered from one of the Al-Hajjar graves. It appears to have been re-cut.

that they were laid out in what might be called 'funerary estates', rather than, as a general rule, being custom-built to order, either by the deceased or by the bereaved. If this were the case, then it might well be that not all the burial mounds would be 'sold' in any one group, for whatever reason, but some, having been built speculatively as it were, remained untenanted.

It is improbable that the two streams of Dilmun's communal life, the sacred represented by the temples, and the secular, the preoccupations of the Dilmunite economy, were ever wholly separate. Trade, in the form of an organized, corporately administered activity, rather than the enterprise of the independent merchant or entrepreneur (who seems, in any case, to have come later on the commercial scene), was originally, in Sumer at least, the province of the temples: worship of the gods and the pursuit of profitable enterprise were twin pillars of the Sumerian religious establishment. This situation, paradoxical to the present-day view (though hardly to people accustomed to the role of the great medieval monasteries) arose from the management of the temples' resources of animals, slaves and land. With the emergence of the *lugal*, however, the civil or military authority in the Sumerian cities began to predominate, eventually leading to the privatization of trade and to the rise of the independent entrepreneur. The merchant might trade in partnership with the temple or the secular ruler but the relationship tended to become more one of equals, rather than perpetuating the merchants' earlier, more dependent status.

Dilmun's reputation for exceptional sanctity is one of the most enigmatic aspects of its history. On the face of it there is no very obvious reason why a small island in the Arabian Gulf should be the site of so many monumental temple structures and shrines, serving, apparently, a community that would not have exceeded a few tens of thousands of inhabitants even at the height of its prosperity. Dilmun's reputation as a primary religious centre which would seem to have ranked equally with the historic centres of Sumerian religion such as Kish or Nippur, may also seem to be at odds with its function as the hub of the Arabian Gulf's wide-ranging trade networks.

In the third millennium in particular the principal Bahrain island must have seemed to its visitors a place especially favoured; the vegetation of its northern regions was exceptionally lush, with massive plantations of palm-trees spreading over much of the land and a rich growth of mangrove reaching down to the foreshore. The island was particularly well supplied with water and the marginally more benign climate which persisted in the third millennium would have contributed to its fertility. Seamen using the island in the course of their voyages from Oman to Sumer carrying supplies of copper and from Sumer south and east to the cities of the Indus Valley would, by their reports of the island's natural resources, have ensured that it was known as a notable exception in a region of generally inhospitable climate and harsh natural conditions.

There may have been another factor involved. To take this into account it will be pertinent to consider for a moment one of the very few scholarly attempts to explore the origins of the Zodiac and the naming of the constellations.[115] It is curious that a phenomenon which has enjoyed so much exposure over the past 2,500 years as the Zodiac has had so little scientific or scholarly attention given to its origins or to the reasons why certain groups of stars were selected to represent the animals or objects which were identified with them. Nor is there any real study of the choice of the names given to the constellations, which, with barely any exceptions, have no apparent similarity to the animal or object with which the constellation is associated.

The study referred to (by the late Michael Ovenden of the Department of Astronomy, Glasgow University) takes as its starting-point the belief that the choice of the constellations which were to make up the twelve 'houses' of the Zodiac shows that it was first made in the early part of the third millennium BC. As this was a time of rapid and exceptional advances all over the ancient world, this is an entirely acceptable time to propose. The observation of the night sky, a preoccupation of the people of Sumer and destined to become one of the triumphs of Babylonian science, had already moved to a level of careful and sophisticated calculation.

The identification of the major constellations would have been undertaken particularly as an aid to navigation, another wholly reasonable assumption. At this time seamen were beginning their first long-distance voyages in search of raw materials and trade; navigation became a necessary science for the success of their enterprises and, indeed, for their very survival. The observations would need to be taken from an island, with a central mountain and with other islands nearby on the horizon to act as fiducial marks.[116]

It is proposed that a northern latitude must be sought for the first naming of the constellations, as their order on the ecliptic would seem to require a point of observation around the middle 30s of latitude. It recognizes that only a people with a highly developed maritime tradition, powered by commercial necessity, would be likely to undertake so elaborate and complex a procedure as the identification and naming of the constellations to serve their purposes. The study suggests that the Cretans were the most probable contenders, pointing to their prowess as seamen and the long-ranging voyages which they undertook. The Babylonians are rather summarily dismissed (whilst admitting that the credit is often given to them for the Zodiac's invention), on the grounds that 'their seafaring would have been in the Persian Gulf and Indian Ocean, too far south for the latitude of the constellations' observers'.[117]

The study is, however, flawed in two particulars. First, there is no evidence that the Cretans were 'great sailors, and undoubtedly therefore, great traders' in the early or mid-third millennium. At that time the island's people were still effectively in a Neolithic stage of culture; it was not until the very end of the third millennium and the beginning of the second that the 'classic' Minoan culture began to emerge in Crete, long after the Sumerians and their successors had taken to the ocean and to the planning of far-ranging voyages.

Second, the Babylonians, in this respect as in so many others, were the heirs of the Sumerians, whose phenomenal abilities affected the course of societal development so profoundly. It is clear that the Sumerians observed the constellations and recorded their observations though these have not survived in the same quantity as is the case with Babylonian star lists.

The contention that the Gulf is too far south for the constellations chosen, which fall along the line of ecliptic early in the third millennium, is also insupportable. The constellations are clearly visible from the Gulf and from the cities of southern Mesopotamia.[118]

It has for long been suggested that the Sumerians and their successors used the ziggurats, the high temple buildings that they constructed in the later part of the third millennium, and which dominated all the important cities, for astronomical observation. Akkadian records show that the movements of the constellations were observed and charted; there is ample, if largely inferential evidence, that they had access to records set down by their Sumerian predecessors in the early third millennium.[119]

The Sumerians divided the sky into three 'ways' or bands.[120] These were the Way of Anu which represented the celestial equator. The Way of Enlil ran to the north of it whilst, significantly, to the south lay the Way of Enki. It is clear that the Mesopotamians were fully aware of the principal regions of the sky and recorded them with careful observation; it is certainly pertinent that the southern sky was associated with Enki, who was the most important divinity connected with the Gulf.

The great towers which are so notable a feature of the Gulf's architecture in the late third and early second millennia may have served a purpose similar to that of the temple platforms on which the priests of Sumer, Akkad and Babylonia made their observations. Given the enthusiasm which the peoples of Western Asia in antiquity demonstrated for astronomical observations, it could hardly be otherwise.

On the criteria that Ovenden proposed, a date early in third millennium, a people with highly developed maritime skills and a wide-ranging trade, and an island with a central prominence from which observations might be taken, attended by other islands on the horizon, the Gulf becomes a much more likely theatre for the observations required and the principal Bahrain island a much more likely candidate for the locus of observation than Crete. Bahrain has its central prominence, the Jebel Dukhan, and, as part of an archipelago, is well provided with attendant islands.

There is, of course, not a whit of evidence at this stage to support this speculation. However, the study's astronomical arguments about the likely role of islands in the naming of the Zodiacal constellations is compelling and if Crete must, on chronological, archaeological and historical grounds, be discarded, Bahrain is a very reasonable, indeed altogether more likely, alternative.

If Bahrain-Dilmun had served as the site for this very important development, both in the maritime affairs of the Sumerians and in the more mystical overlay which such knowledge would certainly have been given, having regard to the management of scientific knowledge in ancient societies, it would account for the very special regard in which Dilmun was held over so many centuries. As the constellations were always identified with the great gods, the island could truly be said to be their original home. It would also be, in a transcendental sense which would have been devised by the priests who would no doubt have been responsible for the original observations, a place of wonder and mystery, the linchpin of the cosmos and the binding-post between earth and heaven.

Note: The epigraphy of the name 'Dilmun' (p. 147) is from Robert Englund 'Dilmun in the Archaic Urk Corpus' in *Dilmun: New Studies in the Archaeology and Early History of Bahrain* (1983), ed. Daniel P. Potts, Berlin: Dietrich Reimer Verlag.

8

DILMUN'S NEIGHBOURING LANDS

The society which evolved in the Gulf in the second half of the third millennium BC and which survived into the early centuries of the second was highly sophisticated and complex. Whilst it clearly possessed many of the characteristics of its great contemporaries, such as the riverine cultures of Egypt and Mesopotamia, a highly structured society, monumental public buildings, far-ranging contacts, extensive and rich burial fields, it was distinct in many of its attributes. For this there were two basic reasons: the particularly mercantile nature of the society, and the fact that it was sea-based with a considerable, and virtually unparalleled, reliance upon islands as its main centres of population and activity.

Dilmun's absorption with international trade makes it quite different from other developed, early urban civilization. Many of these, of course, were concerned with exchange mechanisms and with the onward movement of raw materials or manufactured goods; in all cases the civilizations, centred on cities or royal courts, themselves absorbed substantial quantities of the goods which were the subject of the systems of exchange, which powered their distribution and acquisition. Often this absorption of the society's products found its natural outlet in the large and stately funerary monuments which, from the third millennium onwards, characterized many such societies in the Near East.

In Dilmun's case, trade was the very basis of the society, with one important reservation, which will be considered further. By the time that the epicentre of Dilmun had shifted to the Bahrain islands from eastern Arabia, which seems to have happened some time after the middle of the third millennium, trade was clearly the whole basis of the economy: agriculture and fishing, though present, were relatively unimportant.

Most ancient societies relied on agriculture for their prosperity and for the development of their social systems. Not so in Dilmun's case: as a sea-based economy agriculture was of relatively little importance (other than the harvesting of the sea, though the extent to which this figured in the people's lives is not certain). The extremes of climate did not permit the development of cereal agronomy, though the date-palm, at least in the case of the great oasis of Hofuf in eastern Arabia, was the exception to this principle, for Dilmun's dates were famous.

Dilmun is the only example in the Old World of an island-based society, one, moreover which depended only on four principal components – Failaka, Tarut, Bahrain and, with qualifications, Umm an-Nar. It is this factor which contributes much of Dilmun's special character and marks out its differences from its immediate neighbours and contemporaries. The civilization of south-western Iran was land-based; Sumer to the north depended on the rivers and lagoons for much of its internal communications. The Indus Valley cities, so far as anything is really known of them, were independent elements in a society linked by the rivers and the valley systems in which the cities grew; only Dilmun was a maritime society, looking to the sea for its communications and interconnections. As its prosperity grew and as the demand for its principal product, copper, expanded, important settlements were established along the southern coast of the Gulf, providing access to, and export from, the copper mines of northern Oman.

By the time that the Gulf begins to come to prominence, c. 2400 BC, the polities of the Sumerian cities had been flourishing for upwards of a thousand years. The Gulf – the Dilmun culture or, as it might now be seen to be, the Dilmun state – was, in the early days, the heir of all the complexity of Sumerian civilization. When the second city settlement was established the Qala'at al-Bahrain and the first great temples were built at Barbar, the merchant community was already vigorous and widely travelled. Colonies of merchants were maintained, probably over several generations, often far distant from the home base.

The Sumerians and their Akkadian and Babylonian successors were diligent archivists. Vast quantities of business documents have been recorded as well as libraries of literary material. One of the key archives of the trade with Dilmun was the cache of tablets in Ea-Nasir's house at Ur,[1] which will be referred to in Chapter 9. It is disappointing that so few inscribed tablets have been recovered from Gulf sites, particularly from Bahrain which, as the operational centre of the trade for so long, must have employed extensive and complex filing systems and records. The early Mesopotamians were great ones for making lists and for producing concordances of terms used in different languages. To find such a reference relating to the Dilmun trade would probably reveal what language the merchants, and doubtless the community as a whole, spoke and wrote.

It is, of course, possible that, unlike the Mesopotamians who made use of the almost indestructible properties of baked clay tablets, their Dilmunite counterparts may have used more perishable materials on which to make their records. The date-palm is ubiquitous throughout eastern Arabia and is indigenous to it. Experiments have been conducted to fabricate a writing material from palm leaves, using a process analogous to that employed to make papyrus in Egypt. Such a material was known in early Islamic times; it is therefore entirely possible that it was known in antiquity, for, given the natural inventiveness of the people of the Gulf and their general tendency to make the maximum use of what relatively few raw materials a niggardly providence had given them, it is altogether likely that they would have come upon this application of their most familiar source of fibrous material; after all, they used palm fibres to make ropes.

In this event, given the extreme summer humidity of the Gulf, records written on palm 'papyrus' would not survive long; indeed, given the intensely pragmatic attitude of the people of the Gulf to the business of living, it would perhaps be surprising if they had persisted with the use of such material, rather than adopting baked clay. Be that as it may, there is a dearth of inscribed tablets throughout the Gulf; this may be the happenstance of archaeology or it may be that the absence of written records is the result of their decay. A palm-fibre 'papyrus' would leave no discernible trace in a grave or habitation site when, even if any remains were present, they would simply have been dismissed as matting or an accidental incursion.

If the palm did provide this service to the ancient people of the Gulf – an entirely speculative suggestion – then it might well be another reason for the divinity particularly associated with Dilmun, Enshaq-Inzak, to be identified with a palm branch. By what is no doubt nothing more than coincidence, this god was identified with the planet Mercury, which has often been linked with gods of writing, of learning generally and of commerce.

The movement of goods up and down the Gulf and their eventual distribution to distant markets, the maintenance of proper records and the accounting procedures which were evidently so much a preoccupation for the people, all of these would have required a high degree of organization and of specialization. From the times of the earliest extant records relating to Dilmun we hear of a tax-collector, a post suggesting already a high degree of bureaucracy.

Thus it is that there is a third Dilmun, to be added to the paradisial Dilmun of myth and the mercantile Dilmun of commodities and trade. This third Dilmun is really an extension of the Dilmun of ships and sailors, of merchants harvesting their profits from the city on Bahrain's northern shores. This is the temporal Dilmun, the political organism whose dominion from time to time extended along the east Arabian shore as far as the Bay of Kuwait and included the islands which lie close to the point where the two great rivers of Iraq end their journey in the headwaters of the Gulf.

In the present state of knowledge and at this distance in time it is not possible to speculate meaningfully on what sort of political organization constituted the Dilmunite state in the third and early second millennia when it was at its most important. We know that Ur-Nanshe of Lagash claimed to receive tribute from Dilmun in the twenty-sixth century BC.[2] This implies that even at that time Dilmun was a state, though standing in the status of client to one of the principal Sumerian powers, if Ur-Nanshe is to be believed. Some 200 years later Sargon would seem to have captured Dilmun and added it to his newly founded empire. Other kings after him claimed sovereignty over the Holy Land. We know the names of several of Dilmun's (or, more strictly, Tilmun's) later kings: Uperi, who lived 'like a fish in the midst of the sea', Hundaru and Qanaia, to mention three. Throughout this long period Dilmun as a political entity seems to have extended and contracted, sometimes being confined in extent to the Bahrain islands, at others embracing the whole coast to the west and north. It is not without point, bearing in mind the extraordinarily long currency of names in Arabia, that the Hasa province of Arabia has from time to time been known as Bahrain, though this did not imply any political control over the mainland by the islanders. In his report to the Viceroy's Foreign Department in 1879, Durand reproduces a map from a somewhat earlier date which shows 'El-Bahrein' as embracing the Qatar peninsula as well as the whole of eastern Arabia.[3]

As far as we know Dilmun never incorporated Qatar within its boundaries. There are reports of the remains of settlements on Qatar which include Barbar material but they are scanty and do not seem to represent any major evidence of permanent or long-lasting habitation.[4] More likely they are the result of short-stay expeditions to what, even in antiquity, must have been a pretty inhospitable shore.

It is the mainland which extends from due west of Bahrain up to the edge of the marshlands of southern Iraq which was originally associated with the larger concept of 'Dilmun'. Thus insular Dilmun was able to sustain its territorial links with Sumer, far to the north both by sea and by land. If the Sumerians did come to what was to become their homeland from the south, then this identification of the mainland coastal regions with Dilmun may have served to perpetuate the route of their migration in their collective memory. It may have been because of this migration that they were disposed to retain the ancient name of the mainland region in their new home in the islands, when they moved the centre of Dilmun there in the latter part of the third millennium. We know the Sumerians, on the evidence of some of their far distant settlements in northern Syria, for example, were capable of seeding and sustaining colonies which were essentially Sumerian in character, established in an alien environment far removed from the homeland. It could be that this is how Dilmun began and was then sustained by its landward connection to the north with Sumer, as much as by the sea. The difference is that the Syrian settlements were heavily fortified whilst City I at Bahrain was not. In this connection it has been suggested that the Sumerians turned to the Gulf and southwards in search of trade only after they were driven out of their northern outposts, particularly the settlement which they had established in Anatolia. The evidence, at present, is obscure.

FAILAKA ISLAND

It is on the basis of the partial excavation of the early second-millennium settlements on Failaka island, the great caches of Dilmun seals found there, the occasional inscription and the plentiful pottery recovered from the sites, that the links between Dilmun and Failaka have been established. Parts of the Epic of Gilgamesh may be set in and around the Gulf shores and in Dilmun; in that story the presence of Siduri, a goddess, is important, for she lives in an island on the edge of the ocean which is known as the Garden of the Sun.[5] Gilgamesh visits her at the beginning of his quest. She was, in Sumerian times, the tutelary goddess of the Gulf, who resided in her garden and dispensed drinks to travellers, particularly those who were about to cross the waters of death from which, unlike Gilgamesh, they would not return. It seems most probable that Failaka was Siduri's island, as Burrows indeed proposed.[6] If this were so it would account for the sanctuary on the island and for its reputation as a place sacred to the goddess, under whatever name – a reputation so long enjoyed.

The garden of which Siduri was the mistress was said to bear trees laden with jewels. It has been suggested that this is a reference to the frequently intense phosphorescence of the Gulf's waters, caused by the coral in the shallows. If Failaka is Siduri's island, Siduri is also to be identified with Artemis, to whom Failaka, under its name of Ikaros, was consecrated.

A pretty little Greek temple on Failaka has been excavated by the Danes (Fig. 8.1).[7] This, it must be presumed, was connected with the oracle for which, in Greek times, the island seems also to have been celebrated. The oracle, however, might be less permanent in its structure, a sacred grove perhaps or some wise woman lurking in a cave.

Cornwall, who seems not to have known of the identification between Failaka and Ikaros when he prepared his thesis, recorded Strabo's and Arrian's description of an oracle, said to be dedicated to Diana Tauropolis, situated in Ikaros.[8] He suggests that the oracle's name meant something like 'Diana, of the City of the Bulls': but of what city, what bulls? In fact, Cornwall is incorrect in transcribing the epithet as 'Tauropolis'; it is 'Tauropolos' which is a very different matter. In this form it could mean 'Hunter of Bulls', a very appropriate soubriquet for the Chaste Goddess.

Diana is the Roman form of the Greek Artemis, whom Alexander named as the guardian goddess of Failaka and to whom its animals were sacred. The island in the Aegean after which he is said to have named the Gulf island is Ichara, not Ikaros; but it too had a high bull cult, of the sort which, it increasingly appears, was prevalent on Failaka. Thus it would appear that Alexander, recognizing the sacred character of the Gulf island and its bull cults, which by the evidence of the seals were ceremonies of immense antiquity, brought all these elements together and identified Failaka with Ichara, because of their common preoccupation with rituals involving bulls.[9]

Figure 8.1 Failaka was an important settlement in Hellenistic times, with a Greek community which supported its own temples and shrines and at least one gymnasium.

A most intriguing explanation for the adoption of the name Ikaros for the island has, however, been offered. This suggest that the Greeks knew that in Assyrian times there was a temple on the island called *e-kara*;[10] it was named thus in Aramaic sources also.

The Greeks had a boundless capacity for the distortion of foreign place-names, only to be rivalled by a similar propensity of the British in modern times. Their mangling of such Egyptian expressions as Hikuptah, the name of the principal temple in Memphis produced Aigyptos and, hence, Egypt. Memphis itself was originally Men-Nefer, one of the ancient names of the capital city.

So it may have been with *e-kara*, located on the island in the northern reaches of the Gulf.[11] This would have sounded to a Greek as indistinguishable from Ichara, and the presence of bull cults on both islands would have made their identification very natural. Ikaros was, presumably, a later adaptation of the name, the reasons for which remains obscure though the association with the Daedalus myth set in Crete which culminated in the death of Ikaros, may have had something to do with it.

The ascription of the temple on Failaka island as *e-kara* is based on a bronze bowl inscribed in Akkadian referring to the temple, which is also known from a neo-Assyrian list of Dilmunite temples.[12] The *e-kara* was, according to the Akkadian inscription, dedicated to Shamash, the sun-god who played an important part in the Epic of Gilgamesh and who, it will be seen in Chapter 10, comforts the dying Enkidu.

It is difficult to suggest what might have been the nature of the oracle on Failaka. However, it is not impossible that the ancient goddess who was identified with the island was Siduri herself, who, according to the Epic of Gilgamesh, lived on the Edge of the Ocean in the Garden of the Sun. Her later identification with the Erythraean Sibyl brings her into association with a very visionary and prophetic creature indeed. Perhaps this linking of the island celebrated for its bull cults with a goddess of ancient prophecy accounts, in Alexander's time, for its reputation as the site of an oracle of Diana and the bulls.

Failaka appears only to have become habitable relatively late in the day, at the very end of the third millennium or at the beginning of the second.[13] Prior to this time the island was unstable and, as the level of the Gulf was more than a metre higher than it is today, much of it was under water.[14] The probability is that the island, when it became capable of sustaining a permanent population, was colonized by Dilmunites from Bahrain and eastern Arabia. The island, like its larger sister, was evidently sacred, for cult buildings have been excavated and the island's reputation in the days of Alexander the Great testify to an enduring and special sanctity.

The remarkable concentration of Gulf seals on Failaka will be described in Chapter 9. It is difficult to account for them in such quantity, in the absence of any settlement of the scale of, for example, those known from Bahrain. Thus far, some 500 have been recovered from Failaka,[15] approximately the same number as the much larger and more important Bahrain island.

Two of the seals from Failaka are important, not so much for their aesthetic interest but rather for the hints which they give of wider horizons to the Gulf merchants and the trade which they conducted at the beginning of the second millennium BC.[16] These two seals have conventional Egyptian scarab backs, of the style which was then just becoming popular in the Nile Valley; previously the Egyptians had tended to favour round stamp seals. At the end of the third millennium, however, they began to adopt the scaraboid seal which, whilst it was still a stamp, became oval in shape; eventually Egyptian scarabs became one of the most familiar products of the Egyptian Kingdom, with an extensive repertory of designs of their own. The examples from Failaka, however, though they are Egyptian in the scaraboid form, have Gulf seal designs on their obverse (Fig. 8.2a). This is very remarkable. It suggests either Egyptian traders established in Failaka, since, if they were merely itinerant they would surely have seals which were wholly Egyptian to mark their merchandise, or Dilmunite traders exporting to Egypt and paying their customers the compliment of adopting a degree of Egyptian practice in the manner of the seals which they used.[17]

Figure 8.2(a) Two of the many stamp seals recovered from Failaka look very like Egyptian scarabs. At the time that they were made, this most Egyptian form of seal was just coming into general use in the Nile Valley.

Egyptian (or Egyptianized) sealings have also been recovered from tombs in the Dhahran area. Their datings are uncertain, though some seem certainly to be more likely to be placed in the first rather than the second millennium.

It may be that the evident contact between the headlands of the Gulf and the Nile Valley, which were an important part of the formative process of the Early Dynastic period in Egypt, continued thereafter. How frequently these contacts were made and how they were effected are as yet matters of speculation but the evidence of some form of association in the period which embraces the Middle Kingdom to the Late Period deserves further research.

Figure 8.2 (b) A group of seals from Failaka island; early second millennium BC.

A series of occupation levels has been identified on Failaka, spanning the period from 2000 BC to around 1200 BC; included in this sequence are Kassite levels.[18] There is also evidence of temple building in the Hellenistic period, in addition to the monumental inscriptions which were noted earlier.[19]

Failaka is unusual in the Gulf for having yielded a crop of cuneiform inscriptions. These include inscribed seals, pottery, sherds and some tablets. Several relate to divinities of the Gulf, including Inzak; it is possible that a temple to Inzak existed on the island. The inscriptions tend to be very brief but that they are present in greater quantity than anywhere else in the Gulf is perhaps the consequence of the island's proximity to southern Iraq. It is notable that there do not appear to be any of the burial-mound fields on Failaka, which are so marked a characteristic of the landscapes both of eastern Arabia and Bahrain.

After the Danes' first seasons' work on the sites on Failaka island, there was only occasional and spasmodic activity in the intervening years until the French began operations on the island in the early 1980s.[20] However, the results have been important in adding to the understanding of the sort of role which Failaka played in the Gulf at the beginning of the second millennium BC and, again, in Hellenistic times.

One intriguing discovery made by the French, who have been working extensively on Failaka in recent years, on the south-west corner of the island, was the foundations of what they decided was a high tower which would have been visible, like a *pharos*, from a far distance to seamen as they approached the island.[21] Whether the tower was intended to serve as a marker for the seamen or whether it was defensive for the islanders is not yet known. However, it is striking that a tower, built on Failaka for whatever purpose, should join the list of other towers in the Gulf: the tower tombs at Aali in Bahrain and the defensive towers, probably the earliest examples of the form, which were built near the copper-mines in northern Oman.

The Failaka tower had thick walls and a substantial base, with buttresses, all suggesting that the original structure was of considerable height. Later, another temple was found on Failaka which the excavators believed might be dedicated to Inzak, as recorded in cuneiform inscriptions.[22]

A survey of the Kuwaiti mainland was conducted in the late 1980s. The shoreline was known to have sunk considerably over the past 4,000 years, so it was not expected that extensive early remains would be found.[23] Some Bronze Age pottery sherds were found, however; it is likely that Kuwait would have been occupied at the time of Dilmun's prosperity but any settlement that there might have been must now be lost beneath the silt and the coastal waters.

The Danish expeditions on Failaka had early on identified the island's importance and the rather equivocal role it seems to have discharged in the history of the Gulf at the beginning of the second millennium BC, the time when it was probably first colonized. The Danes found a building that they termed a 'palace',[24] the first phase of which was contemporary with the second temple level at Barbar and with the second city at Qala'at al-Bahrain. It was a substantial building, almost square, measuring 22 × 23 metres. It contained pillars and walls with pilasters, architectural features which were to be found in the temple at Sar, on Bahrain. It seems likely that the population of Failaka abandoned the island precipitantly in the Old Babylonian period, for the houses, built to a regular plan like those at Sar, showed evidence of being left hurriedly.[25]

A second 'palace' was built at Failaka around 1400 BC, by which time the Kassites had been long established in Mesopotamia as in the Gulf.[26] A third 'palace' was built, probably around 700 years later, if an inscription found near the remains which declared 'This palace belongs to Nebuchadnezzar, King of Babylon' is to be believed.[27]

Failaka enjoyed another period of prosperity in the time following the death of Alexander the Great, when the Seleucids who succeeded to the eastern parts of Alexander's empire established their presence in the Gulf. Like Bahrain, Failaka also had hoards of Antiochid coins, one found in 1960, the second the following year.[28] The Seleucid King Antiochos III is commemorated on one of the coins: he reigned from 223 to 187 BC. One of his predecessors was Seleukos II Kallinikos, to whom reference is made in the inscription ordered to be set up on Failaka to record Alexander's special favour to the island.[29]

There is a recent translation of the text of the inscription, which is cut in Greek characters, though now much damaged.[30] It was intended to be set up in a sacred enclosure established on Failaka in the aftermath of Alexander's withdrawal from the east, before his early death in Babylon in 323 BC. The inscription itself dates from approximately a century after Alexander's death. It refers to the 'transfer of the sanctuary of Soteira' which, as we know, was one of the epithets attached to Artemis. It mentions the ordering of a gymnastic contest in honour of the gods; the remains of what may have been the gymnasium of Failaka have been excavated on the island, suggesting that there must have been a sizeable Greek population there to provide enough boys and young men to require the services of such an institution, so familiar in all Greek towns. The King's orders refer to the protection of the rights of the inhabitants: 'everybody shall pay regard to the interests of the community', 'Personal safety and exemption from taxes shall be guaranteed' and, most interestingly, the exemption from taxes is extended to 'those trading with the island and with destinations beyond it'.[31] The remains of the typically Hellenistic temple which has been excavated on Failaka island and the inscriptions and other evidence of the time, indicate the extraordinary ability of the Greeks to flourish in even the most remote and inhospitable circumstances.

EASTERN SAUDI ARABIA

Further down the coast, in what is now the territory of the Kingdom of Saudi Arabia, the situation is markedly different from the apparent archaeological barrenness of the Kuwaiti coastal region. Intensive survey of the surface sites in the eastern region, as in the other parts of the Kingdom, over very recent years has revealed much already and promises more in the years to come.

Unlike other parts of Arabia there appears to be no evidence of human occupation in the eastern quadrant until Neolithic times:[32] what were thought to be Palaeolithic (even 'Neanderthal') facies have now been shown to all come from New Stone Age times.[33] The Palaeolithic is generally well represented in Arabia as a whole, outside the eastern region. In the Najd, the central region, in which lies Riyadh the capital of the Kingdom, extensive Palaeolithic evidence has been recovered, yet there is so far nothing from the east. Indeed, a line can be drawn down the face of the peninsula, somewhat to the east of the city of Riyadh, from the north to the south, which marks the limit of the Arabian Palaeolithic. The explanation can only be that in Palaeolithic times the level of the Gulf was substantially higher and that the east was under water (see Chapter 2). When, in the period between 17,000 BC and 9000 BC, the waters withdrew, leaving the Gulf itself largely uncovered, it is probable that any humans that inhabited the region would have stayed near to the ancient course of the Tigris and Euphrates which then debouched into the Gulf and ran into the sands at the Straits of Hormuz. Such material evidence as they would have left behind them would therefore now lie fathoms deep beneath the Gulf's waters.

Many of the Neolithic tools, the blades for example, the pink tools from Khor in Qatar, the many excellently shaped arrowheads and leaf-shaped artefacts, are distinctive and memorable, suggesting that when Neolithic craftsmen established themselves they were already possessed of a secure industrial tradition. But it is with the first appearance of pottery in the region that the interconnections between the mainland and the islands may properly be said to begin. Much of the prosperity of eastern Arabia, in ancient times as now, depends upon the great Al Hasa oasis and it is from the region peripheral to the oasis that the earliest evidence of settlement comes.

Before modern development the cultivated area of Al Hasa covered about 8,000 hectares, but now the land available for cultivation has been increased to about 20,000 hectares.[34] This, together with its two large towns and over fifty other settlements, makes Al Hasa the largest oasis in Arabia; indeed, it is one of the largest in the world.

The enormous size of this farming area is made possible by an immense volume of water issuing from subterranean rock strata as springs. Each of the four main springs in the oasis has a flow rate in excess of 100,000 litres per minute.[35] Because this water is available – and there appears to have been more in antiquity – the oasis of Al Hasa has a history of continuous human settlement going back to Neolithic times. It is not known when an organized system of irrigation first appeared, but it seems that one was in operation at least by early Islamic times.

The water of eastern Arabia today comes principally from springs in the oases of Al Hasa, al-Qatif and Bahrain. This water is held under pressure in the rock strata of the Alat, Khubar and Umm al-Radhuma formations, whose waters come to the surface in the oases of eastern Arabia, through cracks and faults in the rock. In the springs of Al Hasa, the water is warm (between 29° and 39°C). Carbon-14 analyses of the water show it to be between 24,000 and 30,000 years since it fell as rain. The water belongs to an earlier wet period.[36]

During the Neolithic period, about 7,000 years before the present, an entirely new factor entered the history of the Gulf. It is a factor of crucial importance and it has caused a recurrence of the old controversy about the origin of the Sumerians. The evidence in question was the recognition (originally by two archaeological enthusiasts from ARAMCO, the oil company whose headquarters is in the eastern region) of sherds of pottery which could be classified as belonging to the Ubaid culture of southern Iraq, the first such culture to be established in the land which was, several hundred years later, to become Sumer.[37]

Ubaid pottery, a highly distinctive ware which, once it has been seen, is virtually impossible to mistake for any other, has a rich repertory of elegant, predominantly geometric patterns. It has now been identified on a number of sites in the northern reaches of the eastern Arabian coast, in Qatar, Bahrain and the United Arab Emirates; more sites are probably now lost, submerged as a consequence of the changes which have occurred in the Gulf's sea-levels since Ubaid times. Some forty Ubaid sites have been identified in eastern Arabia clustering around Ain Qannas and Abu Khamis.[38]

From Neolithic times onwards the situation in eastern Arabia reveals evidence of communities, long-distance contact and a growing prosperity. Many of the settlements had domesticated animals but are clearly Neolithic, stone-tool makers and hunter-gatherers.[39] The people who formed these communities are the earliest pottery-users known in Arabia; they are contemporary with the Ubaid period in Iraq. At least thirty sites have been identified which have produced evidence of Ubaid pottery. Already these people were maintaining contact with far-distant regions, from which, by the very earliest manifestation of the region's concern with trade, they imported such natural products as galena, diorite, obsidian, haematite, red ochre and bitumen.

Three important sites in eastern Saudi Arabia from this period have been excavated by the Department of Antiquities. These are Ain Qannas, Al-Dawsariyya andAbu Khamis.[40] At Ain Qannas the remains of an enclosure and the evidence of the domestication of cattle were recovered. The site revealed a succession of minor fluctuations in climate which determined the flow of an extinct spring found at the bottom of the excavation, which was no doubt the reason for the choice of the site for settlement in the first place.[41]

Ubaid pottery in Mesopotamia falls into four categories, the first two named after the southern Iraqi sites where they were first identified.

Ubaid 1, Eridu, c. 5300–5100 BC
Ubaid 2, Hajji Muhammad, c. 5100–4300 BC
Ubaid 3, Standard, c. 4300–3900 BC
Ubaid 4, Late, c. 3900–3500 BC

Ubaid pottery on Arabian sites belongs to the Ubaid 3 and 4 types except at Ain Qannas, where it appears to be Hajji Muhammad (Ubaid 2). Analysis has shown that the Ubaid pottery is of southern Mesopotamian origin, and therefore reached eastern Arabia by exchange or trade.

Other pottery too is found on Arabian settled Neolithic period sites: chaff-tempered, hand-made and red in exterior colour, it was perhaps a locally made imitation ware. A range of flint tools was comparable with those of the early Arabian Neolithic blade cultures.

On the other sites (as in Bahrain and Qatar, further to the south) the pottery is Ubaid 3 and 4.[42] The pottery was originally carried down to Arabia from southern Iraq, particularly from the city of Ur where much of it was fabricated. Amongst the stone tools are fine tanged and barbed arrowheads and flat, tabular flint scrapers.[43]

The site at Al-Dawsariyya also yielded Ubaid pottery. Most notable was the evidence of reed dwellings or enclosures, provided by the many pieces of reed-impressed lime plaster.[44] Traces of red paint were also found, suggesting that the interiors of the dwellings enjoyed some form of decoration. The presence of corner pieces suggests that the 'houses' were rectangular. Al-Dawsariyya maintained long-distance contacts, as witnessed by blades made of obsidian which originates in Anatolia, stone beads, greenstone axes and other ornamental objects, witnesses both to the development of trade and to the appearance – in all probability – of an aesthetic sense amongst the inhabitants. From this site, too, have come small stone borers which could have been used to pierce shell or, conceivably, pearls.[45] Altogether there are seven distinct levels of occupations at Al-Dawsariyya.

Many of the eastern Arabian Ubaid sites are small coastal settlements, probably concerned with fishing, some of which appear to have been occupied over quite extended periods. The pottery, which incidentally is invariably discovered in association with late Neolithic stone tools, is mostly relatively late Ubaid. One more or less complete pot from

Khursaniyah shows that it was made on a slow wheel. Spectrographic analysis has produced the interesting conclusion that all of it was made near Ur.[46]

The presence of Ubaid pottery on eastern Arabian sites is probably evidence of contact, however indirectly, between the makers of the pottery in Ur and small populations of semi-nomads who set up camp seasonally to fish; it is also a testimony to the distances over which pottery might be traded, even in this very early time. It may also be that fishermen from the early Sumerian cities came down to the Gulf in search of seawater catches. The Gulf's waters have for long been exploited; the coastal sites have yielded, from a somewhat later date than the Ubaid sites, evidence of what was most likely to have been the harvesting of the pearl beds. Most pertinent here was the discovery of tiny awls and borers associated with fragments of mother-of-pearl which suggested that even 5,000 years and more ago the pearl was being adapted for ornament. Spindle-whorls, from the same levels, indicate that some form of fabric-making was practised.[47]

The excavation of the Ain Qannas Ubaid-period settlement produced much original and important evidence.[48] Not the least of it was the analysis of spring sediments which showed that during the period 5000–3000 BC the eastern Arabian climate was, from time to time, moister than today.

The large site of Al-Dawsariyya lies 1.5 km from the present-day coastline.[49] Surface finds were abundant, dating both to around 4200 BC and to the Uruk period after 3500 BC. The lowest layer gave a Carbon-14 date of c. 4950 BC. The site is later than Ain Qannas, with the earlier levels overlapping. The surface of the important subsidiary site of al-Khursaniyya gave a date of 4200 BC.[50]

Al-Dawsariyya yielded large quantities of Ubaid pottery, mixed with Neolithic flint debris. It was larger than might have been expected of a site with only infrequent occupation. There were hints of a more complex range of trading contacts and exchanges, not at all typical of small, occasional fishing communities. There were obsidian blades, probably from Anatolia; and semi-precious stone beads, greenstone axes and other ornamental objects suggest a somewhat richer inventory than might reasonably have been anticipated.

The evidence from Al-Dawsariyya, together with that from other sites along the Arabian coast, suggests wide-ranging contact by sea round the peninsula in the Neolithic period, made possible by the use of small craft, making short coastal hops between settlements. Small fishing craft made from the ribs of palm branches, of a type which survives in parts of the Gulf and Oman to this day (called *shasha*), would have been well within the technical capabilities of these Neolithic people.

Seven distinct layers of occupation were interspersed with two layers in which the site may have been abandoned (Fig. 8.3). The whole surface was up to 30 cm deep in shell fragments, and a loose shell layer separated each occupation level from the next.[51]

In antiquity it is likely that there was more water available in eastern Arabia than is the case today. This was certainly true in the third millennium, the time when the region first begins to develop substantially. At Tel el Ramad there is evidence of a considerable settlement, located on a former lake.[52] Microlith blades set in bitumen, coated with the silica sheen which comes from reaping cereals, provide evidence of agriculture. Similar evidence has been gathered from the Yabrin oasis at al-Nussi which is contemporary with Tel et Ramad and Abqaiq.[53] In this area lay thousands of the

Figure 8.3 A reconstruction of an Ubaid period settlement on the eastern Arabian coast *c.* 3800 BC.

burial mounds which are so typical of Bahrain, whose presence suggests a shared or common cultural tradition. The coastal sites formed a culture which was orientated towards the sea but the inland settlements were different. In Oman the culture was based on agriculture but it was to become much involved in the mining and supply of copper to the Mesopotamian cities. At Al Hasa, Abqaiq and Yabrin it is probable that the beginnings of oasis agriculture can be recognized.

At the height of the Gulf's ancient prosperity, when Dilmun flourished and her trade was, in effect, universal since it touched most of the then known world, settlements of substance and wealth were established on the Arabian mainland. The most important to be found so far is probably that located on the small island of Tarut, close to the mainland to which it is now linked by a causeway, somewhat to the north of the Bahrain islands; from Al-Rafi'ah, or Tarut, came the most important steatite, statuary and pottery to be recovered from the region.[54] Tarut, no doubt, served as the point of access to the mainland regions, where the peoples with whom the Dilmunite merchants sought to trade, exchanged their goods for the produce of the region, particularly its dates.[55] Tarut was not the only significant eastern Arabian settlement, however: a substantial site has been identified near Abqaiq, near Dhahran, where there are also large tumulus fields. Complexes of tumuli on the desert ridges once overlooked a large Neolithic lake and an extinct river which apparently flowed from the Al Hasa oasis to the Gulf at this time. Mound fields in great numbers have also been located near the great Yabrin oasis in the southern part of the province. Late fourth-millennium pottery, which some observers have considered might be ancestral to Bahrain's Barbar pottery, has also been noted in this region. It is contemporary with Uruk pottery in southern Mesopotamia; a pot of apparent Umm an-Nar design is thought to have come from Abqaiq.[56]

It is possible to recognize in eastern Arabia at this time the beginnings of two other most enduring social structures which have characterized the area ever since: the establishment of agricultural communities in the rich oases in the hinterland and, on the coast, the creation of coastal settlements. These eventually grew from fishing villages to little towns and formed the basis of the later third- and second-millennia trading entrepôts.

It has not been possible thoroughly to excavate the *tel* at Tarut; that it is of exceptional antiquity is, however, abundantly clear for Ubaid pottery has been observed on its surface. Eventually, no doubt, excavation will begin on what could prove to be one of the most important of east Arabian sites for it is probable that, before the centre of Dilmun in the early third millennium shifted to the island of Bahrain, it was located here.

From the environs of Tarut has come one of the most remarkable, indeed perhaps *the* most remarkable, of the antiquities of eastern Arabia, which suggests something of its importance and prosperity in Dilmunite times. This is a very fine white limestone statue, nearly a metre tall, of a man in an

Figure 8.4 An exceptionally fine limestone statue, with affinities to the Early Dynastic II style in Sumer, of a worshipper or priest *c.* 2700 BC. From near Tarut.

attitude of worship.[57] He has the broad, rather podgy face, with wide, adoring eyes with which the Sumerians were accustomed to portray themselves when engaged in prayer. He is nude, which suggests that he may be a priest or an official, since in early Sumerian times there is evidence that the priests conducted their rites in a state of ritual nudity (Fig 8.4).

The statue is exceptionally well made. If it had been found in a Sumerian city it would have been remarkable enough and would be regarded as a fine piece of particularly high quality; that it was found 1,000 kilometres (600 miles) from the nearest Sumerian city makes it more remarkable still. It is formidable evidence of the prosperity and importance which the Gulf must have enjoyed at the beginning of the third millennium, to which the Tarut statue is to be dated. It was found buried in a field by a farmer ploughing his land. Naturally enough the villagers (for this was in the 1950s before sophisticated notions had reached the region), decided that this shameless object was a petrified *djinn* or evil spirit; the statue was therefore beheaded and cut in half. It has now been reassembled, almost pristine, except for some damage to the face. It is a very remarkable work of high and quite unexpected quality.

Large quantities of worked steatite have been found on third-millennium sites in eastern Arabia, notably at Al-Rafi'ah near Tarut (Fig 8.5).[58] There seems to have been a considerable industry in the carving of this tractable material into bowls, vases and all manner of vessels. The style of carving is extremely distinctive: bold, emphatic and curiously static, often a trifle naive in concept but not in execution. The repertory of designs is remarkable: large felines, bearded men, nude and heroic, and scenes associated with sailing, the sea and fishing. A curious survival is a group of beard curls in chlorite, probably imitating the lapis lazuli beards with which the statues of the gods or the heads of bulls were often adorned.

The origin of the steatite itself, which is found throughout third-millennium levels in the Gulf and adjacent lands, seems to lie in south-western Persia, where evidence of steatite mining has been found at Shahr-i Sokta; a source near Jabrin is also known. The trade which depended upon the mining of the stone was wide-ranging; and it has been extensively studied.[59,60]

Some Dilmun seals have been found in eastern Arabia; three were picked up from the surface, lying in close proximity to each other,[61] to the north of Hofuf. The extent of the Gulf's trading connections and the quality of the craftsmanship employed in the manufacture of the stone which was exported to it is demonstrated by a beautiful lapis lazuli fragment depicting a man wrapped in his cloak (Fig. 8.6). It is a tiny piece but full of vitality; the Sumerians and their neighbours seem always to have worked best in a relatively small scale.

Throughout the eastern region there are extensive mound fields of the same types of tumulus burials familiar from Bahrain. They appear to cluster

Figure 8.5 In the early third millennium there seems to have been a flourishing local industry in eastern Arabia in the manufacture of richly decorated chlorite vessels and containers. The stone was probably obtained from a source near Jabrin.

in the same periods: in the second half of the third millennium to the early centuries of the second and again in Hellenistic times.

The Dilmunite tumulus-building industry, which must have absorbed much of the community's available labour and resources, especially during the late Bronze Age when it was at its height, is an example of the large-scale project which requires the commitment of numerous and permanently engaged cohorts in the society to bring it to realization. The building of the Pyramids is the classic example of such collective, corporate undertakings.[62] They seem not only to have been important by reason of their scale and the effect which they must have had on the economies from which they sprang but also because they exercised a considerable psychological influence on the

Figure 8.6 A small lapis lazuli figurine, of an old man wrapped in a cloak; his hair is dressed with a pigtail. Third millennium BC.

members of the society. By carrying out such massive programmes, requiring the involvement of virtually every level of the society and extending over centuries, the people came to understand the demands of cooperation and the interplay of skills and resources. Such projects are really a form of social management in a society whose mass was growing beyond any previously known level. So it was in Egypt; so it may have been in Bahrain.

One of the main concentrations of mound burials is near the airport at Dhahran. The tumuli in this area had first been noted by Cornwall[63] but they were not surveyed until, first, the Danes in the 1960s[64] and then an expedition in the 1980s, with the larger resources of the Saudi Arabian Department of Antiquities, carried out work on them.[65] As a result of this it was possible, really for the first time, to form some idea of the eastern Arabian society which was probably ancestral to Dilmun when it moved to Bahrain as its 'capital'. The documentary evidence of contact with Dilmun by the early Sumerian communities in Uruk and Kish doubtless refers to this mainland Dilmun.

The tomb fields, and the settlements of sites like Abqaiq, are clearly earlier in date than the communities which appear on Bahrain. The mound fields date from *c.* 2500 BC; they are therefore approximately contemporary with Umm an-Nar in Abu Dhabi.

The Department of Antiquities estimates that the Dhahran field may have numbered some 50,000 mounds.[66] However, unlike most of the Bahraini tombs, the Dharan examples were thought to be communal, used over a number of generations.

A wide selection of pottery has been found in the Dhahran tombs; it includes Uruk, Jemdet Nasr and Barbar wares, suggesting a broad sweep of time and sustained connections with Mesopotamia.

The construction of the tombs is somewhat simple and less diverse than the examples from Bahrain. There are no tombs in eastern Arabia comparable with the massive 'Royal Tombs' at Aali. Generally the Dhahran tombs have an orientation to the east, that is, the deceased is laid with the head in an easterly direction.

From the Dhahran tombs a group of enigmatic seals has been recovered, three of which show clear connections with Egypt or, at the least, with Egyptianizing influences.[67] They come from area B2 in the Dhahran excavations; one is described as 'a finely carved frit seal with the depiction of a lion and two winged cobras wearing the crowns of Upper and Lower Egypt seated on a lotus blossom in two separate panels'.

The other two seals are both stamps. One is rectangular, made from pale blue frit. It shows Horus, in his falcon guise, standing on a cartouche. This design, of great antiquity in Egypt, always proclaims the name of the king, as the reincarnated Horus, the immanent divinity who personified Egyptian kingship. The other, which looks to be less ancient, represents a reclining sphinx wearing the crown of Upper Egypt, with hieroglyphic signs in front of and above it (Fig. 8.7). Taken with the scaraboid seals from Failaka island, dated to around 2000 BC, these seals suggest a degree of contact between the Gulf, eastern Arabia and Egypt which is both greater and more sustained than had been expected.

Goblets, like those found at Aali, were also present in the Dhahran tombs. They had been thrown on a fast wheel. An unusual material for the manufacture of vessels found in the tombs was Muscovite Schist, a comparatively rare, golden-hued stone which must have been imported from western Arabia, its only known source in the vicinity of the Gulf (Fig. 8.8). Chlorite was found in considerable quantity, as might be expected with the precedent of the large amounts found on nearby Tarut in mind. Other mound fields have been identified at Jabrin, to the south of Dhahran and at Abqaiq.

A product of which considerable evidence was also found at Dhahran were reed baskets coated with bitumen.[68] These were also found on Bahraini sites (Fig. 7.25). The excavators suggested that the nearest source of supply of bitumen was Hit, in Iraq;[69] however, Cornwall suggested that in antiquity there was a bitumen source on Bahrain, though he does not appear to advance any very firm authority for the statement.[70]

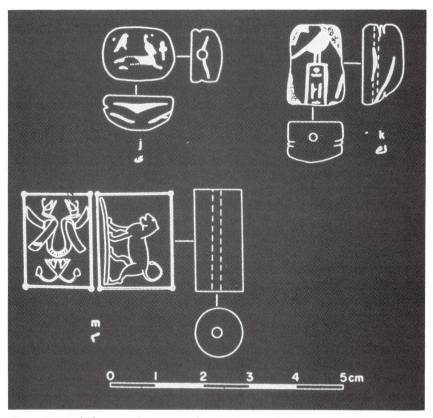

Figure 8.7 Seals from tombs excavated at Dhahran include several with Egyptian, or Egyptianized, motifs.

Figure 8.8 Muscovite schist, also known as 'sunstone', a comparatively rare material, seems to have been handled and carved in much the same way as the more familiar chlorite.

Like Bahrain, eastern Arabia seems to have enjoyed two high points of prosperity and settlement: in the third and early second millennia and again late in the first millennium BC. Nothing yet has been found of the post from which Ili-ippasra complained to his superiors in Babylon about the depredations of the Ahlamu and their seizure of the dates waiting shipment to the capital (see Chapter 7). But in later Hellenistic times the evidence is considerable, including the remains of a substantial city at Thaj.

As yet few sites have been discovered in the eastern region from the second and early first millennia BC. This may be due to the difficulty of identifying the sparse remains. Some Dhahran tumuli, without pottery but with copper and iron arrowheads and personal ornaments, and some of the Jabrin sites may be datable to this time: the Jabal al-Makhruq site has produced a bronze spearhead. In general habitation sites are characterized by rudimentary (probably temporary) structural remains, rough stone tools and occasionally a little crude basket-impressed pottery.

After 1700 BC disruptions in Iraq, Iran and the Levant, and the decline of the Indus Valley civilization slowed the flow of international trade which had made the Arabian Gulf region prosperous for many centuries. However, on the mainland, affecting the coastal sites of eastern Arabia and reaching down into the Gulf's southern limits, crucially important changes took place during this period, made possible by the growing use of the domesticated camel.[71] With increasing aridity after 2000 BC, the people of Arabia separated into more mobile camel-herding nomadic tribes, and settled farmers and traders in the oases.

Evidence from Dilmun suggests that the 'Martu' or Amorites, pastoralist peoples known to the cities of Mesopotamia and the Fertile Crescent, were already active in eastern Arabia around 2000 BC:[72] they, or their ancestors, may well have been the cause of the move of Dilmun's centre from the mainland to the Bahrain islands. As we have seen, c. 1370 BC the governor of Dilmun sent a report to his Kassite overlord in Mesopotamia, complaining about a nomadic people called the 'Ahlamu':

> Around me the Ahlamu have carried away all the dates, thus with me there is nothing I can do. But a single town must not be allowed to be pillaged'.[73]

Elsewhere, in Mesopotamia, the Ahlamu have been identified with early Aramaeans.

In the early first millennium BC Assyrian records refer to Dilmun (now transliterated in its Semitic form, 'Tilmun') from c. 750 to 600 BC during the reigns of Sargon, Sennacherib and Assurbanipal and Babylonian records during the reign of Nabonidus, the king who moved his capital from Babylon to northern Arabia for approximately eleven years.[74] A period of marked prosperity was apparently experienced on the mainland of eastern Arabia, which may have been due to the growth of overland trade. Gerrha is said to have been founded by Chaldaeans, expelled in 694 BC from Babylonia by Sennacherib for piracy.

Tombs from Dhahran of this period, *c.* 800–500 BC, have yielded stamp and cylinder seals which show contacts with the Fertile Crescent and south-west Arabia, pottery, steatite and incense stands, as well as one of the typical New Babylonian 'bathtub' burials, of the type found from the same period at the site of City IV on Bahrain.

Much remains uncertain about the social and political structure of eastern Arabia at this time. The most abiding mystery concerns the whereabouts of the once great city of Gerrha. This is now unknown, though several locations have been suggested for it by commentators and researchers, from Durand onwards.[75]

A number of references to Gerrha and to its famed riches survive in the works of the Roman historians and geographers who wrote of the Arabian Gulf. Thus Strabo, in his *Geography*, writes in AD 23:

> After sailing along the coast of Arabia for a distance of two thousand four hundred stadia one comes to Gerrha, a city situated on a deep gulf; it is inhabited by Chaldaeans, exiles from Babylon; the soil contains salt and the people live in houses made of salt; and since flakes of salt continually scale off, owing to the scorching heat of the rays of the sun, and fall away, the people frequently sprinkle the houses with water and thus keep the walls firm. The city is two hundred stadia distant from the sea; and the Gerraeans traffic by land, for the most part, in Arabian merchandise and aromatics.[76]

Strabo also writes of the already legendary wealth of the Gerraeans and some of their contemporaries and neighbours:

> From their trading both the Sabaeans and the Gerraeans have become richest of all; and they have a vast equipment of gold and silver articles, such as couches and tripods and bowls, together with drinking vessels and very costly houses; for doors and walls and ceilings are variegated with ivory and gold and silver set with precious stones.[77]

Pliny, the historian, observes,

> The Bay of Gerrha and the town of that name, measures five miles around and has towers made of squared blocks of salt. Fifty miles inland is the Attene district; and opposite to it and the same number of miles distant from the coast is the island of Tyros, extremely famous for its numerous pearls.[78]

The reference to the towers made of squared blocks of salt may be a description of the salt-encrusted blocks of the clay taken from the coastal *sabkhas*, which were fired and then used in buildings in Hellenistic times.[79]

Near the frontier between Saudi Arabia and Qatar three Dilmun seals were found lying on the surface.[80] They are amongst the relatively few seals which have been discovered in the Kingdom, and, since they tend to be associated with Dilmun's later centuries, this may be because the centre had shifted from the mainland to the island.

QATAR

Qatar itself would at first sight seem unpromising archaeological territory compared with Saudi Arabia: a small peninsula jutting out into the Gulf, which is wind- and sea-scoured, barren and inhospitable. Yet it has, in fact, much to attract the archaeological eye and all that it has is distinctive and different from the other states in the region. Indeed it is one of the common, if rather curious, features of the archaeology of the Gulf that each little state, superficially similar to its neighbours, with which it has certain elements in common, maintains an individuality which marks it off from the others as firmly as the often somewhat arbitrarily imposed frontiers which now divide one from another.

The neat, painstaking and, in so many ways, persuasive categories into which the Qatar Stone Ages were divided by the Danes, early on in their expeditions to the Gulf,[81] have been somewhat revised by later, French researchers.[82] The earlier divisions suggested that the first Stone Age settlers established themselves on archaic shorelines, well into the Qatar deserts of today, and were characterized by massive, very brutish-looking handaxes. They, the so-called A Group, were, it was suggested, connected with the makers of Middle Palaeolithic axes. They were thought to have been followed by three other principal Stone Age industries, culminating in the so-called D Group, the makers of the fine and elegant tools of the later Neolithic. Now it seems likely that all the Qatar tools are from Neolithic times and in common with all the other parts of eastern Arabia (though not all the rest of the peninsula), there is no evidence of any occupation by humans before the Neolithic period.[83]

However, the fact remains that the Qatar deserts, harsh and grudging to life as they always seem to be, have yielded a fine repertory of stone tools, which remains, indeed, unrivalled in eastern Arabia. No habitation sites have been found from periods earlier than the occasional one with Ubaid material. There are many workshop sites, however, where Stone Age crafts-men made their tools, even the finest, it seems, with speed and precision.

When the French first cast doubt on the idea of a Mousterian (Middle Palaeolithic) date for some of the Qatar artefacts, they suggest that the sea transgressed, leaving the existing *sabkha* behind, about 6,000 years before the present. They believe they have identified Ubaid pottery, recovered from around the edges of what could have been permanent freshwater stands. They identify one site as a fish drying place; whilst extensive fish remains have been found, they do not include vertebrae. There is evidence of

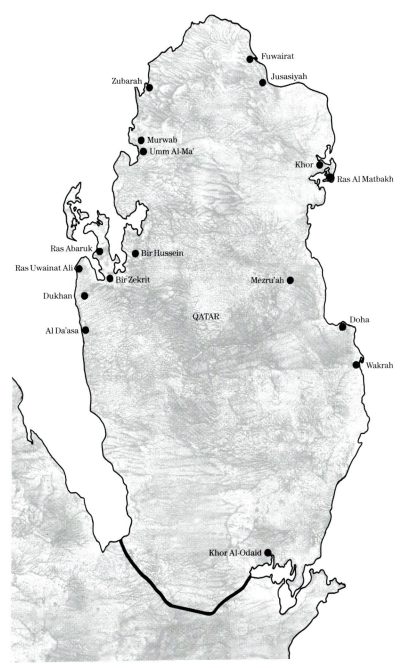

Map 3 Archaeological sites in the Qatar peninsula.

cremation on the site;[84] it appeared to be contemporary with the Ubaid material, which is of obvious importance. There is, however, no other evidence in the Gulf of the people who used Ubaid pottery practising cremation: rather they usually buried their dead, in an extended position.

A small cairn field nearby was perhaps once an island, 3 to 4 metres in diameter. The Ubaid material recovered dates to Ubaid 3. More interesting still is the possibility that the French may have identified a Barbar structure on a small island in the Bay of Khor. Two typical Barbar pots have been recovered from the site.[85]

The products of the Neolithic inhabitants of Qatar are some of the most elegant tools produced by any Stone Age people; they are finely and beautifully made, the best of them fabricated by the technique of pressure-flaking. This consists of striking off tiny, even flakes from the cutting edge of a tool during manufacture, thus producing a consistent edge or, if it is required, a serrated one. This technique reaches perhaps its highest manifestation in Predynastic Egypt, where knives in particular were expertly fashioned to produce works of art of the quality of the justly famous ceremonial knife from Gebel el-Arak, which is one of the Egyptian documents most frequently cited to demonstrate links between Egypt and Mesopotamia in the centuries immediately before the supposed unification of Egypt.[86] The Gebel el-Arak knife displays a whole repertory of Mesopotamian motifs on its ivory hilt, which is as finely made as the blade itself. Only about 2,000 years later were craftsmen in Europe producing pressure-flaked tools of comparable grace.

The flint arrowheads and leaf-shaped scrapers are unquestionably things of beauty. It is, of course, an irresistible if idle speculation to wonder whether their makers themselves saw them as possessing aesthetic as much as utilitarian qualities; probably they did not, though some of them are so sensitively worked, improved apparently far beyond the mere levels of their immediate usefulness, that it is impossible not to ask the question.

Amongst the more distinctive products of the Qatar Neolithic is a fine blade culture which dates from comparatively early in the sequence, from the seventh and sixth millennia. Some of the Qatar Neolithic products could have been used as trimming tools, such as the sickle blades, which were set into hafts. There is no evidence of an early agricultural phase in Qatar (unlike its near neighbour, Bahrain), so it is likely that these tools probably served simply to assist in gathering wild grasses.

Late prehistoric man was physically and intellectually indistinguishable from ourselves, his direct descendants. He comes very near us when the products of his hands are as fine and as appealing as these from Qatar. We know now, from the observation of flint knappers of the present (or near present) day, who have kept alive this oldest of man's technologies, what a marvellous technique is the making of fine stone tools. In fact, though it requires much skill, the knapping of a flint is, to a master, neither onerous nor particularly time-consuming; the finest ripple-flaked blade might be made in a morning or less, a fine arrowhead of the type found in relative profusion in Qatar, in a matter of 30 minutes or so. But one of the qualities that distinguishes the Neolithic craftsman from his predecessors in the working of flint and other friable stones is that his greater industrial efficiency and his ability to select more manageable stone meant that he could produce far more cutting-edged tools per kilo of stone than was possible in earlier times. Evidently something approaching organized industrial processes was by now employed in making stone tools. Preliminary roughing out of the blanks produced from suitable 'cores' would take place at a workshop site, the blanks being taken then to a superior craftsman at a finishing site. Several such workshop sites have been identified in Qatar.

The sites of the Neolithic people, who were almost certainly migrants from outside Qatar and eastern Arabia, were scattered widely over the peninsula. Naturally enough, though, their settlements were concentrated mainly around the shoreline, for they would have been fisherfolk as well as hunter-gatherers, though their fishing would probably have been confined to trapping and spearing.

An incident in the life of a hunter which occurred on a day around 6,000 years ago is preserved dramatically in one Neolithic artefact which has survived in Qatar.[87] Urgent in pursuit of his quarry, the hunter shot his arrow and, it must be presumed, missed his target. The arrow was lost, falling into a shallow pool or on to marshy ground. Over the millennia a calciferous deposit formed around the arrowhead, which is now firmly embedded in what appears to be stone. By so trivial an incident, no doubt exasperating at the time, do the generations communicate with each other, in this case over an immensely long stretch; little could the Qatari hunter of those distant days have dreamed that his lost arrowhead would one day act as a witness to the humanity which links his day with ours.

It is possible to infer more about the way of life of the Neolithic inhabitants of Qatar, a way of life they would have shared in general with contemporaries in eastern Arabia, Bahrain and Oman, where evidence of occupation at comparable periods has also been found. It is reasonable, first of all, to assume that the population would probably have been significantly more numerous than in earlier periods, for just as Neolithic man's techniques of tool-making were more skilled, so his more advanced techniques of hunting, his ability to move over a larger hunting area and to survive in conditions which in earlier times would have been insupportable, meant that a greater number could be fed regularly with a more protein-rich diet. Neolithic Qataris lived on fish, gazelle and onegar and, as was demonstrated perhaps by the small blades which could have been used in sickles, they harvested wild cereals and grasses. This probability in fact is made certain by the recognition of querns, used for grinding meal, though deliberate domestication of plants seems not to have been at their disposal.

The wider horizons which had opened to late Stone Age man as a consequence of his increased skill at managing his environment and its resources had included many new techniques which substantially improved his life. The later Qatar Neolithic sustained some elements at least of this expanded life style: a spindle whorl, an essential device in the spinning of yarn, shows that some form of cloth was produced by the people.[88] Man's insatiable need to ornament himself, in life or in death, is demonstrated by a sea-snail's shell which has been bored (itself quite a skilful procedure) so that it could be threaded and worn, perhaps as an amulet, perhaps simply as a decorative addition to what would have been, at best, a rather sparse wardrobe.[89] This indeed is what may generally be said for the archaeological record in Qatar: despite the rich inheritances of Stone Age artefacts which has descended from the more distant times of human experience and apart from the inferences which can be made from the evidence of Neolithic times, little can be said with assurance about the people who made and used them or about their associations beyond Qatar.

The identification of Ubaid pottery on eastern Arabian sites was followed by a similar discovery in 1973 by a British team invited to conduct an archaeological survey on the Qatar peninsular for Qatar's planned National Museum.[90] There was no reason, at that time, to expect to find any trace of the Ubaid in Qatar: such evidence as had been returned from the Arabian sites had not indicated such an extent of Ubaid influence in the Gulf coastal areas as subsequently became apparent. The presence of Ubaid pottery on the island of Bahrain, for example, had not at that time been established; if it had been, it would have been reasonable to expect that Qatar, too, might contain similar evidence. Anyway, there it was and finding it opened up an entirely new dimension in the archaeology of Qatar and of that part of the Gulf. The pottery is invariably found in archaeological contexts with the stone tools and implements of the Neolithic period. This was indeed the case in Qatar too.

The most important Ubaid site to be found in Qatar was at Al-Da'asa on the north-east coast. The site would seem to have been a small seasonal encampment, probably the lodging of a hunting-fishing-gathering group which returned there from time to time. The site still showed the post-holes of whatever shelter the people used; it was most likely a tent though the posts could conceivably have been the supports of a hut wall.

There was a peculiarly poignant find on the Al-Da'asa site which, like the embedded arrow, seems to bridge the more than fifty centuries which probably separate the time of the Al-Da'asa people and the present day. Near the post-holes was found neatly stacked a group of domestic implements, a grinder, querns, a piece of coral used for scouring and the like. It was the very tidiness of the way they had been piled up together that was particularly moving, as though some Neolithic tent-wife had set them carefully aside intending to return for them or to use them again. For whatever reason they lay undisturbed for many thousand years: whoever put them there so carefully never returned to claim them.[91]

Whilst the pottery found at Al-Da'asa is Ubaid in manufacture, it need not be thought that its discovery in Qatar presupposes the presence of the Ubaid people themselves. Pottery in ancient times was a greatly valued commodity and was traded over considerable distances. The value that would be attributed to a pot of the period is demonstrated by one of the larger Qatar-Ubaid sherds; this was broken in antiquity and then repaired so that it could continue to be used.

There never was, of course, any question of the Ubaid pottery found in Qatar having been made there; it is most unlikely that the region would have permitted the degree of settled occupation necessary for a pottery-producing society to flourish, with all the equipment necessary in the actual production process – kilns, paints, not to mention suitable clays. Indeed, research has shown that the Qatar pottery represented by the scatter of sherds, like those found in the eastern Arabian sites, was actually manufactured in Ur and traded down to the Gulf settlements.[92] It is likely that the Qatar settlements at Al-Da'asa represent the same sort of community as those identified in eastern Arabia. Presumably the sherds are part of the detritus of peoples with a very similar way of life, probably moving seasonally over a comparatively extensive territory, which might well, therefore, have included both eastern Arabia and Qatar in its range.

The later periods in Qatar, when the Gulf was the main artery of world trade and the settlements on the eastern coast of Arabia became cities of great commercial importance, are almost totally barren, with no evidence yet discovered of continuous occupation. If any should be found there it is unlikely that it will prove to be more than occasional or very minor; certain it is that no cities of the scale of those in Bahrain or eastern Arabia were ever a feature of Qatar's landscape. No doubt the environment was too harsh, the country too bleak and barren even for the hardy travellers of Sumerian, Akkadian and Babylonian times. Qatar's is a singularly scoured landscape, torn by constant winds; little vegetation grows there, the grazing is sparse and water is not readily available. There would be little incentive for settlement in times when life was harsh enough anyway.

A recent, if altogether unexpected, discovery has, however, begun to qualify this view of the absence of continuous or significant settlement in Qatar. This was the uncovering by the French Expedition of a small site near Al Khor which yielded a considerable quantity (estimated at some 2 million) of murex shells.[93] The murex is the little creature on which the ancient fame and prosperity of the great city of Tyre in the Levant was based.

From the murex came the superb crimson and scarlet dyes (misnamed purple) which lent glamour and a spectacular flourish to the public assemblies of the Phoenician cities and, later, of Rome. Remembering the legends of the links between the Gulf and the cities of the Levant it is remarkable to find a dye factory (albeit a very small one) in so remote a place on the Qatar peninsula. From the pottery which the site has yielded it can be dated to Kassite times, late in the second millennium BC.

Such archaeological remains as there are in Qatar seem to come from much later periods, which are really beyond the scope of this present study. The Greek presence in the Gulf and eastern Arabia is demonstrated by a quantity of sherds of Seleucid pottery which are of a type dating from around the second century BC.[94] The Seleucids were the rulers of much of Persia in the period following the death of Alexander the Great; they take their name from Seleucus, one of Alexander's generals, who seized the Persian throne in the anarchy which followed the world-conqueror's death. There is no evidence, so far discovered, of a settlement at Ras Uwainat Ali and it seems most likely therefore that the literally thousands of sherds of pottery of the Seleucid period found there by the Danes (who painstakingly restored three whole vessels from the debris) are perhaps the consequence of a shipwreck or some other accidental circumstance.

A more equivocal discovery was made by the Danes by chance when a truck in which some members of their expedition were driving sank into a cavity in the sand at Ras al-Matbakh.[95] On investigating the hole which they had opened up, they found a pithos, a large pot, which had been used as a coffin; the remains of the body were still contained within it. From its orientation it was clearly not Islamic for it was not directed to the west, towards the holy city of Makkah. Since the burial contained no goods nor the possessions of the dead, its dating is a matter of conjecture; however, the use of the pithos, which is nearly a metre high, recalls the 'bathtub' coffins of neo-Babylonian times, examples of which were found at Qala'at al-Bahrain. Some scholars, however, point to pithos burials in eastern Arabia which are more usually attributed to the second millennium BC rather than to the first.

In any event, it is a matter of speculation what so great a pottery vessel was doing in Qatar in the first place, let alone in what circumstances it was used to enclose the body of whoever it was who had the misfortune to die there. Certainly it would seem too large to have been transported by land and, as in the case of the Ras Uwainat Ali pottery, it is uncharacteristic of the people who used the Qatar coast at this time to have produced an artefact so majestic, in size at least. Perhaps the explanation may be that it was part of a shipborne cargo and that its occupant died at sea but that the conventions demanded that he should be returned to earth, cradled in a coffin, albeit a makeshift one. The friends of the dead man may have landed at Ras al-Matbakh and buried him in this lonely place before continuing with their journey.

Two final categories of remains in Qatar must be considered, though briefly, for they too, though obscure chronologically, would seem to belong to periods beyond the *terminus post quem* of this study. The first of these are the fields of cairn burials which are found throughout the Qatar peninsula.

Cairn burial was a common form of grave construction throughout pre-Islamic Arabia: a mound of stones overlying a relatively simple interment. In Qatar the cairns are to be found at Umm al-Ma, Mezruah, Ras Abaruk and Ras Uwainat Ali.[96] In no case is their chronology particularly explicit.

At Umm al-Ma there were two types of cairns identified by the Danes who first investigated them.[97] The first type is rock-cut, the grave lined with trimmed stone blocks. One such grave contained two burials, one on top of the other. The second type of grave in this group also contains worked stone blocks but is triple-chambered in plan. In such a grave a skeleton was found, lying with its legs drawn up.

At Mezruah a burial was found which seems, if only obscurely, to link customs in Qatar in pre-Islamic times with a practice known in other parts of Arabia, including Bahrain: the hamstringing of camels around the grave of a hero.[98] The grave at Mezruah consisted of an oval-shaped cairn of large flat stones; outside it were found the skeletons of camels, crouching on their hocks. In the grave a Sassanian glass, almost intact, was found, suggesting that the burial might have been late pre-Islamic in date. In addition to camel sacrifices there is also evidence of horse sacrifice in pre-Islamic Qatar.

Mezruah produced the most notable of the very sparse grave goods which the cairn burials have so far yielded. The grave in question contained two burials; one at least of the occupants was, it is fair to assume, a warrior, for a handsome iron sword and a group of well-made iron arrowheads had been buried with him. The other skeleton bore the sinister evidence of what was evidently a warrior's last battle; embedded in the principal bone of his forearm was another arrowhead. It remains there to this day, the grim witness of some long-forgotten, but, for the warrior, final encounter.[99]

The last and certainly the most enigmatic of all Qatar's antiquities are to be found on the crests of two low hills in the extreme north of the peninsula, at Fuweirit and Jusasiyah.[100] On these two little hills, both barely more than a sort of rising stone outcrop, there are countless (literally so, since nobody so far has had the determination to count them) carvings, patterns and designs pecked, cut or gouged into the rock beside some of the most desolately beautiful of Qatar's northern shores. The presence of the sea, indeed, adds to the sense of isolation of the two little hills, which are backed simply by the empty desert. It is this very isolation which contributes to the strangeness of these two sites.

Rock carvings are familiar enough over the whole of Arabia (outside the east) to make their discovery in Qatar hardly a matter for comment or even surmise. In fact Qatar is notably bare of inscriptions and graffiti; but the carvings on the two little rocky hills really are very curious indeed. The traveller in the Arabian deserts and the wadis of Oman may be forgiven if he forms the impression that, in pre-Islamic times at least, the peninsula was inhabited by a race of committed artists who, seeing a rock surface, were seized by an urge, universal and irresistible, to carve something on it. The sheer scale of

Arabian rock-carving, which in individual examples must amount at least to hundreds of thousands, suggests an earnestness and application in the decoration of rock surfaces which is perhaps surprising to those who know the desert and its people today. The tradition continues, as demonstrated in Oman, where, alongside what may be third-millennium designs, the outlines of Land Rovers, rifles and other contemporary gear are delineated.

By far the most frequent design to be found on the two hills is that which consists of what are most generally called 'cup-marks': small circular pits cut into the rock surface, their sides curving to a rounded depression; they are usually not more than 3 to 5 centimetres in diameter, and less in depth. In Qatar they are occasionally found singly but far more frequently they are massed together, in a seemingly endless variety of formations, single lines, double and treble lines, sometimes straight and sometimes curving, sometimes circular, sometimes a circle of cups with one in the centre, in formations of six, eight, twelve, fourteen, sixteen and onwards, with no apparent progression or sequence. They seem to be distributed at random over the surface of the little hills; they appear to follow no evident orientation, neither solar, lunar nor stellar.

Those who have studied them have proposed, basically, two explanations for them; neither is entirely satisfactory. It has been suggested, on the analogy with similar formations in Europe, particularly in Scandinavia, that they are in some way associated with fertility, a proliferation of vulvas into which the life-giving rain pours. This may or may not be the explanation of cup forms in northern Europe, dating from the Bronze Age; it seems unlikely in eastern Arabia if only because the cups are so small, and vulvae, other than perhaps in the most febrile imaginations, rarely come in groups.

During the lifetime of man, too, rain in the desert is a comparatively rare phenomenon, at least to the extent that it seems unlikely that so universal a practice in northern Qatar as the making of cup-marks for the purpose of catching rainfall would have prevailed so extensively. A more tenable suggestion was that the cup-mark formations were boards for playing the game called in Arabia *huwais*, but which is known throughout the world under different names and many forms. In essence the game, which is played by two people, consists in moving counters (stones, beans or any other handy alternative) round the board, the moves being determined by the throw of dice or other mechanism. The game is played amongst the Badu to this day; it has been suggested that it is African in origin and of great antiquity.

Convenient though this explanation would be, it is ultimately unsatisfactory on several grounds. The various configurations in which the cup-marks are distributed are not consistent; inconsistent too are their locations, and the fact that at least one example is to be found on the side of a rock, almost in an overhang, demonstrates that it at least could not have been used to contain anything, liquid or solid.

But at the end of the day, the sheer quantity of cup-marks in countless formations destroys the argument that they were used only for *huwais*, unless the making of them had some ritual significance, as though the marking out of a roulette table or tennis court carried with it substantial indulgences, releasing its maker from so many years' penance in some games-playing purgatory, for example. It seems very unlikely that the players either made a fresh board each time they wished to play – by the time they had finished making the board, night, if not their enthusiasm, would have fallen – or that there would have been so many games in progress simultaneously that several hundreds (if not thousands) of boards would be necessary. It seems improbable that this very remote spot in the north of the Qatar peninsula was ever the site of so extensive and feverish a cult of *huwais*-playing as to make the saloons of Vegas or of Monte Carlo seem atrophied and empty either of activity or excitement. It is simply too far-fetched.

Another, more prosaic explanation might be that the cup formations were associated in some way with the pearl trade in which Qatar's pre-oil prosperity was grounded. The sorting of pearls of different sizes and qualities is an essential element in the trade's management and the rewards, often meagre enough, of the fishermen. The cups could have been used for this purpose, though again their quantity, their location so far from the normal habitations of the pearl merchants, and the variety of their composition and disposition over the rocks make this, too, seem unlikely.

But the cup-marks, extensive though they are, are only one form of carving on the two rocky hills, close to the sea shore. Still more enigmatic, because they are quite without precedent in Qatar or, so far as is known, anywhere else, is a series of large carvings, painstakingly cut out on the rock surface, which, at first sight, appear to be representations of boats, seen in plan. Masts, cross-seats, thwarts seem all to be depicted and some of the boats appear to be trailing large anchors. However, the explanation of these carvings, of which there is a particular concentration on Jusasiyah, as showing some sort of sailing-craft, is perhaps too simple: some of the drawings which initially seem to represent boats can, at a second glance, look more like fish, with long feathery tails, whilst others, more remarkably still, seem to be of huge scorpions, crawling across the rock face. They are altogether strange, sinister and, seen at sunset with the dying sun glancing across them, rather disturbing.

Some of the boats, in the view of some authorities, may be pearlers. Thus far only one serious study of the rock carvings has been made.[101] The author recorded many of the carvings and, so far as the ship representations are concerned, concluded that they might be of fourteenth century AD date. Even this conclusion must be regarded as very tentative; but if this dating were to be substantiated, it would still not explain why anyone should have troubled to have portrayed boats, fishes or scorpions (or perhaps something which contains the elements of all three) on such a scale, in so obscure a place.

Other carvings in the same spot add to the mystery, rather than diminish it. Circular pits cut into the rock have been compared with the fire-pits found across the Gulf and associated with Iranian fire-cults of pre-Islamic times. Others seem to be crude offering-tables with long runnels extending from them, as though to allow for the running off of some liquid or other. Some of these sometimes have the look of schematic, horned beasts.

Of quite another sort is a small, elegant and very heavily weathered carving of an ibex or other caprid. This is the most deliberately representational of all the northern group of Qatar rock carvings and would certainly not look out of place in a third-millennium, or even earlier, Mesopotamian context. Once again the question of what it is doing in Qatar, far from any evident signs of occupation with which it might be associated, obtrudes itself – but no answer is forthcoming. But that is the way of Qatar's archaeology as a whole; at present, it proposes more questions than it provides answers.

THE UNITED ARAB EMIRATES

Further still along the coast, eastwards from the Qatar peninsula, lies the most recently invented state in the area, the United Arab Emirates, a confederation of seven little principalities paradoxically united into a highly individual and improbable republic. The seven states, Abu Dhabi, Dubai, Sharjah, Umm al-Qawain, Ras al-Khaimah, Fujairah and Ajman, represent ancient (more or less) tribal or clan territories. The first three are rich, Abu Dhabi immensely so: the latter four are not and depend on the fortunes of their richer brothers.

It now seems likely that the earliest developed culture in the Gulf was located in its southern reaches, on what is today the coast of the United Arab Emirates. Historically speaking, it is difficult not to recognize that this area represents the northern extent of Oman, for the coastal region in which the states and cities of the UAE are today located is really an extension of the piedmont of the northern limits of the Jebel Akhdar and of Ras Musandam to the east. Some of the earliest settlements in the Gulf, dating to the very beginning of the third millennium, were located inland from the coast near the copper-mines; later, the islands which today lie close off shore were the sites from which copper was trans-shipped to Dilmun and the cities of Mesopotamia.

In recent years, more precisely since the mid-1980s, the United Arab Emirates has seen some of the most productive archaeological work to be undertaken in the Gulf. It was known from the early days of the Danish Expeditions that sites in the Emirate of Abu Dhabi were very early and exceptionally important; what only became evident in more recent years was that there had been settlements on the southern coast at least from the late third millennium onwards, the product, no doubt, of the search for copper and the need to keep open the lines of supply from the source of the metal to the customers in Sumer and, in all probability, elsewhere.

What was less to be expected perhaps was that this part of the Gulf, very remote indeed from any of the principal centres of population with which Dilmun maintained contact, was the location for much earlier movements of people. At the time of the floruit of the Jemdet Nasr horizon in Mesopotamia, the people who built the distinctive tombs in northern Oman, identified with the site of Hafit, were active over a considerable geographical area. Evidence of their presence has now been found from eastern Arabia to Dhofar, in the far south of Oman, bordering the Indian Ocean. The activity with which the Hafit people were involved was probably pearling or the fishing of the exceptionally rich seas around the Oman coast, a resource which is sustained to this day. Hafit pottery and the handsome tombs in which the people were buried have been dated to approximately 3100–2900 BC.

It is possible that the people from these early settlements were responsible for the 'colonizing' of the northern Gulf lands, including Bahrain.[102] The earliest burial mounds on Bahrain bear a strong resemblance to those from Umm an-Nar and the building techniques employed in the stone-built structures of Bahrain seem to echo those of the northern Omani coastal settlements. Umm an-Nar tombs usually are designed to hold multiple burials, unlike many, perhaps the majority, of the Bahrain mounds. Probably each tomb was used on many occasions, over a protracted period, for Umm an-Nar forms of pottery as well as funerary architecture continued throughout most of the third millennium. The tombs are circular, the interior divided into a number of chambers, the configuration of which varies considerably. The exteriors of the larger examples were faced with finely cut limestone blocks. A very large quantity of fine pottery and carved chlorite vessels has been excavated from the many tombs which have been examined, the evidence, clearly, of elaborate rituals of offerings for the comfort of the dead.

One of the most frequently encountered architectural forms in the Gulf is the large watch-tower, of which examples have been found from Failaka to Oman. It is probable, to judge by the examples found at Hili in Abu Dhabi and further described below, that these were also the invention of the Hafit people. If so, the towers have had a remarkable survival, since they have continued to be built in Oman in modern times.

The Hafit people were probably either related to or were in considerable contact with the early inhabitants of southern Mesopotamia, for associated with them have been found a characteristic form of brick from the Sumerian cities, plano-convex in shape. They also used a distinctive tanged arrowhead which has been found in some quantity in the southern Gulf sites. In this context, among the Hafit people's associations, it is interesting that the even earlier evidence of people in the Gulf who were in contact with the makers of Ubaid pottery in the early part of the fourth millennium, have been found now in much the same area and in many of the same locations as the Hafit pottery. Ubaid pottery certainly reached the southern coast and probably will be found in Omani sites.

By the beginning of the third millennium some of the sites on the southern coast and further inland were well established and, for their time, quite sophisticated, at least to judge by their architecture. The further excavation of their remains is likely to produce important information on the life of these small and remote settlements in such early times.

On Umm an-Nar island, the principal settlement of the period to be excavated, the remains of stone-built houses have been found; it is the exteriors of these buildings which were finished with mud-brick,[103] which are of the characteristic Mesopotamian form known as plano-convex. The bricks look rather like loaves of bread and are the most typical material from which Sumerian buildings were made. In the context of the Gulf this evidence from Umm an-Nar is particularly intriguing, for further up the Gulf, in Bahrain for example, there is no evidence of the use of such Sumerian building materials, though structures like the temples at Barbar, whilst built in stone, seem to be Sumerian in inspiration and design. If this was so, then it would suggest Mesopotamian influences or indeed the actual presence of people intimately aware of Mesopotamian building techniques, matched with a local Gulf building tradition. Some of the buildings at Umm an-Nar were substantial, one of them occupying more than 300 square metres. Towers similar to those which are to be found at Omani inland sites such as Ibri and Bat have been found at Hili too, which suggests that the inhabitants needed to protect their communities from marauders.[104] The prevalence of the tower as a dominant architectural form in the early Gulf cultures receives further confirmation from these structures.

The inhabitants of Hili in the third millennium were notably robust: the *average* height, based on an anthropological analysis of nearly 200 individuals, was 1.78 m for the males and 1.72 m for females, quite remarkable proportions for people of 4,000 years ago.[105]

From the quality of the architecture and the grave goods recovered, particularly the pottery, it is evident that the Umm an-Nar people, though probably only a very small community, enjoyed a high and rapidly advancing level of prosperity in the early years of the third millennium. This community appears to be considerably earlier even than the first people to live in the original city at the Qala'at al-Bahrain; Umm an-Nar pottery has indeed been discovered at the bottom of the earliest harbour wall there.[106] It becomes increasingly likely that people from Umm an-Nar were involved in the original settlement of the Qala'at site at Bahrain. Graves of Umm an-Nar type or influence are present in Bahrain and are the earliest in that island's long catalogue of funerary architecture. Umm an-Nar burials have now been identified over a wide range of eastern Arabia and down into the southern Gulf, as far as Ras Al-Had on the central Oman coast.

Umm an-Nar pottery is very distinctive. Like the later pottery from other coastal sites such as Ras al-Khaimah, it seems to have affiliations with sites across the Gulf in south-western Iran and, possibly, others in Baluchistan and Afghanistan. The importance of the Umm an-Nar community to the Gulf in the early centuries of the third millennium lies in the fact that it was the point from which copper, mined in what is today the Sultanate of Oman at sites to the south of Umm an-Nar, in the Buraymi and Ibri oases, was shipped via Dilmun to the cities of Sumer.[107]

One of the intriguing elements in the archaeology of the Umm an-Nar community is the evidence of their diet.[108] They were largely a fishing people and amongst the debris of their occupation the remains of a dugong, or sea-cow, have been found.[109] It was evidently butchered at Umm an-Nar to feed the settlers there. The Umm an-Nar settlement also produced evidence of the consumption of the camel, though it is not known whether this should be taken as proof of domestication; probably not, on the basis of more general evidence.[110]

There is some evidence that sorghum was cultivated in this part of the coast. This is particularly significant for it is generally accepted that sorghum was first cultivated in northern Sudan. It appears in very early levels at Hili, at the beginning of the third millennium; it is known in Oman from even earlier times.[111] It appears in India c. 2000 BC and it would seem therefore that it was carried from west to east, from Africa via Arabia to India. It is a nice speculation what people may have effected its transfer over this considerable distance.

At Hili an altogether different situation persisted from that in Umm an-Nar, though the site also dates from early in the third millennium.[112] The funerary architecture at Hili is altogether remarkable. A large circular, drum-like tomb has been restored at Hili and displays a number of remarkable carvings in relief which seem to have served as decorative elements in the architecture of some of the larger tombs (Fig. 8.9). They are quite extraordinary and unlike anything else in their immediate context.[113] Whilst the decoration of rock surfaces is a practice which seems to have engaged the enthusiasm of the ancient inhabitants of much of the Arabian peninsula (though not generally in the east except, as will shortly be seen, in Oman) to an almost obsessional degree, the Hili carvings are of quite a different sort. There are several distinct scenes depicted: an erotic group of an embracing couple (Fig. 8.10), a design which almost exactly repeats much earlier ones from Çatal Hüyük in Anatolia and Ain Sakhri, a Natufian site in Palestine; two felines, possibly leopards, tearing a smaller animal (Fig. 8.11); a group of travellers (Fig 8.10), and two very handsome oryx (Fig. 8.12).[114]

One of the most important developments in the archaeology of the

Figure 8.9 The circular decorated tomb at Hili, Abu Dhabi, as restored, third millennium BC.

southern Gulf has been the identification of Ubaid-period pottery on a number of sites. Thus far, only Oman does not appear to have any evidence of contact with the makers of Ubaid pottery and that situation may well change in the future.

That the southern regions of the Gulf in particular have much more to reveal is clearly demonstrated by the excavations which archaeological teams from a variety of countries have been conducting and which continue to do so in sites all along the coast of the United Arab Emirates. In a number of cases third-millennium shorelines are now located as much as a kilometre or more inland; this is the case, for example, with a large mound at Tel Abraq, on the borders of Sharjah and Umm al-Qawain.[115] This has yielded evidence of continuous settlement from the middle of the third to the middle of the first millennium BC.

Tel Abraq was obviously a substantial community. A very large tower structure has been excavated there, with a diameter of 40 metres.[116] This means that it is considerably larger than contemporary towers to the south at locations such as Hili and Bat, which are approximately half the size of the Tel Abraq tower.

The repeated discovery of towers throughout the Gulf, which are represented from Failaka island in the north to the copper-related sites in Oman and which are now to be recognized as almost as typical a Gulf architectural feature as the fields of grave mounds, is a remarkable aspect of the archaeology of the past two decades. The oldest examples of the towers seem to be on the northern coast of the Oman peninsula, in what is today the territory of the United Arab Emirates and in Oman itself.

The Tel Abraq site has already augmented considerably knowledge of the Umm an-Nar period on the coast and added to the repertory of pottery of the periods during which it flourished.

Whilst the work on the early sites in the UAE has tended to dominate reports of archaeology from the country, important excavations from later periods have been recorded over recent years. Most of the remains, whilst they testify to continuing international connections, and are doubtless to be associated with trade in the region, are quite distinctive and not merely reflections of the apparently much more advanced and assertive Dilmun culture located further up the Gulf.

One type of grave which seems to have been specific to this part of the Gulf coast during the second millennium BC is a long, narrow, communal tomb, partly sunken into the ground. Chlorite vessels (Fig. 8.13) with a bulbous base and tapering to a narrower neck, inscribed with pierced circles and a number of dress ornaments including some made in gold, silver and bronze, were recovered from such graves. Tombs of this type have been found at Qattara (Fig. 8.14), Al Qusais near Dubai, and at Shimal in Ras Al-Khaima;[117] in the case of the last some Harappan artefacts, pottery and a weight were excavated, suggesting connections with the Indus Valley.[118] There appears to have been an extensive settlement at Shimal, located at the foot of the small mountain range (Fig. 8.15);[119] a similar settlement was located at Dhayah.

A sizeable Iron Age settlement was established at Hili and another at Rumailah.[120] Large, well-built tombs were associated with the settlements and there is evidence of cults including the worship of snakes, approximately contemporary with the snake cults which seem to be evident up the Gulf in Bahrain.[121]

In Hellenistic times, when the Gulf was actively involved with the incense trade from the southern Arabian kingdoms, a major port was established at Ed-Dur, in Umm al-Qawain.[122] This has been excavated by a British team; a French expedition has been responsible for the excavation of a contemporaneous town at Mleiha, further inland from the coast, located, like Shimal, at the foot of the mountains.[123]

The interest of the various states in their archaeology has been mixed and they have only been described here in a general and cursory fashion. Abu Dhabi has encouraged excavation and some ambitious reconstructions of some of her important and very early monuments. Dubai has carried out spasmodic surveys whilst Ras Al-Khaimah commissioned a distinguished British researcher to survey its northern regions, which resulted in some

Figure 8.10 A man riding a donkey, accompanied by another (*left*) and an embracing (or dancing?) couple (*right*); the Hili tomb.

Figure 8.11 Two felines tearing a smaller animal; the Hili tomb.

of the better publications on the area.[124] Recently some evidence of copper-smelting has been found there, which suggests that Ras Al-Khaimah was also one of the points from which copper was trans-shipped up the Gulf from its source in Oman.[125] There has also been identified at Ghadilah a form of tomb unlike the others for which this part of the Ras Al-Khaimah coast is known, with a profile 'like a pill-box'.[126]

Figure 8.12 Two oryx in confrontation, with two figures between and beneath them, holding hands; the Hili tomb.

THE SULTANATE OF OMAN

The last of the Gulf territories which contributed much to its culture in antiquity is that which is today contained within the northern part of the Sultanate of Oman. The second largest country in the Arabian peninsula, often spectacularly beautiful, diverse in its topography and with a rich admixture of peoples and traditions, Oman is markedly different in character from its neighbours. It is one of the few distinct nation-states in the Arab world, with a firmly defined identity of its own. This it seems always to have had; the mediaeval Arab geographers and historians tend to emphasize its essentially individual and homogeneous character.

245

In the texts of the ancient Sumerians and their successors, Dilmun is frequently linked with two other lands, Melukhkha, which is now considered to be the Indus Valley region, and Magan or, as it is sometimes transliterated, Makkan. From Magan came much of the Sumerian city-states' most important imported commodity, the staple of their economies, copper. Magan is today identified with Oman and parts of the northern coast now within the political boundaries of the United Arab Emirates; sometimes the term may also have included areas of the coast across the Straits of Hormuz.

Oman occupies much of the south-eastern quadrant of the Arabian peninsula though it is geographically, as it has always tended to have been historically, isolated from its neighbours. This isolation has contributed much to the Sultanate's particular character.

Indeed, strictly speaking, Oman is only in part a Gulf state; much of her extensive coastline borders the Indian Ocean. It is this geographical isolation which has most contributed to the Omani experience throughout history, a history which has been most notably a record of Oman's marriage with the sea. Oman is cut off from her northern and western neighbours by the central and southern Arabian deserts which divide the coastal strip, in which most of Oman's historic towns are concentrated, from the rest of the peninsula. This division is strengthened by the presence of the great range of mountains, the Jebel Akhdar, which runs north to south down most of the length of the country. To the west of Oman, and north of her fertile southern provinces, lies the Rub' al-Khali, the Empty Quarter or, more simply, the Sands, as they are called by the local people. This gigantic waste, some 400,000 square kilometres (250,000 square miles) of deep and constantly moving sands, was, in late Neolithic times, a region of swamps and marshes, in particular on its northern periphery, where evidence of Neolithic settlements has been found in abundance.[127] Then, bodies of water ran down from the Rub' al-Khali to the sea, making the coast of what was once called Trucial Oman, and which today is the United Arab Emirates, a string of islands of which Umm an-Nar is a survivor.

Sailing southwards from the Gulf, a vessel must pass through the Straits of Hormuz (to the Iranian shores of which the Empire of Oman once extended in middle Islamic times) out into the Gulf of Oman, the beginning of the Arabian Sea, and the first ocean water that the sailor meets on the route to the Indian subcontinent. The prevailing winds and currents of this region have had a considerable influence on the development of Omani history, bringing her ships eastwards to India and beyond, and westwards to the east African coast.

Thus Oman's long coastline has had a profound influence on the course of her history; her people have always been energetic and courageous seamen, probably from the earliest times. Oman's ships are distinctive and her sailors

Figure 8.13 A chlorite beaker from Wadi Asimah, third millennium.

Figure 8.14 A communal tomb at Qattara, showing its entrance and reused Umm an-Nar stonework, second millennium BC.

Figure 8.15 An excavated tomb at Shimal, Ras Al-Khaima, second millennium BC.

were foremost amongst the seamen of Islam, their fame spreading through-out the world in the time of the Arab empires. Omani seamen opened up the sea routes to China and the east, and at the height of the Arab caliphates her cities were reckoned amongst the most populous and splendid in Islam – which effectively meant, at that time, in the entire world.

Oman differs from other parts of Arabia in respect of the variety of climate and the consequently varied ecology which she enjoys. Much of the country is desert, the home of camel-rearing nomads; the mountain valleys and terraces, however, are in parts richly fertile and bear a variety of fruits and crops impossible to cultivate in other parts of eastern or central Arabia, whilst in the far south the green and undulating foothills of Dhofar are the home of Arabia's only cattle-breeders, archaic tribes which still speak non-Arabic languages in the confines of their family groups. The south of the country catches the tail of the monsoon season, its rains bringing the prospect of intense cultivation to the land which it touches. Again, Oman is unique in this for it is the only part of the peninsula within the monsoon's reach.

It appears that even as early as the late fourth millennium, and certainly by the beginning of the third, Oman was in touch with other centres in the region of the Gulf. The evidence for this degree of wide-ranging contacts is

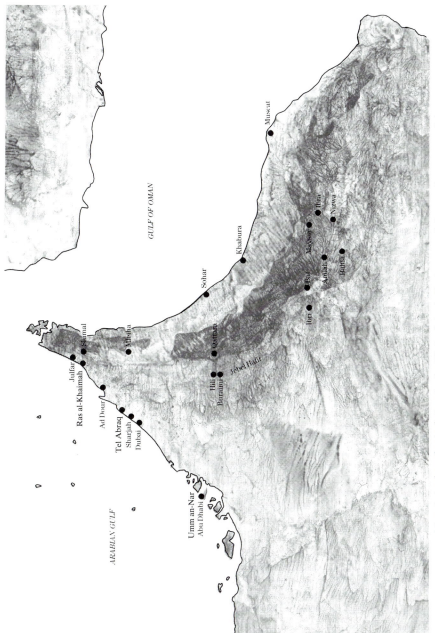

Map 4 Archaeological sites in the United Arab Emirates and the northern part of the Sultanate of Oman.

the pottery found on several sites in the Sultanate which show connections with Umm an-Nar to the north, with Kulli across the Gulf in Baluchistan, with western Iran and, later, with the Barbar levels at Bahrain. So far no other Gulf site has produced comparable material to show, apparently, so broadly cast a net of interconnections which, as this pottery suggests, Oman enjoyed in such very early times. The reason for this evident concentration of foreign contact was once again trade and in particular, in Oman's case, almost certainly trade based on the ancients' search for hard stones for building and sculpture and for sources of one of the most important elements in their economies, copper.

In the early inscriptions relating to trade and the carriage of merchandise, the term 'Magan-boat' is often employed; a case in point is the myth *Enki and the World Order* in which, it may be recalled, the god declares that he 'moored the Dilmun-boat to the ground, loaded the Magan-boat sky-high'.[128] This presumably is to be taken as a demonstration of the exceptional prosperity that Enki brought to both places, as witnessed by the heavy loads borne by their craft; it may also refer to the type of boat which it was customary to use on the run between Magan and the markets with which it had dealings, no doubt Dilmun-Bahrain, perhaps the Indus cities, maybe Sumer itself. In the light of Oman's subsequent history of intense involvement with the sea and seamanship it is conceivable that even this early the Maganites were renowned sailors and reference to them in such a context would produce the same degree of recognition and response which might be expected from a similar reference to the better known lands of Dilmun and its sailing ships. It may be, too, that 'Magan-boat' meant something like 'China Clipper' would have done to a nineteenth-century participant in the Far Eastern trade.

It is, of course, even possible that a particular type of boat originating in Magan is also meant. Oman has produced at least one vessel which may be peculiar to itself and which is of great antiquity: the 'sewn-boat' whose planks are stitched together without the use of nails and which is used extensively in Omani waters to this day.[129] This explanation would also require the 'Dilmun-boat', referred to in the same text, to represent a specific type; for this there is no evidence, though the representations on seals, for example, do seem to show a variety of types of boat in use, several of which might have originated in the Gulf trade.

What particularly lured merchants and seamen to Oman in Early Dynastic times as well as later was the prospect of copper, present in substantial quantities and relatively easily mined. References in early texts to 'the Mountain of Copper'[130] are thought to refer to Magan, for Oman might well be memorable to its early visitors by reason of the high mountains which are so dominating a feature of the landscape in the northern half of the country, where the copper deposits are located. This assumption is less definite now, in most scholars' views, but there is no doubt that Oman was an important source of copper in antiquity; the areas which were mined are still visible, as are the great heaps of slag remaining from the smelting operations which were evidently carried out close to the source of supply. The fact that Oman's copper contains a relatively high concentration of arsenic, which is also found in Mesopotamian copper artefacts, is suggestive, but it cannot yet be regarded as decisive proof of an Omani provenance for specific samples of Sumerian copper until analytical techniques are further refined.

There are extensive workings in copper-rich areas of the Wadi Jizzi system in northern Oman which have been worked since the third millennium; the surface workings which are to be seen today date from Islamic times when Oman was once again developed as an important source (Fig. 8.16). There are, in addition, extensive third-millennium workings in the Wadi Andam and Wadi Ibra. There seems little doubt that the communities which existed there depended upon the exploitation of the copper resources. The devastation which smelting on this scale must have wrought on the forests,

Figure 8.16 Ancient copper workings in the wadis of northern Oman

particularly on the acacia trees which grew extensively on the mountain slopes of Oman, and hence the effect on Oman's ecology and perhaps on its climate, has already been noted (see Chapter 2).

Nothing very precise is known about the actual mechanism of the third-millennium copper-trade in the Gulf. How the copper was mined, whether by slaves or by freemen, what was the nature of Oman's political and mercantile systems at the time, are all unknown. We do not know whether colonies of Sumerian merchants were established in Oman on the model of other outposts of their culture, or whether Oman's traders themselves travelled up the Gulf to Dilmun and Sumer. The name of only one king of Magan is known to us at present. This is Manium, whose only claim to fame is that he was defeated by Naram-Sin, the grandson and eventual heir of the great Sargon of Akkad. Manium has sometimes been confused with Menes, the putative unifier of the two Egyptian kingdoms, but Menes lived a thousand years earlier than Manium. Naram-Sin faced a general rebellion in his empire when he assumed power. Evidently control of the copper-trade was worth mounting what must have been a substantial expedition, with greatly extended lines of supply, from Akkad down the Gulf to Magan. But it seems he was victorious and recorded his victory on various objects which were dedicated to his gods in gratitude.[131]

In Bahrain, on the foreshore at the Qala'at al-Bahrain city site, copper fragments and the remains of whole ingots were found, suggesting that the ore may have been exported to Bahrain and smelted into ingots before being sent on to Sumer. In the workshops of the little cities it would have been converted into tools and traders' vessels, weapons, statues and offerings for the gods, inlays and ornaments for furniture – a thousand different uses for a metal which helped to transform the old Neolithic communities into the civilized city populations of the third millennium and later. The amalgam with tin, in which copper becomes the even harder-edged bronze, gave a name to this period of third- and second-millennia development, the Bronze Age, in the nomenclature of nineteenth-century archaeology.

Early in the third millennium, at the beginnings of the Mesopotamian cities' prosperity, Oman too was prosperous, supporting a sizeable population, some of whom lived in fortified townships of an architectural sophistication and of a character, so far as it is yet possible to judge, distinct from that of other urban centres of the third-millennium Gulf.[132] Indeed, some of the earliest material in the Gulf region, other than the Ubaid (which seems not to be present in Oman) comes from these early Omani settlements. A Jemdet Nasr horizon has been identified in sites such as Jebel Hafit, Ibri and Bat, amongst others.[133] This dates to around 3000 BC and is consequently earlier than any settlements known in Bahrain or eastern Arabia, other than the Ubaid-connected ones on the coast. The Ubaid is not known in Oman though of course it is present on the coast of what is today the United Arab Emirates.

Figure 8.17 The round fortified tower at Nizwa before the modern development of the town. This demonstrates the relationship of the tower to the settlement; the Nizwa tower is the descendant of those built in northern and central Oman, from the early third millennium BC.

Amongst the most remarkable phenomena in Oman, and another testament to the longevity of architectural forms in these parts, are the observation towers which have been identified on some of these early sites.[134] They were, in all probability, observation posts protecting the little settlements against raiders; they seem generally to have contained water wells which presumably they also protected and they would have provided protection for the villagers in case of attack. The most notable are situated at Ibri and at Bat; there are also examples in the United Arab Emirates at Hili, where one tower was surrounded by a moat.[135] One of the towers at Hili appeared to date from around 3000 BC, much earlier than any other similar structure.[136] The towers are the direct ancestors of towers such as that at Nizwa, built in the eighteenth century in the form in which it now stands and which thus has an ancestry of at least 5,000 years (Fig. 8.17).

An otherwise unprecedented but probably very early fragment of pottery came from an unrecorded excavation of a grave in northern Oman. The sherd derives from a spouted vessel; it is of a fairly coarse red ware painted with black. It is significant because of its decoration, which suggests connections with other lands, particularly Iran, perhaps as early as the late fourth millennium BC.

The decoration on the sherd is particularly interesting for it shows a group of dancers, hand in hand in a landscape dominated by three triangles, which look suspiciously like pyramids but which, since the sherd is clearly a good deal earlier than the earliest pyramid, they certainly are not. In fact they are probably intended to represent mountains, perhaps the great central Oman chain, the Jebel Akhdar. What is notable is that the motif of the dancers holding hands appears in Elam, and in Egypt from Predynastic times, whilst the two elements, of dancers and mountains, are frequently combined in late Predynastic Egyptian pottery.[137]

The distinctive character of Oman in antiquity is further borne out by the funerary architecture of its early inhabitants. Oman shares in the extraordinarily widespread practice of tumulus building but her tombs are different from those in, for example, Bahrain or Saudi Arabia. One group is similar to those identified at Umm an-Nar in Abu Dhabi, but the Abu Dhabi examples must really be regarded as the Omani type reaching up to the northern coastline; there can be little doubt that the form of the Umm an-Nar tombs is Omani in origin, as the same type is to be found throughout northern Oman, distributed over a widely dispersed area.

Many examples of these formidable, beehive-shaped tombs are to be found, generally built on level ground, occasionally singly but more frequently concentrated in groups; a notable concentration of beehive tombs is to be found at Bat (Fig. 8.18).[138] Each tomb is probably a communal burial-place, most likely for a clan or extended family group and was probably used over a quite considerable period of time, representing the burials of several generations. They are themselves monuments of Oman's prosperity in the early third millennium for even as communal graves they must have represented a substantial expenditure of material and effort.

The tombs must have been remarkably conspicuous monuments for they were cased in fine white limestone blocks, skilfully shaped and fitted to the contours of their beehive form. So far none has been found intact and all were plundered in antiquity.

The second type of tomb of this period is again most distinctive: a cairn of stones, often standing up to 6 metres (20 feet) and more in height.[139] These are often to be found on ridges built evidently with the deliberate intention of setting them against the skyline and, perhaps, of providing their owners

Figure 8.18 Omani tombs of the mid- to late third millennium have a distinctive 'beehive' shape. They are well constructed and were finished with a 'skin' of finely shaped limestone blocks.

with an agreeable view (Fig. 8.20). In this they may be reminiscent of Egyptian 'houses of millions of years'.

It may be assumed that both of these tomb types, which each represent such a substantial investment in labour and materials, were the sepulchres of the more prosperous citizens of ancient Oman. From the quantity, it may be inferred that the population of northern Oman in the third and early second millennia, was, like Bahrain in the same period and for this same reason, relatively substantial, a community certainly to be reckoned in thousands of inhabitants. The poor, it may be assumed, were not laid to rest in these handsome monuments but were buried simply in the eternally receptive desert.

But there was even earlier communal activity in Oman which has left its traces in the archaeological record. At Ras al-Hamra, not far from the capital Muscat and close to Qurum, evidence of very early groups of fishermen has been found.[140] On the several promontories which mark the coastline of this part of Oman, burials have been found of fishermen dating back as early as the sixth millennium BC.

At this time conditions were evidently very primitive; the communities would have presented a distinctly savage appearance. Their graves, however, are well formed and the occupants were laid in them with some ritual.

255

Figure 8.19 Three typical cairns on an escarpment in northern Oman, built from local flint.

Ornaments and weapons have been found as well as the evidence of animal (particularly turtle) sacrifices.

The Ras al-Hamra communities flourished before the invention of pottery. Their existence, though long lasting, for they continued to fish Omani waters down to the end of the fourth millennium, must have been sparse indeed. Also on the coast, to the south of Muscat, traces have been found which suggest the presence of Harappan voyagers or at least of a people who were sufficiently in touch with the Indus Valley people to have acquired their pottery.[141]

In common with what seems to have been the situation in much of the rest of the Gulf, Oman appears to have experienced a decline in activity and in the evidence of such substantial and prosperous communities after the beginning of the second millennium; the possible reasons for this

Figure 8.20 A finely built Umm an-Nar tomb excavated at Bat, near Ibri, third millennium BC.

phenomenon have been outlined earlier. In the case of Oman it must not be thought that so large a country, well endowed with water and fertile soil, was abandoned totally; this is most unlikely but the changed economic circumstances of the Gulf did not support large urban populations. In the case of the upper Gulf towns, whilst those in Bahrain and the mainland were probably never actually abandoned, their populations fell to a low level, to be represented perhaps by the equivalent of squatters, with an occasional military force garrisoned there. The situation generally is obscure. In Oman it is likely that the population reverted to a closer relationship with the land, living in villages or even in mobile communities which have left few identifiable traces behind them. It is to be hoped that more intensive exploration will reveal what evidence there may be of occupation during most of the second millennium and much of the first: so far, there is little to go on.

It is significant that Alexander the Great's advisers evidently knew nothing of Oman when he was seeking information about the peoples of Arabia as he contemplated its conquest in the last months of his life. Although he had endured the appalling rigours of the march through the Gedrosian desert on the coast opposite Oman, it is evident that he knew nothing of what conditions were like on the western shore. This suggests strongly that after its earlier prosperity the downturn in the commercial and trading activity of the Gulf had resulted in the onset of barbarism in south-eastern Arabia and the towns which had grown up to serve those who searched for Oman's copper fell into decay and into the oblivion from which they are only now being recalled.

Prosperity once again returned to Oman when the extreme south of the country, the region which is now called Dhofar, came into prominence as one of the principal sources of supply of aromatics and spices, and, in particular, of frankincense. Expeditions had been sent out from Egypt at least as early as the third millennium in search of incense. Such expeditions sailed down the Red Sea to the land of Punt, sometimes also called the Land of the God in the Egyptian inscriptions which record the journeys. The Egyptians burned large quantities of aromatics in their religious and state ceremonies. A famous relief in the funerary temple of Hasheshowi (or Hatshepsut) at Deir al-Bahari shows an expedition setting out for Punt and, later, returning with Punt's dwarfish, stout and steatopygous Queen, a visitor of State, if of improbable proportions, to the equally formidable, though evidently more elegant, Egyptian Queen.

Mesopotamia's comparative lack of interest in incense evidently meant that the sources of supply in south-eastern Arabia and in Oman were not exploited by the powers in Mesopotamia; there is as yet no evidence that the Egyptians ever went there themselves. It is possible that they acquired their supplies from middlemen, for the Egyptians themselves do not seem particularly to have honoured the calling of merchant. However, the growth of European powers such as Greece and later Rome, appearing for the first time on any real scale in the later first millennium, brought about an enormous increase in demand and, in consequence, the need to find permanent and reliable sources of supply.

The quantities of incense which Greece, Rome and the post-Alexandrian kingdoms consumed were prodigious. The altars of all the gods were perpetually wreathed in it; emperors and city corporations alike would seek to honour their chosen divinity by the consumption of yet greater amounts of costly fragrances. Thus Alexander himself, in his own lifetime renowned for his piety and the service of the gods, was never sparing in his observances. When, as a young prince, he was reproved for wasting incense by his first tutor, he stored the memory in his mind and when he had conquered the world sent him a large quantity of incense, of near-incalculable value, warning him not to be parsimonious in paying honour to the gods.

The cult of luxury in Rome and in the post-Alexandrian world added still further to the demand for Arabian aromatics. By their use as perfumes and unguents, the wealthier citizens, whose nostrils might be expected to be sensitive, could make living bearable in a teeming, malodorous city like Rome.

All of this meant an unparalleled prosperity for Arabia, the surest and most accessible source for the aromatics which these cults and customs demanded. Soon, kingdoms grew up in southern Arabia whose sole reason for existence was the cultivation, marketing and distribution of frankincense. Caravans, powered by the camel, which now came into its own for the first time (though introduced into the desert as early as the late fourth millen- nium, even if it probably was not domesticated), began to move up and down both littorals of Arabia, along the Red Sea coasts and up the Gulf shores.[142]

At points along the route duties levied on the camel trains and the provision of food and services for the master of the caravan and his men led to the creation of permanent communities which lived almost exclusively on this trade; from these caravanserai developed the great trading cities of Arabia. Those in the west, like Makkah, were later to exercise a still more stupendous role in world history when they witnessed the birth of Islam in the seventh century of the present era.

Soon the riches of Arabia entered into the mythology of Europe, never wholly to be forgotten. 'Fortunate Arabia' – 'Arabia Felix' – counted its wealth in the resins which were tapped from the trees, on which, it could for once be truly said, their fortunes grew. As the rumours of Arabia's limitless wealth circulated in the political centres of the world (fuelled, no doubt, by the sumptuous apparel and rich retinues of its princes and merchants, who began to become familiar figures in Mediterranean cities), so European ambitions, notably those of the Roman Republic and its successor Empire, began to focus on Arabia, with the object of controlling if not subsuming the kingdoms which seemingly contained so much of the world's wealth. The parallel with circumstances today is irresistible; then as now, Arabia's wealth was based essentially on a one-product economy and one which was vir- tually unique in quantity and accessibility. Then, as now, Arabia's resources were the envy of the world and the target of the acquisitiveness of the powers. Oman enjoyed great wealth at this period and cities like Sumharam (Khor Rori) in Dhofar were extensive in size and very rich.

There is another survival from the remote past in which Oman is excep- tionally rich – rock carvings. In this too her heritage is different from that of her Gulf neighbours, for in general eastern Arabia has little to show of the practice of carving on rocks, though it is one which is found throughout the north and west of the peninsula from very early Neolithic times (Fig. 8.21).[143]

Figure 8.21 Rock carving in Oman.

The distribution of rock carvings in Arabia and beyond is interesting and suggestive. Oman represents the most easterly manifestation of the phenomenon; to the west they run into the south-western desert regions of Saudi Arabia and up the Red Sea coastal areas, in some cases penetrating quite far inland. They appear in great quantity in the wadi systems of the Egyptian eastern desert. In different forms, rock drawings are to be found still further to the west in the Sahara and to the east in Iran. Some of the themes seem to be common to several of the regions, though they are separated by great distances.

Winkler, who first attempted a scientific analysis of rock carvings, using those in the Wadi Hammamat in Egypt, tried to apply a chronology to the drawings he examined.[144] In this he was followed, though cautiously, by Anati,[145] who has analysed and published many examples from the south-west Arabian repertory. They both believed they could detect various styles of drawings which, from internal evidence of the dress, weapons and manners depicted, together with the recurrence of iconographic elements familiar from other contexts, made it possible to ascribe a time-scale to them. Any such attempt at applying a chronology was necessarily broadly generalized, and depended much upon the establishment of sequences of styles for the different groups of drawings.

Any attempt to date rock carvings absolutely is fraught with difficulty. Only the palimpsest, provided it is interpreted correctly, can allow the presumption to be made that a drawing imposed on top of another is younger than the drawing which it overlies. The patination of the rock on which the drawings lie was once thought to be a reliable indicator of age; this is no longer so, for a prevailing wind constantly dusting a rock surface with sand particles can build up the most convincingly ancient-looking patination relatively quickly.

In Oman the problem is further complicated by the fact that some of the desert people have continued the practice of engraving on rocks into very recent years.[146] Thus one case showed a replica of a drawing of an embracing couple, known from the Hili tombs of early third millennium BC; the replica appeared in Oman in a context which made it clear that it was of very recent date. Such is the persistence of certain themes in folk art the world over.

Great horned beasts make frequent appearances in the drawings; some of them are of considerable size. Felines, mountain lion or leopard perhaps,

Figure 8.22 The enigmatic carvings on the face of 'Colman's Rock' have puzzled all those who have examined them. They appear to be ancient and have been attributed to the Bronze Age. The figures, carved in high relief, are somewhat larger than life-size. South of Jebel el Abri, near Al-Hamra (Bahla).

both of which were native to Oman in the past, are also depicted; in one dramatic scene a huge feline is depicted in the act of devouring a little man. One handsome carving seems to show a warrior with a high-crowned helm or a feather in his hair very similar to a style known from Iran. One of the most remarkable groups to be found in Oman is at Colman's Rock, in the interior south of Jebel el Abri (Fig. 8.22). On the rock, a large boulder in fact, are carved, expertly and in relief, four great figures, the largest of which is more than 2 metres tall. One of the figures, the central one of a group of three, wears a flat cap and has distinctly Caucasian features; at his side stands a huge negroid figure.[147]

This enigmatic group is quite without precedent, as is the manner of their representation, fine relief carving not being among the usual techniques of rock artists, in Oman or anywhere else in Arabia, except of course in Hili. It is conceivable that the figures on Colman's Rock may bear some relationship to the Hili carvings, though it would be difficult to be more specific at this juncture.

The horse appears in a number of carvings, including spirited combat scenes where warriors brandish their little swords perpetually. These are sometimes associated with inscriptions in pre-Islamic south Arabian scripts, which allows them to be dated approximately to the first century of the Christian era. As would be expected, the horse is a relatively late arrival in this part of Arabia. Many are the representations of camels, from around 2,000 years ago, by which time they had become a familiar part of the economy.

The siting of the carvings is often very remarkable. Naturally many are found in rock shelters, under rocky overhangs and in places generally of reasonably easy access. Some, however, are engraved high on the face of wadi cliffs, prompting the speculation as to how the artists worked in such difficult locations. They recall, in terms of the difficulties which they must have imposed on the artist, some of the more inaccessible places chosen by the cave artists of European Palaeolithic times 10,000 years or more before the Omani examples.

The archaeology of Oman is potentially very rich. Settlements in the country are long established and it may well hold at least one or two of the keys to the fuller understanding of the Gulf region in antiquity. Some historians of the earlier part of this century speculated that the Sumerians themselves originated in Oman: the preoccupation in the art of the people of the Land of the Two Rivers with mountains suggests that their origins lay in a mountainous land and Oman seems a fair candidate. There is no evidence yet to support the idea but enough has been said about the *possible* southern origins of the Sumerians not to dismiss absolutely any reasonable guess about their original home.

However, it must be said that the Sumerians seem to have known from very early on that Oman was very rich in copper. If it had also been their original home, or close to it, they surely would have remembered it from this fact alone. How else would they have known of the existence of copper there, at least by the end of the fourth millennium? It may be that the years ahead will answer this question, as the years past have answered so many others.

Most of the communities which lived on the western side of the Gulf were concerned, one way or another, with the development, management or supply of Dilmun's trade, the staple of which was the mining and conversion of copper. The gods now began to fade from this narrative, to be replaced, for the moment, by the businessmen of Dilmun and of Sumer, exploring the world's markets and seeking new contacts, all in the hope of earning an honest *mina*.

9

THE MERCHANTS OF DILMUN

During the time of Sumer's greatness and the prosperity which its successor states maintained, life went on busily in the cities, despite the sombre, occasional courts-in-death of the kings or their surrogates, the instability of the prevailing political system and the perennial threats of invasion and unrest. But as the Sumerians were essentially a down-to-earth people, much of their life consisted of concentrating on the simple process of making a living. The profit motive was strong in Sumer and its pursuit was more agreeable and the play of market forces was certainly more dear to the average Urite, for example, than the pursuit of an uncertain immortality by dead courtiers or the pretensions and schemes of aggrandizement of little princes.

Most of the earliest city-states of Sumer were concentrated near the confluence of the two great rivers on which the black-headed people's civilization depended, the Tigris and the Euphrates. It was natural, especially if the legends of their origins were based upon any sort of recollected reality, that they should explore the sea routes to the south, down through the Gulf, the Lower Sea, and out into limitless ocean, which they believed, reasonably enough at the time, circled the world. Very soon the Sumerians became considerable, though sometimes rather apprehensive, seamen; they constitute, indeed, the first great maritime trading nation in the world's history. The boats which they sailed were probably not greatly different from the present day *boum* (often erroneously called a dhow) and the high-prowed *tarafa* of the Marsh Arabs.

Trade and legend are inextricably mixed in Sumer's history. Dilmun stands at the centre of both, just as the Bahrain islands occupied a conveniently central position between Mesopotamia, the Arabian coast, Oman (the source of much of Sumer's copper and stone) and the markets of the Indus Valley.

For many centuries Bahrain-Dilmun provided the natural entrepôt and distribution centre for the trans-shipment of the raw materials vital to Sumer's economy. Like the Vikings of a later age, the princes of Sumer were merchants on a lavish scale and the most substantial records of Dilmun come from the trading activities of the little states, particularly from the city of Ur.

TRADE

Trade became possible when man had learned to exploit nature and to produce beyond his immediate needs. The surplus he thus created he could exchange with other peoples, taking from them their surplus in turn.

The exchange of artefacts, which clearly began very early, probably arose out of simple admiration, an admiration which could not be satisfied merely by clubbing the owner of the object admired. Sophisticated techniques of warehousing, distribution, banking, a system of exchange based on value-based rates and commodities, and all the other facets of a complex economic system, were developed over the period from the middle of the fourth to the middle of the third millennias, as the result of the recognition of a need in each case and of a reasoned response to it. The dialogue, often as acrimonious as in our own day, between the needs of the state and those of the private sector of the economy began very early on, and complaints against the level of taxation and the incursions of central government into the affairs of commerce can be heard rising clearly above the chatter of the most ancient of market-places.

Great cities rose and fell because of economic factors and their attendant political responses. In the documents which survive from Mesopotamia a significant proportion are commercial records of one sort or another, bills, memoranda and even dunning letters from anxious creditors seeking the repayment of a debt.

In the trade of the ancient Near East, certainly in its earliest centuries when the great civilizations of Mesopotamia were widening the range of their influence and contacts, the Gulf, and particularly the islands and Oman, had an important part to play in the most vital trade route by sea of the day, that which went south and eastward from Mesopotamia to India. At the time when the Gilgamesh legend was written down in something like the form that has reached us, a millennium or more after the actual reported voyage of Gilgamesh to Dilmun, it is a thriving and important entrepôt, with its kings recognized throughout the region as powerful merchant princes. Dilmun is no longer simply the faeryland of Sumerian legend but a place of trading ships and thronged harbours, its storehouses stacked with the wealth of the states on whose trade routes it was so strategically placed.

Trade routes were of immense antiquity and well travelled, both those which extended over land and, later, the sea routes. Along the principal routes was strung a chain of trading posts and one of the most frequently repeated claims of a reforming monarch was that under his rule merchants could travel securely and speedily over the great distances, provisioned by caravanserai at regular stages and protected by imperial agents along the way.

The mechanics of ancient trade took as many forms as its modern counter-part today. In some cases, as we know from the documentary evidence, merchants would base themselves abroad, far from their homes. From this distant posting, living in small colonies, they would maintain contact with their headquarters and manage the acquisition, exchange or distribution of products with the communities amongst which they had established them-selves. Artefacts themselves, of course, sometimes travelled far further than even the most dauntless merchant reached. A fine vessel, a piece of jewellery or a weapon might be handed on across an immense distance and pass through the hands of many different intermediaries.

THE MECHANISMS OF ANCIENT COMMERCE

For the Sumerians trade was inextricably linked with every phase of their lives. By harnessing the waters of the two great rivers on which their prosperity and even their lives depended, they created abundance; by plan-ning their year carefully in relation to the rivers' inundations they created leisure in which to develop crafts and technical skills of a very high order. Because Sumer was a land barren of trees and of minerals these resources, essential for the well-being of the land and its ambitious and intensely creative people, could only be obtained from outside their own frontiers. The abundant fertility of their crops and herds gave them scope to trade their surplus for their other needs.

From very early times the Sumerians had established a flourishing import–export economy, at first directed by the temples, later by the secular authorities and merchants operating on their own account.[1] As the cities grew, they became important trading points for the caravans which came up out of the plateaux of Iran. The early cities of Iran straddled the overland routes for many of the most sought-after raw materials of the fourth and third millennia, such as chlorite (steatite) and lapis lazuli. It has indeed been postulated that these cities, some of which were considerable in scale and extensive in influence, came into being simply in response to the demands of trade and the search for raw materials (Map 5).[2]

The great highway of Sumerian and later, of Akkadian and Old Babylonian trade, however, ran north–south. The two rivers themselves were the most expeditious and direct means for trade to flow from the Gulf, up through Sumer proper, onwards towards the Mediterranean into what was to become Assyria, travelling further north still, into Anatolia and to the west across the Upper Sea, possibly as far as distant Cyprus. As will be seen later, one of the most important items of trade was copper, both in the form of ingot and converted into manufactured products. The Euphrates' part in moving this trade may be commemorated by the fact that its

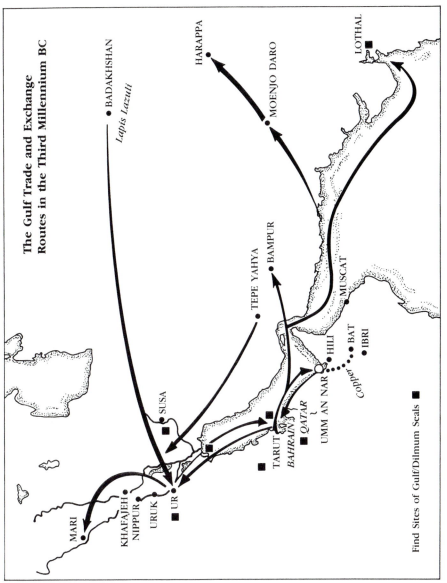

The Gulf Trade and Exchange Routes in the Third Millennium BC

Map 5 Trade routes in Western Asia, in the third and second millennia.

267

Sumerian name was *Urudu*, 'the copper river'; the Tigris, on the other hand, a swift-flowing stream, was appropriately named *Idiglat*, 'the arrow'. The various cities on the river routes also became the principal system for the distribution of manufactured goods and for interurban trade.

The excavation of the mound at Tel Mardikh in Syria, the location of the city of Ebla, produced evidence of the extent of Dilmun's trade, as early as the mid-third millennium.[3] The importance of the Ebla site, apart from revealing it as the capital of a large and complex kingdom which maintained relations with other states on an international scale and which controlled a substantial area of Syria and upper Mesopotamia, lay in the rich caches of cuneiform tablets, written in an early Semitic language, that were excavated in profusion.

From these tablets, whose translation is still proceeding, many references to the Dilmun trade have been identified.[4] Even by around 2500 BC tin was recorded as being brought from Dilmun. A considerable number of goods and products seems to have been identified with the term 'Dilmun –' followed by the word for the product. This suggests that, even as early as this, Dilmun represented some sort of criterion of quality or was a synonym for excellence. 'Harps' (in Eblaitic, *ber-lag*) 'beer-bread' (*bappir*), 'date-palm' (*gis*), tin (*nagga*) and copper (*urudu*) all are recorded in this way.[5]

It is clear from this list that Dilmun was regarded as an important commercial centre even in distant Ebla. It makes another appearance, in a list of geographical locations, where it is named amongst some of the most famous of Sumerian cities. These are Uruk, Lagash, Nippur, Adab, Shurupak, Umma, Elam and Dilmun. There is then a break (the translator believes that three place-names are missing) and the list ends with a repeated sign which he suggests may represent Egypt.[6]

The list of toponyms is particularly interesting. Uruk was the city of Gilgamesh, who sought his deified ancestor Ziusudra, King of Shurupak, in a place which can only have been the Dilmun of myth. Lagash was the state whose ruler, Ur-Nanshe, boasted that the ships of Dilmun unloaded their merchandise at his quays. Nippur and Umma were sacred centres, of great antiquity, with a reputation for sanctity comparable with Dilmun's. Elam, like Dilmun itself, is out of place with the others for both were countries or specific regions rather than city-states.

It is an intriguing reference because it indicates that Dilmun must have been recognized as being of considerable importance, even before the migration of its centre to the Bahrain islands. At the time of the Ebla texts it must be presumed that Dilmun was still located in eastern Arabia. However, as yet no early or mid-third-millennium site of sufficient size and status has been identifed which would be convincing as the centre of a state worthy to be ranked with some of the most prestigious of Sumerian cities.

Further evidence of Dilmun's status, at least as far as the merchants of Ebla were concerned, is revealed by references to a 'Dilmun-shekel'. This appears to have been a unit of weight which was accepted as being comparable with Ebla's own units of measurement, a tribute presumably to the standing of the merchants of Dilmun, though they came from far away.[7]

DILMUN: ENTREPÔT OF THE GULF

From the marshlands where the Tigris and Euphrates debouch into the Gulf another route lay open to the enterprising Sumerian merchant, south to Arabia and away to the east, to the rich and powerful cities of the Indus Valley, Moenjo-Daro and Harappa. On this route, Dilmun occupied a crucial position, lying some 480 kilometres (300 miles) from the head of the Gulf, and the only safe harbourage in what was often a dangerous and unpredictable sea. By the middle of the third millennium Sumerian rulers are to be found dealing directly with Dilmun. Ur-Nanshe, king of Lagash c. 2520 BC, records the fact that, in his reign, ships of Dilmun brought tribute to him, in what is otherwise a catalogue of the temples that he built for the honour of the gods of Sumer. The inscription is from a door socket dedicated by the king:

> Ur-Nanshe, the king of Lagash, the son of Gunidu, the son of Gurmu, built the house of Ningirsu: built the house of Nanshe: built the house of Gatumdug: built the harem: built the house of Ninmar. The ships of Dilmun brought him wood as a tribute from foreign lands. He built the Ibqal: built the Kinir: built the sceptre-house.[8]

Thus, as early as the first recorded kings of Lagash, at the time when the pyramids in Egypt were sparkling new, Sumer was actively promoting an extensive trade with Dilmun. The king and queen of Lagash (if such titles may be used, however anachronistically) were directly involved and in exchange for Dilmun's copper and splendid dates they offered barley, cedar, oil, flour, dresses and silver.

Records of the shipment of dates and onions, both specialities of Dilmun, again occur in the reign of Ur-Nanshe. The wife of Lugalanda, another ruler of Lagash, exported wheat, cedarwood, cheese and shelled barley to the island: '234 mina of copper ore; copper ore, property of Luqunntu (wife of Lugalanda) which Ur-Enki the merchant has brought from the mountain of Dilmun, Lugalanda, Ensi of Lagash, has paid for in the palace.'[9] Copper from Dilmun was called, in the Sumerian language, *urudu NiTuk^{ki}*. Ur-Enki, whose name is compounded with that of Enki, the benign god, is one of the earliest merchants to be known by name; it is interesting that by his time the temporal power, in the person of the sovereign's wife (or, more accurately, one of the sovereign's several wives), was engaging in trade, rather than its being the province of the temple authorities, which is generally thought to have been the case in Early Dynastic times. The wives of rulers also engaged, like their husbands, in the fish trade.[10]

The records of Lagash in Sumerian times reveal something of the mechanics of trade in the city-states, before the merchants had achieved fully independent status. The ruler evidently provided goods from some sort of central warehousing system to the merchants, enabling them to trade (in this case, with Dilmun) and to exchange Lagash merchandise for Dilmun's products.

Presumably the merchants were working on a basis of commission payments. Ur-Enki operated on quite a large scale: he is recorded as having moved something like 100 kilograms of copper in one shipment from Dilmun. 'From the central warehouses Shubur, the Inspector, gave him a quantity of cedarwood, grain and flour for exchange in Dilmun. This was in the fifth year of the rule of Lugalanda.'[11]

Lugalanda was evidently favoured with at least two commercially minded wives. Apart from Luqunntu we are told that 'Barrambara, wife of Lugalanda, counted out copper to the merchant Dugilam, to take to the city of Umma and exchange for silver.'[12]

It may be inferred by various objects, including the distinctive Barbar ware pottery found in Sumerian sites, that Dilmun early on had its own export industry, probably originating at the time of the Sumerians' first accession to supremacy in the land, towards the later centuries of the fourth millennium. The earliest textual reference to Dilmun, as we have seen, comes from this time and refers to trade.

THE INDUS VALLEY

The Indus Valley cities spread north-west in a chain along the banks of their great river. There is little early evidence at present of developed cultures having flourished in the region, most of which is now contained within modern Pakistan, at the time of the foundation of the Sumerian cities. However, as many of the early levels of the Indus cities are hopelessly waterlogged, caution must be expressed about this view. The sites of the Indus cities are impressive and suggest a considerable awareness of the importance of town planning; most of them are designed on a formal pattern with a preponderance of large public buildings and wide, regular streets. Indus Valley architecture tends to be monolithic, lacking in relief or features, and their cities must have been oppressive places to live in.

The people of the Indus cities had developed a pictographic script, evolved seemingly to a relatively high degree and apparently demonstrating, for example, the understanding and use of accent markings. It occurs on the pottery of the region and on their characteristic square stamp seals, of which many examples survive.[13] It is still generally considered to be undeciphered.

At the height of the Indus Valley civilization, about a hundred cities made up what was, to a large extent, a centrally organized state. The two cities of Harappa and Moenjo-Daro were much the largest and, it has been suggested, may have been twin capitals of a large and monolithic state. Throughout the Indus Valley there are hints of Mesopotamian, even of Sumerian, associations, but these are too slight to suggest a profound and continuing influence of what is probably the older civilization on the younger. There is, however, little doubt that the Indus Valley people, whoever they were, drew some of their initial inspiration from Mesopotamia. Beyond that fact, contact was maintained between them principally by way of trade through Bahrain-Dilmun and the Gulf, particularly in the early days through Oman.

The little of Indus Valley art that survives suggests the presence of Sumerian influences. The so-far-unique carved stone bust of a 'priest-king' or divinity from Moenjo-Daro *could* be a provincial, orientalized Sumerian work.[14] Pottery figures of divinities display the pinched, almost reptilian faces of their much earlier Mesopotamian colleagues, with similar rather bizarre ideas about the head-dress proper for a god.

Kidney-shaped beads found in Dilmun may have their origins in the Indus Valley and there is little doubt that the ivory which was so important a part of Dilmun's trade with the Sumerian cities came from there. A little ivory figurine, unhappily only a fragment, found by Mackay in one of the tumuli in the desert near Aali,[15] is reminiscent, no more, of one of the most celebrated pieces from Moenjo-Daro, which in its elegance and mastery of form is quite uncharacteristic of the little that we know of the Indus people's art. This is a little bronze dancer, pert and nude, full of charm;[16] comparable with it, if suspect as far as the relatively early period to which it has been ascribed is concerned, is the torso of a youth, whose impressively developed genitals and general chubbiness may lack appeal to those accustomed to judge such figures by the more slender charm of a *kouros*.[17]

Indus Valley pottery has been found in the Arabian Gulf at Abu Dhabi, at the oasis of Buraimi and, arguably in that the Indus provenance is disputed, on the island of Umm an-Nar.[18] However, the evidence in Bahrain itself is reasonably conclusive, and, *prima facie*, there is no reason why other points on the coast of the Gulf should not have been visited by traders journeying to or from the Indus Valley. Harappan material has also been identified on the Omani coast at Ras al-Hamra, not far from Muscat.[19]

THE ROLE OF THE MERCHANT

Documents from the very ancient and holy city of Shurrupak, once ruled by Ziusudra, show that the dealers and sailors engaged in the trade were known as *gal-Dilmun*.[20] This compares with the Old Babylonian term *Alik Tilmun* which described the guild which represented the merchants who traded with Dilmun in the early second millennium.

The land routes from Sumer to the Indus ran through Persia and were long and dangerous, beset with rapacious and deplorably uncommercial tribes. The sea route was to be preferred, therefore, and it was because of this that in the third and early second millennia Dilmun, the sacred island, assumed another, more mundane role as the great emporium of trade between east and west. Equally important, it was well placed between the southern, richly endowed but primitive lands and the northern states, hungry for the raw materials and for copper, stone, ivory and gold, which were needed for their rich, consumer-orientated economies.

In pre-Sargonid times trade was largely the perquisite of the temple administrations even when it was conducted in the ruler's name, a logical enough practice since, technically at least, all land and goods belonged to the god of the city and the authorities, the governors and priests, merely administrated them on the god's behalf. Thus it was the practice for the temples to fit out trading expeditions, hiring sea-captains and a class of merchant who specialized in the brokerage of the temple-financed trade. Apart from the merchant's payment, the profits went to the temples and they grew exceedingly rich.

Later, however, as a result of an as yet unknown change in the Sumerian social system, individual merchants appear, trading on their own behalf or as members of privately financed syndicates. It may well be that the merchants who had traded in the temples' interest grew rich and, over generations, saw the prospect of even more substantial profits as a motive still more compelling than the favour of the gods, whose payment of dividends was likely, in the Sumerian view of things, to be long deferred if, indeed, forthcoming at all. During the time when free enterprise flourished, however, the palace and sometimes certain of the temples levied a duty on imports, particularly on the all-important copper trade.

In the first year of the reign of King Ibbi-Sin of Ur (c. 2029–2006 BC) a sea captain, Ur-Gur, who commanded a large boat and thought it worth recording the fact, shipped 10 talents' worth of wool 'of ordinary quality' to Dilmun. There is some evidence that he was acting under the aegis of one of the temples in this transaction.[21]

Over a century later a woman, Amad-Ningal, in all probability a native of Ur, made an offering to the goddess Ningal from the proceeds of an expedition to Dilmun.[22] It is a matter of speculation whether she was making the offering, the customary tithe, on behalf of another or whether, as is equally possible, since women were at no disadvantage in Sumerian society (as witness Lugalanda's wives), she was trading in her own right.

Trade did not only flow one way, directed from Sumer to the impressionable natives of Dilmun and other distant regions, for several unmistakably Dilmunite names in texts of the time make it clear that the islanders themselves also traded in Ur and other Sumerian cities. Thus from Larsa, at the end of the twentieth century BC, gifts to the temple of Ningal are recorded from one Idin-Nin-Inzak, the last part of whose name commemorates Dilmun's tutelary god.[23] Included amongst the merchandise listed in Idin-Nin-Inzak's inscription are 'fish-eyes', almost certainly the pearls of

Dilmun, the trade of which was of very high antiquity. Idin-Nin-Inzak was prosperous enough for gold, a comparatively rare product in Sumer, to figure amongst his benefactions to the temple of Ningal.

Another inscription is a catalogue of the items found in the great burial tumuli of Bahrain: carnelian beads, rods of iron, copper and ivory combs, all recorded as the proceeds of an expedition to Dilmun.[24]

A Dilmunite, Iddin-ilum, appears making a tithe of silver whilst Dumu-dugga certifies the correctness of the amount.[25] The Dilmun merchants were prosperous and influential men; indeed, so considerable was their reputation that in Babylonian times *lu-tilmun-a*, 'the men of Dilmun', became a synonym for the profession of trader. The Sumerian term for merchant, incidentally, and itself of great antiquity, is *dam-gar*; it may be one of the supposed pre-Sumerian words taken into the language from some earlier stratum.

One of the techniques of early trading, developed to aid the interchange of goods and contacts between distant peoples, was the establishment of merchant colonies in cities linked by mutual trading interests. This obviously was desirable amongst peoples who did not possess a common language (although Akkadian was employed for this purpose by the middle of the second millennium) and whose literacy was, to say the least, limited. Thus communities grew up whose function was to broke the argosies which plied to and from the land from which the settlers came. Sometimes they lived outside the city walls; often they were independent communities, governed by their own magistrates who were responsible for the general maintenance of order and the return of taxes to the central authority. Their rights were respected, but they were aliens, forming a sort of ghetto in the midst of a foreign city or living on its periphery. Seals found at Ur, obviously Indian in origin, demonstrate the existence of such communities in the Mesopotamian cities.

The Sumerians, more than their successors the Babylonians and Assyrians, seem to have been by inclination a seafaring people, but their attitude to the sea and sailing was one of extreme caution and respect; in this way they were typical of most ancient peoples. Although in one mood they would salute the Gulf as the father of all oceans, in another they spoke of it as 'the fearful sea'. They were forced on to the sea to gain additional and, because they were far distant, more lucrative markets for their exports. The fact that the waters of the Gulf flow in a counter-clockwise motion (see Chapter 3) would have assisted the development of sailing. The merchant ships would have set out from the head of the Gulf holding to the west shore and being driven south by the counter-flow. On their return they would have lugged along the coast of what is now Iran with the Gulf's flow carrying them home.

They were more confident of their merchanting ability than of their seamanship: many ex-votos survive proclaiming the gratitude of these nervous merchant venturers to the gods who have ensured their safe return from the perils of ocean. Ningal was the recipient of most of the offerings of Urite seamen; she has been well described as a sort of Sumerian Notre Dame de la Garde.[26] The Mesopotamians were, however, far from being as alienated from the sea as some of their contemporaries. The Egyptians, the most conservative of all the ancients, regarded 'the Great Green' with positive distaste and considered the fact that Egypt was but little dependent on the sea for any of its wants as another singular mark of the favour of the gods who had, they felt, made Egypt as perfect a land as it was possible even for the gods to do.

But the extent of the Dilmunite trade overland was equally formidable and is demonstrated by the appearance at the court of the king of Mari, a city on the Euphrates far to the north of Sumer in northern Syria, of messengers from the island in the eighteenth century BC.[27] That its emissaries could travel these distances, apparently independently, attests to the prosperity and influence of Dilmun at that time. The king of Assyria, Shamsi-Adad I (1814–1782 BC) commanded that the Dilmunites should be given gifts of oil, sesame, boxwood and sandals. The Assyrians sent a caravan to Dilmun, which on its return was directed to deliver its goods to Hammurabi of Babylon, who reigned from 1792 to 1750 BC. Before it reached the city, however, it seems to have met with difficulties on the way.[28]

Hammurabi's successor as king of Babylon was Samsu-iluna, who reigned from 1749 to 1684 BC. In the twenty-first year of his reign traders from Dilmun are mentioned in a text from a provincial city, Legaba.[29] This document records the delivery of a quantity of barley, perhaps the property of a Dilmunite, Samas-Nasir, resident in the Babylonian kingdom, to two others, one of whom, Inzak-gamil, has a traditional Dilmunite compound in his name.

Most ancient history is the record of the doings of kings and conquerors, figures who loom larger than life and whose shadows obscure the people whose lives went on despite them. But an engaging feature of the records of early Mesopotamia is that individuals play their part, private citizens who would be wholly recognizable today, mocking the grave significance which history gives to the events happening around them, like jesters chuckling sardonically at the feet of emperors.

THE ARCHIVES OF TRADE

The largest group of cuneiform tablets to have come down from the city mounds of Mesopotamia over these 4,000 years is unquestionably that which is concerned, in general terms, with trade. Many of them are contracts between one merchant and another, with captains of ships hired for specific voyages, and bills, notes of exchange, and even agreements over the financing of trading expeditions. These last are particularly interesting in that they appear to describe the earliest examples of banking, whereby a financier would advance funds against a particular project at an agreed rate, the contract specifying, in the manner of bankers ever since, that the borrowers alone would be responsible for all losses. Hammurabi tried unsuccessfully to change this and make the banker equally liable.[30] That even he, one of the most powerful kings of antiquity, could not do so suggests that the legendary political power of bankers has deep historical roots. There is one particularly interesting document which appears to be a 'joint and several guarantee' by a number of partners to the banker who had advanced them a loan.

Credit makes its first helpful appearance in commercial history and is recognized as a factor in assessing how much money might reasonably be advanced to a trader. The Sumerian term *tadmiqtu* approximates to the concept of 'goodwill' as a factor in assessing the value of a business and thus in securing a loan.[31] A system of letters of credit enabled a merchant to operate at a distance far from his home base without the need for carrying large amounts of treasure with him, with all the risks attendant upon so doing. Relationships between one merchant firm and another in a foreign market were built up and enabled members of the firm to trade together to the advantage of both. Many firms existed for long periods, often for several generations.

The idea of a currency standard first appears at the end of the third millennium, for values of goods are often expressed in terms of an equivalent in silver. Whilst the Sumerians used the silver standard, they did not go to the next stage and actually produce a currency for exchange, although they did possibly exchange discs or rings of standard weight silver for services or products; coinage had to wait for its invention until the seventh-century Lydians of Asia Minor. But its absence did not prevent the Sumerians from developing a highly sophisticated system of merchant banking by using the silver standard as an agreed basis on which loans or interest might be assessed. This was largely achieved by comparisons of weights. Silver was handled in bars, with official markings and a certification of weight.

Dilmun seems to have been of sufficient importance as a trade centre around the beginning of the second millennium to have had its own measurement of weight, differing from that of the great commercial metropolis of the time, Ur. It appears that the Dilmun weight may have been of the same value as that used in the Indus Valley cities.[32] A set of weights found in the City II site at the Qala'at al-Bahrain is equivalent to the weights used in the Indus Valley cities and may be evidence of the actual presence of merchants from those cities in Dilmun.[33]

EA-NASIR, THE DILMUN MERCHANT

In the reign of Rim-Sin (1822–1763 BC), one of the kings of the Elamite dynasty which ruled the kingdom of Isin-Larsa, there flourished in the city of Ur, for centuries one of the most important of the Sumerian trade centres, a member of the guild of Dilmun merchants whose name was Ea-Nasir. The guild, the *Alik Tilmun* as it came to be called in the Babylonian form, consisted of those merchants who, trading on their own behalf down the Gulf, based their trans-shipment business on Dilmun's prosperous and hospitable quays. By a fortunate chance an extensive correspondence, if it is sometimes anxious and acrimonious, between Ea-Nasir and his business associates survived in the ruins of his house in Ur, to which he had withdrawn in the hope of enjoying a prosperous retirement after his evidently not wholly scrupulous business career.[34] He was active in business around the turn of the nineteenth century BC.

It is, incidentally, important to recognize that this particular trade, of which we have relatively detailed knowledge, was between Dilmun and Ur. There may well have been other merchants of the status of the Urites who dealt with Dilmun but nothing is known of their organization, if any such existed. Ea-Nasir was a substantial dealer in copper, a wholesaler of copper ingots; sometimes he dealt in finished products made from the metal and, indeed, in anything else from which he could see the chance of a profit.

Amongst the mass of often tedious, but historically very important cuneiform commercial correspondence which survives inscribed on tablets of baked clay, Ea-Nasir's letters gleam mischievously, for much of what survives of his archives may be categorized as 'dunning tablets' from his creditors, often expressed in those terms of hurt surprise and reproach which would be familiar to many a debtor today. Ea-Nasir, the first part of whose name is the Semitic or Babylonian form of Enki, was obviously considered a reasonably good risk at the outset, judging by the amounts which he was advanced; the records credit him with substantial borrowings in copper. Evidently at the outset of his career he was acting for the palace, buying and selling on the king's behalf. But later there appears a series of sharp and sometimes rather petulant cries of financial anguish directed to him by his backers in Ur whilst he is away in Dilmun. The usual formal injunction 'Speak to . . .' precedes the text of most of the letters, indicating that in all probability neither the sender nor the recipient was literate. A letter, in fact, was known as 'a say to them' and was written and read by professional scribes who thus themselves became men of influence and power, privy as they were to all the commercial and political secrets of the time.

Nanni is particularly hurt at Ea-Nasir's casual, even discourteous, attitude: after all, are not both of them gentlemen and surely they should behave as such?

Speak to Ea-Nasir; thus says Nanni. Now when you had come you spoke saying thus: 'I will give good ingots to Gimil-Sin' this you said to me when you had come, but you have not done it: you have offered bad ingots to my messenger, saying 'If you will take it, take it, if you will not take it, go away.' Who am I that you are treating me in this manner – treat me with such contempt? and that between gentlemen such as we are! I have written to you to receive my purse but you have neglected it – who is there among the Dilmun traders who has acted against me in this way?[35]

Sumerian and Babylonian businessmen frequently demonstrate a strong sense of their own gentility and deplore the absence of it in their correspondents. They were, in fact, right to do so. The status of 'gentleman' was defined at law, certainly in Hammurabi's time. It was, for example, considerably more expensive, in terms of the compensation which had to be paid, to wound a gentleman than it was to injure a commoner or a slave.

In another letter Nanni seems to resent the fact that Ea-Nasir has removed a quantity of silver from his house and now 'you make this discussion'.[36] He is worried too that he and others have sworn as to the legality of the contract in the temple of Shamash. The sun-god was traditionally the witness of all such oaths, thus rendering them sacred, and he had a special care of merchants. In a hymn of praise to the god it is said of him, 'The merchant with his pouch, thou dost save from the flood.' Abituram follows, more concisely and with the threat that he will call in Ea-Nasir's mortgages; Abituram, wisely one feels, had actually pinned Ea-Nasir down in writing. Nigga-Nanna, the bearer of a name that it would be difficult to take seriously today no matter how much one might owe him, makes the first of his several appearances. 'The silver and its profit give it to Nigga-Nanna . . . I have made you issue a tablet. Why have you not given the copper? If you do not give it, I will bring in your pledges.[37]

Exasperation dominates the opening of the next letter, still as curt in its address to Ea-Nasir as the others have been: 'Speak to Ea-Nasir: thus says Abituram. Why have you not given the copper to Nigga-Nanna?' He ends on a kinder note, but still with a plea for his copper: 'The work you have done is good. . . . The copper . . . give it to Nigga-Nanna.'[38]

The next is no doubt familiar to the modern reader, for it gives the impression of a weary banker dismissing a tiresome client:

Speak to Ea-Nasir: thus says Imqui-Sin. May Shamash bless your life. Give good copper under seal to Nigga-Nanna. Now you have had one issue ten shekels of silver. In order that your heart shall not be troubled give good copper to him. Do you not know how tired I am? And when you arrive with Itsu-Rabi take it away and give it to Nigga-Nanna.[39]

Nanni's place in the correspondence is now taken by Appa, who has the same sort of problem with Ea-Nasir and who also wants, slightly improbably, a copper kettle.

> Speak to Ea-Nasir: thus says Appa. The copper of mine, give it to Nigga-Nanna – good copper in order that my heart shall not be troubled . . . and one copper kettle which can hold 15 qa of water, and 10 minas of other copper send to me. I will pay silver for it.[40]

Ea-Nasir evidently has a partner, Ilsu-ellatsu, for one of the letters is addressed to them both. Another, a rather cagey one in which Ilsu-ellatsu seems to be worried that his partner will upset the client, is addressed by him to Ea-Nasir.

> Speak to Ea-Nasir: thus says Ilsu-ellatsu, with regard to the copper of Idin-Sin. Izija will come to you. Show him 15 ingots so that he may select 6 good ingots and give him these. Act in such a way that Idin-Sin will not become angry.[41]

It would be agreeable to think that in the end Ea-Nasir honoured all his commitments and lived happily ever after with the other financiers of Ur on the profits of the Dilmun copper trade. He appears again, this time in the garment business, a very profitable export line to Dilmun and one which it is difficult not to feel was particularly suited to the egregious Ea-Nasir.

Unhappily, all may not have gone well with Ea-Nasir in the long run. According to Woolley, who excavated his house at Ur, part of it was incorporated into the house next door at the end of the Isin-Larsa period when Ea-Nasir lived and flourished hopefully.[42] In Ea-Nasir's private records, Woolley found evidence of a diversity of interests and a variety of commercial involvement to a degree which would impress a modern entrepreneur. Land speculation, real estate, usury and second-hand clothing were all, apparently, grist to Ea-Nasir's mill.

His ambition, however, seems to have outrun his ability, at least in Woolley's view, and to have forced on this agile and adventurous merchant a significant reduction in his standard of living and in the size of his house. At this distance in time, it is probably merely sentimental to hope that part of Ea-Nasir's house was incorporated into his next-door neighbour's residence because his neighbour offered him a good price for it.

It is to Woolley that we owe the location and layout of Ea-Nasir's house in Ur, at the time of Rim-Sin. Woolley was a splendid excavator and a perceptive archaeologist: he was also often idiosyncratic. When he published the results of his epoch-making researches at Ur, so much more remarkable than the findings of the burial of Tutankhamun in the same period (the 1920s), Woolley produced a clear and precisely drawn street plan of the city as it was in Ea-Nasir's time. For some reason he chose to give the streets, or at least the principal ones, the names of the streets of Oxford where he had been an undergraduate (a contemporary of T.E. Lawrence) in the early years of the century. This produces some curious consequences: Ea-Nasir's address thus becomes 1 Old Street; after his house was combined with his neighbour's it became 7 Church Lane. It would be a courageous archaeologist today, incidentally, who would inscribe two lanes on his city plan as Gay Street and Straight Street respectively,[43] even if he had been at Oxford.

It is easy to be amused by the bickerings and craftiness of these ancient businessmen whose attitudes, behaviour and even language are so totally those of their modern successors. Yet it must not be forgotten that to the immediate predecessors of Ea-Nasir and his companions, one of the supreme and most glorious achievements of the human race is due.

As far back as the middle of the fourth millennium, trade in Sumer had achieved such proportions that those engaged in it required the means to record their sales and purchases and the stocks of goods and animals which they maintained. From the system which they developed, the earliest known examples of which are baked tablets from Gilgamesh's city of Uruk and from Kish, dated roughly 3500 BC, all writing, so far as we know, descends. From its earliest form, when it was little more than the association of symbols of quantity with the representation of the object concerned, writing quickly evolved to become a sophisticated and flexible instrument for recording not merely the number of sheep a temple possessed, but the aspirations, fears and delights of men. By the early centuries of the third millennium a formal literature already existed which culminated in the story of Gilgamesh's quest, perhaps the most moving and majestic of all the legends of antiquity; but it is wholly in character with the Sumerians that one of the earliest phonetically written words should be *dam-gar*, 'a merchant'.

Ea-Nasir, the Dilmun merchant, was clearly more concerned with profit than with poetry. But he has his modest place in the line which runs from the archaic scribes of Uruk and Kish, through the spiky elegance of Sumerian cuneiform and all the written languages of the world to Virgil, Dante and Shakespeare.

Agreeable though it is to associate Ea-Nasir and his colleagues with poets and poetry, it is only part of the story; arguably, it is not the most important contribution which such ancient commercial enterprises made to human progress and development. Before the creation of armies, a relatively late development, the social and cultural character of one land was most likely to be influenced by another through trade and the contacts and exchanges which it brought about. Merchants were, of necessity, travellers, by nature observant and keen to take advantage of any opportunity which might present itself. Finding a society less developed than that from which they themselves had come, they could introduce new ideas, new ways of doing things, even new beliefs and religious practices. This must have been especially true when there was something, metal perhaps or timber, that they wanted from a less sophisticated land. From those countries that had developed crafts, they brought goods which they had bartered, leaving behind the products of other lands which in turn exercised their influence and contributed to change and progress.

From the earliest times this traffic had extended far across the known world. It is to the merchants, and probably in particular to the seafaring merchants, that much of the credit must go for the bringing of the arts of civilization to backward lands and not, as so many legends would have it, to gods such as Enki or, in Egypt, to the followers of Horus, unless they too combined business with divinity.

Writing is one thing; the immediate, day-to-day responsibilities of running a business quite another. It is clear that few merchants were themselves literate: each firm would have had scribal staff members who were responsible for the archives and for the management of the firm's correspondence. The production of literary texts could be left to the temple scribes or to ladies of a literary turn of mind, like Sargon the Great's daughter who was a High Priestess in Uruk in the twenty-fourth century BC, and was given to occasional composition.

SEALS AND SEALINGS

For the ordinary affairs of the businesses on which so much of the prosperity of Sumer and Dilmun was founded, a technique other than the laborious, labour-intensive and no doubt costly process of scribal composition was devised: the practice of marking merchandise, documents or other movable property with the impression of a design cut into the face either of a cylinder or of a stamp seal. The latter form, the stamp seal, is one of the special glories of the Gulf cities. Its use made general literacy unnecessary for, whilst it might be difficult for a hard-pressed merchant or his assistants to decipher a written text, anyone could recognize a design, their own or another's, whose repetition would make it familiar very quickly. Before the various caches of Dilmun seals from Bahrain and other sites in the Gulf are described, it may be appropriate to consider more generally the purpose of seals in antiquity, for they are amongst the most enduring objects frequently to survive from these remote times. They are of special appeal to those who approach the ancient world from what is nowadays perhaps an outmoded and unfashionable humanistic standpoint, for they are highly personalized objects, most of them unique and hence attributable to a single ownership.

Man has an interesting tendency to seek mechanical solutions to any problem that confronts him. In central Anatolia, at Çatal Hüyük in the seventh and sixth millennia before the present era, he seems, remarkably enough, to have devised a method for the repeated impression of stylized designs by means of baked clay stamp seals, with the design scored on the flat undersurface of the seal.[44] Because the designs which they reproduced were often regarded as sacred and celebrated the gods, the seals themselves may have served as amulets and thus transmitted the benefit of their protection to the wearer. There is, further, a strongly probable link between the use of seals, writing and urbanization. As man began to live in permanent communities, the idea of individual property evolved and with it the need to protect and to identify it. To meet these needs, first the seal and then writing itself were invented, with the use of 'tokens', whose extraordinarily long history has been demonstrated, as a stage preliminary to the development of scripts.[45]

The use of seals was to become one of the most characteristic practices of the peoples, particularly the traders, of the ancient Near East. Whether they originated in Anatolia it is not at present possible to assert positively but certainly none older are known. If they did first emerge there it seems that, although a dark night of oblivion descended on the Anatolian settlements which has only been lifted in the past generation, the practice spread from there, since some of the early forms and symbolisms seem to be preserved, travelling down into Syria, across to Mesopotamia and Iran and southwards to the Indus Valley; in time, each region developed a form or shape of seal peculiar to it, although, as will be seen later, many of the elements of their designs were common or were diffused from one culture to another. The excavator of the remarkable pre-literate, pre-urban 'cities' on the Anatolian plain proposed that the original use of the stamp seals found there was as a means of decorative tattooing on the body and, in what is surely the first glimmering of printing as a mechanical reproduction process, the imposition of designs on textiles.[46] This beginning of the practice of making seals may be dated to the seventh millennium BC.

In the Gulf, the seals are the harbingers of capitalism; but they are also talismanic, powerful amulets which invoked the protection of a divinity over the goods which they marked, or even, since some have been found in positions which indicate that they were attached to their owners in their tombs, over the owner himself.

Seals fall broadly into two types: 'stamp' seals, of which those from the Gulf are typical, and 'cylinder' seals of which the Akkadian, Old Babylonian and Assyrian empires in Mesopotamia were notable producers. Their purpose is the same, to identify property in a largely illiterate society; not, it should be noted, in specifically pre-literate societies, for the use of seals and the practice of writing frequently coexist. The method employed in the actual business of sealing differs in the two types of seal: in the case of the stamp seal a single 'print' of the seal is impressed in the clay either on the object to be identified, a pottery jar, inscribed tablet or a bulla which could be attached to the article concerned; the cylinder seal, by contrast, is rolled out and gives a continuous, repeated impression of the design by which its proprietorship is to be distinguished.

Stamp seals were the earlier of the two types to be invented; the cylinder seal is a product of the later fourth, early third millennium in Mesopotamia. One of the pieces of evidence which shows Mesopotamian influences in late

Predynastic and Archaic Egypt (*c.* 3200–2800 BC) is the appearance of cylinder seals which bear designs with Mesopotamian or Elamite elements.[47] The adoption of cylinders in Egypt was, however, a temporary phenomenon, Mesopotamian influence or not; they were replaced at the end of the Old Kingdom by one of the most typical of Egyptian products, the scarab, which is in fact a stamp seal. However, at certain times, notably during the First Intermediate Period, immediately prior to the formation of the Middle Kingdom (*c.* 2000–1780 BC) Egypt developed a type of circular stamp seal sometimes called a 'button seal', very reminiscent of the Gulf forms. Whilst there is certainly no evidence to prove it, it is not beyond the bounds of possibility that the early second millennium, a time of great mercantile and commercial activity in the Gulf and far beyond it, saw some contact between the Dilmunite merchants and Egypt; the remarkable evidence of the 'scaraboid' seals from Failaka noted in Chapter 8 will be recalled in this context (Fig 8.2). It was a time of renewed Asiatic penetration of the Nile Valley. Later, in the New Kingdom and subsequently, the scarab became one of the most common of all Egyptian artefacts, and replaced the circular stamp.

The cylinder seal was in many ways a more efficient device than the stamp seal, for it allowed a larger surface to be exposed. Thus many cylinders carry textual inscriptions, which is not usually the case with Gulf seals; cylinders are in consequence more frequently capable of being attributed to named owners than are stamp seals.

The latest and most typical Gulf seals are of a highly distinctive form which seems to have evolved over a period, from the latter part of the third millennium, and subsequently into the early centuries of the second millennium. When the Kassites moved in to control the Mesopotamian plains and the Gulf, the stamp seal virtually disappeared, to be replaced by the cylinder seal, which thus finally asserted its functional superiority. The fully evolved form of the Gulf seal is a round stamp, rarely more than 2 or 3 centimetres in diameter and often smaller. Its obverse is flat and on it the design is carved: animals, cultic scenes or what often appear at first sight to be random elements which are frequently found in various combinations on different seals. The motif of the pierced circle or 'eye' found on the domed reverse very frequently appears on other Gulf products of the period and is often an element in the decoration of, for example, the steatite vessels which are found often in large quantities on sites throughout the region.

The earliest-known seals, other than those from the early Anatolian sites, date from the fourth millennium and have been recovered from Syrian and Iranian sites.[48] The earliest of these tend to be stamp seals, which had to be impressed firmly, held with the fingers, into the clay that was to take their image; often, like the seals from early Mesopotamia, they portray formalized animals, perhaps with a fetishistic or totemic significance. Each level of the Sumerian cities' sites and those of their successors has yielded its crop of seals, the earliest showing highly stylized, abstract designs, whilst the latter ages settled upon graphic designs which often appear to be narrative in their purpose. These seals show scenes which can be associated with Mesopotamian myth, such as the hero and the bull-man wrestling with animals, a design which is customarily (though probably anachronistically) ascribed to the Gilgamesh Epic, or, later still, scenes of worship and ritual observance, of which the most common is the seal's owner, or perhaps his patron, being presented to one of the great divinities. Episodes from the stories of the gods are displayed, with Enki, Shamash, Nanna and Inanna being amongst those most frequently portrayed.

The Mesopotamian variety demonstrates well the dual function of the seals for, in addition to serving as amulets and thus conferring the protection of the divinity whose presence they invoked over the object that they sealed, they also became the means, in predominantly non-literate societies, for property to be identified. Thus, and in time, temple administrations, the rulers of cities and later still the merchants themselves developed their own marks which made the identification of their property easy and certain. However, it is unlikely that the seals ever wholly lost their amuletic quality. They were also used on legal documents to attest the presence of witnesses or the consent of the parties concerned.

Although the princes of antiquity used their seals to engross treaties and official papers, there seems little doubt that the majority of the seals which survive are the personal signets of merchants and businessmen. They are, it might be said, the originals of the trade mark; certainly they served the function of a personal crest and represent the beginnings of heraldry.

In Crete, where the extent of ancient trade is incidentally evidenced by the presence of Old Babylonian seals, the custom of seal-making was taken up keenly, and that elegant civilization predictably produced some of the most elegant examples of all. Indeed, with what appears to be the Cretan habit of over-sophistication demonstrating itself in this as in other departments of their society, the Cretan seals are really gems and are frequently classified as such. Amongst the Cretan seals are some which are prismatic in shape. Oddly enough, prismatic seals are known from Maysar in Oman, from an earlier date than the Cretan examples, derived in fact from an Umm an-Nar horizon, in the third millennium.[49]

In the Indus Valley cities a distinctive form of stamp seal was evolved, usually square in shape and with a remarkable massivity in the design elements which were incorporated on the face. The Indus Valley script appears on many of them, often in juxtaposition with the huge, hump-backed bulls which are a significant factor in the subcontinent's agronomy even today. The reverse of the Indus Valley seal usually shows a slight elevation through which the suspension-hole has been bored. Some of the seals, incidentally, seem to portray divinities who were later assumed into the Vedic pantheon.

That trade routes had been open between the Sumerian cities and those of the Indus Valley has long been known by the discovery of Indian seals in cities such as Ur. A third, highly individual type of seal was recognized, which was clearly neither wholly Indian nor wholly Mesopotamian, though the examples recovered seem to contain design elements which could be related to both societies. This third category of seals found in Sumer, and later in Indus Valley sites, was felt to lie between the other two and so gave rise to the speculation that it might have had its origins in the Gulf. The excavations in Bahrain and Failaka have confirmed this and that these seals are peculiar to Dilmun; as such they are now designated.

Seals, especially those from sites in the Gulf, are frequently miniature works of art of great complexity and appeal. The art of the lapidary must have been highly valued in the communities of the ancient world and the stone carvers or craftsmen, as precise as the most exact jewellers, repaid whatever respect they were accorded by the high standards of their craftsmanship. No seal-cutter's tools have survived but what was probably a workshop has been found in Bahrain; no doubt small drills, of copper, bronze or stone,were employed in cutting the fine detail of the design once the face of the seal had been prepared by grinding and polishing the surface.

The best of the seals demonstrate one of the special glories of ancient art in the miniature dimensions employed by these archaic craftsmen: the designs can be enlarged to a monumental scale and still retain their proportions and their power. In the Gulf, seals are almost invariably made of chlorite, a relatively soft stone which is easily worked and which engraves well. Sometimes, in the manner of seals from the Indus Valley cities, they are washed with an alkaline solution which gives them a milky-white finish; equally often they are found in the uncoloured stone. The fact that seals from Dilmun are stamps and that several of the earliest of them bear Indus Valley inscriptions has led to the suggestion that the form originated from the Indus Valley cities which were the destinations of much of the Gulf's merchandise.

THE SEALS OF THE GULF

Nearly 1,000 Gulf seals have now been recovered; over 400 come from the island of Failaka, in the Bay of Kuwait.[50] A similar number, perhaps more, has been found in Bahrain itself, though not all of them have yet been published. It is generally believed that the type originated in Bahrain.

There are two types of seal: the earlier with one or two parallel grooves on the obverse of the dome, the later with four quarters in which are often set pierced circles. The earlier type tends to emphasize animal figures and astral and solar symbols; the later ones, what appear to be ritual scenes.

The seals from Barbar are all of the second, later type, as are those from Failaka. The transition from the earlier to the later form seems to have taken place during Ur III times. *c.* 2025 BC.

The distribution of the Dilmun seals follows the routes which the merchants who owned them plied between Sumer and the Indus Valley; the excavations at Ur produced the first group, several of which are now in the British Museum.[51] These seem to show particular Indus Valley relationships. Others have been found at Lothal, one of the seaports on the coast of what is now Pakistan, serving the Indus cities.

The dome shape of the reverse, in the case of the earliest forms, is frequently more of a cylindrical projection from the seal face than the fully integrated dome of the typical Dilmun seal. Some examples are simpler still and are merely round stones bisected horizontally: it is possible that it was from this form of simple 'button' seal that the dome itself later evolved. The designs, with one or two exceptions, are equally simple, in general being confined to one subject, frequently an abstract form or an animal. Already, though, two creatures which will be found throughout the lifespan of the Dilmun seals are in evidence, the scorpion and the bull.

Amongst the crop of seals from the temple complex at Barbar several seem to have been deliberately cast into the 'sacred well'. This group is fully realized in format and the designs are highly sophisticated and aesthetically pleasing; full and sensitive use is made of the circular face of the seal (Fig. 7.7). The design of these seals is noticeably uncluttered when compared with some of the later examples, where the craftsmen have seemingly not been able to resist filling every available millimetre of the surface. The figures of men and animals are full of grace and vitality, with that curious sense of arrested motion which is always one of the glories of ancient art.

The largest group of seals from Bahrain comes from the second city level at Qala'at al-Bahrain and the Bahrain temples associated with it. They are thus to be dated from the end of third millennium and the beginning of the second. The latter period was the time of the *Alik Tilmun*, the guild of Dilmun merchants; it was the zenith of Dilmun's commercial influence and importance. All obvious traces of Indian influence have now been subsumed in Gulf forms, though some elements are retained from earlier times and with them some Mesopotamian and Elamite influences are still evident.

Probably contemporary with these seals, a number of which were found among the debris of a seal-cutter's workshop, are those found in the remarkable caches amounting to nearly 500 seals discovered in the remains of an early second-millennium settlement at Failaka. Whilst these conform to the general pattern of Dilmun seal forms, for Failaka was a province of the Dilmun culture at this time, they have their own distinctive iconography and, in many ways, are the most striking and attractive of all the seals found in the Gulf.

These later seals are remarkable for their precision, elegance, vitality and craftsmanship; the last characteristic only requires the slight and occasional qualification that the seal-cutter apparently was never able to leave well alone and displayed a tendency to over-elaboration.

The seals are also remarkable from one further point of view: that, at the present stage of knowledge, their iconography is largely incomprehensible. Of course, many of the elements can be identified but it is not yet possible to advance a coherent explanation of each seal's design. This, of course, presupposes that they are capable of being 'read' and are not merely amalgams of different elements (for no two seals are ever wholly alike) which served to differentiate one owner's property from another. It seems, on balance, and with the precedents of both the Mesopotamian and the Indus Valley seals to go on, that they probably did convey some specific ideogrammatic significance to the people who used them.

It has already been noted that in the case of Mesopotamian seals, ritual scenes were customarily depicted, whilst the Indus Valley seals frequently incorporated inscriptions, although these are also unintelligible. The Dilmun seals are different in that they often contain groupings of apparently random elements; but the repetition of certain ones, the ibex, gazelle, goat, bucranium, bird, tree, foot, scorpion and others in a variety of permutations, suggests that each element had a particular significance or that the whole design could be 'read'.

The ibex, the creature particularly sacred to Enki, is one of the most frequently depicted animals, as often found on the Gulf seals as the bull or the scorpion. Often the animal is shown in a curious juxtaposition with the other elements of the seal's design, even sometimes upside down; not infrequently, it appears with its head turned back, looking behind it (Fig. 9.1). This may be an attempt to suggest some sort of astronomical significance and relationship between the various elements of the design, each of them perhaps signifying one of the celestial bodies or constellations. Many of the recurring elements of the design on the seals are identified with the constellations specifically: the bull, the scorpion, the lion, the goat, the snake, the bird (sometimes the eagle).

Many of the designs on the seals seem to be associated with the fertility of animals and men. Some of them may symbolize good and evil, the one to be identified with the owner of the seal, and the other to be propitiated and its malignancy deflected. In the case of the later seals, especially those from Failaka, there are hints in the designs of a connection with Syria and eastern Anatolia.[52] This is interesting in the light of the possibility that there may have been some contact between the people of the Gulf in the early second millennium and the Levantine coast.

Attempts have been made to identify specific seals with known Sumerian myths, and to suggest that they illustrate, for example, incidents from the story of Gilgamesh or the creation myths associated with Dilmun. There is no warrant for such attributions, however, and to describe, as often has been the case, two male figures on a seal from Failaka as Gilgamesh and his friend Enkidu, whilst it is appealing, is misleading. Not enough is known, for example, of the understanding which the Sumerians themselves had about

Figure 9.1 The ibex, often depicted with its head turned back, is frequently included in the iconography of the Gulf seals. The ibex was identified with the god Enki, himself the most important of the Gulf's divinities, and may represent him on the seals.

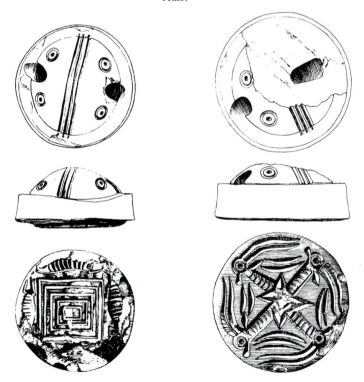

Figure 9.2 A Dilmun seal showing scorpions circling a maze-like design of enclosed squares.

Figure 9.3 Linked protomes of ibex heads, whirling in a design of great antiquity.

their own myths, and the possibility must be recognized that the duality of Gilgamesh and his friend and the dualism of two figures on a seal, whilst probably representing the same principle, do not necessarily represent each other. The fact that every figure of a hero wrestling with lions or bulls tends to be labelled with Gilgamesh's name, even in cases which clearly preceded his historical existence, has already been remarked upon and demonstrates the problem of this sort of over-simplification. However, it is only fair to add that it does not in the least matter what interpretation is put upon the seals as they are quite sufficiently potent and attractive to be admired in their own right. Indeed, they are thoroughly engaging, if minor, works of art, tiny documents which throw a light, however wavering, on the minds of the men who lived in this region 4,000 years and more ago.

To date the seals of the Gulf, other than those from Failaka,[53] have not been published fully, so that knowledge of them even in archaeological quarters is very limited. It is to be hoped that eventually, when the complete corpus of Dilmun seals is published, they will be recognized as having an important part to play in the history of art. In the meantime, it is possible to single out some of the seals and some of the elements which frequently appear in their design, for even what must of necessity be only a cursory examination of a few, produces considerations of great interest.

The gods, or at least superhuman beings, appear on many of the seals. They are identified with animals, with ships and with a companion figure, a mysterious part-man, part-bull (whether he is monster or mask is not clear). Often the gods wear the typical horned crown or horned turban of Sumerian divinities.

Amongst the Bahrain seals, one of the most common designs represents the scorpion, which appears by itself and in conjunction with other elements, sometimes literally represented and at others portrayed schematically. Several of the scorpion seals are closely similar to examples from Tel Brak in northern Syria but may be earlier in date. It seems possible that the scorpion motif may have originated in the Gulf, perhaps in Bahrain itself. One of the Barbar seals appears to show four scorpions circling a series of superimposed squares, which perhaps represent a sacred area or building; this design would admirably represent the successive levels of a ziggurat, seen in plan (Fig. 9.2).

A design inherited from earlier times is to be recognized in a class of seals, from Failaka as well as from Bahrain, which depict whirling ibex or gazelle heads, four, five or six joined at the neck (Fig 9.3). These Gulf forms mark a return to literal representations of this symbolization of the creature's fleetness, for the shape became highly abstracted after its introduction in Samarra ware from northern Mesopotamia in the fifth–fourth millennia BC.

One class of seals, that was categorized as 'erotic' in the eyes of later classifiers, though perhaps less certainly in the minds of those who created them, is represented by two black seals from Barbar and the second city at

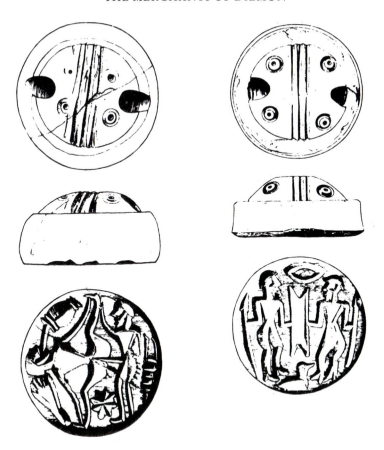

Figure 9.4 A seal which recalls Enki's penetration of a succession of goddesses.

Figure 9.5 A seal showing two warriors in confrontation, holding a shield or buckler between them.

Qala'at al-Bahrain. The first shows a gigantic, steatopygous female with her massive legs spread apart being penetrated by a more modestly proportioned male (Fig 9.4). It is a remarkably athletic copulation for he grasps one of her ankles and she appears, oddly, to be standing on one leg as he enters her, a difficult enough manoeuvre one would have imagined, even for a divinity. It is possible that she is lying above him in what an older generation of anthropologists believed was the conventional position for intercourse in a matriarchal society. More surprising still is that she appears to be vomiting into a jar: even the most fervid imagination might find it difficult to know what to make of this scene. The other seal appears to depict the two same principals and shows the male, not ithyphallic this time as in the previous example, lying passively by the female's opened thighs. This scene does of course recall the myth of the healing of Enki by Ninhursag who laid him by her vulva (see Chapter 6). These two seals are matched by two others from Failaka which appear to depict in one case an act of sodomy and in the other a frieze of men and monkeys (perhaps boys?) indulging in some rather curious acts. Monkeys are very frequently depicted, often in association with bulls or other horned animals.

Two seals stand out from the Bahrain group, both of them from Barbar, for their technique and content seem different from the others, demonstrating, as other examples from Failaka do, that despite the normally rigid conventionalism of ancient art there was still considerable scope and opportunity for the individual artist. The first shows two men in confrontation, holding a shield between them, each with a spear grasped in his other hand (Fig 9.5). Above them appears an 'eye', an extremely ancient symbol which perhaps signified the all-seeing divinity of the sun; countless examples are known from, for example, the so-called Eye Temple at Tel Brak, and many other sites. The men appear to be wearing either helmets or 'topknots' with their hair shaved to the crowns of their heads.

The other seal shows a male figure standing in a rectangular surround, two sides of which each have a pot, a larger and a smaller one, fixed to them (Fig. 9.6). Beyond the enclosure, on the left, a gazelle turns its head to look at the figure enclosed within it, whilst on the right a scorpion is shown. It may be that the two creatures represent life and death and that the scene suggests a burial, with the pots that were customarily placed in the tomb; equally possible is that a figure in a shrine is intended.

Curiously, a painting from an Egyptian tomb of the First Intermediate period (c. 2000 BC), now in the Egyptian Museum in Berlin, appears to show much the same elements; it and the seal are probably roughly contemporary.[54] A seal from Failaka certainly depicts a complicated ritual scene with two figures standing in an enclosure which bears Mesopotamian symbols of divinity.

A frequent representation on Mesopotamian seals is of the 'symposium', two or more figures, sometimes human, sometimes divine, drinking through

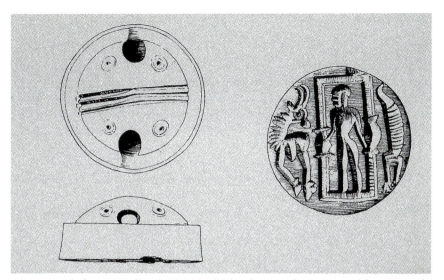

Figure 9.6 A figure standing (or lying) within what may be a grave, with two vessels built into the walls. The ibex and scorpion outside the enclosure may represent life and death respectively.

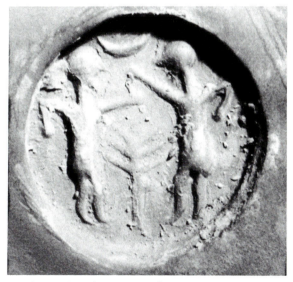

Figure 9.7 An impression showing two figures gesticulating under a palm-tree.

long straws from a shared pot. This scene also appears in the Gulf and shows two figures gesticulating at each other by a palm-tree, with the moon's crescent riding over them (Fig 9.7). It is difficult not to see two Dilmun merchants here, perhaps making their way home together after a hard day's commercial drinking. More formal representations of two figures drinking through long straws also exist on other Dilmun seals.

An important category of seals comprises those made from seashells, in contrast to the chlorite or steatite examples which represent the vast preponderance of seals recorded.[55] The shells employed for the making of the seals are drawn from the family Conidae. This is a common shell in the Gulf and is distinguished by its helical form. The adaptation to a seal shape is obtained by sawing off the base of the shell, the Dilmunites evidently having realized that each shell has a distinctive configuration in its interior.

So far, the shell seals have been found only in tombs. In this they are different from most Gulf seals, which only occasionally were buried with their owners. The shell seals have been found in most types of burial in Bahrain, particularly in those from the earlier Dilmunite period.

Some of the seals have designs drilled on them in a technique which has been compared with that used by seal-cutters in Mesopotamia during the Jamdet Nasr period, though the Bahraini examples must be chronologically much later. Some of them seem to reproduce design elements, particularly of animals and solar and stellar symbols, which appear on the Gulf seals proper.

It is not at present clear whether the shell seals are earlier in date than the chlorite seals or whether they are contemporary. As they are only found in funerary contexts it is, of course, possible that they are simply replicas of the real thing, a relatively inexpensive way of ensuring that the dead did not go wholly seal-less to the afterlife.

A notable group of seal impressions was recovered from Barbar.[56] These are flattened pellets of clay on which impressions from small seals appear to have been made, in some cases on both sides of the bullae. Their function is not known and the term 'bullae' has only been applied to them as they are in appearance similar to the seal impressions customarily attached to official documents in mediaeval Europe. They introduce a range of quite new designs, one of which appears on several of them; this seems to be a bundle of reeds, bound together at the centre and thus looking rather like the Roman *fasces*.

A motif which appears on the Bahrain seals and is also to be found on those from Failaka, though apparently less frequently, is a single human foot; this may be connected iconographically with the Mesopotamian 'fringed triangle'. The frequency with which the foot appears in Gulf iconography and in other contexts in Arabia is striking, to the extent indeed that it is difficult to avoid the idea that its appearance in the Barbar temple is not accidental. Perhaps it is intended to convey the idea of eternal contact with the chthonic gods, of whom Enki was certainly one and perhaps the first and greatest, by means of the one part of the human body which is generally in permanent contact with the earth, beneath whose surface the gods of the underworld dwell.

THE FAILAKA SEALS

The sheer quantity of seals from Failaka, where there does not seem to have been an important settlement or large port, is remarkable and frankly puzzling. No part of the site yet suggests a settlement in any way approaching in size and importance as an urban centre the Bahrain City II site. Yet from the latter fewer seals have been recovered than from Failaka and fewer still from the temple site at Barbar. The one site on Failaka has provided a substantial number of all the known examples. The eastern province of Saudi Arabia has yielded five seals but, of course, no major city site of the period has yet been excavated there.

One explanation, though it must be regarded as wholly speculative, for this concentration of seals on Failaka, would relate to the island's sacred character; perhaps it was customary to dedicate the seals to the presiding divinity, on a merchant's death, for example, or on his retirement from business. But until more of the Failaka site is excavated it is really idle thus to speculate. However, it is likely that Failaka acted as some sort of customs post for goods intended for onward shipment to Mesopotamia and the seals may simply have formed some sort of deposit or recording system.

The Failaka seal designs are generally, though not always, more complex and involved than the Bahraini examples. Animal forms predominate with scenes of sacrifice being common. The principal sacrificial animal appears to be the bull, but gazelle and ibex are also selected, and scenes of the chase are frequently depicted. Arrian makes the point that, in the time of Alexander, deer and wild goats were bred on Failaka for sacrifice to the island's goddess.

A variety of elements recurs in the Failaka seals. A large bird, perhaps an ostrich, or, since two of them are shown on a seal surmounting a large bull of Indus type, possibly 'the bird of Melukhkha' which is thought to have been the peacock, are often included in the iconography. Whatever species it is, the bird on the seals is clearly the same as the copper bird excavated at Barbar.

A puzzling feature on many seals, from both Bahrain and Failaka, is a chequer design of regular squares, sometimes 9, 15, 16, 20, 24, 28 and, in one case, 40 in number (Fig. 9.8). These chequers are usually shown in close association with significant human or divine figures who may be standing on or over them as if they were altars, holding them or presenting them. Like the Egyptian hieroglyph which has a similar form, this symbol may represent a town or settlement and the figure with which it is associated, either

Figure 9.8 One of the finest and most monumental seals recovered from Bahrain.

Figure 9.9 A design of striking modernity, recalling Matisse, of three figures in
a boat.

Figure 9.10 Two *lahmu* depicted on a
seal banded in gold.

the king or its tutelary divinity. Occasionally, animal heads project from the chequer design.

It is notoriously difficult to interpret the intentions of ancient craftsmen and artists or to attempt to determine what purpose was in their minds. However, there is one category of seals that is especially interesting and, by the frequency with which one particular motif is present, perhaps one of special significance to the whole region, though the seals come principally from Failaka. This group of seals seems to display evidence of an extensive and highly developed bull cult.

If it were possible to speculate about the principal religious cult at Failaka, it would be reasonable to suppose this to have been concerned with bulls, as some of the most remarkable of the designs feature the bull in what are obviously ritual contexts. A figure who appears on both the Failaka and the Bahraini seals introduces a mysterious and hieratic personage: a man with hoofed feet and a tail, wearing what may be a bull-mask, a variation of the horned turban of Sumerian divinities, is frequently portrayed (Fig. 9.8). In one seal he holds the severed head of a bull, standing on the chequer symbol as two ibexes turn their heads away; in another two masked figures support a third, less distinct, personage upon an altar. Above them, one of the great eight-petalled rosettes which frequently occur on the Failaka seals dominates the middle ground with two more beside the officiants at the sacrifice, if that is what the scene depicts. Above them, two bulls stand whilst monkeys leap on their backs. The altars depicted on these seals are crescent-shaped, similar to the crescent 'horned' altars which are to be found in the 'temple' at Sar, in Bahrain.

The last of the seals featuring bulls to be described here is one which recalls, however anachronistically, the treasure of the Royal Tombs at Ur. Some of the most spectacular of the Ur finds were the great ceremonial harps and lyres which were buried with the dead princes and their courtiers. These were notable for the finely worked bull-heads which decorated the sounding boxes of the lyres. On the Failaka seal a man is shown, seated and drawing his fingers across the lyre's strings. But the lyre itself has turned into a bull with the instrument's front strut projecting from the animal's back, an artist's extension, obviously, of the idea of the bull-headed sounding-box. Gudea, the king of Lagash, incidentally, records that a lyre, which he dedicated to a temple in his city, 'bellowed like a bull' when played.

The 'harp-bull' is standing on the back of another, larger bull, before which stands a man with an axe raised over the head of the animal, which is clearly intended to be a sacrifice. A palm branch, a bird, an open square and what are probably planetary symbols complete an intricate and remarkable design. It is possible that the votive axes at Barbar commemorated the bull sacrifice, here seemingly depicted. There is evidence that animals were sacrificed in the temple and all or part of their carcases burned as offerings to the waiting gods.

These bull motifs on the Failaka seals do prompt speculations which, in their implications, are tantalizing. If a cult of the bull existed in the Gulf at the end of the third millennium, this itself is surprising enough: but taken with the seeming evidence of rituals and symbolism which became, in later centuries, associated with the northern Levantine coast and from there were transmitted to Crete, the prospect opened up is, in archaeological and historical terms, extraordinary.[57] Perhaps, as so frequently has been confirmed by others about his reports, which once were regarded as wholly unreliable and then were proved to be accurate, Herodotus had sound reasons for relating the belief that the Phoenicians came originally from the Gulf. In this case, however, it perhaps was not the Phoenicians of whom he ought to have been speaking but their predecessors, the peoples who populated the Levantine coast at the beginning of the second millennium and who brought with them bull cults which were to be transplanted so spectacularly to that other island, Crete, in the second millennium.

If it could be substantiated that the islanders of the Gulf emigrated to the Levant, perhaps around the beginning of the second quarter of the second millennium, it would explain why there seems to have been a sudden break in continuity, at least in religious practice, in Bahrain and in Failaka at that time. Though several small objects from the second millennium have been found, the ruins of the third-millennium settlement at Failaka do not seem to have been succeeded by any important buildings until Hellenistic times, just as the last temple at Barbar, c. 2000 BC, seems to be followed by an abandonment of the site.

Other seals from Failaka may be mentioned briefly: a beautiful and almost Matisse-like design of two men apparently masked, standing in a boat with an animal-headed prow; one of the men holds a bow (Fig. 9.9). A third, smaller figure is leaping from it, his leg thrown up over the stern; he holds a baton or sword. One of the most handsome of all the seals, and so far unparalleled, is double-sided with a milled edge which, with the dignity of its design, gives it the appearance of a Renaissance medallion; on one side two men are seen in a boat, in the act of worship, one of them holding a palm branch; on the other side, a divinity is enthroned, with a worshipper standing before him.

Of particular interest to the cults of Dilmun is the seal which shows a tall, etiolated, standing figure in the centre of the seal with the remainder of the surface incised with vertical registers of a cuneiform text, so far the only one to be found on any seal from Dilmun. The text is an invocation to Inzak, god of Dilmun, and recalls the Durand inscription with which it is approximately contemporary. Another seal unique in form and technique is cut in a fine green steatite. Two men stand, looking outwards from the seal, caught for ever in some ritual, perfectly symmetrical action. They are naked but for belts around their waists, which are of an almost Cretan narrowness; their fingers are entwined. Both have elegantly curled wigs and beards of a form known from Sumerian precedents: they are perhaps *lahmu* 'hairy ones' who were creatures of Enki living in the Apsu (Fig. 9.10).[58] On the other face of the seal a circle encloses an eight-rayed star and at the four cardinal points, an ibex stands, the creature of Enki; between each ibex is an eight-petalled rosette. The seal is banded with gold, suggesting that its owner might have been royal, and in this it has no precedent.

From a group of Dilmun-type seals excavated at Ur and now in the British Museum comes one which has a design strangely different from any others and which would seem more appropriate to a later age.[59] A man is portrayed bearing on his shoulders a pole from which hang two large pots; above him there are two stars or rosettes, and beside him, two indeterminate creatures. This design is most evocative of the water-carrier; perhaps it is Akki, the drawer of water, commemorated in the legend of Sargon's birth and upbringing, who is here depicted.

One late Sumerian cylinder seal, dating to the very early second millennium, has been found on Bahrain; it comes from the time of the Isin-Larsa dynasty. It is thought to be comparable in date with a Dilmun seal impression found on a tablet, probably from Ur, which can be dated precisely to the tenth year of King Gugunum of Larsa, in 1923 BC. This is one of the few reasonably certain dates in the history of the region. A small number of cylinder seals bear Gulf designs, adapted to the form of seal which predominated in Mesopotamia.[60]

The study of ancient seals is profoundly revealing of the societies which made them; seals also exercise a special appeal in that they are wholly personal objects and, although this cannot positively be asserted, may well represent in their design and symbolism the direct choice of the men who first owned them so long ago. It may be said that some of the Dilmun seals equal the finest achievements of gem-cutters from far more celebrated cultures and that they deserve to rank high in the history of glyptic art. It would be difficult to have imagined a more unlikely prospect when excavations first began in Bahrain but, in many ways, the seals of Dilmun may prove to be among the most significant additions to the corpus of knowledge of the ancient world to have been gained in recent years.

It is becoming increasingly clear that the Gulf's commercial and trading network in antiquity was a good deal more extended and complex, and its mechanisms much more sophisticated, than seemed to be the case only a few years ago. Then it appeared that its principal role was to serve as a link between the cities of Sumer on the one hand and the movement of raw materials and manufactured goods on the other, on a north–south axis.[61]

The geographical range of the trading centres which were linked by the networks was very extensive. Whilst Mesopotamia appears to have been the focus of the trade, this may be illusory; in the earliest times, in the fourth millennium and the early third, the area which was associated through common trading links, ran from Anatolia through northern Syria and

Mesopotamia to Iran and onto Central Asia in the east, and the Indus Valley to the south. The border lands with Afghanistan were regularly involved and provided access, for example, for the distribution of the precious lapis lazuli which was brought down from the far north of Afghanistan and eventually reached markets as far away as the little courts of the Nile Valley in late Predynastic times.

The city-states which were emerging in Sumer in the fourth millennium and which flourished for most of the third, undoubtedly provided much of the dynamic for the system of exchange which operated over this vast area. By the middle of the third millennium there was a significant merchant class in the cities, which was replicated in more distant centres such as Ebla. It is also becoming clear that the cities (to use a term which may be marginally anachronistic) in Central Asia, which served the trade routes, were the products of societies which in many ways were comparable with those in Mesopotamia, though it is not certain whether they supported the type of organized commercial systems that the Mesopotamians developed.

However, whatever may have been the part played by other of the various centres in sustaining the wide-ranging commercial structures on which the region depended, there is no doubt that the Gulf itself was one of the principal factors in the creation of this international trading network. It provided the medium for contact and exchange between regions which were of crucial importance for the movement of goods and influences. The Gulf served not only the cities of Sumer and their hinterland but Elam and Iran and provided access to the Indus Valley cities. It also served as an outlet for the traders moving across the Iranian plateau.

The dynamic focus of the region's trade shifted from time to time. Thus, in the Uruk period (late fourth millennium) it was the Sumerian cities which dominated the exchanges; then, Uruk's influence seems to have been replaced by Elam, centred in Susiana.[62] This is of particular interest for it is at this time that the so-called Mesopotamian influences, which are more accurately to be categorized as Elamite (or proto-Elamite), appear as far away as Egypt, suggesting a considerable influence of the traders from the northeastern end of the Gulf at this time. There is also a notable diffusion of bureaucratic technologies at this time, in the use of recording systems, writing and the use of cuneiform, and the ubiquitous employment of baked clay tablets.

There has been a tendency to focus especially on the importance of the Sumerians' search for metals as the key factor in the development of the Gulf as a commercial waterway. The discovery of sources of metals was clearly of great value to the cities of the north – and, perhaps to a lesser degree the settlements of Central Asia – but of equal importance was the search for high-quality stone, a resource which was generally lacking, especially in Sumer. Stone was essential for the building and adornment of the public buildings in the Sumerian cities; one of the enduring mysteries of the

Sumerian cultural dynamic was the creation of great buildings at the very beginning of the process of urbanization in the fourth millennium, when there seems to have been no antecedant tradition on which the people of Sumer might draw.

This need for the acquisition of stone may be why Oman was of such significance in the early third millennium, at a time when the rest of the Gulf was really only just beginning to develop advanced communities. Expeditions to recover the fine stone of which Oman is generously possessed, are recorded in the later centuries of the third millennium, which suggest that the trade was of long standing. This is further borne out by the discovery of Jemdet Nasr (late fourth millennium) to Early Dynastic II (c. 2700 BC) pottery in graves excavated in Oman.[63]

The expeditions to Oman in search of stone may have provided the opportunity by which sources of copper were identified in the north of the country. Oman became an important supplier of copper ore for Sumer from the second quarter of the third millennium; prior to this it is likely that Sumer received its copper from Anatolia but, for reasons that are not yet clear, this source became unavailable and an alternative had to be found. How the Sumerians knew that Oman was copper rich is obscure; they may well have found ore-bearing rocks when they were quarrying for stone, but that in turn begs the question of how they knew that the stone which they needed was to be found in Oman in the first place.

10

GILGAMESH, THE GULF AND THE LAND OF THE LIVING

The Sumerians were the first people to create an heroic literature, the record of the deeds of great men, in part historical personalities and in part the figures of legend. They were followed, with evident enthusiasm, by the Akkadians and Babylonians, who also recorded myths which have become part of the common literary currency of western man. In these stories the Mycenaean heroes of Homer and the doom-ridden protagonists of Northern myth have their forebears.

Dilmun, represented as a secure, peaceful and temperate land, figures in the first great epic poem which has survived from the earliest records of civilized urban man. In it is contained one of the great archetypes of legend found in lands all over the world, the story of the universal Deluge. It is also the story of one of the most completely realized figures of heroic myth, the generous-hearted Shepherd King of Uruk, Gilgamesh, and of his journey across the waters of death, ferried by a solitary boatman, to the Land where the Sun Rises in search of the illusion which still obsesses man, the restoration of lost youth.[1]

Probably for as long as speech has been possible, men have invented stories in an attempt to explain the purpose of their existence, of their relationship with the natural world around them and in the hope that they might make the unseen world less fearful. Myth is of overwhelming importance in the development of human culture. Not only does it embody many of the fundamental beliefs which man has formed about himself, but in it is often enshrined much historical reality, even if it is dimly and uncertainly recalled. The themes and subjects of myth lie at the threshold of man's discovery of art.

When myth coincides with historical experience it becomes especially powerful, for then reality mirrors the deepest longings and fears of the human psyche. Such may have happened if ever Oedipus was a limping king in Thebes or when a local catastrophe was magnified to enclose the Sumerians' fears of a recurring universal deluge. In these circumstances the event recalled in myth becomes inextricably welded into the pattern of human experience.

The oldest recorded cycle of epic myth in the world tells of the triumphs and disasters of a Sumerian king, Gilgamesh of Uruk. In his struggle against the tremendous odds which beset him, Gilgamesh is the archetypal hero, ranking with Herakles – of whom indeed he may be the inspiration – and Siegfried but a great deal more agreeable than either. Those who have described Akhnaton,[2] the god-possessed Pharaoh of the fourteenth century BC as the first individual in history, overlook Gilgamesh.

Gilgamesh (his name is said to be a Babylonian corruption of the Sumerian form of the name *Bilga-mes*, which apparently means 'the old man is a young man')[3] reigned in Uruk during the twenty-seventh century BC. He is thus approximately a contemporary of Djoser, the second king of the Third Dynasty of Egypt's Old Kingdom and the inspiration of the titanic stepped pyramid at Saqqara. Little is known of the historical events of Gilgamesh's reign but it is clear that he was a sovereign well loved by his people and remembered gratefully by them. He was the fifth king in the post-diluvian dynasty of Uruk, after the reigns of the gods. His immediate predecessors included Lugalbanda, who seems to have been an historical figure, and Dummuzi, who is described as a shepherd and is almost certainly the god later known to the peoples of the Levant as Tammuz, whose name is perpetuated in the Jewish and Arabic names of the month which commemorates him to this day. Gilgamesh speaks of Lugalbanda as his father, although his paternity is disputed. He was said to be two-thirds divine for his mother was a goddess Ninsun, 'The Lady Wild Cow': his birth was probably the consequence of his mother's participation in one of the sacred marriage rites, the temple ceremony which year by year ensured the fecundity of the city.

Gilgamesh is one of the most popular subjects in Sumerian and Babylonian art, in which he is depicted as a young man, bearded and vigorous, enacting scenes from his epic history. Frequently he is shown in the company of gods and animals, reflecting an early belief that man stood somewhere between these two orders of creation. Almost invariably he seems to be smiling and exulting in the twin powers of his kingship and his manhood, and as a king walks as happily with beasts as with divinities. He fortified his city against invasion and gave laws to his people which anticipated the code of Hammurabi, another great Mesopotamian sovereign who was to rule in Babylon a thousand years after Gilgamesh.

The story of Gilgamesh's journey to Dilmun is recorded in the Epic of Gilgamesh which in the form in which it substantially survives today was written down during the eighteenth century before our era.[4] But this version undoubtedly drew on a much older Sumerian original, reaching us from the third millennium; parts of this earlier text survive and the other versions call on parts of the original now lost. The most complete text is preserved in twelve tablets of baked clay, written in the wedge-shaped cuneiform script of the first Babylonian empire. The tablets were found in the ruins of the library of King Assurbanipal (668–633 BC) who, in addition to being a great conqueror, was a conscientious antiquarian, who collected with enthusiasm and appreciation the records and legends of those who had preceded him on the thrones of Mesopotamia.

Over the past century or so various recensions of the myth have been published. A problem arises in relating them out of a scholarly context, in that the names of the principal characters are different in each version; only Gilgamesh himself seems to preserve his own consistent identity. Thus the character of the immortalized king of Shurupak, the prototype of Noah, is called Ziusudra in the Sumerian text, but Utanapishtim in the Babylonian and Assyrian. The mysterious boatman who ferries Gilgamesh across the Waters of Death is Sursunabi and Urshanabi respectively. In the outline which follows, the names are used as they appear in the original versions though the incident quoted may only appear in the non-Sumerian recensions which survive.

The story is as follows: Gilgamesh, the young and vigorous king of one of the oldest and most important of Sumer's states, is loved by his people, but with certain distinct reservations. His nature, two-thirds divine and one-third human by his descent from the Great Goddess of Sumer and a High Priest (or from Lugalbanda, who by his kingly office would also have been a cult-priest), is tempestuous and uncontrolled. The citizens of Uruk have become increasingly unenthusiastic about his assaults on their wives and daughters and his appropriation of their sons for his campaigns. However, since the inhabitants of Uruk are a responsible people with a proper respect for both the divine parentage and earthly rank of their king, they seek the advice of the great god Enlil. They beg him to devise some distraction for Gilgamesh which will turn his energies away from their relations. The god sympathizes with their problems and creates Enkidu to be the king's companion, a wild, untamed man living in company with the animals. Enkidu may symbolize the second mainstream of the people of Mesopotamia other than the settled city-dwellers, the Semitic-speaking nomads who entered the land from earliest times, often intermarrying with the Sumerians themselves. Enkidu's destiny is to become the twin of Gilgamesh, the king's *alter ego*. Not altogether surprisingly, in view of his record of fairly indiscriminate sexuality, Gilgamesh is deeply attracted by him and they swear eternal friendship; there are indeed hints that their relationship is a sexual one. In the manner of boys who ultimately become inseparable, this relationship only develops after they have fought a great battle, in which Gilgamesh defeats Enkidu. 'They grappled, each other holding fast like Bulls.'

Unhappily, the seeds of the destruction of their friendship have already begun to germinate: Enkidu has only been coaxed to the habitations of men by the wiles of the town whore, probably a priestess of the Mother in her character of the goddess of love and lust, who seduces him by the river bank. Hitherto he has run wild, as free and untrammelled as the gazelles and other fauna with whom he has shared the desert. But now, because the animals who have been his companions to this point sense the corruption of human-ity on Enkidu, they withdraw reproachfully from him, leaving him to the fortunes of gods and men. However, it is by the power of love that Enkidu, the wild man of the steppe, becomes civilized. Despite his primitive charac-ter Enkidu is a complex figure: he is the first innocent in all literature, the literary ancestor of Parsifal.

To some commentators, those who seek an astrological significance in events and personalities which probably would have considerably surprised those concerned had they known of them, Gilgamesh and Enkidu may represent the Twins, the eponyms of the epoch of Gemini superseded by that of the Bull in the concept of the Universal Zodiac which, some believe, may descend from ancient Mesopotamia.[5] The only problem with this interpretation is, of course, that the Twins overthrow the Bull, as will shortly be related, and not the other way about. Sometimes Gilgamesh and Enkidu (or rather those two characters from an earlier time who seem to prefigure them) appear as Bull and Ram, thus symbolizing the poetic Precession of the Equinoxes. The Twins even overthrow the Bull of Heaven when it is sent precipitately to earth to destroy them. They represent, too, that constantly returning principle of the dualism of all the created world which so obsessed the ancients. It has been suggested that the whole Gilgamesh cycle is in fact a solar myth with an occult, astrological signifi-cance. There are twelve divisions in the epic – but who knows?

Gilgamesh's love for Enkidu brings him to a sense of his responsibilities for his kingdom, and he no longer concerns himself with leaping upon the more personable members of the Uruk community. With the blessing of Shamash, the benevolent sun-god, the two friends set out on a quest to conquer evil manifest in the form of Huwawa, the Keeper of the Wood. Gilgamesh is anxious to create a 'name' which will endure. Enkidu is his companion and occasionally his protector. Huwawa is the prototype of the sad monster, with whom it is difficult not to feel a similar degree of sympathy as with Fafnir when he is overcome by the doltish Siegfried. Dragon- or monster-slaying was a major preoccupation of the heroes of antiquity; Horus, the Archangel Michael, even Yahweh, were all given to the practice.

After many trials the pair defeat Huwawa and when he is at their mercy, Gilgamesh is inclined to be compassionate and to spare his life. Weeping, Huwawa pleads to be saved: but Enkidu, fulfilling what is evidently his destiny, is inflexible and demands his death. Huwawa is swiftly slain.

The heroes return to Uruk and are fêted in a splendid and triumphant entry to the city. But they are guilty of hubris; Enkidu has angered the gods both by his refusal to spare Huwawa and because he joined with Gilgamesh in insulting Inanna-Ishtar, a goddess of uncertain temper at the best of times. She tries to persuade Gilgamesh to her bed but he, prompted by Enkidu, reminds her of the dismal fate of her previous lovers. The friends mock her unmercifully and with deadly accuracy. She complains to heaven of the wrong which has been done her, the more annoying as all the taunts and accusations of libidinousness and treachery which are flung at her by Gilgamesh and Enkidu when they spurn her, she knows only too well to be true. But for these faults and also because they have killed the Bull of Heaven, sent to avenge the goddess, one of the two must die. Enkidu dreams of the congress of the gods when the fearful decision is spoken by the supreme God; it is Enkidu who is stricken.

The mortal illness of Enkidu, which lasts for twelve days, is the occasion for a remarkable and moving exchange between the dying man and Shamash the sun-god, who has taken a benevolent interest in the affairs of the two companions. He alone opposed the ruling of the gods when they agreed upon Enkidu's death and now he comes to solace the last hours of one of his protégés.

Enkidu tosses miserably on his death-bed; Gilgamesh is powerless to help him. Enkidu curses his life with a bitterness made utter by his realization of the futility even of his cursing. Frenziedly he reproaches the events which drew him away from his natural existence to the haunts of men, and even inanimate objects in his delirium become the focus of his dreadful sorrow. He curses the hunter who led the people of Uruk to his steppe-lair; most bitterly he execrates the whore who was the instrument of his ensnaring. But in Heaven, Shamash hears Enkidu and speaks to comfort him. He reminds him that life with Gilgamesh has been glorious; the princes of the world have honoured him because he was Gilgamesh's companion; indeed they have kissed his feet as he was the king's beloved friend. He has lived magnificently and now he must die knowing that Gilgamesh will command the most elaborate obsequies for him.

In the words of the myth: 'when Enkidu heard the words of valiant Shamash, his vexed heart grew quiet.' Now he blesses those whom before he cursed and, although he has a dark vision of the afterworld before his eyes, he dies reconciled by the sun-god's words.

Gilgamesh mourns his dead friend with the frenzy and inconsolable grief of Achilles bewailing the death of Patroclus and, like Alexander of Macedon weeping beside Hephaestion's corpse, he clasps the body of his friend until the horrifying evidence of corruption begins to display itself. He speaks a lament for Enkidu which anticipates that of David for Jonathan. He orders sumptuous funeral ceremonies in Uruk and then, horror-stricken, realizes that the same mortality which has claimed his friend must one day bring an end to his own life, splendid, powerful and just though he knows himself to be. The death of Enkidu and Gilgamesh's mourning for his friend, inevitably perhaps, seem to be an especially contemporary theme.

Again he sets out, this time alone, to search for the secret of eternal life, the most constant and the most fruitless of man's quests. He is still bitterly saddened by Enkidu's death and constantly speaks of his love for him, his own awareness of life's transience feeding upon his melancholy. In the words of the epic, 'the Lord towards the Land of the Living set his mind' across the marshlands and southwards to the Gulf.

The rejection of Inanna-Ishtar and the subsequent death of Enkidu represent a curious episode in Gilgamesh's story because, of all divinities, it might have been expected that she was the one whom Gilgamesh would most honour. She was the patroness of Uruk itself, Gilgamesh's own city and his mother was probably a priestess of her cult; yet the king is clearly in opposition to her.

Some might speculate whether this episode does not record, in mythological terms, a rejection by Gilgamesh of the ultimate payment exacted for the kingship in societies which still honoured the Mother. Gilgamesh conforms admirably to the character of the Sacred King. The myth of Tammuz-Dummuzi, which still echoes in the Near East to this day, was the story of the dying king for whom the goddess mourns but always recreates that he may again be sacrificed. When male gods began to predominate in ancient societies there was revulsion from the archaic sacrifice of the Sacred King, consecrated to destruction for the honour of the Goddess. The transitional phase, between the sacrifice of the king and its rejection, was marked by the recognition that a surrogate might die in the king's place and his royal life be thus renewed. In Greece the practice seems to have been well attested and there are hints of it amongst the ancient Jews.

In Egypt, the king underwent the ordeal of rebirth at the *heb-sed* festival, when his powers were renewed. It is generally proposed that the *heb-sed* is a surrogate act for the ritual sacrifice of the king, though in fact there is no evidence for the practice.[6] Christianity, it has long been recognized, enshrines the age-old concept of the dying god, whose physical death is re-enacted – as, similarly, was the death of Osiris in Egypt through the mystery plays which were a feature of the earliest rituals – by the sacrifice of the Mass, in which the central event is the ingestation of the consecrated bread, rather than the celebrant. The bread is thus a substitute for the living flesh, once consumed in a more dreadful eucharist.

It may also be that this episode in Gilgamesh's story contains some of the essential elements of the sacred marriage rite of old Sumer and that Gilgamesh was in truth intended to be the successor of Dummuzi in the love of Inanna, the city-goddess of Uruk. In later ages the rite of the sacred marriage recurs frequently and it was clearly an integral part of the Sumerian canon, surviving into times after Sumer itself had passed away and was forgotten. It has been suggested that the burial pit at Ur, in which the unbelievably rich accoutrements of a presumed Sumerian royal interment were found, contains the principal actors in the same ceremony. The later deification of certain Sumerian kings – in itself a wholly un-Sumerian practice – in the time of the Third Dynasty of Ur may be yet another echo of this ancient ceremony in which the king and the god who ensures the continued fertility of crops and herds are identified. But in Gilgamesh's case, great though his love for his people unquestionably is, he is not prepared to die at the whim of the goddess and, by his rejection of his role, marks the end of her domination. Gilgamesh's denial of his sacrificial character cannot be absolute, however, and therefore his surrogate, Enkidu, his twin as dear to him as any living thing, must die in his place.

North-east of Gilgamesh's city of Uruk lay the Kingdom of Shuruppak, the modern Fara. Shuruppak was the home of Ziusudra ('Long of Days') or, as the Babylonians called him in their version of the myth which survives, Utanapishtim, a name which may mean, appropriately as it turns out, 'I have found Life'; he was known, evocatively, as 'The Faraway'. He was said to have reigned in Shuruppak for 36,000 years, a period which reflects the Sumerians' enthusiasm for the sexagesimal scale, which they invented. He was destined to become the hero of the Deluge story, like the Biblical Noah and the Greek Xisuthros, the good and wise king singled out by the gods for salvation when they determined to destroy the rest of the human race, with whom they had become disenchanted. In a long digression which must be reflected here, the Epic explains the reason for their displeasure.

The gods of Sumer were even more arbitrary in their relations with mankind than the Hebrew god Yahweh was to be, for at least in the version contained in Genesis the Deluge was occasioned by God's wrath being visited upon the sins of the created world. The gods of Sumer, and their leader Enlil in particular, could not, it seems, tolerate the noise that mankind was making and on this petulant pretext determined to destroy the race of men by flood. Man was not destined to be wholly annihilated, however. Despite the stern decree of the High Gods in council, Enki, the friend of man and ruler of the floodwaters, decided to intervene, thus risking the wrath of Enlil. But so that he might not be accused of betraying the gods' decision, he came to Ziusudra's city and, with the cunning and resource which rarely deserted the most crafty of the gods, whispered his warning to the wall of the king's reed hut. Through the wall he urged Ziusudra to build an ark, put his family and retainers on board and, with a cargo of all living creatures, to set out upon the rising waters.

The Sumerian epic contains many dramatic passages which differ from the Biblical story; the description of the mounting terror of the storm, led by the black powers of wind and thunder, is particularly striking.

> With the first glow of dawn
> A black cloud rose up from the horizon
> Inside it Adad thunders
> While Shullat and Hanish go in front
> Moving as heralds over hill and plain
> Erragal tears out the posts;
> Forth comes Ninurta and causes the dykes to follow

The Annunaki lift up the torches
Setting the land ablaze with their glare
Consternation over Adad reaches to the heavens
Who turned to blackness all that had been light
The wide land was shattered like a pot
For one day the south storm blew.
Gathering speed as it blew submerging the mountains
Overtaking the people like a battle
No one can see his fellow
Nor can the people be recognized from heaven
The gods were frightened by the deluge
And, shrinking back, they ascended to the heaven of Anu
The gods cowered like dogs crouched against the outer wall.[7]

Ever since the last century when the 'Deluge' tablet was first deciphered, the argument has swung back and forth as to whether the story recalls a major catastrophe actually experienced by the Sumerians and subsequently impressed deeply on their memory, or whether it is merely the literary expression of what must have been a constant and deep-seated fear of a people living between two such unpredictable streams as Tigris and Euphrates.

Woolley, who excavated so diligently and with such effect in Sumerian cities, firmly believed in the historicity of the Biblical flood, admittedly on slender evidence;[8] in more recent years it has been usual to adopt the contrary view. But floods in Sumer there certainly were and one – or all of them – may have been immortalized in the original of the myth, told around the camp fires, perhaps even before Enki founded his first city at Eridu.

More recent evidence has become available, however, which opens the question again. First, it now seems likely that Ziusudra/Utanapishtim/Noah was an historical figure and not simply the man with the amiable manner and a taste for zoology whom the legends, both Sumerian and Biblical, portray. At Shuruppak, Ziusudra's capital, and at Kish, one of the most respected religious sites of ancient Sumer, extensive flood deposits have been un-covered since Woolley's time which are almost certainly contemporary with Ziusudra's supposed reign and are more widespread than had been earlier believed.[9] It is clear that the floodwaters covered considerable areas of the land and could quite easily have been mistaken for a universal deluge by the survivors, so terrible must have been the havoc they wrought. The flood would seem to have covered an area many square kilometres in extent to a considerable depth, and the persistent legend which has survived the millennia may thus be based upon a real and fearful experience. This deluge at Shuruppak may have taken place towards the end of the Jemdet Nasr period, c. 3000 BC.[10]

To return to the version of the Flood which the Epic relates: like Noah when the deluge had abated, Ziusudra releases birds as his messengers to find dry land, but it is the raven rather than the dove which makes the landfall in the Sumerian legend. On the mountain-top where his ark – a peculiar, perfectly cubical vessel – comes to rest, Ziusudra offers sacrifices to the gods who are said, rather gracelessly, to hover around the sacrifices 'like flies' hungry for the worship which has been denied them by the destruction of the creatures they created, in part for this very purpose. A slightly acid view of the behaviour of the Sumerian pantheon is not unreasonable; it is apparent from the passage quoted earlier that at one stage the whole operation was beginning to get out of hand when the gods, obviously inexperienced in directing cosmic disasters, withdrew cravenly to the higher heavens. The image of them crouching 'like dogs' against the outer wall of Anu's most distant Heaven is a telling one.

Ziusudra is rewarded with immortality by the now calmer gods, a state which is to be shared by his wife, a peculiarly thoughtful touch. They are translated to 'the land of crossing', Dilmun:

> Ziusudra, the King
> Prostrated himself before Anu and Enlil.
> Anu and Enlil cherished Ziusudra,
> Like that of a god they gave him,
> Breath eternal like that of a god they bring down for him
> Then Ziusudra the King,
> The preserver of the name of vegetation and of the seed of mankind
> In the land of crossing, the land of Dilmun, the place where the sun
>   rises they caused to dwell.[11]

In some versions of the myth, Ziusudra is said to be placed by the gods in a mysterious land 'at the mouth of the rivers'.[12] It had generally been thought that this location must be somewhere near the outflow of the Tigris and Euphrates into the Gulf through the marshlands near the Shatt al Arab. However, some light may be thrown on this typically vague piece of Sumerian geographical description by the fact that local legend in Bahrain and on the Arabian mainland maintains that the sea's freshwater springs, which feature later in Gilgamesh's story, are the 'subterranean mouths' of the two rivers. This they are not: but it is certainly possible that the legend persisting today descends from very ancient times and that it was to these springs that the Ziusudra legend refers, when it speaks of 'the mouth of the rivers' as the eternal home of the justified king of Shuruppak – and Bahrain means, in Arabic, 'the two seas'.

Gilgamesh goes out to search for Dilmun, for nowhere is it more likely that he will find the secret of eternal life than there, a land blessed by the gods, ruled by the one man who has already been transformed by them into an immortal. He travels by foot from his city, alone and meeting more adventures on the way, including an encounter with a sort of celestial hostess,

Siduri, who urges Gilgamesh to forget his concern for man's condition and to eat, drink and be merry.

Gilgamesh, whither rovest thou?
The Life thou pursuest thou shalt not find
When the gods created mankind
Death for mankind they set aside
Life in their own hands retaining.
Thus Gilgamesh let full be thy belly
Make thou merry by day and by night,
Of each day make thou a feast of rejoicing,
Day and night dance thou and play!
Let thy garments be sparkling fresh,
Thy head be washed; bathe thou in water
Pay heed to the little one that holds on to thy hand
Let thy spouse delight in thy bosom!
For this is the task of mankind.[13]

Siduri is an intriguing, enigmatic character. The Gulf in ancient times was well populated with goddesses; Siduri is, by any standards, one of its principal divinities. She lives on an island at the edge of the Ocean, that mysterious generalization for all unknown seas. Her land is a garden in which the Sun walks in the mornings: the trees bear jewels. Siduri has sisters, or perhaps the other goddesses are really herself in other guises. One of them, Sinara, is described as the goddess of the Gulf, given charge of it by the Lord Enki himself. Lakhamum is conflated with Sarpanit of Dilmun[14] and is represented bearing the scales of a mermaid or a fish-goddess. Then there are the several goddesses associated with holy Dilmun: Ninsikilla, the Lady of Pure Decrees and spouse to Enki, and Ninhursag, the great goddess whose terrible epiphany brought death near to Enki, are but two of them.

Siduri survived her encounter with Gilgamesh to become, in Hellenistic times, the Erythraean Sibyl. She was then represented, anachronistically, as the daughter of Berossus, the Chaldaean historian whose *Babyloniaca* contained the weird story of the appearance in the Gulf in legendary times of the *apkallu*, the part-men part-fish who brought the arts of civilization to the black-headed folk of Sumer.[15]

After his meeting with Siduri, Gilgamesh continues on his way: he meets sinister scorpion men, the guardians of the Gates of Yesterday and Tomorrow (also known as the Keepers of the Place of Sunrise), and is fearful of them: they warn him that no one has accomplished the journey which he has set himself. He meets Shamash and even the god is awed by Gilgamesh's presumption:

Shamash was distraught, as he betook himself to him;
He says to Gilgamesh

'Gilgamesh, whither rovest thou?
The life thou pursuest thou shalt not find.'
Gilgamesh says to him, to valiant Shamash:
'After marching [and] roving over the steppe,
Must I lay my head in the hearth of the earth
That I may sleep through all the years?
Let mine eyes behold the sun that I may have my fill of the light!
Darkness withdraws when there is enough light.
May one who indeed is dead behold yet the radiance of the sun!'[16]

But Gilgamesh is not to be turned from his course: he crosses the marshlands and reaches what must be the head of the Arabian Gulf. There he summons Ziusudra's boatman to take him to Dilmun. It is clear that Gilgamesh intended to make the journey by water, suggesting that by the time this element of the story had been taking into the myth, the insular Dilmun, the Bahrain islands, was intended as the object of Gilgamesh's journey. Ziusudra's boatman is a mysterious character, whose responsibility, like Charon's in Greek mythology, is to ferry the dead to Paradise. He agrees to carry Gilgamesh across the waters of death which separate Dilmun from the living world. However, it is essential that Gilgamesh shall not touch the waters and Sursunabi instructs him to cut 120 poles 60 cubits in length to punt the boat (the Sumerian cubit was just under 50 centimetres long). This generous allocation of gigantic poles, each one about 30 metres long, is necessary so that Gilgamesh may let each one fall back into the sea of death; thus he will avoid touching the lethal waters.

The journey according to the Epic might reasonably be expected to take a month and fifteen days; Gilgamesh and Sursunabi, however, reach Dilmun in three days, a testimony to Gilgamesh's more than human qualities. In fact, three days is about the time it would have taken a ship of Sumerian times to sail from the head of the Gulf to Bahrain.

As the boat approaches Dilmun, Ziusudra is watching from the shore; at once he recognizes that Gilgamesh is no man of his, for Gilgamesh is living. It is of some significance that the Epic makes this point, the recognition by Ziusudra that the figure standing in Sursunabi's boat is untouched by death and thus is not truly ready to be brought to his (and Dilmun's) shores. This suggests, however tentatively, that the place to which Ziusudra had been transported was a place to which others were to be brought; since they had to cross the waters of death to reach it, it may be presumed that they, too, were dead. This may be an echo of the belief which gave occasion to Dilmun's sepulchral reputation. The deeply evocative concept of the 'island of the dead' which so haunted the imagination of nineteenth-century Romantic artists may have had its remote beginnings here. Boeklin's celebrated painting, transposed to the blood-warm waters of the Gulf, may lose something of its mournful, cypress-haunted solemnity but it gains in antiquity.

Ziusudra welcomes Gilgamesh, but asks the reason for his mournful appearance; Gilgamesh at once rehearses the story of Enkidu's death and their love for one another, his fears of his own dissolution and his quest for immortality. He realizes that unless he finds the secret, one day soon he too will die and be laid in the earth for ever. He pleads with Ziusudra to tell him how he may find the eternal life which he has dedicated himself to seeking, enduring all hardships and tribulations in the quest for it. Ziusudra is emphatic and discouraging:

> There is no permanence. Do we build a house to stand for ever, do we seal a contract to keep for ever, does the flood of rivers endure? It is only the nymph of the dragonfly who sheds her larva and sees the sun in his glory. From the days of old there is no permanence. The sleeping and the dead, how alike they are, they are like a painted death. What is there between the master and the servant when both have fulfilled their doom? When the Annunaki, the judges come together, and Mammetum the mother of destinies, together they decree the fates of men. Life and death they allot but the day of death they do not disclose.[17]

Yet Ziusudra is the only mortal to escape the universal fate of mankind; to explain this destiny he begins to tell the weary Gilgamesh of the story of the Flood and his part in it. What Ziusudra, presumably delighted to have a new audience for the recital of his life-story, has to tell him seems to have little relevance to Gilgamesh's problems, except perhaps to demonstrate that the king of Shuruppak was merely fulfilling the role which destiny and the gods had determined for him.

When his recital is finished, Ziusudra puts Gilgamesh to another test; all he needs to do to become immortal, he tells him, is to resist sleep for six days and seven nights. Gilgamesh tries his best, but wearied by his journeys, and in all probability by the story of the Deluge, he falls asleep. So tired is he that, far from remaining awake for seven nights, he sleeps for all that time, outside Ziusudra's reed hut in Dilmun.

The immortal, who has watched over him with affectionate compassion, wakens him at last and Gilgamesh, endearingly and wholly in character, cries that he had only just dropped off into a light sleep. Gently Ziusudra tells him it is not so, and the realization that he cannot resist even the little death of sleep brings panic and despair to Gilgamesh. 'Already', he says, 'the thief in the night has hold of my limbs, death inhabits my room: wherever my foot rests I find death.'

Ziusudra offers Gilgamesh some consolation, but it is tinged with irony, for if he cannot give him eternal life he can give him a new set of clothes which will keep their pristine quality until he returns to his own city.

Sometimes even mere possessions outlive their owners.

Gilgamesh is about to leave Dilmun and return despondently home to Uruk, when Ziusudra's wife prompts her husband to reveal one mystery of the island to him. At its revelation Gilgamesh becomes greatly excited, for it seems to be the very object of his quest. Under the water, Ziusudra tells him, there grows a plant, similar to the buckthorn, which if plucked will bring the possessor the return of lost youth. At once Gilgamesh joyously prepares to set off in search of it convinced, mistakenly, that it is the secret of immortality that awaits his grasp.

At this point in the narrative, the story-teller comments specifically that it is a sweet-water current that bears Gilgamesh to the sea-bed where the plant grows. He weights himself by tying heavy stones to his feet in the way which is the practice of the pearl-fishers of the Bahrain seas to this day. It seems not impossible that it might have been one of the sea's freshwater springs that carried Gilgamesh down to find the flower of restored youth.

These springs, it has already been remarked, are a peculiar feature of the seas around Bahrain, fountains of brackish water which burst up surprisingly from the shallows about a kilometre and a half offshore. It is clear from the poem that Gilgamesh is in the sea, for it is stated that when he picked the flower he cut the weighted stones from his feet 'and the sea carried him and threw him on the shore'.

The actual nature of the 'plant' that Gilgamesh seeks is unknown. One possibility is that it is the coral which is the object of his quest.[18] Coral grows abundantly in the Gulf; its phosphorescence has already been referred to in connection with Gilgamesh's encounter with Siduri. One of the candidates for the place where Gilgamesh plunged into the sea must be Fasht Khor, off the north shore of the principal island, for there is located a substantial freshwater spring which forces its way up out of the seabed itself.

Now Gilgamesh reveals one of the traits of his nature which may have caused him to be so loved by his people while he was king of Uruk and which ensured that the recollection of him grew over the centuries until he assumed heroic and semi-divine proportions in the memory of the generations that delighted in his story. Excitedly he shows the magic plant to Ziusudra's ferryman; he announces that he will return to Uruk with it and there give it to the old men to eat that they may become young again. Only when the old men are restored will he, the king, eat it himself.

Gilgamesh leaves the house of Ziusudra on the shores of Dilmun and begins his journey home, bearing his magic plant and accompanied by Sursunabi, who has been banished from Dilmun for bringing a mortal to its shores; but he is now Gilgamesh's friend. This time, presumably because Sursunabi has had his boat taken away from him, they are on foot. But Sursunabi is something more than a simple boatman, a Sumerian Charon ferrying the dead to Dilmun. He is a member indeed of the principal family of gods, for he married the daughter of the great god, Enki of the Abyss; his name, it has been suggested, means 'Servant of Enki'. Thus Enki's dominion over Dilmun is again demonstrated by the presence of his henchman.

After a while upon their journey, they stop by a cool and inviting pool. Gilgamesh flings off the splendid clothes given him by Ziusudra and plunges in, leaving the precious flower of youth on the bank.

Deep in the pool, a serpent lives. Disturbed by Gilgamesh splashing joyfully above it, the serpent rises to the surface and smells the sweetness of the magic plant. Quickly it rears out of the water, seizes the plant, swallows it, and at once sloughs its skin, the invariable sign of the snake's immortality in the eyes of the ancients.

Thus destiny and the gods played their final deception upon Gilgamesh. He wept by the waters, mourning now not only Enkidu and his own certain dissolution, but also the hopelessness of his quest and the wreck of his hopes to change man's destiny.

In Bahrain near the north-east end of the island is the Pool of Adari; though there is not the slightest evidence to warrant it, it is pleasant to think of it as the place where Gilgamesh, having pitted himself as the champion of mortal man against the fates, was finally conquered. Today it is a happier place, full of boys bathing, few of whom have ever thought of the king who might have bathed there before them.

The pool is a few kilometres to the south of the two principal Sumerian-connected sites in Bahrain, Barbar and Qala'at al-Bahrain. Offshore, about a kilometre and a half due north of Barbar lies another of the freshwater springs which bubble up from the seabed, called al-Sharaiba in Arabic. It is tempting to place all the main events of Gilgamesh's visit to Dilmun in this corner of the island. Adari, incidentally, was probably a place of ritual sacrifice in pre-Islamic times, for in Arabic the word means 'virgin' and this suggests that an ill-fortuned girl was once marked out as an offering to the island's divinities, and cast into its depths. To this day popular belief in Bahrain insists that a serpent in Adari pool demands an annual sacrifice and that every year a swimmer will be drowned there.

But there is another possibility: in some versions of the myth Gilgamesh is said to have bathed in a well. Given the frequently recorded practice of goddesses bathing their heads in wells or fountains, this seems a reasonable possibility. There was a well, clearly of some ritual importance, in the temple site at Barbar.

A recurring factor in mythology and ancient belief has appeared in the Epic at this point in the form of the serpent which stole Gilgamesh's hope of eternal youth. Snakes were sacred from the earliest times and the serpent was as frequently a creature of good omen as it was of evil, for it was one of the attendants of the ambiguous Great Mother, the original divine creative force recognized and worshipped by man from Upper Palaeolithic times onwards. The serpent that played so deplorable a part in the Garden of Eden was almost certainly Sumerian or Babylonian in its mythical origins, though the

Biblical story was probably based upon a misunderstanding of the original source. A snake cult was still maintained in Bahrain 1,000 years after the time from which the earliest versions of the Epic of Gilgamesh dates and 2,000 years after the events which it describes.

Gilgamesh returned to Uruk with the knowledge that man's life is destined to be brief and that there is no escaping the ultimate summons of death and the rule of the Iggigi, the dark and terrible gods who were the judges of the Underworld. However, he finds some cause for pride in his city and he points out to Sursunabi (for he has befriended the now unemployed boatman) the high ramparted walls he has built of burnt brick, dependable and strong, and the orchards and temple lands which march with the city's limits. At least his life has not been wholly wasted if he can build a strong city and bring good government to his state; is he not Gilgamesh, the king, the shepherd of his people?

> Go up and walk upon the wall of Uruk,
> Inspect the base terrace, examine the brickwork,
> Is not its brickwork of burnt brick?[19]

At length the number of Gilgamesh's days in Uruk are realized; still protesting against his fate and the fate of all men, he dies and must descend into the sombre underworld of the spirits. His people prepare a solemn funeral for him, for the panoply of death is as splendid as that which marks the progress of a living king. The young Gilgamesh, wild and insatiable, is forgotten and only the royal shepherd who suffered much for his people is remembered. Gilgamesh the king who was enjoined by Enlil, the master of the gods, to deal justly before the face of the sun, is taken to his tomb lamented by all the people of the city:

> The King has laid himself down and will not rise again
> The Lord of Kullun will not rise again;
> He overcame evil, he will not come again
> Though he was strong of arm he will not rise again
> He had wisdom and a comely face, he will not come again
> He is gone into the mountain, he will not come again
> From the couch of many colours he will not come again.[20]

The foundations of the walls of Uruk, so proudly acclaimed by Gilgamesh, may still be made out and they are nearly 10 kilometres (6 miles) in circumference.[21] The city itself has become a mound raked over earnestly by archaeologists, the splendour of its temples and towers reconstructed from fragments and impressions in the Mesopotamian soil. But Gilgamesh has achieved eternal life, at least to our day and, it is to be hoped, for as long as men are moved by heroes and the sagas of their exploits. And surely he warrants such remembrance, for he symbolizes man's protest against the little time which he is allowed to wander in the garden of this world and his eternal struggle against the harsh lottery of the gods.

It would be foolish to try to trace too literally, step by step, Gilgamesh's journey to Dilmun. The voyage described in the Epic may well *not* be capable of being placed in any real location at all; for all we know today, it may be astronomical, cosmological or purely fictional.

The majesty of the myth and its expression through the medium of the Epic is, however, neither increased by being rooted in place or time nor diminished by not being so. It is part of the universal heritage and its real significance in the present context is that the culmination of Gilgamesh's journey is sought for and, in a sense, fulfilled in Dilmun's land, which in this case lies beyond the borderlands of reality. Again, it is the faery quality of Dilmun which pervades those parts of the Epic which touch it.

So many strands of myth run into this most ancient of all sacred lands that those of Gilgamesh's story are only part of the warp and woof of the Dilmun tapestry. The gods cluster around Dilmun as once they were said to cluster, like flies, around Ziusudra's sacrifices after the Flood, and, in addition to Gilgamesh, the most splendid among heroes, there is a significant company of other heroic figures whose stories, like his, find much of their expression in Dilmun and the lands of the Gulf. The heroes, passing in review, are the Lord Enki, Oannes, Ziusudra, Al-Khidr and Alexander.

These heroic figures are a special element in the Gulf's mythology. Thus Gilgamesh and his counterpart, Alexander, distant in time but comparable in their heroic status and enduring legend, are not alone as the most powerful figures who bridge the realms of myth and reality. Enki himself is there, the most puissant of divinities, who has his *alter ego* in Oannes, part-man, part-fish, the aquatic didact after whose time no new knowledge had been imparted to mankind. Ziusudra, too, must qualify as an heroic figure, certainly as someone more than mortal. But there is another still more mysterious being, who enters the story of the Place of the Two Seas and who may subsume all of these mighty entities – at least in the version of his legend with which we are dealing – in his own shadowy self, one of the most complex and mysterious figures in Near Eastern myth.

The myth relates the activities of one of Al-Khidr, the Green One. Al-Khidr features in the archaeology of the Gulf by virtue of a shrine dedicated to him on Failaka island, close to the site excavated by the Danes. The shrine and the legends which attend it have been obscured by Bibby; it is obviously of considerable antiquity, demonstrated by the mound on which the present shrine stands.

The shrine is particularly venerated by the Shi'ite sect of Islam, the second great stream of dogma and practice of the Faith of which the orthodox Sunni branch is the larger part, dominant on the Arabian shores of the Gulf. Kuwait is overwhelmingly Sunni in observance but respect for belief, even if it may appear to be heterodox, prevents any interference with a shrine sacred even to a small minority. Thus the shrine of Al-Khidr is not available for the probings of archaeologists, a triumph for Faith if a loss for knowledge. There can be little doubt that the site would repay excavation, for it has obviously been a sacred place over many millennia: indeed, it is likely that its position today is a consequence of the ancient concept that certain points on the earth's surface were immemorially sacred and hence were for ever consecrated to a divinity. Thus did the ziggurat originate in Sumerian cities and no doubt, if it were possible to penetrate the lower levels of Al-Khidr's Failaka shrine, evidence would be found of its own origin; it might even reveal who, and what, Al-Khidr was.

In Islamic lore Al-Khidr is an intriguing figure; he has no precise analogy in Christian or Jewish mythology. In the Quran it is never clear exactly what Al-Khidr is, other than that he is a messenger and a servant of God (like Sursanabi, who was a servant of Enki); he is, presumably, a spirit who, since he is visible to men, can assume human form. He is one of the agents of the divine power and is himself something of an elemental force, with much of the apparent capriciousness and unpredictability of a primaeval divinity.

Al-Khidr is the protagonist of one of the most remarkable, complex and disturbing Surahs (chapters) of the Quran. This is Surah 18, commonly titled *The Cave*.[22]

The Cave contains many different elements: stories, precepts and injunctions, as well as the account of Moses' meeting with and attachment to Al-Khidr. Al-Khidr is never named as such in the Quranic accounts; he is called 'one of Our Servants to whom we have vouchsafed Our mercy and whom we had endowed with knowledge of Our own'. But all the commentaries agree that it is Al-Khidr's intervention in human affairs, an intervention wholly countenanced by God, that is described in the episode.

The Cave is many-levelled; the Surah begins with the sequence which gives it its name, but which is not immediately relevant to our purpose here. It relates the story of the Seven Sleepers (and their dog) who, in the Quranic version of a widespread myth, are boys who fall asleep for an unknown time in the depths of the cave. When this story is told the Surah goes on to warn of the catastrophes which await the nations of unbelievers and wrongdoers; then, suddenly, Moses appears and an entirely different narrative begins. It is at this point that *The Cave* begins to assume a particular significance and interest in the context of the Gulf. It must, however, be remembered that the account belongs essentially to the realm of legend; nothing is precise and clearly defined but all is hazy and allusive. *The Cave* has much of the quality of a dream sequence.

Moses announces to his servant that he plans to journey to 'the place where two seas meet'. It must be said that traditionally the commentaries on the Quran have always assumed the objective of Moses' journey to have been Suez where two seas, the Red Sea and the Mediterranean, may be said to meet.[23] However, modern scholarship has tended to suggest that the

Quran means precisely what it says and that it is to 'the place of the two seas'; that is, to Bahrain in the Gulf, that Moses directs his wanderings.

Moses is himself attended by a servant whose name, in the commentaries on the Quran, is Joshua son of Nun. Joshua is Jesus; Nun is the Deep, the primaeval waters. He is also sometimes identified as a fish. Thus all the elements in the story of Al-Khidr constantly run together in the most intriguing way.

Moses and his servant journey on together, and the Quran reads: 'But when they came at last to the place where the two seas met, they forgot their fish, which made its way into the water, swimming at will.' The loss of the fish, a miraculous creature evidently, which has not been referred to before in the account, is not realized by Moses until he asks his servant for food. The servant admits the loss of the fish; Moses recognizes that the event is a miraculous one and 'they return by the way they came' – presumably once more to the place where the two seas meet. Here they find the Servant of God – was he perhaps the fish, disguised? Recognizing him for what he is, Moses begs to be permitted to follow him that he may learn from his wisdom. The Servant of God warns Moses that he will find it difficult to bear with him and with the accession of knowledge which is beyond him; Moses insists, however, and they set off together.

Then follow three episodes in each of which Al-Khidr carries out an action which appears to Moses to be either malignant or inexplicable. In the first Al-Khidr bores a hole in the bottom of the boat in which they are travelling and sinks it; in the second they meet a youth on the road and at once Al-Khidr kills him; in the third they find a wall on the point of collapse and Al-Khidr restores it, but seeks no payment for doing so.

Moses has promised Al-Khidr not to question his acts, but cannot contain his bewilderment at what Al-Khidr does, so perplexing do his actions seem to be. At each event, therefore, Moses (who in this episode is presented as a rather frivolous and irresponsible chatterer) demands an explanation from Al-Khidr, only apologizing abjectly as, each time, the Servant reminds him of their bargain. Al-Khidr, when he is pressed by Moses, now warns him that they must part but first he explains each of his strange proceedings. He knew that an enemy was in pursuit of the boat in which they were travelling so, to thwart him, he scuttled it. The boy he killed was the only son of his parents, true believers to whom the boy would bring much distress by reason of the sinful life which Al-Khidr knew lay in his future; he would beg his Lord to give them another, more pious son whose worth would bring them joy. The wall he rebuilt, because beneath it was buried a treasure which belonged to two orphan boys, which they would find when they grew to manhood and could protect it. All these events were directed, not by Al-Khidr's will but by the will of God.

Apart from his appearance in *The Cave* Al-Khidr is an important figure in popular Muslim and Near Eastern myth. Sometimes he is said to be the son of Adam: sometimes his true name is given as Elijah. On occasion he is identified with St George.[24] As well as being a contemporary both of Moses and of Alexander, he is said to have been living in the time of Abraham. He lives, variously, on an island or on a green carpet in the midst of the sea. In some of the legends associated with the life of Alexander he is the commander of the king's vanguard, his vizier, even his cousin, certainly his friend. They journey together to the spring of life and Al-Khidr discovers a miraculous well.[25]

Al-Khidr is said to worship God on an island. By his association with islands he is taken to be the patron of seamen and seafaring folk; indeed, on the sea he is said to be God's 'Khalifa' or successor. In India he is a river-god, a spirit of wells and streams who is portrayed seated on a fish. One of his principal shrines is on an island in the Indus river. He can find water below ground and speaks the languages of all peoples. He is a particular friend of the archangel Raphael and his name is even substituted sometimes for that of the still greater Michael.

After relating the story of the three episodes involving Al-Khidr and Moses, *The Cave* abruptly changes the course of its narrative once again. Al-Khidr and Moses vanish, to be replaced by yet another powerful figure in Islamic lore, Dhul-Qarnein, the Two-Horned One.

There is general agreement among the commentators as to the identity of Dhul-Qarnein; to their collective mind he is Alexander, son of Philip, king of Macedon and customarily surnamed the Great. Alexander's legend lives on fervently in the Near and Middle East, even to this day; he is, moreover, enshrined in the Quran as one chosen by God and particularly favoured by Him. In *The Cave* we learn that Dhul-Qarnein is given by God the rulership over many peoples. He journeys to the west where he sees the sun setting in a pool of black mud and to the east where he builds a rampart of iron and molten brass against the depredations of those two familiar figures in the mythology of London, Gog and Magog, who, perhaps rather surprisingly, make their appearance here. Then the Two-Horned One in turn disappears and the narrative of *The Cave* is concluded.

The Cave is a text of great subtlety and complexity; to unravel all of its many strands would require the invention of a Quranic scholar of deep learning and skill. However, it may be possible to detect one or two more elements which are relevant to the larger theme and which contribute to an understanding of the importance of myth in the development of the Gulf's historical character.

C.G. Jung, the most perceptive magus of our century, who probed deeply into the nature and structure of myth, chose Al-Khidr as one of his 'four archetypes'.[26] For Jung, Al-Khidr stood for the figure of the Trickster, the almost elemental and catalytic force which produces effects but conceals their (and his) reality. Thus, nothing is wholly what it seems to be under Al-Khidr's dispensation and the victim of his wiles must be careful neither to seek for premature understanding of what his actions mean nor to attribute to them solutions which are rooted simply in what seems to be.

A better candidate than Al-Khidr for the Trickster would, however, surely be Enki himself, the wise divinity who, by a cunning device, saved the race of men from the Flood and the misdirected wrath of the other gods; often in his dealings with his fellow divinities Enki adopted subterfuge and displayed a predilection for obscuring the reality of his actions. Jung probably did not know of Enki's existence when he was considering the origins of myth. Then the Greek and Hebrew legends, with the addition of the occasional Egyptian example, were considered to be formative to man's developing consciousness. The immensely more ancient Akkadian and, more ancient still, Sumerian myths were then largely unknown. It is interesting to speculate what Jung might have made of them had he known of their existence, in the form in which they are understood today. Had he known Enki, the god's enigmatic and ambiguous nature could hardly have failed to intrigue him.

It is reasonable to assume that the story of Moses and Al-Khidr takes place in the Gulf waters where the two seas meet, somewhere therefore in the general location of Bahrain, perhaps on the Arabian mainland rather than on the island. The miraculous fish and the appearance of Nun recall the fish cults which are known to have been a feature of early religious practice in Sumer as witnessed by the evidence of such cults in the earliest shrines at Eridu. Enki's priests were often represented wearing a sort of fish costume, emphasizing the god's concern with the creatures of the deep.

A popular myth of great antiquity, still current in Bahrain in this century, has a giant striding up the Gulf, its waters only up to his ankles, who reaches down into the water to take a fish for his meal. Having caught it, he holds it up against the sun to grill it. Clearly the giant is another fish-connected wonder-worker, still haunting these waters. His name is Ishnaq bin Inak and it obviously recalls, over these several thousand years, Enki and his son, Enshag or Inzak.[27]

The Two-Horned One is Alexander as he is most frequently portrayed on his coinage, after his coronation as King of Egypt. He is shown, often in Herakles' lion-skins, wearing the horned head-dress by which his descent from ram-headed Amon, the ruler of the Egyptian pantheon in his day, is portrayed. But horned men and horned gods are powerful symbols from long before Alexander's time, particularly in Mesopotamia and the Gulf; it should not be forgotten that Moses himself is often portrayed wearing the ram's horns, particularly in mediaeval iconography. Horned men abound in the seals of the Gulf, particularly those from Failaka island.

Of the real nature of both cult and myth we can only guess. Indeed, the whole of this topic is essentially speculative but it seems not impossible that the elements of fish, horned divinity and sacred king may suggest that Al-Khidr, who is the common denominator of them all, may in reality be

Enki, the benign god of Dilmun and Eridu, on the one hand; and at the other end of the chronological sequence with which we are concerned, he emerged as the figure of Alexander Dhul-Qarnein, when he assumed legendary proportions and the status of universal myth. Many of the aspects of Alexander's legends recall those of Gilgamesh, who is thus further brought into the equation. But the appeal which Gilgamesh has exerted on the world over the forty-five centuries which divide his time from the present day is that he represents one of the most enduring archetypes of man in historical time, the hero who sets out on a quest and, despite sufferings and all the odds agains him, endures. That Gilgamesh failed in *his* quest only adds another dimension to his essential humanity.

11

THE ENIGMA OF DILMUN

Over 100 years of archaeology in the Gulf and Bahrain have revealed much about the material culture which flourished in the centuries during which the archipelago of islands was the heart of the far-famed land of Dilmun.[1] The post-war period has provided at least the beginnings of an understanding of the part played by the lands of eastern Arabia and Oman in the development of a Gulf-wide culture over the past fifty or so centuries. But two fundamental questions remain as inpenetrably unanswered as ever they were:

Who were the Dilmunites and where did they come from?

We are reasonably certain that the Dilmunites were not Phoenicians; we are by no means certain now that the Phoenicians were not Dilmunites.[2] There is no evidence that the Dilmunites were Sumerians, though the destinies of the two peoples were closely linked. We do not know what was the language of Dilmun. That inscriptions in most of the historic languages associated with the region have been found either in the insular or the continental Dilmun (the islands or the mainland) prove only that Dilmun had contact with the peoples of many lands and that, in all probability, people to whom these languages were native resided there.

We may be reasonably sure that there would have been a significant component in the Dilmunite stock drawn from the proto-Arabians (if such a term may be permitted) who inhabited the eastern part of the Arabian peninsula in the historic period and who probably had done so since the earliest times of human settlement or occupation.[3] These were the relatives of the Mar-tu, the Ahlamu and eventually of the Arameans; they tended, all of them, to have connections with the Western Semitic linguistic groups but whether the Dilmunites spoke a Western Semitic tongue, in post-Sumerian times, must be considerably in doubt.

We do not know what a Dilmunite looked like. We do not know what his customs of dress were, other than the odd fragments of jewellery which have survived. We do have the mildly satisfying information that the reputation of Dilmun as a particularly favourable place in which to live seems to have been borne out by the fact that the Dilmunites' skeletal remains show them to have been rather taller, better built and somewhat longer living than the average of their contemporaries.[4]

On the matter of the origins of the Dilmun civilization, it may now just be possible to discern some tentative landmarks through the haze which surrounds them, which may in time lead to their fuller recognition. Even this, however, will not necessarily tell us all that we would wish to know about the Dilmunites themselves, though it may begin to suggest at least some associations for them.

It now appears more and more likely that the essential impetus which led, in the later centuries of the third millennium, to the establishment of what was evidently a rich and sophisticated society on the principal Bahrain island, came from the south and east.[5] There are more and more hints of connections in the third millennium between the island of Bahrain and what is today the Sultanate of Oman, particularly its northern reaches and beyond Oman to the Indus Valley and its coastal regions. There is no doubt also, that, as matters stand at present, the settlements in Oman are earlier in date than the earliest so far known in Bahrain.

There is a curious chronological hiatus in Bahrain's archaeology, which in effect seems to mean that between the late Ubaid period in the fourth millennium BC and the latter part of the third millennium, a gap of several hundred years, there was apparently no significant settlement in the Bahrain islands. Since the Mesopotamians of the earlier period evidently had some contact with the eastern Arabian seaboard and since people using Ubaid pottery landed on Qatar, on the little offshore island to Bahrain, which is now the inland site of Al-Markh, and down the Gulf at several points on the coast, this is puzzling. In particular it is odd that Bahrain itself does not appear to have been visited.

It is the more strange since the holy character of Dilmun-Bahrain seems to be bound up with its insular nature and clearly it is strongly identified in the minds of the Sumerians with the origins of their society. It is considered the place where many of the benefits of civilization originated: this ought to refer, in terms of the Sumerians' own chronology, to some time in the middle of the fourth millennium.

The Sumerians were certainly capable of sailing the Gulf's waters as early as this. We can presume that they did so in pursuit of the raw materials which they so earnestly sought in lands far from their own home. The conversion of copper was very ancient; by the late fourth millennium it was a familiar medium and by the early third its use was virtually industrialized. Oman represents the most convenient source of copper that the Sumerians could tap, but nonetheless it is about 1,000 kilometres distant from the most southerly Sumerian settlement. The odds against their finding it accidentally must be formidable; the idea cannot be wholly discarded, therefore, that the Sumerians themselves *did* come up the Gulf from the south, perhaps from Oman itself or somewhere near to it and brought with them the knowledge of its resources. As was proposed earlier, the affection in which they seem always to have held Dilmun-Bahrain may have originated because it sheltered them on their northward journey. In which case, why did they apparently delay establishing the temples (if they are, in any real sense, Sumerian) at Barbar until virtually the end of the Sumerian period? Or are there still earlier shrines awaiting discovery?

It would seem that the Sumerians either maintained contact with or themselves established bases on the eastern Arabian seaboard. They could hardly have failed to be aware of Bahrain's existence, yet apparently they did not use the island during the time of their own greatest prosperity and creative outpourings.

It may be that the explanation lies in the erratic character of the Gulf itself over this period. The Gulf is significantly lower today than it was in the fourth and early third millennia; it is conceivable that any early settlements that there might have been were built of very fragile materials, such as *burasti*, and simply perished. The sites themselves would be beyond the original shorelines and may now be buried beneath wind-blown sand, a substantial distance inland. But, despite the many surveys which have been undertaken of Bahrain's land surface over the past thirty years, no trace of earlier settlements has, in fact, been found.

The extensive structures at Barbar which still wait for the spade of the archaeologist (and for the even more sophisticated survey equipment which he has at his disposal today) could well reveal earlier evidence than has so far been the case. Indeed, it would be very surprising if they did not. The architecture of Barbar is strange, taken in the context of the presumed Sumerian associations of the rites practised there. The architecture, of finely dressed stone blocks, is distinctly un-Sumerian; in what architectural tradition therefore did the builders of Barbar work?

Similarly, who were the builders of the great tomb at Hili, with its carved decoration? Were they perhaps the precursors of the architects of Barbar?

Whether the discovery of fourth- or early third-millennium remains on Bahrain would resolve the long-disputed matter of the Sumerians' own origins is another matter altogether. Perhaps it will; certainly no one seems inclined nowadays to suggest any convincing alternative, so a southerly approach may be at least as defensible as any other and more so than most. If, in the closing pages of a book which has tried to take a broad-based but reasonably objective view of the evidence of the past of this region, it were permissible to speculate, then there is one prospect which teases the imagination, once it is planted there.

In late Neolithic times, between 7,000 and 6,000 years ago, the Gulf and the eastern reaches of the Arabian peninsula presented a markedly different appearance from its present-day topography. With the level of the Gulf significantly higher, by as much as 2 metres, the sea reached far into parts of the coastal area and beyond, which are now well removed from it.

Al-Markh would have been only one of many such little islands, strung along the coast; Umm an-Nar, off the northern coast of the Omani peninsula, was another. The sea ran deep into the Empty Quarter, ar-Rub'al-Khali, and into the Omani desert. The little communities of hunters who lived on the edges of the lakes which were formed along the desert's perimeter and who subsisted on the larger game which the region could then support were, by the evidence of their stone tools, talented craftsmen; we do not know what other products they produced since these would have been made from perishable materials. As the sea withdrew and the desert supervened, this people must have been driven away to find a new homeland. As they were lake-dwellers, they were probably competent boatmen; the Gulf (which would hardly have been recognizable to them as such) would not have represented any insuperable barrier to their movement; rather, indeed, the opposite.

As the environment changed, the lake-dwellers may have moved eastwards and south to form the root population of Oman, whilst others may have moved northwards, working up the Arabian coast or, some of them, skirting it by sea. Eventually the most adventurous of them – and perhaps they were also amongst the earliest to undertake this putative 'trek' – reached the southern Mesopotamian marshlands and founded Eridu. They were unquestionably fisherfolk, wherever they came from, and as such they would be primary candidates to know the Gulf islands intimately; Enki, after all, was their patron. If they were the progenitors of the later Gulf populations, this would explain their attachment to its habitable islands: Umm an-Nar, Bahrain, Tarut and Failaka were all important centres of the Dilmun culture or its contemporaries.

These early migrants may have been the ancestors of the Ubaid pottery-makers. This is not to assert that they were responsible for the Ubaid pottery found in east Arabian sites, Qatar, Bahrain and the UAE. This is later in time than the period about which we are now speculating. The earlier Ubaid pottery has, however, been identified with early levels at Eridu. The first wave of migrants may have been followed by others, not all of whom perhaps went all the way to Sumer but stayed on the Arabian mainland, though, if they did, they seem to have kept some contact with their cousins to the north.

Over the centuries the south-east Arabian lake-dwellers could have fanned out over a wide area.[6] There may even have been a corresponding movement towards the west which, if it is not wholly fantasy, might account for some of the similarities which seem to exist between, for example, the rock art of the early inhabitants of Oman and that of the western Arabians, who lived far away from the Gulf in the region now called the Hijaz and there energetically undertook the decoration of most available rock faces in the area, using forms and motifs strikingly similar to those in the south-east quadrant of the peninsula.[7] These western Arabians were probably the carriers of many of the Asiatic influences which appear in late Predynastic

Egypt, in the second half of the fourth millennium. Even some of the rock art of Egypt seems to echo forms to be found in the wadis of Oman. But this is more speculative still, and, for the present, must remain so. However, it may be recalled in passing that the Egyptians seem to have sustained a memory of an island, in the midst of the sea, far away beyond the eastern horizon, the Island on the Edge of the World.[8]

The chronology of the Gulf, which is now reasonably secure, raises the question of the chronology of other parts of the ancient world. Most ancient chronologies are based on the succession of the kings of Egypt; in the third millennium this is less sure than in later periods. Indeed, the correspondences between Egypt and the Gulf would look a good deal more comprehensible if the chronology of Egypt were to be lowered by some 800 years.

It may well be that one of the most tantalizing omissions from the catalogue of Bahrain antiquities, the archives of Dilmun, still survives and will one day be recovered, perhaps from the library of a Dilmunite king, the tablets room of a great temple or the filing system of a member of the Alik *Tilmun*: for all of these there are precedents in Mesopotamia. In recent years the discovery of the huge cache of tablets at Ebla (Tel Mardikh), in northern Syria, which reveals an entire literature in a language previously unknown, demonstrates the wonders which chance or the archaeologist's skill can still recall. The archives of Dilmun must exist somewhere; it is unthinkable that what must have been a substantial body of records and, conceivably, literature should have been irrevocably lost. The possibility that they may have been written on organic materials which would have decayed cannot, of course, be wholly rejected. However, given the number of references, official as well as literary or liturgical, to Dilmun in Mesopotamian records, it seems unlikely that no cache of tablets awaits discovery in Bahrain.

The discovery of such an archive might conceivably throw light on one of the most enigmatic elements in the character of Dilmun-Bahrain in antiquity. It is early enough to comprehend the importance of the island in trade and to accept it as the centre of an important late third-millennium culture in the central Gulf whose influence spread to quite distant lands. What is more difficult to understand is why it occupied so very special a place in the Sumerian (and later) traditions, why, in particular, it was celebrated as the *the* Holy Land.[9] Its essential holiness is possibly Dilmun's most powerful characteristic; it is the first of all sacred lands and its legend endured over long ages. Its influence was, as has been seen, profound. It was even more important than the shrines of Greece, even of Egypt's holiest place at Abydos, where Osiris was reputed to have been buried.

If we assume that by the time the Sumerian cities established themselves, the temple administrators flourished and the scribes of Sumer found time from their recording of the numbers of sheep the temple owned to compose the marvellous songs and stories which are the glory of Sumer, the people of the islands and the Arabians were distinct (or thought themselves to be) from their cousins in the north, their view of the holiness of their land might well be impressive to a visiting Sumerian merchant. The merchant, or the scribe, or court official or whoever, might thus take back to Sumer the story of a distant land lit by a strange and numinous light.

Well and good. But why did the Dilmunites themselves consider their land to be so uniquely, so exceptionally sacred? It cannot have been simple chauvinism ('*my* land is holier than *your* land') or merely the consequence of ample supplies of fresh water, *pace* Enki, in an otherwise desert environment. There must be some other, more compelling explanation, but thus far it evades us. In this context a connection with astronomical observation and navigation, postulated here, may repay consideration.

The rich and complex designs of the seals will clearly repay further study, containing, as they must do, much information waiting to be released. It may eventually be possible to 'read' the seals: it certainly should be possible to understand the significance of some of their symbolism, particularly of the interrelationship of the symbols and the frequency with which some of them are repeated.

In the southern Gulf there are also important issues to be resolved. The nature of the relationship between the Umm an-Nar culture of the north of Oman and the high Dilmun culture needs to be further refined. In Oman itself the extent and character of its third-millennium society needs to be clarified; it may be that even earlier, perhaps fourth-millennium, connections will be established as a consequence of further study.

In eastern Arabia, possibly the coastal regions, and others which are now quite deep into the desert, will almost certainly produce evidence that will be at least as remarkable as that which Bahrain can provide. The nature of early third-millennium settlements, the influence, if any, which the mainlanders exercised on the people of the islands (if they were not the same people), need to be analysed still further.

If this book has a theme, other than the simple presentation of the evidence of a high culture which, since it is ancestral to us all, demands to be known, it is the quest: the quest for the Terrestrial Paradise, Gilgamesh's quest for the flower of eternal youth, the merchant's search for materials and profit, are all elements which go to make up the story of Dilmun, of Bahrain and the Arabian Gulf in centuries long past. It is fitting that it should end with a small and tentative signpost pointing directions (even if they prove to be hopelessly misguided) for those who enjoy quests for their own sake, or who engage in them for the sake of archaeology, where yet more remarkable discoveries may still await those who search for them.

THE CHRONOLOGY OF THE
ARABIAN GULF 7000–300 BC

The chronology of the Arabian Gulf is, at least in its early phases, quite complex; nonetheless, it is a good deal more straightforward than many ancient chronologies, if only because it is relatively self-contained and compact. It does, however, repay some consideration.

The earliest evidence of human settlement in the Gulf, the various Neolithic, aceramic industries whose products have been identified in many parts of the region, comes from around 7000 BC; prior to this time the Gulf islands and much of eastern Arabia would still have been inaccessible to human habitation. The makers of the fine tools associated with the hunting communities which lived on the edge of the Rub' al-Khali flourished from around the beginning of the sixth millennium BC until late in the fifth.

Stone industries are important components in the Gulf's archaeological store. Most of the tools found in the central and northern Gulf are defined by reference to those originally recorded in Qatar, first by the Danes and then revised by the French. It would now appear that the earliest tools in the Gulf are those found on the eastern Arabian coast *c.* 5000 BC and from Qatar itself, perhaps earlier, *c.* 5500 BC. Other tools have been recovered from the ar-Rub' al-Khali, dating to the early fourth millennium; others, earlier still, come from the early fishing communities at Ras al-Hadd in Oman.

By the early decades of the fourth millennium BC pottery-users were establishing small settlements, which are probably seasonal in the first instance, in coastal eastern Arabia; the earliest of them may be dated to around 3800 BC. They are recognized by the pottery fragments which they left behind them, known as Ubaid from the southern Iraqi site at which they were first identified. From this point onwards the chronology of the Gulf tends to be fixed by reference to the various cultures and periods attributed to the southern Mesopotamian communities. The earliest records which speak of Dilmun, the Gulf's own long-lasting culture, date from around 3000 BC and were recovered from the cities of Kish and Uruk.

Dilmun seems to have been established as an entity, probably primarily concerned with trade rather than with any status it may have enjoyed as the original home of the gods, by the end of the fourth millennium BC, first on the eastern Arabian mainland, later, from around the middle of the third millennium, on the islands of Bahrain. However, before this time, other small but notably sophisticated communities, who looked mainly to the sea for their livelihoods, were established far to the south, on the northern coasts of Oman in what is today the United Arab Emirates' states of Abu Dhabi, Ras Al-Khaimah, Umm al-Qawain and the northern limits of the Sultanate of Oman. Here, on the island of Umm an-Nar and inland at Omani sites like Hili and Hafit, communities with an assured architectural tradition are identifiable around 3000 BC: in other words, at the time when the first records of Dilmun are known from far to the north, in the land of Sumer.

The Umm an-Nar people, if they can be so described, were skilled potters, producing a distinctive decorated ware which is found throughout the Gulf and its neighbouring lands. There is some evidence that the makers of this pottery, who were also the builders of some very notable grave mounds, may have been the people who first settled the Bahrain islands, setting up a village on the north shore of the principal island which the Danish excavators described as 'City I'. The date of this crucial development in the Gulf's history was around 2400 BC. It was crucial because the settlement on the north shore of Bahrain was destined to be the precursor of the true city which succeeded it ('City II') and which was rapidly to become the centre of the far-reaching Dilmun trade.

Prior to the second half of the third millennium Dilmun seems to have been located in the coastal regions of eastern Saudi Arabia. The Epic of Gilgamesh, which descends from third-millennium times though with the accretions of many later and some earlier myths, has echoes of what may have been a Gulf journey, undertaken by Gilgamesh, who was king of Uruk around 2700 BC. He approaches by sea the home of Ziusudra, who had reigned in Shurrupak around 3000 BC but who was remembered principally as the protagonist of the Deluge myth, the origin of which is contained in the Epic. Ziusudra had been translated by the gods to Dilmun after the Flood waters receded. However, Gilgamesh returns to his city, in southern Mesopotamia, overland, and thus the two locations associated with Dilmun are perhaps here recollected and reconciled.

At sometime around 2400 BC – and certainly by 2730 BC when Sargon of Akkad is believed to have succeeded to the control of most of central and southern Mesopotamia – the centre of Dilmun had shifted from the mainland to the island of Bahrain. The first settlement at the Qala'at al-Bahrain site was succeeded by City II, the foundation of which is dated prior to 2100 BC. There are six building phases associated with the second city site, extending into the Old Babylonian period, c. 1700 BC. This was the period of Dilmun's greatest prosperity, spanning more than four centuries.

The first temple at Barbar probably spans the transition between the end of City I and the first building phase at City II. The second temple level, consisting of two building phases, is contemporary with the second phase of building at City II. The third temple is from the same period as the last development of City II in the Old Babylonian period. Barbar therefore seems, with the exception of the very earliest levels of the site, to be a product of this extraordinary period in Dilmun's history when so much was concentrated into a few hundred years.

The most enduring survivals from this period are the vast fields of grave mounds in Bahrain and in eastern Arabia. Some of the earliest tombs are derived from Umm an-Nar: by the latter part of the third millennium, however, the distinctive local forms of mound burials predominate in Dilmun's islands and coastal lands.

One minor anomaly of the chronological record of the Gulf is the evident lack of settlement on Failaka prior to 2000 BC, although a site with Ubaid material has been reported from the Kuwaiti mainland. Bearing in mind the considerable activity which had been taking place throughout the Gulf in the preceding many centuries, this would be puzzling were it not for the realization that the shoreline at the head of the Gulf has been exceptionally volatile. Prior to the end of the third millennium Failaka, lying in what is today the Bay of Kuwait, would have been waterlogged, if not under water.

A glance at the chart of comparative chronologies will show the extraordinary concentration of building and political and social activity generally in the central and northern reaches of the Gulf around 2000 BC. This was a time of exceptional prosperity and it continued almost until the middle of the second millennium; then the Kassites replaced the Babylonians in control of Mesopotamia and extended their interests to Dilmun and the Gulf.

The decline of the Gulf's importance in world politics and trade is evident from the relative poverty of action and events in the region during the latter part of the second millennium compared with the expansion which the rest of the ancient world enjoyed. There are points at which the Gulf reappears in the record, of course: at the end of the second millennium, again in neo-Assyrian times, when City IV was built in Bahrain, and again after the death of Alexander the Great. The region as a whole enjoyed something of a revival in Hellenistic times, the result, no doubt, of the Greek world's interest in the aromatics trade.

It is pleasing to identify individuals and events which are contemporary. Thus Gilgamesh was king in Uruk when Djoser Neterikhet was king of Egypt, for whom the Step Pyramid at Saqqarah was built; when the Old Kingdom in Egypt collapsed into anarchy Dilmun was enjoying the early years of its greatest period of prosperity. The mercantile civilization which grew up in the Gulf at the end of the third millennium is matched in Egypt by the First Intermediate Period, when many foreign influences streamed into the Nile Valley.

The death of Alexander the Great in Babylon in July 323 BC marks the end of a cycle of history in all the lands reflected in the chronology of the Gulf and the principal lands with which it was in contact.

Chronological table

Years BC	Eastern Arabia	Bahrain	Qatar	Failaka	United Arab Emirates	Oman	Mesopotamia (Iraq, Syria)	Iran	Crete	Egypt	Anatolia
7000											Cattle domesticated Çatal Hüyük, c. 6400
6500											
6000 — Gulf level +1.3 m asl	Al Rub ar-Khali Lacustrine settlements		Qatar 'B' Stone tools	PRE-POTTERY NEOLITHIC							Çatal Hüyük Level II
5500			Khor (shells, hearths)			Ras al-Hamra Fishing communities	Hassuna / Sammara Halaf Eridu (Ubaid I)	Ali Khosh			Hacilar Level IX
5000 — Gulf level –1.3 m bsl	Ain Qannas (Ubaid II–III) Al-Dawsariyya		'D' Group tools	QATAR 'B' TOOLS			Eridu Archaic temples / Ubaid II				Hacilar Level I
4500	Abu Khamis	Al Markh (Ubaid IV)	Al Da'asa (Ubaid III–IV)		Ras al-Khaimah Arrowheads	Ras al-Hamra	Ubaid III			Fayum El Tasi El Badari	
4000 — Gulf level +1.5 m asl	HUNTERS – GATHERERS – FISHERS						Ubaid IV	Susa I (Proto-Urban)		Naqada I Naqada II Ma'adi	
3500 — Gulf level +0.5 m asl						Ras al-Hamra Burials	Uruk White temple	Yahya Va Susa II		Hierakonpolis Dynasty I Royal tombs – Abydos Magnates' tombs – Saqqarah Helwan tombs	
3000	Tell el Ramad Abqaiq Al Rufiyah – Tarut statue Yabrin – carved chlorite vessels Dhahran South Tarut				Hafit burial mounds Al-Ain Qarn bint Saud Hili tower Sorghum cultivated	? Evidence of camel domestication at Hili Towers at Bat, Ibri Copper mining: Wadi Samad Wadi Jizzi	Jemdet Nasr Early dynastic I–II Gilgamesh, King of Uruk 'Royal' graves at Ur Temple oval at Khafajeh	Proto-Elamite Yahya IVc Susa III Yahya IVb	Early Minoan I	Dynasty II Old Kingdom Dynasty III King Djoser: Step Pyramid at Saqqarah Hierakonpolis: Temple oval Dynasty IV Giza pyramids	
2500											

NEOLITHIC — MOIST PHASE

2500 Gulf level +1 m asl	——→ Dilmun Chain-ridge ware	Qala'at al-Bahrain I Early Dilmun seals QaB IIa Barbar Ia–b IIb IIa 'Aali tombs Diraz ——→			Umm an-Nar Decorated tomb at Hili Hili tower Indus Valley influences Hili north tomb Ajman tombs	Umm an-Nar: Bahla, Bisyah, Bat Stone towers Maysar 'Magan trade'	Early Dynastic III *Ur-Nanshe* *Lugalzaggesi* *Sargon of Akkad* *Manistusu* *Shar-Kali-Shari* *Naram-Sin* *Gudea of Lagash* *Shulgi Ur-III* *Amar-Sin* *Ur-Nammu* *Su-Sin Ibbi-sin*	Susa IV Neo-Elamite *Puzu-in- Shushinak* *Simash* Shahr-i-Sokta IV	Early Minoan II–III	Collapse of Old Kingdom Middle Kingdom

2000
Gulf level
5 m asl
	*Martu/
	Amorites*
	Emergence of
	camel
	nomads
		IIc IIb
		IId Sar
		Ea-Nasir Umm es
		flourishes Sejour III
		         Gulf seals
		End of Dilmun
		copper trade
		IIIa Kassites
		Rimum inscription
			Bir Abaruk
			Khor
			Evidence of
			contact with
			Eastern
			Arabia,
			Bahrain
				First
				settlements
				(from Eastern
				Arabia and
				Bahrain?)
				Failaka I
				Gulf seals
				IIIa
					Qattara 'long
					tomb'
					Shimal
					Chlorite vessels
					Al Quasais
						Wadi Suq
						→
							Gugunum–
							dated Gulf seal
							Sumnol
							Warad-Sin
							Sumumabum
							Samsi-Adad
							Hammurabi
							Samsuiluna
							Kassites
								Yahya IVa	Middle
									Minoan I
									       II
									       III
									Knossos
										Dynasty XI
										       XII
										Amenemhet II
										Senwosret I
										            II
										            III
										Dynasty XIII
										'Hyksos' invasion
										Dynasties XV–XVII

1500	Kassite traces
	Dhahran
	Uqayr
		IIIb
		I-ilipasra
		correspondence
		Tikulti-Ninurta,
		'King of Dilmun'
			Khor South
			Murex
			deposits
				IVa
				IVb
					Iron Age
					settlements →
					Ghalilah →
						Iron Age
						settlements
						→
							Burnaburiyas II
							Kurigalzu II
							Tikulti-Ninurta
									Late Minoan I
									       II
									       III
									Mycenaeans
										Dynasty XVIII
										Amenhotep III, IV
										(Akhenaton)
										Tutankhamun
										Dynasty XIX
										Ramses II
										Dynasty XX
										Ramses III

1000 Gulf level −1 m bsl	Dhahran: Egyptianizing seals ?Foundation of Gerrha *Nabonidos* in Arabia	Burials at Al Hajjar *Uperi* *Hundaru* *Qanaia* Kings of Dilmun Assyrians Neo-Babylonians Qala'at al-Bahrain IV			Rumailah Qarn Bint Saud →	Amlah Wadi Sumail Maysar ?Introduction of Falaj irrigation	*Sargon II* *Sennacherib* *Assurbanipal* *Nabonidos*	Achamaenids *Cyrus I* *Cambyses I* *Cyrus II*	Protogeometric	Late Period Persian Conquest
500	*Thaj* *Nearchos* exploration of the Gulf	'Seleucid' pottery Qala'at al-Bahrain V	'Seleucid' pottery	Ikaros 'Hellenistic' temple	Mleiha, Ed-Dur		Death of *Alexander the Great* in Babylon	*Darius I* *Xerxes II* *Darius II* *Darius III* *Alexander,* Great King	*Alexander,* King of Macedon	*Alexander, King* of Egypt

ABBREVIATIONS

AfO	Archiv für Orientforschung, Berlin
ANET	*Ancient Near Eastern Texts*
AOMIM	*Arabie Orientale, Mesopotamie, et Iran Méridional*
Arab. Arch. Epig.	*Arabian Archaeology and Epigraphy*
Atlal	*The Journal of Saudi Arabian Archaeology*
BASOR	*Bulletin of the American School of Oriental Research*
BBVO	*Berliner Beitrage zum Vorderen Orient*
BTAA	*Bahrain Through the Ages: the Archaeology*, Proceedings of the 1983 Bahrain Historical Conference.
CNRS	Centre National des Recherches Scientifiques
EW	*East-West*
JAOS	*Journal of the American Oriental Society*
JCS	*Journal of Cuneiform Studies*
JESHO	*Journal of the Economic and Social History of the Orient*
JNES	*Journal of Near Eastern Studies*
JOS	*Journal of Oman Studies*
JRAS	*Journal of the Royal Society for Asian Affairs* (New Series)
JRCAS	*Journal of the Royal Central Asian Society*
Kuml	Journal of the Jutland Archaeological Society
MDP	Mémoires de la Délégation en Perse
PSAS	*Proceedings of the Seminar for Arabian Studies*

NOTES

INTRODUCTION

1 *Atlal, the Journal of Saudi Arabian Archaeology* and the *Journal of Oman Studies*.
2 Al-Khalifa and Rice, 1986.

1 THE ARABIAN GULF IN ANTIQUITY

1 Glob, 1954d, 1968b.
2 Kramer, 1963a.
3 Rawlinson, 1880; Burrows, 1928.
4 Wilson, 1928.
5 Rice, 1984a.
6 Frankfort, 1968.
7 See Daniel, *The Arabs and Medieval Europe*, London, 1975.
8 M. Izzard, *The Gulf*, London, 1979.
9 H. Frankfort, *Kingship and the Gods*, Chicago, 1948; Rice, 1990.
10 K. Kenyon, *Digging Up Jericho*, London, 1957.
11 Mellaart, 1967.
12 Ibid.
13 Rice, 1990.
14 Kramer, 1961a.
15 Cornwall, 1946b; Kramer, 1963b.
16 Alster, 1983.
17 On the Sumerian view of the date-palm generally, see B. Landsberger, *The Date Palm and its By-products according to the Cuneiform Sources*, Graz, 1967.
18 See Kramer, 1944, revised as Chiera's original.
19 Kramer, 1969.
20 Ferrara, 1979.
21 W.F. Albright, 'Cuneiform texts from Babylonian tablets', in Cornwall, 1952.
22 Bibby, 1969.
23 Ibid.
24 Sandars, 1972.
25 trans. A. de Selincourt, Harmondsworth, 1954.
26 trans. A. de Selincourt, London, 1970.
27 Ptolomaeus, Claudius 'Tabula Asiae Sexta', in C.J.R. Tibbets, *Arabia in Early Maps*, Cambridge, 1978.
28 See Ratnagar, 1981, for a broadly based discussion.
29 McClure, 1971.

30 Ibid.
31 Nielsen, 1959.
32 Lloyd, 1978.
33 N Groom, *Frankincense and Myrrh*, London, 1981.
34 Lombard, 1986.
35 Herodotos, ed. de Selincourt.
36 Ibid.
37 Ezekiel 27: 3–4 (see D.N. Talbot, *The Saturn Myths*, New York, 1980).
38 Bowersock, 1986.
39 Calvert, 1989.
40 Potts, 1986a.
41 C. Niebhur, *Travels in Arabia*, Edinburgh, 1792.
42 Wilson, 1928.
43 But see Shaikh Sultan bin Mohammad Al-Qasimi, *The Myth of Piracy in the Gulf*, Beckenham, Kent, 1986.

2 THE PROGRESS OF GULF ARCHAEOLOGY

1 Durand, 1880.
2 Rawlinson, 1880.
3 Durand, 1879.
4 W. Palgrave, *Central and Eastern Arabia*, London, 1865.
5 Burstein, 1978.
6 J.T. Bent, 1890.
7 M.V.A. Bent, 1900.
8 Prideaux, 1912.
9 T.E. Lawrence, *The Letters of T.E. Lawrence*, London and Toronto, 1938.
10 W.M.F. Petrie, *Ancient Egypt*, London, 1917.
11 W.M.F. Petrie, *The Making of Egypt*, London, 1939.
12 Mackay *et al.*, 1929.
13 Burrows, 1928.
14 Cornwall, 1943a.
15 A. Diemel, *Sumerischer Lexicon* II.
16 Cornwall, 1946a.
17 Cornwall, 1943a.
18 Kramer, 1944.
19 Cornwall, 1952.
20 Glob, 1954a; Bibby, 1986.
21 Bibby, op. cit.
22 The late Sir Charles Belgrave, pers. comm.
23 *Atlal, The Journal of Saudi Arabian Archaeology*, published by the Department of Antiquities and Museum, Riyadh, Saudi Arabia.
24 *The Journal of Oman Studies*, published by the Department of Antiquities, Muscat, Sultanate of Oman.
25 See Winifred Thomas, 'The Third International Conference in Asian Archaeology', *Archaeology*.
26 *The Qatar National Museum: Its Origins Concepts and Planning*, The Ministry of Information, Doha, Qatar.
27 *A Handbook for Visitors* (Arabic and English Language editions), Museum of Archaeology and Ethnography, Riyadh, Saudi Arabia.
28 Al-Khalifa and Rice, 1986.

3 CLIMATE, SEA-LEVELS, MAN
AND HIS COMPANIONS

1 McClure, 1971.
2 H.B. Baker, 'The structure patterns of the Afro/Arabian rift system in relation to plate tectonics', *Phil. Trans. Royal Soc.*, Series AV 267, 1970.
3 Al-Asfour, 'The marine terraces in the Bay of Kuwait', in Brice, 1978.
4 P. Kassler, 'The structures and geomorphic evolution of the Persian Gulf', in Purser, 1973.
5 G. Child and J. Granger, 'A system plan for protected areas for wildlife conservation and sustainable rural development in Saudi Arabia', The National Commission for Wildlife Conservation and Development, Riyadh, Saudi Arabia, 1990.
6 Kassler, op. cit.
7 De Cardi, 1978.
8 P. Andrews, W.R. Hamilton and P.J. Whybrow, 'Dryopithecine from the Miocene of Saudi Arabia', *Nature*, 224, 1978.
9 McClure, op. cit.
10 Ibid.
11 Ibid.
12 Ibid.
13 Ibid.
14 See Peter J. Whybrow, British Museum of National History, quoted in *The Society for Arabian Studies Newsletter*, December 1989.
15 Anati, 1968.
16 McClure, op. cit.
17 Ibid.
18 Ibid.
19 Ibid.
20 Roaf, 1974.
21 Al-Sayari and Zötl, 1978.
22 Kassler, op. cit.
23 Ibid.
24 Larsen, 1983b.
25 Kassler, op. cit.
26 Ibid.
27 Masry, 1974.
28 McClure, op. cit.
29 J. Zarins, pers. comm.
30 Masry, op. cit.
31 See J. Mellaart, *The Neolithic of the Near East*, London, 1975.
32 M. Khan *et al.*, *Atlal* 9, 10, 11 (1985–7). Also Rice, forthcoming, *The Power of the Bull*.

4 DILMUN, THE CULTURE OF THE ANCIENT GULF

1 Frankfort, *Kingship and the Gods*, Chicago, 1948.
2 Ibid.
3 Solecki, 1972.
4 See E. Strommenger and M. Hirmer, *Art of Mesopotamia*, London, 1964.
5 J. Mellaart, *Neolithic of the Near East*, London, 1975.
6 Masry, 1974.
7 See De Cardi, 1977.

8 Masry, 1974 and De Cardi, 1977.
9 C.L. Woolley, *Ur Excavations – The Early Periods*, London, 1955.
10 J. Oates, 1960.
11 Rice, 1990.
12 J. Oates, op. cit.
13 Kramer, 1963a.
14 Ibid.
15 Ibid.
16 Cornwall, 1943a; Kramer, 1963a; Pritchard, 1969.
17 A. Marshack, *The Roots of Civilization*, New York, 1972.
18 See H. Müller-Karpe, *Handbuch der Vorgesichte*, vol. II, Munich, 1968.
19 Schmandt-Besserat, 1977.
20 Ibid.
21 Nissen, 1986.
22 Ibid.
23 Kramer, 1963a.
24 Leemans, 1950.
25 Leemans, 1960a.
26 Muhly, 1973.
27 Goettler, Firth and Huston, 1976; Weisgerber, 1978.
28 Bibby, 1969.
29 For example, Barton, cited in Cornwall, 1944.
30 J. Oates, Kamilli and McKerrell, 1977.
31 Burstein, 1978.
32 Kramer, 1961b.
33 Ibid.
34 Larsen, 1975.
35 Lloyd, 1978.
36 Witzel cited in Goetz's Appendix to Cornwall, 1952.
37 See R. McC. Adams and H.J. Nissen, *The Uruk Countryside*, Chicago and London, 1972.
38 J. Oates, 1960.
39 J. Oates *et al.*, 1977.
40 F. Safar, M.A. Mustafa and S. Lloyd, 1981.
41 J. Crowfoot Payne, *Lapis Lazuli in Early Egypt*, Iraq, 1968; Rice, 1990.
42 Jacobsen, 1970.
43 Kramer, 1961a.
44 Ibid.
45 Woolley, 1934..
46 Whitehouse, 1977.
47 Woolley, op. cit.
48 P. Amiet, *Élam*, Paris, 1966.
49 Amiet, 1961.
50 Kohl, 1978.
51 Lamberg-Karlovsky, 1972.
52 Vallat, 1983.
53 E. Baumgartel, *Predynastic Egypt*, I and II, London, 1947 and 1960 (but see also Rice, 1990).
54 Petrie, 1939.
55 For example, W.B. Emery, *Archaic Egypt*, London, 1961.
56 Rice, 1990.

5 THE POLITY OF THE ANCIENT GULF

1 Tigay, 1982; Sandars, 1972.
2 *ANET*, The Sumerian King-List.
3 Kramer, 1963a.
4 Nissen, 1986; Englund, 1983b.
5 Woolley, 1934.
6 Ibid..
7 *ANET*, I.
8 Kramer, 1969, for reference to the *hieros gamos*.
9 *ANET*, I.
10 Bibby, 1986b.
11 Bibby, 1958a.
12 *ANET*, I.
13 *ANET*, II.
14 Roux, 1966.
15 Leemans, 1950, 1960a.
16 Nielsen, 1959.
17 *ANET*, II.
18 Cornwall, 1943a.
19 Ibid.
20 Cornwall, 1952.
21 Rice, 1972.
22 Cornwall, 1952.
23 Ibid.
24 Zarins, 1984; Buccellati, 1966.
25 See Zarins, 1984.
26 *ANET*, I.
27 Luckenbill, 1926.
28 Cited D.D. Luckenbill, *The Annals of Sennacherib*, cited in Alster, 1983.
29 Cornwall, 1943a.
30 Werdner, in Cornwall, 1943a.
31 *ANET*, I.
32 Ibid.
33 Oppenheim, 1954.
34 Lombard, 1986.
35 A. De Sélincourt, *The Life of Alexander the Great*, London, 1970.
36 Salles, 1984a, 1984b, 1986.
37 R. McC. Adams and J.H. Nissen, *The Uruk Countryside*, Chicago and London, 1972.
38 See E. Badian, 'Alexander the Great and the unity of mankind' in G.T. Griffith, *Alexander the Great, the Main Problems*, Cambridge, 1968.
39 Bibby, 1969.
40 *Gulf Mirror*, Bahrain.
41 Bibby, 1969.
42 A.R. Al-Ansary, *Qaryat Al-Fau: A Portrait of Pre-Islamic Civilization in Saudi Arabia*, London, 1981.
43 Bibby, 1969.
44 Jeppersen, 1989.

6 THE MYTHS OF SUMER AND DILMUN

1 Kramer, 1961b.
2 Heidel, 1963; *ANET*, The Epic of Gilgamesh; Sandars, 1972.
3 See 'The birth of man', in T. Jacobsen, *The Harps that Once . . .*, Sumerian poetry in translation, New Haven and London, 1987.
4 Kramer, 1961b.
5 Rice, forthcoming.
6 Kramer, 1961b.
7 Albright, cited in Cornwall, 1943a.
8 After Kramer, 1961b.
9 Witzel, in Goetz, *The Texts Ni 615 and Ni 641 in the Istanbul Museum*.
10 Kramer, 1963b.
11 *ANET*, I.
12 Cornwall, 1943a.
13 Cornwall, 1952.
14 Kramer, 1961b.
15 Rice, 1990.
16 F.Ll. Griffith, *The Conflict of Horus and Set from Egyptian and Classical Sources*, Liverpool, 1960.
17 Kramer, 1961b.
18 Cornwall, 1943a.
19 Burstein, 1978.
20 Ibid.
21 Nagel, 1968.
22 Rawlinson, 1880.
23 *ANET*, The Epic of Gilgamesh.

7 BAHRAIN: THE BLESSED ISLAND

1 Durand, 1880.
2 Vallat, 1983.
3 Rawlinson, 1880.
4 Bowersock, 1986.
5 Nissen, 1986.
6 See T. Heyerdahl, *The Tigris Expedition*, London, 1980.
7 Rice, 1990.
8 McNicholl, 1975.
9 Glob, 1954c.
10 Bibby, 1958a.
11 Bibby, 1986b.
12 Bibby, 1977–8.
13 Kohl, 1978; Zarins, 1978.
14 J. Laessoe, 'A cuneiform inscription from the island of Bahrain', *Kuml*, 1957.
15 Mortensen, 1986.
16 Frohlich, 1986.
17 Bibby, 1969.
18 Krauss, Lombard and Potts, 1983.
19 Luckenbill, 1926.
20 Glob, 1958b.
21 Ibid.
22 Frifelt, 1975b.
23 Burstein, 1978.

24 Andersen, 1984; Doe, 1984a, 1984b; Mortensen, 1986.
25 Durand, 1880.
26 Glob, 1955.
27 Mortensen, 1986.
28 Glob, 1954d.
29 Andersen, 1956; Rice, 1983.
30 Glob, 1955.
31 Ibid..
32 Mortensen, 1971.
33 Kjaerum, 1983.
34 Mortensen, op. cit.
35 Frankfort, 1968; Rice, 1990.
36 W.M.F. Petrie, *Ancient Egypt*, London, 1917; *Egypt and Mesopotamia, The Geography of the Gods*; *The Making of Egypt*, London, 1939; Rice, 1990.
37 Glob, 1955.
38 Kjaerum, op. cit.
39 Glob, 1955.
40 Potts, 1983b.
41 Woolley, 1934.
42 Nissen, 1986.
43 Kramer, 1961b.
44 Mellaart, 1967.
45 W.B. Emery, *Great Tombs of the First Dynasty*, 3 vols, Cairo and London, 1949, 1954, 1958.
46 Ibid.
47 Cornwall, 1943a.
48 Ibid.
49 Ibid.
50 Rice, 1990: see also its bibliography.
51 Ibid.
52 Potts in Potts, 1983b.
53 Bibby, 1986a.
54 Doe, 1986b.
55 Mortensen, 1956, 1971, 1986.
56 Rice, 1983; Doe, 1986a, 1986b.
57 Bibby, 1954.
58 Burkholder and Golding, 1971; Masry, 1974.
59 De Cardi, 1978.
60 McNicholl and Roaf, n.d.
61 Roaf, 1974.
62 Ibid.
63 Ibid.
64 Ibid.
65 Ibid.
66 Shaikha Haya bin Ali Al-Khalifa, pers. comm.
67 Frohlich, 1983.
68 Højgaard, 1983, 1986.
69 Rice, 1990.
70 Bahrain National Museum: palaeontological exhibits.
71 Lamberg-Karlovsky, 1982, 1986.
72 Frohlich, 1986.
73 For a discussion of the various types see Potts, 1990.
74 Ibid.

75 Mackay *et al.*, 1969.
76 Calvet, 1989.
77 Ibrahim, 1983; Mughal, 1983.
78 Cornwall, 1943b.
79 I.E.S. Edward, *The Pyramids of Egypt*, London, 1947, revised edn 1985.
80 Mackay *et al.*, op. cit..
81 Ibid.
82 Ibid.
83 Cornwall, 1943b.
84 Durand, 1879.
85 Durand, 1880.
86 P.V. Glob, 'Arabian Gulf archaeology', *Kuml*, 1964.
87 Woolley, 1934.
88 Rice, 1983.
89 C. Vermeule and E. Vermeule, 'An Aegean gold hoard and the court of Egypt', *Illustrated London News*, 2l March 1970.
90 M.J. O'Kelly, *New Grange*, London, 1982.
91 Vermeule and Vermeule, op. cit.
92 Prideaux, 1912.
93 Cornwall, 1946b; Piesinger, 1983; *Atlal, passim*.
94 Ibrahim, 1983.
95 Rice, 1990.
96 Ibrahim, op. cit.
97 R.G. Killick, H.E.W. Crawford, K. Flavin, H. Ginger, A. Lupton, C. Maclaughlin, R. Montague, J.A. Moore and M.A. Woodburn, 'London–Bahrain Archaeological Expedition: 1990 excavations at Saar', *Arabian Archaeology and Epigraphy* 2, 1991.
98 Ibid.
99 Ibid.
100 Roaf, 1974.
101 Killick *et al.*, op. cit.
102 Ibid.
103 Ibid.
104 Ibid.
105 Ibid.
106 H.E.W., Crawford, 'Seals from the first season's excavation at Saar, Bahrain', *Cambridge Archaeological Journal* 1:2, 1991.
107 Kjaerum, op. cit.
108 Crawford, op. cit.
109 Ibrahim, 1983; Mughal, 1983.
110 Ibid.
111 Rice, 1972.
112 Lloyd, 1978, reference to Eridu burials: see also *Illustrated London News*, 11 September 1948.
113 Rice, 1972.
114 Killick *et al.*, op. cit.
115 Michael W. Ovenden, 'The origin of the constellations', *The Philosophical Journal* 3, 1966.
116 Ibid.
117 Ibid.
118 G. De Santillana and H. von Dechend, *Hamlet's Mill – An Essay on Myth and the Frame of Time*, Macmillan, 1969.
119 Ibid.
120 Ibid.

8 DILMUN'S NEIGHBOURING LANDS

1 Leemans, 1950, 1960a.
2 Kramer, 1963a.
3 Durand, 1879.
4 *Mission archeologique française à Qatar*, I, Doha, Qatar, 1980.
5 *ANET*, I; Sandars, 1972.
6 Burrows, 1928.
7 See K. Jeppersen, 'The Ikaros inscription', in *Ikaros – the Hellenistic Settlement*, vol. 3: *The Sacred Enclosure in the Early Hellenistic Period*, Aarhus, 1989.
8 Cornwall, 1943a.
9 See *The Power of the Bull* (forthcoming) by the author for an extensive discussion of these associations.
10 See Potts, 1990, vol. 1, for references.
11 Potts, 1990, vol. 2.
12 Ibid.
13 See Potts, 1990, vol. 1.
14 Kassler, 1973.
15 Kjaerum, 1983.
16 Ibid.
17 Rice, 1990.
18 Potts, op. cit.
19 Jeppersen, op. cit.
20 See Calvet *et al.*, 1984.
21 Calvet, 1989.
22 Potts, op. cit.
23 T. Al-Asfour, in Brice, 1978.
24 Potts, op. cit.
25 Ibid.
26 Ibid.
27 See Jeppersen, op. cit.
28 Potts, 1990, vol. 2.
29 Jeppersen, op. cit.
30 Ibid.
31 Ibid.
32 Potts, 1990, vol. 1.
33 Ibid.
34 Al-Sayani and Zötl, 1978: C.H.V. Ebert, 'Water resources and land use in the Qatif Oasis of Saudi Arabia', *Geographical Review* 55 vol. 4, 1965.
35 Ibid.
36 Ibid.
37 Burkholder and Golding, 1971.
38 Masry, 1974.
39 Ibid.
40 Ibid.
41 Ibid.
42 Ibid.
43 J. Oates, 1976.
44 Masry, op. cit.
45 Ibid.
46 Oates, op. cit.
47 Masry, op. cit.
48 Ibid.

49 Ibid.
50 Dates are from Masry, 1974, uncalibrated.
51 Ibid.
52 Piesinger, 1983.
53 Ibid.
54 Bibby, 1973.
55 Piesinger, op. cit.
56 Said to be from a site near Al-Uyun.
57 Rashid, 1972; the handbook of the Museum of Archaeology and Ethnography, Riyadh: Strika, 1984.
58 Zarins, 1978.
59 Kohl, 1978.
60 Emery, op. cit.; Rice, 1990.
61 Golding, 1974.
62 Rice, 1990.
63 Cornwall, 1946b.
64 Bibby, 1973.
65 Zarins *et al.*, 1983.
66 Ibid.; Cornwall, 1946b.
67 Zarins *et al.*, 1983.
68 Ibid.
69 A. Clark, *Bahrain Oil and Developments 1929–1989*, London, 1991.
70 Cornwall, 1943a.
71 R.W. Bulliet, *The Camel and the Wheel*, Cambridge, Mass., 1975.
72 Zarins, 1986.
73 Cornwall, 1952.
74 H.I. Abu Duruk, *Introduction to the Archaeology of Taima*, Department of Antiquities and Museums, Riyadh, 1986.
75 See Potts, 1990, vol. 2, for various alternatives.
76 Translation, Loeb Classical Library, amended W. Facey.
77 Ibid.
78 Ibid.
79 Pers. comm. to Sir Charles Belgrave, supplied to author.
80 Golding, op. cit.
81 Kapel, 1967.
82 *Mission archéologique française à Qatar.*
83 Ibid.
84 Ibid.
85 Ibid.
86 Rice, 1990.
87 De Cardi, 1978.
88 Ibid.
89 Ibid.
90 Ibid.
91 Ibid.
92 J. Oates, in De Cardi, 1977.
93 *Mission archéologique française à Qatar*, vol. 1.
94 *Kuml*, 1964.
95 Ibid.
96 Ibid.
97 Ibid.
98 Ibid.
99 Ibid.

100 Ibid.; also Facey, 1987.
101 H. Kapel, 'Report concerning indexing and examination of rock carvings at Jebel Jessessiyah, Qatar', in Dainser, *Rock Carvings at Jessessiyah*, no. 8, 1983.
102 Bibby, 1986b.
103 Cleuziou, 1986.
104 Frifelt, 1971, 1975b, 1976.
105 S. Kay, *Emirates Archaeological Heritage*, Dubai, 1986.
106 Bibby, 1986a.
107 Weisgerber, 1978, 1986.
108 Tosi, 1974.
109 Ibid.
110 Tosi, op. cit.; *Kuml*, 1962.
111 Potts, 1990, vol. 1.
112 Frifelt, 1975a, 1978b.
113 Cleuziou, 1978–9.
114 Ibid.
115 Potts, op. cit.
116 Ibid.
117 B. Vogt, and U. Franke-Vogt, *Shimal* 1985–86, Berlin, 1987.
118 Potts, op. cit.
119 Vogt and Franke-Vogt, op. cit.; Potts, op. cit.
120 Potts, op. cit.
121 Ibid.
122 Ibid.
123 R. Boucharlat and M. Monton, 'Excavations at Mleiha site: a preliminary report', in Boucharlat, ed., *Archaeological Surveys and Excavations*, Sharjah and Lyons, 1986.
124 De Cardi, 1971, 1975b.
125 Potts, op. cit.
126 Ibid.
127 McClure, 1971, 1984; see also *Atlal* 4, 5, 6 *passim*.
128 Kramer, 1963a.
129 Ibid.
130 H. Peake, *The Copper Mountain of Magan*, Antiquity 2, 1928.
131 Cornwall, 1943a.
132 Frifelt, 1970, 1975b.
133 Frifelt, 1975a.
134 Frifelt, 1976.
135 Frifelt, 1975b.
136 Frifelt, 1968.
137 E.J. Baumgartel, *The Cultures of Prehistoric Egypt*, vol. 1, London, 1955; Rice, 1990.
138 Frifelt, 1975b.
139 Ibid.
140 Durante and Tosi, 1977.
141 M. Tosi, *A Possible Harappan Sea-port in Eastern Arabia. Ras Al-Jurrayz in the Sultanate of Oman*, 1st International Conference on Pakistan Archaeology, Peshawar, 1982.
142 N. Groom, *Frankincense and Myrrh*, London, 1981.
143 *Atlal, passim*.
144 For example, H. Winkler, *The Rock Carvings of Southern Upper Egypt*, 2 vols, London, 1938 and 1939.
145 Anati, 1968.

146 Clarke, 1975.
147 Ibid.

9 THE MERCHANTS OF DILMUN

1 V. Diakonoff, *Structure of Society and State in Early Dynastic Sumer*, 1974.
2 Lamberg-Karlovsky, 1972.
3 Pettinato, 1991.
4 Matthias, 1977.
5 Potts, 1986a.
6 Pettinato, op. cit.
7 Potts, 1990.
8 Kramer, 1963a.
9 Cited in Leemans, 1950.
10 Ibid.
11 Ibid.
12 Cornwall, 1943a.
13 W.A. Fairservis, *The Roots of Ancient India*, London, 1971.
14 Ibid., pls 33, 34.
15 Mackay, 1928.
16 Fairservis, op. cit., p. 279, fig. 39.
17 Ibid., pl.46.
18 Potts, 1990, vol. 1.
19 Durante and Tosi, 1977 (Ch. 9).
20 Diemel in Cornwall, 1943a.
21 Leemans, 1960a.
22 Ibid.
23 Ibid.
24 Ibid.
25 Ibid.
26 Oppenheim, 1954.
27 In Potts, 1986a.
28 Ibid.
29 Leemans, 1960a.
30 Oppenheim, op. cit.
31 Ibid.
32 Bibby, 1971b.
33 Ibid.
34 Leemans, 1960a, from whom much of the following material is taken.
35 Ibid.
36 Ibid.
37 Ibid.
38 Ibid.
39 Ibid.
40 Ibid.
41 Ibid.
42 C.L. Woolley, *Ur of the Chaldees*, London, 1955.
43 Ibid.
44 Mellaart, 1967.
45 Schmandt-Bessaret, 1977.
46 Mellaart, op. cit.
47 Rice, 1990.
48 Amiet, 1961.

49 Potts, 1990, vol. 1.
50 Kjaerum, 1983.
51 Gadd, 1932.
52 See Potts, 1986b, quoting Briggs, Buchanan, Porada, Amiet and Kjaerum, op. cit.
53 Kjaerum, op. cit: a study of the Bahrain seals is promised.
54 Rice, 1990.
55 Al-Khalifa, 1986.
56 Mortensen, 1971.
57 Rice, 1990 and, forthcoming, *The Power of the Bull*.
58 See S. Dalley, *Myths from Mesopotamia*, Oxford, 1991.
59 Gadd, op. cit.
60 Kjaerum, op. cit.
61 See T.F. Potts, 'Patterns of trade in third-millennium BC Mesopotamia and Iran', in *World Archaeology* vol. 24, no. 3, February 1993.
62 Ibid.
63 See K. Frifelt, 1991, 'The islands of Umm an-Nar', vol. 1, in *Third Millenium Graves*, Aarhus.

10 GILGAMESH, THE GULF AND THE LAND OF THE LIVING

1 Sandars, 1972; Tigay, 1982.
2 Particularly Sigmund Freud.
3 Tigay, op. cit.
4 Ibid.
5 See Rice, forthcoming, *The Power of the Bull*.
6 Rice, 1990.
7 *ANET*, I.
8 C.L. Woolley, *Ur of the Chaldees*, London, 1955.
9 E.E. Schmidt, quoted in Campbell, *Oriental Mythology*, Harmondsworth, 1976.
10 Ibid.
11 *ANET*, I.
12 Ibid.
13 Ibid.
14 Burrows, 1928.
15 Burstein, 1978.
16 *ANET*, I.
17 Sandars, op. cit.
18 During-Caspers, 1982.
19 *ANET*, I.
20 Sandars, op. cit.
21 Bibby, 1969.
22 *The Koran*, trans. N.J. Dawood, Harmondsworth, 1956.
23 *Shorter Encyclopaedia of Islam*, Leyden and London, 1961.
24 Ibid.
25 Ibid.
26 C.G. Jung, *The Archetypes and the Collective Unconscious, Collected Works*, vol. 9, London, 1959.
27 Y.A. Shirawi, pers. comm.

11 THE ENIGMA OF DILMUN

1 Rice, 1983, and Chapter 2 above.
2 Bowersock, 1986.

3 Zarins, 1986.
4 Frohlich, 1986.
5 Bibby, 1984b.
6 McClure, 1971.
7 Zarins, *Atlal* 5, 1981.
8 Rice, 1986, 1990.
9 Bibby, 1984a.

BIBLIOGRAPHY

There is now an extensive bibliography of books, articles and references to the Gulf states in antiquity. Certain works are essential reading: Durand's report and Bibby's *Looking for Dilmun* in particular. The pattern of publication throughout the states is very uneven: Bahrain and Saudi Arabia are generally well referenced; Kuwait is woefully under-published. The United Arab Emirates is now better represented. The Sultanate of Oman is relatively well served.

Several important journals concerned with archaeology have been introduced in the course of the past decade: *Atlal, the Journal of Saudi Arabian Archaeology*, published by the Department of Antiquities and Museums of the Kingdom of Saudi Arabia, and the *Journal of Oman Studies*, published by the Ministry of National Heritage of the Sultanate of Oman. Bahrain has *Dilmun*, published by the Bahrain Historical and Archaeological Society. These journals contain a wealth of references to sites and specific aspects of their own and their neighbours' archaeology and history. *Arabian Archaeology and Epigraphy*, Munksgaard, Copenhagen, the latest introduction to the field and probably the most authoritative, aims to provide 'a forum for the publication of studies in the archaeology, epigraphy, numismatics and early history' of the Arabian peninsula states.

Year by year the Proceedings of the Seminar for Arabian Studies, held on a rotating basis in London, Oxford and Cambridge since 1970, contain a great deal of important material contributed by the most committed researchers in the field.

Volume 1 of the Proceedings of the 1983 Conference *Bahrain through the Ages – the Archaeology* (KPI, London) has a wealth of important papers contributed by the principal scholars in the field. Whilst it concentrates its interest on Bahrain, it is of primary value in achieving an understanding of the Gulf as a whole in antiquity.

More comprehensive still is D.T. Potts, *The Arabian Gulf in Antiquity* (Clarendon Press, Oxford) in two volumes, which contains references of virtually all published studies on the Gulf culture.

Adams, R. McC., Parr, P.J., Ibrahim, M., Al-Mughannum, A.S. 1977, 'Saudi Arabian archaeological reconnaissance – 1976', Preliminary Report on the First Phase of the Comprehensive Archaeological Survey Program – Eastern Province, *Atlal* 1

Alster, B. 1983, 'Dilmun, Bahrain, and the alleged Paradise in Sumerian myth and literature', in Potts, ed., *BBVO* 2.

Amiet, P. 1961, *La Glyptique mesopotamienne archäique*, Paris, 1966.

—— 1975, 'A cylinder seal impression found at Umm an-Nar', *EW* n.s. 25 (3–4).

—— 1986, 'Suse et la civilization de Dilmun', *BTAA*.

Anati, E. 1968, *Rock Art in Central Arabia*, Vol. 1: *The Oval- headed People of Arabia*; Vol. 2, part 1, *Fat-tailed Sheep in Arabia*; part 2; *The Realistic-dynamic Style of Rock Art in Jebel Qara*, Université de Louvain, Institut Orientaliste.

Andersen, H.H. 1956, 'The building by the Barbar temple', *Kuml*.

—— 1986, 'The Barbar temple: its stratigraphy, architecture and interpretation', *BTAA*.

Barrelet, M.T. 1978, *L'Archéologie de l'Iraq du début de l'époque néolithique à 333 av. n. ère: perspective, et limites de l'interprétation anthropologique des documents*, CNRS Colloque no. 580, Paris, June 13–15.

Bent, J.T. 1890, 'The Bahrein islands in the Persian Gulf', *Proceedings of the Royal Geographical Society* 12.

Bent, M.V.E. 1900, *Southern Arabia*, London.

Bibby, T.G. 1954a, 'Fem af Bahrains hundrede tusinde gravhoje' (Five among Bahrain's hundred thousand grave-mounds), *Kuml*.

—— 1954b, 'Tyrebronden' (The Well of the Bulls), *Kuml*.

—— 1958a, 'Bahrains oldtidshovedstad gennem 4000 ar' (The hundred-metre section), *Kuml*.

—— 1958b, 'The "ancient Indian style" seals from Bahrain', *Antiquity 32*.

—— 1965, 'Arabiens arkaeologi' (Arabian Gulf archaeology), *Kuml*.

—— 1966, 'Arabiens arkaeologi' (Arabian Gulf archaeology), *Kuml*.

—— 1967, 'Arabiens arkaeologi' (Arabian Gulf archaeology), *Kuml*.

—— 1969, *Looking for Dilmun*, New York.

—— 1971a, *I Dilmun Tier Ravnen*, Højbjerg.

—— 1971b, '. . . efter Dilmun norm' (according to the standard of Dilmun'), *Kuml* 1970.

—— 1973, 'Preliminary survey in east Arabia 1968', *Jutland Archaeological Society Publications* 12, Aarhus.

—— 1977–8, 'Gensyn med Bahrain', *Sfinx 1*.

—— 1986a, 'The land of Dilmun is holy', *BTAA*.

—— 1986b, 'The origins of the Dilmun civilization', *BTAA*.

Bowersock, G.W. 1986, 'Tylos and Tyre: Bahrain in the Graeco-Roman world', *BTAA*.

Brice, W.C., ed., 1978, *The Environmental History of the Near and Middle East*, Academic Press, London, New York and San Francisco.

Brunswig, R.H., Jr, Parpola, A. and Potts, D. 1983, 'New Indus type and related seals from the Near East', in Potts, ed., *BBVO* 2.

Buccellati, G. 1966, *The Amorites of the Ur III Period*, Istituto Orientale di Napoli, Pubblicazioni del Seminario di Semitistica, Naples.

Bulliet, R. W., 1975, *The Camel and the Wheel*, Harvard University Press, Cambridge, Mass.

Burkholder, G. and Golding, M. 1971, 'A surface survey of Ubaid sites in the Eastern Province of Saudi Arabia', informal paper (mimeographed) delivered at the Third International Conference on Asian Archaeology, Bahrain, March 1970.

Burrows, E. 1928, 'Bahrain, Tilmun, Paradise', *Scriptura Sacra et Monumenta Orientis Antiqui*, Pontifici Istituti Biblici, Rome.

Burstein, S.M. 1978, *The 'Babyloniaca' of Berossus*, Undena Publications, Malibu.

Butz, K. 1983a, 'Zwei kleine Inschriften zur Geschichte Dilmuns', in Potts, ed., *BBVO* 2.

— 1983b, 'Dilmun in altbabylonischen Quellen', in Potts, ed., *BBVO* 2.

Callot, O., Gachet, J. and Salles, J.-F. 1978, 'Some notes about Hellenistic Failaka', *PSAS* 17.

Calvet, Y. 1989, 'Failaka and the northern part of Dilmun', *PSAS* 19.

Calvet, Y., Caubet, A. and Salles, J.-P. 1984, 'French excavation at Failaka 1983', *PSAS* 14.

Carter, T.H. 1972, 'The Johns Hopkins University Reconnaissance Expedition to the Arab-Iranian Gulf, *BASOR* 207.

— 1981, 'The tangible evidence for the earliest Dilmun', *JCS* 33.

— 1984, 'Eyestones and pearls', *BTAA*.

Child, G. and Grainger, S. 1990, *A System Plan for Protected Areas for Wildlife Conservation and Sustainable Rural Development in Saudia Arabia*, The National Commission for Wildlife Conservation and Development, Riyadh, Saudi Arabia.

Clarke, A. 1981, *The Islands of Bahrain*, The Bahrain Archaeological and Historical Society.

Clarke, C. 1975, 'The rock art of Oman', *JOS* 1.

Cleuziou, S. 1986, 'Dilmun and Makkah during the third millennium and the early second millennium BC: a tentative view', *BTAA*.

— n.d., *Archéologie aux Emirats Arabes Unis* (Archaeology in the United Arab Emirates), Department of Tourism and Archaeology, Abu Dhabi, UAE.

— 1978–9, *Archéologie aux Emirats Arabes Unis* (Archaeology in the United Arab Emirates), Vols 2–3, Department of Tourism and Archaeology, Abu Dhabi, UAE.

Cleuziou, S., Lombard, P. and Salles, J.-F. 1979, *Excavations at Umm Jidr, Bahrain*, Editions ADPF, Paris.

Cornwall, P.B. 1943a, 'Dilmun: The History of Bahrain Island before Cyrus', Ph.D. dissertation, Harvard University.

— 1943b, 'The tumuli of Bahrein', in *Asia and the Americas*, 43.

— 1946a, 'On the location of Dilmun', *BASOR* 103.

— 1946b, 'Ancient Arabia: explorations in Hasa, 1940–41', *Geographic Journal* no. 107, p. 28.

— 1952, 'Two letters from Dilmun', *JCS* 6.

Costa, P.M. 1978, 'The copper mining settlement of Arja: a preliminary survey', *JOS* 4.

Dani, A.H. 1984, 'Bahrain and the Indus Civilization', *BTAA*.

De Cardi, B. 1967, 'The Bampur sequences in the 3rd millennium BC', *Antiquity*, 41.

— 1971, 'Archaeological survey in the northern Trucial States', *EW* n.s. 21 (3–4).

— 1975a, 'Survey and excavations in Oman', *JOS* 1.

— 1975b, 'Archaeological survey in northern Oman', *EW* n.s.21.

— 1977, 'Surface collections from the Oman Survey, 1976', *JOS* 3, Part 1.

— 1978, *Qatar Archaeological Report, Excavations 1973*, Oxford.

— 1986, 'Harappan finds in a tomb at Ras Al-Khaimah,' UAE, *PSAS* 16.

De Cardi, B., Bell, R.D. and Starling, N.J. 1979, 'Excavations at Tawi Gilaim and Tawi Sa'id in the Sharqiyah 1978', *JOS* 5.

De Cardi, B, Collier, S. and Doe, D.B. 1971, 'Archaeological survey in the northern Trucial States', *EW* n.s. 2l (3–4).

— 1976, 'Excavations and survey in Oman 1974–5', *JOS* 2.

De Cardi, B., Doe, D.B. and Roskams, S.P. 1977, 'Excavation and survey in the Sharqiyah. Oman 1976', *JOS* 3 part 1.

Doe, D.B. 1977, 'Gazetteer of sites in Oman, 1976', *JOS* 3.

— 1986a, 'The Barbar temple site in Bahrain', *BTAA*.

— 1986b, 'The masonry of the Dilmun temple at Barbar', *BTAA*.

Durand, Captain E.L. 1879, 'Notes on the Islands of Bahrain and Antiquities, as Submitted from the Political Resident, Persian Gulf, to the Foreign Department, Calcutta.

—— 1880, 'The islands and antiquities of Bahrain', *JRAS* n.s. 12, part 2.

Durante, S. and Tosi, M. 1977, 'The aceramic shell middens of Ra's al-Hamra: a preliminary note', *JOS* 3, part 2.

During-Caspers, E.C.L. 1971a, 'New archaeological evidence for maritime trade in the Persian Gulf during the late protoliterate period', *EW* n.s. 2l.

—— 1971b, 'The bull's head from Barbar Temple II, Bahrain: a contact with Early Dynastic Sumer', *EW* n.s. 21.

—— 1972–4, 'The Bahrain tumuli', *Persica* 6.

—— 1973a, 'Sumer and Kulli meet at Dilmun in the Arabian Gulf', *AFO* 24.

—— 1973b, 'Dilmun and the date tree', *EW* n.s. 23.

—— 1973c, 'Harappan trade in the Arabian Gulf in the third millennium BC', *PSAS* 3.

—— 1976, 'Cultural concepts in the Arabian Gulf and the Indian Ocean: transmissions in the third millennium and their significance', *PSAS* 6.

—— 1977, 'A Dilmun seal cutter's misfortune', *Antiquity* 51.

—— 1979a, 'Westward contacts with historical India: a trio of figurines', *PSAS* 9.

—— 1979b, 'Statuary in the round from Dilmun', in J.E. van Louhuizen-de Leeuw, ed., *South Asian Archaeology* 1975, Brill, Leiden.

—— 1980, *The Bahrain Tumuli: An Illustrated Catalogue of Two Important Collections*, Uitgaven van het Nederlands Historisch-Archaeologisch Instituut te Istanbul 47.

—— 1982, 'Corals, pearls and prehistoric Gulf trade', *PSAS*.

—— 1986, 'Animal designs and Gulf chronology', *BTAA*.

During-Caspers, E.C.L. and Govindakutty, A. 1978, 'R. Thapar's Dravidian hypothesis for the location of Meluhha, Dilmun and Makkan', *JESHO* 21 (2).

Edens, C. 1982, 'Towards a definition of the western Ar-Rub Al-Khali "Neolithic"', *Atlal* 6.

—— 1986, 'Bahrain and the Gulf: the second millennium crisis', *BTAA*.

Englund, R. 1983a, 'Exotic fruits', in Potts, ed., *BBVO* 2.

—— 1983b, 'Dilmun in the archaic Uruk corpus', in Potts, ed., *BBVO* 2.

Facey, W. 1987, 'The boat carvings at Jabal Jusasiyya, N.E. Qatar', *PSAS* 17.

Fairservis, W. 1971, *The Roots of Ancient India*, Allen & Unwin, London.

Falkenstein, A. 1967, 'The prehistory and protohistory of Western Asia', in E. Bottero et al., eds, *The Near East*, Delacorte Press, New York.

Ferrara, A.J. 1979, *Nanna-Suen's Journey to Nippur*, Biblical Institute Press, Rome.

Field, H. 1958. 'Stone implements from the Rub' al-Khali', *Man* no. 30.

—— 1960, 'Carbon-14 date for a "Neolithic" site in the Rub' al-Khali', *Man* no. 214.

Foster, B. 1977, 'Commercial activity in Sargonic Mesopotamia', *Iraq* 39.

Frankfort, 1968, *The Birth of Civilization in the Near East*, Benn, London.

Frifelt, K. 1968, 'Archaeological investigations in the Oman peninsula', *Kuml*.

—— 1970, 'Jemdet Nasr fund fra Oman', *Kuml*.

—— 1971, 'Excavations in Abu Dhabi (Oman)', *Artibus Asiae* 33 (4).

—— 1975a, 'A possible link between the Jemdet Nasr and the Umm an-Nar graves of Oman', *JOS* 1.

—— 1975b, 'On prehistoric settlement and chronology of the Oman peninsula', *EW* n.s. 25 (3–4).

—— 1976, 'Evidence of a third millennium BC town in Oman', *JOS* 2.

—— 1986, 'Grave mounds near Aali excavated by the Danish Expedition', *BTAA*.

Frohlich, B. 1983, 'The Bahrain burial mounds', *Dilmun* 2.

—— 1986, 'The human biological history of the Early Bronze Age in Bahrain', *BTAA*.

Gadd, C.J. 1932, 'Seals of ancient Indian style found at Ur', *Proceedings of the British Academy* 18.

Gelb, I.J. 1970, 'Makkan and Meluhha in early Mesopotamian sources', *Revue d'Assyriologie* 64.

Glob, P.V. 1954a, 'Bahrain, Oen med de Hundredtusinde gravhoje' (Bahrain – island of the hundred thousand burial-mounds), *Kuml*.

—— 1954b, 'Bahrains oldtidshovedstad' (The ancient capital of Bahrain), *Kuml*.

—— 1954c, 'Flintpadser i Bahrains orken' (The flint sites of the Bahrain desert), *Kuml*.

—— 1954d, 'Templer ved Barbar' (Temples at Barbar), *Kuml*.

—— 1955, 'Udgravninger pa Bahrain, Dansk Arkaeologisk Bahrain-Ekspeditions 2. udgravningskampagne' (The Danish Archaeological Bahrain Expedition's second campaign), *Kuml*.

—— 1956, 'Et nybabylonisk gravfund fra Bahrains oldtidshovedstad' (A neo-Babylonian burial from Bahrain's prehistoric capital), *Kuml*.

—— 1958a, 'The prosperity of Bahrain five thousand years ago: solving the riddle of the 100,000 burial mounds of the island', *Illustrated London News* 232.

—— 1958b, 'Slangeofre i Bahrains oldtidshovedstad: Dansk Arkaeologisk Bahrain-Ekspeditions 4. Udgravningskampagne' (Snake sacrifices in Bahrain's ancient capital), *Kuml*.

—— 1958c, 'Investigations in Kuwait', *Kuml*.

—— 1959a, 'Alabasterkar fra Bahrains templer. Dansk Arkaeologisk Bahrain-Ekspeditions 5. Udgravningskampagne' (Alabaster vases from the Bahrain temples), *Kuml*.

—— 1959b, 'Arkaeologiske undersogelser i fire arabiske stater' (Archaeological investigations in four arab states), *Kuml*.

—— 1960, 'Danske arkaeologer i Den Persiske Golf' (Danish archaeologists in the Persian Gulf), *Kuml*.

—— 1968, *Al-Bahrain, De danske ekspeditioner til Oldtidens Dilmun*, Gyldendal, Copenhagen.

Glob, P.V. and Bibby, T.G. 1960, 'A forgotten civilization of the Persian Gulf', *Scientific American* 203.

Goettler, G.W., Firth, N. and Huston, C.C. 1976, 'A preliminary discussion of ancient mining in the Sultanate of Oman', *JOS* 2.

Golding, M. 1974, 'Evidence for pre-Seleucid occupation of eastern Arabia', *PSAS* 4.

Hallo, W.W., and Buchanan, B. 1965, 'A Persian Gulf seal on an old Babylonian mercantile agreement', *Assyriological Studies* 16 (Landsberger volume).

Hamilton, W.R., Whybrow, P.J. and McClure, H.A. 1978, 'Fauna of fossil mammals from the Miocene of Saudi Arabia', *Nature* 274.

Hansman, J. 1973, 'A periplus of Magan and Meluhha', *Bulletin SOAS* 36(3).

Hastings, A., Humphries, J.H. and Meadow, R.H. 1975, 'Oman in the third millennium BC', *JOS* 1.

Heidel, A. 1963, *The Gilgamesh Epic and Old Testament Parallels*, 2nd edn, University of Chicago Press.

Herrmann, G. 1968, 'Lapis lazuli: the early phases of its trade', *Iraq* 30 (1).

Højgaard, K. 1983, 'Dilmun's ancient teeth', *Dilmun* 2.

—— 1986, 'Dental anthropological investigations on Bahrain', *BTAA*.

Højlund, F. 1986, 'The Chronology of City II and III at Qala'at al-Bahrain', *BTAA*.

—— 1989, 'The formation of the Dilmun state and the Amorite tribes', *PSAS* 19.

Hruska, B. 1983, 'Dilmun in den vorsargonischen Wirtschaftstexten aus Suruppak und Lagas', in Potts, ed., *BBVO* 2.

Humphries, J.H. 1974, 'Some later prehistoric sites in the Sultanate of Oman', *PSAS* 4.

Ibrahim, M. 1983, *Excavations of the Arab Expedition at Saar El-Jisr*, Ministry of Information, State of Bahrain.

Jackli, R. 1980, *Rock Art in Oman. An Introductory Presentation*, Zug, Switzerland.

Jacobsen, T. 1970, *Towards the Image of Tammuz*, Harvard Semitic Series, Harvard, Cambridge, Mass.

Jeppersen, K. 1989, *Ikaros – The Hellenistic Settlements: The Sacred Enclosure in the Early Hellenistic Period*, Jutland Archaeological Society Publication, Aarhus.

Joshi, P.J. 1986, 'India and Bahrain – a survey of cultural interaction during the third and second millennia', *BTAA*.

Jouannin, M. 1905, 'Les tumuli de Bahrein', MDP 8.

Kapel, H. 1967, *The Atlas of the Stone-Age Cultures of Qatar*, Jutland Archaeological Society Publication 6, Aarhus.

Kay, S. 1986, 'Emirates' archaeological heritage', Motivate Publishing, Dubai.

Kervran, M. 1986, 'Qala'at al-Bahrain: a strategic position from the Hellenistic period to modern times', *BTAA*.

Al-Khalifa, H.A. 1986, 'The shell seals of Bahrain', *BTAA*.

Al-Khalifa, H.A. and Rice, Michael, eds, 1986, *Bahrain through the Ages*. Vol. 1: *The Archaeology*, Kegan Paul, London.

Kjaerum, P. 1983, *Failaka/Dilmun: The Second Millennium Settlements*, Vol. I.I.: *The Stamp and Cylinder Seals*, Jutland Archaeological Society Publications, 17: 1.

—— 1984, 'The Dilmun seals as testimony of long distance relations', *BTAA*.

—— 1986, 'Architecture and settlement patterns in 2nd millennium Failaka', *PSAS* 16.

Kohl, P.L. 1978, 'The balance of trade in southwestern Asia in the mid-third millennium BC', *Current Anthropology* 19(3).

—— 1981, *The Bronze Age Civilization of Central Asia*, M.G. Sharpe Inc., New York.

—— 1986, 'The lands of Dilmun: changing cultural and economic relations during the third and early second millennia', *BTAA*.

Komoroczy, G. 1977, 'Tilmun als "Speicher des Landes" in Epos "Enki und Ninhursag"', *Lag* 39, Part 1.

Kramer, S.N. 1944, 'Dilmun, the land of the living', *BASOR* 96.

—— 1961a, *History Begins at Sumer*, Thames & Hudson, London.

—— 1961b, *Sumerian Mythology*, Harper Torch Books, New York.

—— 1963a, *The Sumerians*, University of Chicago Press.

—— 1963b, 'Dilmun: quest for Paradise', *Antiquity* 37.

—— 1969, *The Sacred Marriage Rite*, Indiana University Press, Bloomington and London.

Kramer, S.N. and Maier, J. 1989, *Myths of Enki, the Crafty God*, Oxford University Press, Oxford and London.

Krauss, R., Lombard, P. and Potts, D. 1983, 'The silver hoard from City IV, Qala'at al-Bahrain', in Potts, ed., *BBVO* 2.

Laessoe, J. 1958, 'En Kileskrift fra Bahrain' (A cuneiform inscription from the island of Bahrain), *Kuml*.

Lamberg-Karlovsky, C.C. 1972, 'Trade mechanisms in Indus- Mesopotamian inter-relations', *JAOS* 92(2).

—— 1982, 'Dilmun: gateway to immortality', *JNES* 41.

—— 1986, 'Death in Dilmun', *BTAA*.

Lambert, W.G. and Millard, A.R. 1969, *Atra-Hasis. The Babylonian Story of the Flood*, Oxford University Press.

Larsen, C.E. 1975, 'The Mesopotamian delta region: a reconsideration of Lees and Falcon', *JAOS* 95(1).

—— 1983a, *Life and Land Use in the Bahrain Islands: The Geoarchaeology of an Ancient Society*, University of Chicago Press.

—— 1983b, 'The early environment and hydrology of ancient Bahrain', in Potts, ed., *BBVO* 2.

—— 1986, 'Variations in Holocene land use patterns in the Bahrain islands: construction of a simple land use model', *BTAA*.

Leemans, W.F. 1950, *The Old Babylonian Merchant*, Brill, Leiden.

—— 1960a, 'Foreign trade in the Old Babylonian period', *Studia et Documenta ad Iura Orientis Antiqui Pertinentia* 6, Brill, Leiden.

—— 1960b, 'The trade relations of Babylonia and the question of relations with Egypt in the Old Babylonian period', *JESHO* 3.

—— 1968, 'Old Babylonian letters and economic history: a review article with a digression on foreign trade', *JESHO* 11.

Lees, G.M., and Falcon, N.L. 1952, 'The geographical history of the Mesopotamian plain', *Geographical Journal* 118.

Lloyd, Seton 1978, *The Archaeology of Mesopotamia from the Old Stone Age to the Persian Conquest*, Thames & Hudson, London.

Lombard, P. 1986, 'Iron Age Dilmun: a reconsideration of City IV at Qala'at al-Bahrain', *BTAA*.

Lombard, P. and Salles, J.-F. 1983, *La Nécropole de Janussan, Bahrain*, Maison de l'Orient Ancien, Lyons.

Luckenbill, D.D. 1976, *Ancient Records of Assyria and Babylonia*, Oriental Institute, University of Chicago.

Macadam, H.I. 1990, 'Dilmun revisited' (review of *BTAA*), *Arab. Arch. Epig.* 1.

McClure, H.A. 1971, *The Arabian Peninsula and Prehistoric Populations*, Field Research Projects, Coconut Grove, Miami, Fla.

—— 1984, 'Late Quarternary palaeoenviroments of the Rub'Al-Khali', Ph.D. dissertation, London.

Mackay, E., Harding, G.L. and Petrie, F. 1929, *Bahrein and Hemamieh*, Publications of the British School of Archaeology in Egypt, Vol. 47, London.

McNicholl, A.W. 1975, *Al-Markh Excavations*, Committee for Arabian and Gulf Studies, Vol. 6, 1976, Institute of Archaeology, London.

McNicholl, A. and Roaf, M. n.d., 'Archaeological investigations in Bahrain 1973–75', unpublished. MS, Dept. of Antiquities, Bahrain.

Masry, A.H. 1974, *Prehistory in Northeastern Arabia: The Problem of Interregional Interaction*, Field Research Projects, Coconut Grove, Miami, Fla.

Matthias, Paolo, 1977–80, *Ebla – An Empire Rediscovered*, Hodder & Stoughton, London.

Mellaart, J. 1967, *Çatal Hüyük*, Thames & Hudson, London.

—— 1970, *Excavations at Hailar*, Edinburgh University Press for the British Institute of Archaeology at Ankara.

de Miroschedji, P. 1973, 'Vases et objets en stéatite susiens du musée du Louvre', *Cahiers de la Délégation Archéologique Française en Iran* 3.

Mitchell, T.C. 1986, 'The Indus and Gulf type seals from Ur', *BTAA*.

Morkholm, O. 1973, 'En hellenistisk montskat fra Bahrain' (A Hellenistic coin hoard from Bahrain), *Kuml*.

Mortensen, P. 1956, 'Barbartemplets ovale anlaeg' (The temple oval at Barbar), *Kuml*.

—— 1971, 'On the date of the Barbar temple in Bahrain', *Artibus Asiae* 33.

—— 1986, 'The Bahrain Temple – its chronology and foreign relations reconsidered', *BTAA*.

Moscati, S. 1959, *The Semites in Ancient History*, University of Wales Press, Cardiff.

Mughal, M.R. 1983, 'The Dilmun burial complex at Sar', *The 1980–82 Excavations in Bahrain*, Ministry of Information, Directorate of Archaeology and Museums, State of Bahrain.

Muhly, J.D. 1973, *Copper and Tin*, Connecticut Academy of Arts and Sciences, New Haven, Conn.

Muller, W.H. 1986, 'Tylos, Hagar, Gerrha – a triangle of Arabian oases in antiquity', *BTAA*.

Nagel, W. 1968, *Frühe Plastik aus Sumer und Westmakkan*, Verlag Bruno Hessling, Berlin.

Nashef, K. 1986, 'The deities of Dilmun', *BTAA*.

Nielsen, V. 1959, '-vidt beromt for dens mange perler' (Famed for its many pearls), *Kuml*.

Nissen, H.J. 1986, 'Mentions of Dilmun in the earliest Mesopotamian texts', *BTAA*.

Oates, D. 1986, 'Dilmun and the Assyrian Empire', *BTAA*.

Oates, D. and Oates, J. 1976, *Rise of Civilization*, Elsevier-Phaidon, Oxford.

Oates, J. 1960, 'Ur and Eridu, the prehistory', *Iraq* 22.

— 1976, 'Prehistory in northeastern Arabia', *Antiquity* 50.

— 1986, 'The Gulf in prehistory', *BTAA*.

Oates, J., Kamilli, D. and McKerrell, H. 1977, 'Seafaring Merchants of Ur?' *Antiquity* 51.

Oppenheim, A.L. 1954, 'The seafaring merchants of Ur'. *JAOS* 74.

Pettinato, G. 1991, *Ebla – A New Look At History*, trans. C. Forth Richardson, Johns Hopkins University Press, Baltimore and London.

Philby, H. 1933, *The Empty Quarter*, Constable, London.

Phillips, C.S. and Wilkinson, T.J. 1970, 'Recently discovered shell middens near Quriyat', *JOS* 5.

Piesinger, C.E. 1983, 'Legacy of Dilmun: the roots of ancient maritime trade in eastern coastal Arabia in the fourth/third millennium BC', Ph.D. dissertation, Madison, Wis.

Porada, E. 1965. 'The relative chronology of Mesopotamia. Part II', in R. Ehrich, ed., *Chronologies in Old World Archaeology*, University of Chicago Press.

— 1971, 'Remarks on seals found in the Gulf states', Third International Conference on Asian Archaeology in Bahrain, March 1970, *Artibus Asiae* 33, (4), Institute of Fine Arts, New York University.

Potts, D. 1978, 'Towards an integrated history of culture change in the Arabian Gulf area: notes on Dilmun, Makkan, and the economy of ancient Sumer', *JOS* 4.

— 1983a, 'Dilmun: where and when?' *Dilmun* 2.

— 1983b, *Dilmun: New Studies in the Archaeology and Early History of Bahrain*, in Potts, ed., *BBVO* 2.

— 1983c, 'Barbar miscellanies', in Potts, ed., *BBVO* 2.

— 1984, 'The chronology of the archaeological assemblages from the head of the Arabian Gulf to the Arabian Sea (8000–1750 BC)', in R.W. Ehrich, ed., *Chronologies in Old World Archaeology*, 3rd edn, University of Chicago Press.

— 1986a, 'Dilmun's further relations: the Syro-Anatolian evidence from the third and second millennia BC', *BTAA*.

— 1986b, 'Nippur and Dilmun in the 14th c. BC', *PSAS* 16.

— 1990, *The Arabian Gulf in Antiquity*, Vol. 1. *From Prehistory to the Fall of the Achaemenid Empire*; Vol. 2: *From Alexander the Great to the Coming of Islam*, Oxford.

— n.d. 'Proto-Elamite problems', paper read at the 25th Rencontre Assyriologique Internationale, Berlin, 3–7 July 1978.

Potts, D., al-Mughannum, A.S., Frye, J. and Sanders, D. 1978, 'Preliminary report on the second phase of the Eastern Province survey 1397/1977', *Atlal* 2.

Powell, M.A. 1983, 'The Standard of Dilmun', in Potts, ed., *BBVO* 2.

Preston, K. 1976, 'An introduction to the anthropomorphic content of the rock art of Jebel Akhdar', *JOS* 2.

Prideaux, Captain 1912, 'The sepulchral tumuli of Bahrain', *Archaeological Survey of India*, Annual Report, 1908–9.

Pritchard, J.B., ed. 1969, *Ancient Near Eastern Texts Relating to the Old Testament*, Princeton University Press.

Pullar, J. and Jackli, B. 1978, 'Some aceramic sites in Oman', *JOS* 4.

Purser, B.H. 1973, *The Persian Gulf: Holocene Carbonate Sedimentation and Diagenesis in a Shallow Epicontinental Sea*, Springer, New York.

Raikes, R.L. 1967, *Water, Weather and Prehistory*, John Baker, London.

Rao, S.R. 1969, 'A bronze mirror handle from the Barbar temple, Bahrain', *Kuml*.

— 1973, *Lothal and the Indus Civilization*, Asia Publishing House, London.

— 1986, 'Travel and cultural contacts between Bahrain and India in the third and second millennia BC', *BTAA*.

Rashid, S.A. 1972, *Eine frühdynastische Statue von der Insel Tarut in Persischen Golf*, Bayerische Akademie der Wissenschaften, Munich.

Ratnagar, S. 1981, *Encounters, the Westerly Trade of the Harappan Civilization*, Oxford university Press, Delhi.

Rawlinson, Major-General Sir H. 1880, 'Notes on Capt. Durand's Report upon the Islands of Bahrain', *JRAS* 12.

Reade, J.E. 1986, 'Variations in the Mesopotamian-Dilmun relationship', *BTAA*.

Reade, J.E. and Burleigh, R. 1978, 'The 'Ali cemetery: old excavations, ivory, and radiocarbon dating', *JOS* 4.

Rice, Michael 1972, 'The grave complex at Al-Hajjar Bahrain', *PSAS* 2.

— 1983, *The Barbar Temple Site, Bahrain*, Ministry of Information, State of Bahrain.

— 1984a, *Dilmun Discovered*, London.

— 1984b, *The Search for the Paradise Lane*, London.

— 1986, 'The island on the edge of the world', *BTAA*.

— 1988, 'Al Hajjar revisited: the grave complex at Al-Hajjar, Bahrain' (revised, with photographs), *PSAS* 18.

— 1990, *Egypt's Making*, Routledge, London.

Roaf, M. 1974, 'Excavations at Al Markh, Bahrain: a fish midden of the fourth millennium BC', *Paleorient* 2.

Roux, G. 1966, *Ancient Iraq*, Pelican Books, London.

Safar, F., Mustafa, M.A. and Lloyd, S. 1981, *Eridu*, Ministry of Culture and Information, Baghdad, Republic of Iraq.

Salles, J.-F. 1981, 'Le Golfe arabe dans l'antiquité', *Annales d'Histoire de l'Université Saint-Joseph*, Fasc. I.

— 1982, 'Gulf area during the first millennium', *Dilmun* 10.

— 1983, 'Bahrain "hellénistique": données et problèmes', in Boucharlat and Salles, eds, *AOMIM* 157.

— 1984a, 'Le Golfe entre le Proche et l'Extrême Orient à l'époque hellénistique', in E.C.L. During-Caspers, ed., *Beatrice De Cardi Felicitation Volume*, Academic Publishers, Leiden.

— 1984b, 'French excavations at Failaka 1983', *PSAS* 14.

— 1986, 'The necropolis of Janussan and burial customs at the end of the first millennium BC', *BTAA*.

Sandars, N.K. 1972, *The Epic of Gilgamesh: An English Version with an Introduction*, Penguin Books, London.

Sanlaville, P.J. 1986, 'The evolution of Bahrain shore levels through the ages', *BTAA*.

Al-Sayani, Saad S. and Zötl, Josef G. (eds) 1978, *The Quaternary Period in Saudi Arabia*, vol. 1, Springer-Verlag, Berlin.

Schmandt-Besserat, D. 1977, *An Archaic Recording System and the Origin of Writing*, Undena Publications, Malibu.

Smith, G.H. 1977, 'New prehistoric sites in Oman', *JOS* 3, part 1.

Solecki, R. 1972, *Shanidar*, Allen Lane, The Penguin Press, London.

Sollberger, E. 1970, 'The problem of Magan and Meluhha', *Bulletin of the Institute of Archaeology* 8–9, 1968–9.

Strika, F.L. 1986, 'The Tarut statue as a peripheral contribution to the knowledge of early Mesopotamian plastic art', *BTAA*.

Suell, D. 1982, *Ledgers and Prices – Early Mesopotamian Merchant Accounts*, Yale Babylonian Collection.

Thapar, R. 1975, 'A possible identification of Meluhha, Dilmun and Makkan', *JESHO* 17(1).

Thorvildsen, K. 1962, 'Burial cairns on Umm an-Nar', *Kuml*.

Tigay, J.H. 1982, *The Evolution of the Gilgamesh Epic*, University of Philadelphia Press.

Tixier, J. 1978, 'La mission archéologique française au Qatar', in Barrelet 1978.

—— 1986, 'The prehistory of the Gulf', *BTAA*.

Tosi, M. 1974, 'Some data for the study of prehistoric cultural areas on the Persian Gulf', *PSAS* 4.

—— 1975, 'Notes on the distribution and exploitation of natural resources in ancient Oman', *JOS* 1.

—— 1976, 'The dating of the Umm an-Nar culture and a proposed sequence for Oman in the third millennium BC', *JOS* 2.

—— 1986, 'Early maritime cultures of the Arabian Gulf and the Indian Ocean', *BTAA*.

Vallat, F. 1983, 'Le Dieu Enzak: une divinité dilmunite vénérée à Suse', in Potts, ed., *BBVO* 2.

Weisgerber, G. 1978, 'Evidence of ancient mining sites in Oman: a preliminary report', *JOS* 4.

—— 1986, 'Dilmun – a trading entrepôt, evidence from historical and archaeological sources', *BTAA*.

Wheeler, Sir M. 1953, 'The Indus Civilization', in *Cambridge History of India*, Cambridge University Press.

—— 1968, 'The Indus Civilization', Cambridge University Press.

Whitehouse, R. 1977, *The First Cities*, Phaidon Press, Oxford.

Wilson, A.T. 1928, *The Persian Gulf*, George Allen & Unwin, London.

Winkler, H.A. 1938–9, *Rock Drawings of Southern Upper Egypt*, 2 vols, The Egyptian Exploration Society, London.

Woolley, C.L. 1934, *Ur Excavations*, Vol. 2: *The Royal Cemetery*, Oxford University Press.

—— 1956, *Ur Excavations*, vol. 4: *The Early Periods*, British Museum and the University Museum of the University of Pennsylvania, Philadelphia and London.

Zarins, J. 1978, 'Steatite vessels in the Riyadh Museum', *Atlal* 2.

—— 1986, 'Martu and the land of Dilmun', *BTAA*.

Zarins, J., Whalen, N., Ibrahim, M., Morad, A. and Khan, M. 1980, 'Preliminary report on the Central and Southwestern Provinces Survey', *Atlal* 4.

Zarins, J., Mughannum, A.S. and Kamal, M. 1983, 'Excavations at Dhahran South – the tumuli field. A preliminary report', *Atlal* 8.

INDEX

Anatolia
MEDITERRANEAN
Akkad
Sumer
ARABIAN
Dilmun
Egypt
Arabia
RED SEA